Annual Editions:
Early Childhood Education,
36/e

Edited by Karen Menke Paciorek

http://create.mheducation.com

ISBN-10: 1259384683   ISBN-13: 9781259384684

Contents

Preface

*A*nnual Editions: Early Childhood Education has evolved during the 36 years it has been in existence to become one of the most used resources for students in early childhood education. This annual collection of the best relevant articles is used today at over 550 colleges and universities. In addition, it may be found in public libraries, pediatricians' offices, and teacher reference sections of school libraries. As the editor for 30 of the 36 years, I work diligently throughout the year to find articles and bring you the best and most significant readings in the field. I realize this is a tremendous responsibility to provide a thorough review of the current literature—a responsibility I take very seriously. I am always on the lookout for possible articles for the next *Annual Editions: Early Childhood Education.* My goal is to provide the reader with a snapshot of the critical issues facing professionals in early childhood education. The overviews for each unit describe in more detail the issues related to the unit topic. I encourage everyone to read the short, but useful unit overviews prior to reading the articles.

Early childhood education is an interdisciplinary field that includes child development, family issues, educational practices, behavior guidance, and curriculum. *Annual Editions: Early Childhood Education, 36th edition* brings you the latest information in the field from a wide variety of recent journals, newspapers, and magazines.

There are four themes found in the readings chosen for this 36th edition of *Annual Editions: Early Childhood Education.* As editor I read a preponderance of articles on these key issues. They are the:

(1) focus on providing developmentally appropriate learning experiences for all children but especially kindergartners

(2) role of the adults in choosing appropriate materials for play and exploration by young children

(3) key role educators play in advocating for and supporting hands-on, exploratory, play-based learning activities for all children, but especially our youngest learners, and

(4) evidence that creative and problem-solving experiences early in a child's life are critical for life-long learning.

It is especially gratifying to see issues affecting children and families addressed in sources other than professional association journals. The general public needs to be aware of the impact of positive early learning and family experiences on the growth and development of children.

Also included are learning outcomes and Internet references for each article that will guide the student in his or her reading of the article. Readers are encouraged to explore these sites on their own or in collaboration with others for extended learning opportunities. All of these sites were carefully reviewed by university students for their worthiness and direct application to those who work with young children on a day-to-day basis.

Given the wide range of topics *Annual Editions: Early Childhood Education, 36th edition* may be used by several groups—undergraduate or graduate students, professionals, parents, or administrators who want to develop an understanding of the critical issues in the field.

I appreciate the time the advisory board members take to provide suggestions for improvement and possible articles for consideration. The production and editorial staff of McGraw-Hill ably support and coordinate the efforts to publish this book.

To the instructor or reader interested in current issues professionals in the field deal with regularly, I encourage you to check out *Taking Sides: Clashing Views in Early Childhood Education,* 2nd edition (2008), which contains 18 critical issues. The book can be used in a seminar or issues course and opens the door to rich discussion.

I look forward to hearing from you about the selection and organization of this edition and especially value correspondence from students who take the time to share their thoughts on the profession or articles selected. Comments and articles sent for consideration are welcomed and will serve to modify future volumes. I encourage you to follow my semi-regular thoughts and updates on the Early Childhood Education profession on twitter @karenpaciorek or contact me at kpaciorek@emich.edu.

Editor

Karen Menke Paciorek is a professor of Early Childhood Education at Eastern Michigan University in Ypsilanti. Her degrees in early childhood education include a BA from the University of Pittsburgh, an MA from George Washington University, and a PhD from Peabody College of Vanderbilt University. She is the editor of *Taking Sides: Clashing Views in Early Childhood Education* (2nd ed.) also published by McGraw-Hill. She has served as president of the Michigan Association for the Education of Young Children, the Michigan Early Childhood Education Consortium, and the Northville School Board. She presents at local, state, and national conferences on curriculum planning, guiding behavior, preparing the learning environment, and working with families. She served for nine years as a member of the Board of Education for the Northville Public Schools, Northville, Michigan. She is on the Board of Directors for Wolverine Human Services, serving over 600 abused and delinquent youth in Michigan and many other volunteer service boards. Dr. Paciorek is a recipient of the Eastern Michigan University Distinguished Faculty Award for Service and the Outstanding Teaching Award from the Alumni Association.

Academic Advisory Board

Members of the Academic Advisory Board are instrumental in the final selection of articles for the *Annual Editions* series. Their review of the articles for content, level, and appropriateness provides critical direction to the editor(s) and staff. We think that you will find their careful consideration reflected in this book.

Paul Anderer
SUNY Canton

Elaine M. Artman
Mercer University

Fredalene Barletta Bowers
Indiana University of Pennsylvania

Leilani M. Brown
University of Hawaii, Manoa

Erin Brumbaugh
Davis & Elkins College

Joyce Chang
University of Central Missouri

Evia L. Davis
Langston University

Linda C. Edwards
College of Charleston

Paulina Escamilla-Vestal
Modesto Junior College

Colleen Fawcett
Palm Beach State College, Lake Worth

Kathleen E. Fite
Texas State University, San Marcos

Josephine Fritts
Ozarks Technical Community College

Bernard Frye
University of Texas, Arlington

Sara Garner
Southeast Missouri State University

Cindy Gennarelli
William Paterson University

Alyssa Gilston
South University

Jane Elyce Glasgow
Tidewater Community College

Corrie Gross
Santa Fe College & Palm Beach State

Deborah Harris-Sims
University of Phoenix

Carlene Henderson
Sam Houston State University

Alice S. Honig
Syracuse University

Christy Hopkins
Stanly Community College

Glenda Hotton
Masters College

Joan Packer Isenberg
George Mason University

Lois Johnson
Grove City College

Richard T. Johnson
University of Hawaii, Manoa

Katharine C. Kersey
Old Dominion University

Sherry King
University of South Carolina

Michelle Larocque
Florida Atlantic University—Boca Raton

Dennis A. Lichty
Wayne State College

Leanna Manna
Villa Maria College

Michael Martinsen
Edgewood College

John W. McNeeley
Daytona State College

Charlotte Metoyer
National Louis University

Gayle Mindes
DePaul University

George S. Morrison
University of North Texas

William A. Mosier
Wright State University

Barbie Norvell
Coastal Carolina University

Caroline Olko
Nassau Community College

Christine Pack
Westmoreland County Community College

Jessie Panko
Saint Xavier University

Karen L. Peterson
Washington State University

Peter Phipps
Dutchess Community College

Laura Pierce
University of West Alabama

Frankie Denise Powell
University of North Carolina, Pembroke

Jack V. Powell
University of Georgia

Frank Prerost
Midwestern University

Anne Marie Rakip
South Carolina State University

Mary Eva Repass
University of Virginia

Claire N. Rubman
Suffolk County Community College

Jana Sanders
Texas A & M University, Corpus Christi

Thomas R. Scheira
Buffalo State College

Stephen T. Schroth
Knox College

Hilary Seitz
University of Alaska, Anchorage

Laura Shea Doolan
Molloy College

Paulette Shreck
University of Central Oklahoma

Wallace Smith
Union County College

Dolores Stegelin
Clemson University

Ruth Steinbrunner
Bowling Green State University, Firelands

Robert Stennett
University of North Georgia, Gainesville

Sandra M. Todaro
Bossier Parish Community College

Joan Venditto
Albertus Magnus College

Lewis H. Walker
Lander University

Valerie Wallace
California Lutheran University

Robin A. Wells
Eastern New Mexico University

Janette C. Wetsel
University of Central Oklahoma

Harriet S. Worobey
Rutgers University

Jang-Ae Yang
Northwest Missouri State University

Unit 1

UNIT ——————

Prepared by: Karen Menke Paciorek, *Eastern Michigan University*

Building a Strong Foundation

The title for this unit, "Building a Strong Foundation," is representative of the work we do with our youngest learners and their families. Any builder will tell you, if you want a structure to stand for many years, even centuries, you must initially do significant foundation and preparation work before the first stone, steel beam, or load of cement is set. Shoddy construction will not last and will only lead to more problems in the years to come. The same holds true when planning for the care and education of young children. The articles in this unit all point to the importance of quality early childhood programs to develop necessary learning skills, contribute to closing the achievement gap, and advocate for early childhood programs. This unit also broadens the job description of anyone in the profession from one who cares for and educates young children to one who educates family and community members about our field, advocates for our profession, and works to be an informed professional who takes responsibility for the work we do. In short, we are in a profession, not just a job which is performed during specific work hours and then forgotten about when not at work. The early childhood profession requires you to be alert and focused on the field at all times.

Unfortunately, I continuously read multiple articles each year on the benefits of play in my search for the best articles for inclusion in this anthology. On one hand I want to say, "Really, do we still need to tell people about the importance of play?" But I know the message is not being heard by large numbers of individuals. Play has been called as important to our survival as other basic needs such as nutrition or sleep. I wonder why our message about the many benefits of play and the deep need for all children to have multiple opportunities throughout each and every day to engage in freely chosen creative play is not being heard. The play children need is different from playing video games, or playing an organized game. This play is what is necessary for developing skills creatively, socially, cognitively, physically, and emotionally; in short, developing the whole child. Please join me in becoming a strong advocate for play in formal educational settings as well as in homes and communities. Educators who are pushing young children to learn in ways that are not developmentally appropriate and which rob them of their special time to learn by manipulating

materials and engaging in active play need education about how children best learn. We should not have to build a case for play in programs serving young children but should instead be able to foster and support the play in which children engage and help them learn. James L. Hymes, Jr. is one of my favorite early educators from the past century. Dr. Hymes was the director of the Kaiser Ship Yards Child Service Centers in Portland, Oregon from 1943–1945 during World War II and on the initial planning committee for Head Start in 1965. In 1959, he wrote about play in the following way:

> We need a new word to sum up what young children do with themselves—how they occupy their time, what they give themselves to, the activity that is the be-all and the end-all of their days.
>
> We have words to say all this for other ages. We can talk about adults and say that they are "working." That sounds right and reasonable. We can talk about the elementary or high school or college age and say that they are "studying." That is a dignified description that sounds legitimate and right for the age. But we say that young children "play." That is the reason for our schools: to let this age do what it has to do, with more depth and richness, to let these children play. But to many people the word sounds weak and evasive, as if somehow this age was cheating.
>
> If we say "free play" we put two bad words together. Free and soft, and easy, casual, careless, sloppy, pointless, aimless, wandering, senseless. Play of pleasure and ease and waste and evil.
>
> The words to violence to the deeds. Can't we find a word or coin a word that conveys the respect this time in life deserves? Must we always minimize it, or hasten it, or deny it? (Hymes, *The Grade Teacher,* 1959.)

A startling examination of what most call, "day care" but those in the field refer to as, "child care" is an issue many parents face on a daily basis. If you have looked for child care, or worry about facing that task in the future, it most likely sent chills down your spine. Licensing rules are very different from state to state and the economic downturn across the country means most states are sending fewer inspectors out to growing caseloads with shorter visits to homes and child care centers each year. There is a crisis waiting around every corner and parents must be vigilant when looking for quality care for their children. At some point in the pregnancy of any single working parent or dual income family the question changes from, "When is the baby due?" to "What are you going to do for child care?" This dilemma hangs heavy over all parents and requires a comprehensive approach supported by employers, communities, and the family. I am always struck that a family can easily get a loan at most financial institutions to pay for college but would be denied for a loan for child care even though at most state supported colleges and universities the cost of child care at the campus-based early childhood program is more for the child to attend full time than the parent to attend classes full time. Both the quality of care available and the cost must undergo extensive changes.

How to best close the achievement gap found between children living in an environment that may not offer the necessary support for learning and children who are stimulated and challenged at home continues to be an issue educators wrestle with on a daily basis. There are a number of articles in this edition that come from journals aimed at school administrators. School administrators must have an understanding of the developmental needs of all children, not just those in the age group in their school. That means an elementary school principal must be familiar with child development and the early care and education experiences children have prior to entering kindergarten. He or she must also work to build a smooth transition from one setting to the next and understand how pre-kindergarten experiences can establish life-long learning attributes early in one's life. This issue is also significant for the sheer number of articles that have been written addressing the achievement gaps and how to best narrow those gaps. Some would argue that good teaching and quality educational experiences inside the school setting should prepare all students to achieve at the same level while others indicate experiences, or lack there of, in the home and local community can greatly affect learning in the classroom. There are always exceptions to each argument where outstanding academic achievement is found in schools located in extreme poverty areas. The many barriers that prevent children from coming to school each day well rested and fed do affect academic performance and teachers who are aware of the many stumbling blocks children and their families must overcome prior to entering the classroom are better prepared to assist them in their quest to achieve in school. Legislators across the country are addressing these gaps in a number of ways. Some states offer universal preschool, programs that are free and available for all preschool children living in that state. Other states are taking a different approach and targeting specific state funded preschool programs for those children who need, and would benefit from, preschool the most. This need is often determined by a child

meeting two or more risk factors such as a low income family, a non-English speaking family, a speech, language, or hearing deficit, a teenage parent, and so on. There are pros and cons to each approach and this issue will continue to play out in state legislatures across the country as they look for the most effective way to help all children succeed.

One of the classes this editor teaches as a professor of Early Childhood Education at Eastern Michigan University is a graduate class titled Trends, Issues, and Advocacy in ECE. In that class we read writings by many of the individuals who laid the foundation for our profession. John Locke (1632–1704) is one of those individuals. I share with my students one of my favorite quotes written by Locke back in the mid-1600s, "Accommodate the educational program to fit the child; don't change the child to fit the program." That quote is so relevant today as we work to ensure that schools are ready for all children. The analogy of an arborist trying to revive a dying tree but not paying attention to the roots which would allow the tree to take hold and develop a strong foundation has been used to describe the need to focus on our youngest learners as school reform issues are discussed. Of course some private funds can support quality programs for preschool children, but without a commitment from the federal or state government to learning prior to kindergarten we will not be successful in reaching all children who will benefit from attending preschool.

Care and education of young children is a profession as defined by the need for initial preparation and ongoing professional development. Early childhood educators must see the importance of ongoing advocacy and professional development and the need to be an active, lifelong learner and advocate in the field. Just as we would not want to go to a physician who graduated from medical school over 25 years ago and has never attended a conference or read a professional journal, we would not want that same lack of professional development for our field. We have an added responsibility in our profession because the people with whom we work are unable to speak for themselves to tell others about the issues they face.

The benefits of developing a professional advocacy and development plan include the ability to interact with others who share your passion for the care and education of young children and interaction with their families. It is a wonderful way to build your network of contacts and friends, whether you are new to an area or a long time resident. Get out and get involved in our wonderful profession. Become an active member of a student ECE organization on your campus or start one if none exists. Look to attend professional development opportunities in your community. If funds are available, consider joining a professional organization and contact legislators and educate others who make important decisions that affect our jobs.

I am reminded of one of the more popular perceptions of early care and education held by those outside of the profession. For the past 50 years, "early childhood education was viewed as a panacea, the solution to all social ills in society" (Paciorek, 2008, p. xvii). This is a lot of pressure to put on one profession, especially one that is grossly underpaid and undervalued. We do have outside forces carefully watching how early education practices affect long-term development and learning. Early childhood professionals must be accountable for practices they implement in their classrooms and how children spend their time interacting with materials. Appropriate early learning standards are the norm in the profession, and knowledgeable caregivers and teachers must be informed of the importance of developing quality experiences that align with the standards and assessment practices. Teachers can no longer plan cute activities that fill the child's days and backpacks with pictures to hang on the refrigerator. Teachers must be intentional in their planning to adapt learning experiences so that all children can achieve standards that are based on knowledge of developmental abilities.

As the editor, I hope you benefit from reading the articles and reflecting on the important issues facing early childhood education today. Your job is to share the message with others not familiar with our field and to explain impact that attending a quality program can have on young children throughout their life. I always feel good when I realize that others outside of the field of early childhood education recognize that quality care and education for young children can have tremendous financial benefits as well as educational benefits for society. Of course we would always welcome the interest from more people outside of the profession, but the field is receiving increased attention from others for a number of reasons. The nation is learning that high-quality programs are beneficial for young children's long-term development. Much of this interest is, in part, due to some state legislatures allocating resources for state-operated preschool programs. In many states, early childhood education program options for at-risk children are growing. We need to continue to demand that the adults who work with young children on a daily basis are highly qualified and highly effective in what they do. Coupled with the knowledge of the importance of ECE programs is a realization that the quality of these programs should be of utmost importance.

Article

Prepared by: Karen Menke Paciorek, *Eastern Michigan University*

What Exactly is "High-Quality" Preschool?

CLAUDIO SANCHEZ AND CORY TURNER

Learning Outcomes

After reading this article, you will be able to:

- Describe the role of the teacher in a high-quality preschool program.

- Explain the importance of high-quality preschool in the life of young, at risk children.

- List some components of high-quality preschool.

For years, President Obama has been a vocal booster of early childhood education. In his past two State of the Union addresses, he has called on Congress to help fund preschool for every child in the country.

"Research shows that one of the best investments we can make in a child's life is high-quality early education," Obama told Congress in January.

The president even put a price tag on his plan: $75 billion over 10 years, he said, would help every state provide preschool to every 4-year-old—to be paid for by raising cigarette taxes by 94 cents a pack.

But just what *is* quality preschool? It's difficult to debate the merits of early childhood education, and to argue that every child—indeed, the nation as a whole—will benefit from better access to preschool, without first defining what exactly constitutes a "high-quality" model.

NPR's new education team set out to unpack those two words and to understand what separates the nation's best preschool programs from the rest. That journey led us to a surprising place: Tulsa, Oklahoma, where the public school system is now a leader in early childhood education.

Education: One Approach to Head Start: To Help Kids, Help Their Parents

Interrupting "A Spiral of Failure"

The federal government currently spends almost $8 billion a year on preschool programs. States spend billions more, mostly geared toward low-income 4-year-olds. And while state-run programs today reach twice as many kids as they did back in 2002, that's still only 30 percent of all eligible children.

Even so, Obama's $75 billion plan was a nonstarter with Congress. One big argument critics make against spending more on preschool is that the benefits don't last.

Some researchers counter that many kids don't see lasting benefits because early childhood education programs are often underfunded. That can mean poorly trained teachers and a weak curricular patchwork.

"Those kids are going to be in a spiral of failure," says Steve Barnett, director of the National Institute for Early Education Research at Rutgers University. "And we set that up by not adequately investing before they get to kindergarten."

Barnett says a majority of low-income 4-year-olds are in poor-quality programs. If there is a silver lining, it's that even substandard preschool is better than the more common alternative: none at all. Children who get no preschool start kindergarten already a year or more behind developmentally.

"It's very clear from the research," Barnett says, "that our problems with inequality . . . are set when children walk in the school door."

So . . . what to do? One answer can be found at Porter Early Childhood Development Center in Tulsa, Oklahoma.

There, each morning begins with the school secretary, Tracy Jones, standing outside as the yellow school buses pull up. She greets the kids as they make the big step down to the curb, some still groggy from their 45-minute ride. Once the last student files past, Jones asks the driver to make sure no one's still aboard, fast asleep in the back. It happens.

Inside, through Porter's sturdy, steel doors, Howard Wible waits in the gymnasium. The principal is an affable, burly man in his late 50s, known to dress up as Winnie the Pooh for special school occasions.

Today, he's happy to lead the children in a few stretching exercises, then a song about the seven continents. From there, the hungry 4-year-olds make their way down the stairs to the cafeteria and breakfast. On the menu today: scrambled eggs, toast, potatoes, milk, and cereal. Shovel, chew, and repeat . . . before it's time to see Ms. Nikki Jones.

Jones, 32, brown hair bobbed at the shoulders and held behind her ears by a pair of upturned reading glasses, has only been teaching for a few years, but she has the classroom presence of a veteran. She's firm yet gentle as she rounds up her 20 kids and sits them down on a thick, shaggy rug. It's time for one of the day's first and most important rituals: morning storytelling.

It's 10 A.M., and instead of reading to the kids herself, Ms. Jones has brought in a kindergartner from down the hall to read aloud. All eyes turn to 5-year-old Madison as she makes her way confidently, sentence by sentence, through Dr. Seuss' *The Foot Book*. Madison is a hit. The kids watch her, cross-legged and enraptured. When she finishes, Jones leads the class in a thank you "Hip Hip Hooray!"

Now, the play begins. The class disperses to various stations of their choosing: a cluster of computers, a tiny kitchen tucked into the corner, or an art center known affectionately as "the fort." For Jones, play should be the beating heart of a child's preschool experience.

"I try to have an hour-and-a-half to two hours of uninterrupted play," she says. "The play is open-ended, so we put out objects that aren't task-oriented. That way they aren't limited to what they can do with them. It builds problem-solving, imagination . . . creativity."

The results are all around the room, hanging from the ceiling and stuck to the walls: square cows, a snowman with rabbit ears, lots of stick figures (hearts and squiggly lines really). And the children are encouraged to roam freely, from one experience to another. All the while, Jones keeps a watchful eye, assessing everything they do: their vocabulary, their familiarity with numbers . . . even how they resolve disputes.

"They're having to collaborate," Jones says, "and to collaborate during a phase when they're still very egocentric and all about themselves."

The Role of the Teacher

The role of the teacher in all of this, researchers say, is the foundation of a high-quality preschool program. Deborah Phillips, a developmental psychologist and professor at Georgetown University, has devoted her entire career to studying early childhood education.

"What you're going to look for," Phillips says, "is a teacher who knows how to instruct children in pre-math, pre-literacy, who gets down on the child's level when talking to them, who's respectful toward them."

Phillips was the lead researcher in an exhaustive study of the Tulsa program. For seven months, she and her team observed teachers in dozens of classrooms across the city, and found four pillars of quality.

First, as is clear within minutes of setting foot in Nikki Jones' classroom, the city employs a rich curriculum that doesn't just include play—it revolves around play. Second, the program is well-funded. Tulsa spends about $7,500 per child per year. Third, the teacher-student ratio is balanced: 1 teacher for every 10 kids. And fourth, all teachers are highly qualified.

Take Jones, for example. She is just a few credits shy of her master's degree and has already been accepted into a doctorate program. Tulsa requires at least a bachelor's degree of its preschool teachers. They must also be fully certified in early childhood education. And, once they're hired, they receive still more training—monthly.

As a result, Nikki Jones arrives each morning brimming with ideas and strategies rooted in research and good pedagogy. Indeed, what looks like an art project with acorns, pine cones, glass beads, and a film projector is also a stealth math lesson. Jones says her kids love to count, add and subtract with little or no direct instruction.

A Link to Parents

But does this kind of program have lasting benefits? That's one of the arguments now being used against increased funding for preschool: that the benefits fade as kids move through elementary school.

Not so, says researcher Deborah Phillips—not in Tulsa. She found evidence of lasting impacts there, at least through third grade.

"The children who went through Tulsa pre-K, compared to those who didn't, are doing better in math," Phillips says. "That's especially true for boys and lower-income children."

Nikki Jones says preschool is all about building that lasting foundation—though it's not easy for most 4-year-olds.

"You're asking kids to do things they've never done before. They've never been in school before, never raised their hand and stood up and given an answer before. So it's scary to them."

They're scared to fail, Jones says. Because many of these kids have seen failure. Many of Jones' students are growing up with just one parent in Tulsa's toughest neighborhoods, poverty and failure all around them. And she says part of her job, as a teacher, is to establish a direct line of communication with whoever is looking after her students when they're not in her classroom.

"Without the family connection, we wouldn't know if so-and-so didn't have dinner or if so-and-so's mom got put in jail last night. Because parents aren't going to tell you that if they don't trust you," she says.

Georgetown's Deborah Phillips agrees—and takes things a step further. She argues that a high-quality preschool teacher does many of the things parents are supposed to do.

"She provides strong emotional, social support for children, makes them feel safe, protected, loved, valued," she says.

And if they get that, Phillips adds, "they're motivated. They love school. We're setting children along a much sturdier, promising pathway into their futures."

That's what Tulsa's preschool program is doing, says Phillips, and why she argues that it's a model for the nation.

"If it can happen in Oklahoma, it can happen everywhere."

And, with some 30 states now expanding their preschool offerings, someday soon Tulsa could be the rule, not the exception.

Critical Thinking

1. Develop a list of criteria you would share with parents looking for a high-quality preschool program for their 4-year-old.

2. How is the job of a highly effective preschool teacher different from a teacher who may teach elementary age students?

3. Describe the ramifications if some children receive high-quality preschool and others don't. What are the long term consequences for the country?

Internet References

American Institute for Research
http://www.air.org/resource/what-look-high-quality-preschool

HighScope Educational Research Foundation
http://highscope.org/

National Association of Early Childhood Specialists in State Departments of Education
http://www.naecs-sde.org/

National Association for the Education of Young Children
http://naeyc.org/

Article   Prepared by: Karen Menke Paciorek, *Eastern Michigan University*

Head Start

A Bridge from Past to Future

BLYTHE S.F. HINITZ

Learning Outcomes

After reading this article, you will be able to:

- Articulate the importance of Head Start programs on the development of young children in poverty.

- Advocate for quality Head Start programs for your community.

- Explain why programs related to Head Start were developed and the need they serve.

H ead Start was built on a strong base of civil rights advocacy and a long history of private and government-funded US early childhood education programs. At the 50th anniversaries of the Civil Rights Act of 1964 and the Economic Opportunity Act (EOA) of 1964, it is fitting that we remember that Head Start was born of President Lyndon B. Johnson's War on Poverty in the middle of the civil rights movement of the 1960s.

At the time of Head Start's creation, 10 years had already passed since the Supreme Court's momentous *Brown v. Board of Education* (1954) decision that racial segregation in public schools was unconstitutional. The Reverend Dr. Martin Luther King Jr. and others were helping the United States focus on the needs of under-represented groups. President Johnson announced the creation of Head Start in a special message to Congress on January 12, 1965, in which he focused on the expansion of "preschool program[s] in order to reach disadvantaged children early" (Osborn 1991). Lady Bird Johnson launched her role as a national spokeswoman for the Head Start program with a tea in the Rose Garden, attended by members of the Head Start planning committee. The gathering, which was covered on newspaper society pages, gave the program "an aura of respectability" (Kuntz 1998, 8–9).

Varying Views on Head Start

Views varied on what kind of program Head Start should be. It was widely believed at the time that "poverty and welfare dependencies are transmitted intergenerationally [because] . . . education, independence, ambition, [and] concern for the future are not reinforced during a childhood spent in poverty and dependence on welfare" (Washington & Bailey 1995, 21). Those who held this view believed that since parents were accountable for their children's condition, anti-poverty programs—including Head Start—should either remove children from the influence of parents who were not meeting their needs or work to improve the parents for the benefit of the children. This attitude led to the cultural deprivation theory, which "suggested that the poor needed to be educated, to have opportunities to learn the values embraced by middle-class America and that, if introduced to these ideas—most important to the work ethic—the poor would straighten up and act like real Americans" (Kuntz 1998, 4).

Others, believing that parents should personally benefit from a program and that community buy-in was important, suggested a combination of parent education and participation in decision making. Those espousing the least supported view—that poverty is a systemic issue—proposed that parents should be involved in actual program governance.

Although the EOA legislation authorized Community Action Programs (CAPs) to assist local communities in establishing and administering their own antipoverty efforts, some local governments opposed the proposed placement of administrative control and resources in the hands of poor people and refused to apply for program grants. In an effort to make the CAP more palatable to local officials, while using what would have been an embarrassing budget surplus, the Head Start project was born (Zigler & Styfco 1996, 133).

From a feminist history perspective, Greenberg (1998) wrote,

Probably the many men involved in the original planning of Head Start were so exhilarated by the heady thrill of inclusion in such an exciting and important project that they neglected to notice the relevant pioneering work in early education, social work, child health, and parent education that women had been thoughtfully engaged in—and teaching and writing about—for several generations. (63)

Greenberg points out that although the wives and mothers of some of these men were kindergarten and nursery school teachers, and most of their children had attended early education programs, "the several dozen men at the head of Head Start never appeared to realize that there was an early childhood profession, with leaders, usually female, of its own" (63).

Early Education and Social Justice

From its inception Head Start had a dual role. It would provide comprehensive health, nutrition, and education services for young children, including early identification of physical and mental health problems and medical, dental, and psychological services. An overarching goal of the program was enhancing social competence (now termed *social and emotional competence*), which included "the child's everyday effectiveness in dealing with his environment and later responsibilities in school and life" (Osborn 1991, 152).

But Head Start wasn't only about early education; as a CAP, the program was envisioned as a vehicle to give families with low incomes a voice, and for doing things *with* them rather than *to* them. Osborn's concept of the child development center, which emphasized all resources—family, community, and professional—that could contribute to children's development, was adopted as a model.

Parent Involvement

To help achieve the goal of giving families a voice, Head Start legislation called for the "maximum feasible participation" of parents. Programs would form Parent Policy Councils. Parents on the councils would have executive responsibilities, including engagement in planning the center environment and curriculum, obtaining jobs as classroom assistants, participating in the hiring process, and learning empowerment strategies to become catalysts for community action efforts. In practice,

however, there was a dichotomy of implementation of the parent involvement initiative. In the initial stages of the project, some Head Start programs provided for community control. Parents in these programs handled funding for training, supervisory staff, monitoring, and evaluation. Parents participated equally with professionals in decision making. In the majority of programs, however, the emphasis was on parent *involvement,* which meant parents were participants on the perimeter rather than at the core.

The program was envisioned as a vehicle to give families with low incomes a voice, and for doing things *with* them rather than *to* them.

In 1975 the standards for parent involvement were codified into the national Head Start Performance Standards, Section 70.2, which mandated that parents of children in the program constitute a majority on the policy board and described the ways in which that board must have input and decision-making power in different areas of operation. These standards set Head Start apart from other social service programs and the public schools by providing for specific, active roles for families in such areas as curriculum, finance, staff hiring and firing, and policy. "These parent roles, though perhaps without as radical a potential as community control could have had, do give parents significant official control of programs" (Ellsworth & Ames 1998, xiii).

Serving Diverse Populations

In addition to giving parents more prominent roles in their children's education and in their community, Head Start has been "seen as a special opportunity for our minority groups" (Hymes & Osborn 1979, 33). Head Start programs for children from migrant families (beginning in 1969) and children living on federal Native American reservations meet some of the specialized needs of these children and families. The emphasis on respect for, and serving the needs of, diverse populations in communities was underscored by Dr. Julius B. Richmond, Head Start's first project director, in his 1991 address to Head Start's First National Research Conference: "We can no longer afford to neglect groups that will become even larger segments of our population. This bespeaks the need to have many approaches, both quantitative and qualitative, covering diverse domains" (Zigler et al. 1992, 23).

Head Start's Early Days

Initially a summer-only program, Head Start served 562,000 children in 2,500 centers across the United States during its first summer. There were 41,000 teachers (including the author), 46,000 teaching assistants (mothers who were hired to assist the teaching staff), 256,000 volunteers (including Lady Bird Johnson and her daughter, and many congressional wives), and 170 early childhood consultants. Thanks to the efforts of Keith Osborn and James Hymes, classes had a favorable adult-child ratio: each class consisted of 15 children, 1 teacher, 1 paid aide, and at least 1 volunteer. Training materials included the Rainbow Series of booklets and pamphlets, along with a phonograph record and 20 films developed by Dr. Joseph L. Stone of Vassar College and Dr. Jeannette Galambos Stone of Sarah Lawrence College. Head Start was offered as a nine-month, half-day program beginning in 1966 (Zigler, Styfco, & Gilman 1993).

Theoretical and Research Influences on Head Start

There is general agreement that Sargent Shriver, director of the Office of Economic Opportunity (OEO) created under the Economic Opportunity Act (EOA), his staff, and the consultants they engaged were influenced by the following theories and writings in creating Project Head Start:

- Sigmund Freud's emphasis on the importance of the early years
- Beth Wellman's argument that IQ is not a fixed element
- Jean Piaget's genetic epistemological studies
- Benjamin Bloom's and J. McVicker Hunt's writings
- John Kenneth Galbraith's *The Affluent Society*
- Michael Harrington's *The Other America: Poverty in the United States*
- Daniel Patrick Moynihan's *The Negro Family: The Case for National Action* (the Moynihan Report).

These theories and writings still impact Head Start today. In addition, research carried out during the early stages of the program by Bettye Caldwell, Blanche Persky, Susan Gray, Cynthia and Martin Deutsch, and David Weikart and the Perry Preschool Project staff led to program models in use across the country today.

Research on results of the Head Start program has been mixed. The scathing 1969 Westinghouse report (Westinghouse Learning Corporation & Ohio University 1969); the Jensen article (1969), which stated that "compensatory education has been tried, and it apparently has failed" (p. 2); and Bronfenbrenner's 1974 report on the fade-out hypothesis all caused much concern, but such reports also triggered major revisions to the Head Start program. Research conducted by Irving Lazar and the Cornell Consortium, and studies done in Ypsilanti, Michigan; Syracuse, New York; and Philadelphia, Pennsylvania, provided more supportive data (see Washington & Bailey 1995).

Professional Development

The Child Development Associate (CDA) Credential—a major professional development component of Head Start created in 1972 to meet the need for qualified child care staff—now extends to early childhood programs beyond Head Start. The CDA, a national certification, celebrated its 40th year by revising its assessment model to take advantage of recent technological innovations. (For information about the CDA and technology, visit the Council for Professional Recognition website at www.cdacouncil.org.) The CDA is based on a set of core competencies: providing safe and healthy learning environments, advancing children's physical and intellectual competence, supporting children's social and emotional health, building positive relationships with families, responding to the needs of program participants, and maintaining professionalism (Council for Professional Recognition 2013).

The Strong Foundation Stands

Head Start today retains in practice and philosophy many ties to its roots. It remains a comprehensive health, nutrition, and education program addressing the needs of a diverse group of young children with differing abilities. The original goal of enhancing children's social competence also remains important. Despite the fact that "maximum feasible participation" of parents has more often meant limited parent involvement rather than active participation in decision making, governance, and establishing and administering their own antipoverty efforts, Head Start has maintained its commitment to giving families with low incomes a voice, as mandated in the Head Start Program Performance Standards. As Head Start nears its golden anniversary, it continues to build on its strong early education and social justice foundation.

Head Start Planning Committee and Related Programs

Julius B. Richmond, MD, was Head Start's first project director. The planning committee was formed in 1964. The early childhood education field was represented by John H. Niemeyer, D. Keith Osborn—who became the project educational director—and James L. Hymes Jr. Other committee members included Urie Bronfenbrenner, Mamie Clark, Jacqueline Wexler, and Edward Zigler, who later became the first director of the federal Office of Child Development.

Project Follow-Through (1966–1996) was an intervention program for Head Start graduates from kindergarten through the third grade. Its aim was to enable children to maintain the gains made in Head Start and establish continuity between the children's preschool education and later schooling. It initially included comprehensive health, social, mental health, nutrition, and other support services similar to those offered in Head Start and retained an emphasis on parent involvement. The planning committee, chaired by Gordon Klopf of Bank Street College of Education, included Zigler and Bronfenbrenner from the original Head Start planning committee. Robert Egbert, the first Follow-Through director, established a pilot program of planned variation and sponsored curriculum models similar to that of Head Start. When the Office of Economic Opportunity delegated Follow-Through to the US Office of Education, funding cuts drastically reduced the comprehensive services provided and eventually forced the program to

close. Head Start generated several related programs that address the needs of a variety of populations. In 1967 the first of **33 Parent and Child Centers** (PCCs) opened, offering supportive services and parent education to families and children from birth to Head Start entry. PCCs were intended as preventive programs to protect young children from physiological trauma, leading to a reduction in developmental disturbances.

Beginning in 1972, **Home Start** provided rural and isolated families access to health, education, and social services through home visitors. These visitors were usually community residents who had participated in training in child development principles and Head Start's goals. An advantage of the home-based program was that siblings of the child for whom the services were intended also benefited. Some Head Start and related programs continue to employ home visitors today.

Early Head Start began in 1998 under the sponsorship of the Advisory Committee on Services for Families With Infants and Toddlers, established by Department of Health and Human Services Secretary Donna Shalala. It is currently operated by the Office of Head Start, with training and technical assistance provided by the Early Head Start Resource Center at Zero to Three.

For more information about Head Start and related programs, see Lascarides & Hinitz 2011, 401–59.

References

Bronfenbrenner, U. 1974. *Is Early Intervention Effective?* Vol. 2 of *A Report on Longitudinal Evaluations of Preschool Programs.* Washington, DC: Department of Health, Education, and Welfare, Office of Child Development.

Council for Professional Recognition. 2013. "Child Development Associate (CDA) Credential." www.cdacouncil.org/the-cda-credential

Ellsworth, J., & L.J. Ames, eds. 1998. *Critical Perspectives on Project Head Start: Revisioning the Hope and Challenge.* Albany, NY: State University of New York Press.

Greenberg, P. 1998. "The Origins of Head Start and the Two Versions of Parent Involvement: How Much Parent Participation in Early Childhood Programs and Services for Poor Children?" Chap. 2 in Ellsworth & Ames, 49–72.

Hymes, J.L., Jr., & D.K. Osborn. 1979. "The Early Days of Project Head Start: An Interview With D. Keith Osborn." In *Early Childhood Education Living History Interviews: Vol. 3— Reaching Large Numbers of Children,* ed. J.L. Hymes Jr., 28–55. Carmel, CA: Hacienda.

Jensen, A.R. 1969. "How Much Can We Boost IQ and Scholastic Achievement?" *Harvard Educational Review* 39 (1): 1–123.

Kuntz, K.R. 1998. "A Lost Legacy: Head Start's Origins in Community Action." Chap. 1 in Ellsworth & Ames, 1–48.

Lascarides, V.C., & B.F. Hinitz. 2011. *History of Early Childhood Education.* New York: Routledge.

Osborn, D.K. 1991. *Early Childhood Education in Historical Perspective.* 3rd ed. Athens, GA: Daye.

Washington, V., & U.J.O. Bailey. 1995. *Project Head Start: Models and Strategies for the Twenty-First Century.* New York: Garland.

Westinghouse Learning Corporation & Ohio University. 1969. *The Impact of Head Start: An Evaluation of the Effects of Head Start on Children's Cognitive and Affective Development.* Vol. 1. Athens, OH: Ohio University; New York: Westinghouse Learning Corporation.

Zigler, E., L. Datta, J. Richmond, & S. White. 1992. "Head Start's Future: The Challenge for Research." Plenary session. In *New Directions in Child and Family Research: Shaping Head Start in the 90s,* Conference Proceedings, June 24–26, 1991, eds. F.L. Parker, R. Robinson, S. Sambrano, C. Piotrkowski, J. Hagen, S. Randolph, & A. Baker, 14–26. New York: National Council of Jewish Women Center for the Child; Ann Arbor, MI: Society for Research in Child Development.

Zigler, E., S.J. Styfco, & E. Gilman. 1993. "The National Head Start Program for Disadvantaged Preschoolers." Chap. 1

in *Head Start and Beyond: A National Plan for Extended Childhood Intervention,* eds. E. Zigler & S.J. Styfco, 1–41. New Haven, CT: Yale University Press.

Zigler, E.F., & S. Styfco. 1996. "Head Start and Early Childhood Intervention: The Changing Course of Social Science and Social Policy." Chap. 8 in *Children, Families, and Government: Preparing for the Twenty-First Century,* eds. E.F. Zigler, S.L. Kagan, & N.W. Hall, 132–155. Cambridge, UK: Cambridge University Press.

Critical Thinking

1. Why is it important for Head Start to include families in the daily operation of the program?

2. Interview a teacher in a local Head Start program and ask about their initial preparation for the job and their ongoing professional development.

3. Ask 10 friends not in the early childhood profession what they know about Head Start. Develop a two to three sentence information speech you can share with those who are unfamiliar with the program.

Internet References

Early Head Start
http://eclkc.ohs.acf.hhs.gov/hslc/tta-system/ehsnrc/Early%20Head%20Start

National Head Start Association
http://www.nhsa.org/

Office of Head Start
http://www.acf.hhs.gov/programs/ohs

Blythe S.F. Hinitz, EdD, is Distinguished Professor of Elementary and Early Childhood Education at The College of New Jersey. The author of publications about the history of early childhood education and about teaching social studies to young children, she shares her research in national and international venues.

Author's Note—This column is dedicated to the work and spirit of friend and colleague Polly Greenberg (1932–2013), who chronicled the history of Head Start as a social justice advocate, a feminist, and an early childhood educator.

Hinitz, Blythe S.F. From *Young Children,* May 2014, pp. 94–97. Copyright © 2014 by National Association for the Education of Young Children. Reprinted by permission. www.naeyc.org

Article   Prepared by: Karen Menke Paciorek, *Eastern Michigan University*

Play Is the Way . . ."

Play is not merely a break from useful and productive activities. It is, as Dr. Stuart Brown and Kristen Cozad of the National Institute for Play contend, a fundamental survival drive, as important as adequate nutrition or sleep.

STUART BROWN AND KRISTEN COZAD

Learning Outcomes

After reading this article, you will be able to:

- Advocate for time for daily play for all children.

- Explain to parents the lifelong learning skills developed through play.

What exactly is play? Why did Mother Nature make it so much fun? And what is its purpose when play seems so . . . "purposeless"?

Scientists from many different disciplines are now beginning to understand the importance of play. Mother Nature didn't embed joyful play throughout the animal kingdom for no reason.

"Play Science" is an emerging discipline that is making its way into academic scholarship, onto university campuses and into the most leading-edge companies. Play Scientists now know that play covers a wide range of experiences and behaviors not only in humans, but throughout the animal kingdom. They are discovering that play is much more than simply a "fun activity."

Integrated into the human biological design, play is both highly individualized and a shared experience, and difficult to define. Like love, play is impossible to measure. And like love, play has unifying qualities.

We know play when we see it. We all light up when we watch puppies frolicking. We also know when we have played; we feel refreshed, revitalized and reinvigorated. Perhaps that is why George Bernard Shaw said, "We don't stop playing because we grow old; we grow old because we stop playing."

Play occurs in unlimited ways, and not everyone plays the same. What unifies the myriad expressions of play is an incredibly deep engagement where experienced fragmentation of our inner and outer worlds yields to the integration of unity and wholeness.

Attunement

This deep engagement is called *attunement*. If you open yourself up to it, you will discover and experience attunement all around you.

Consider an orchestra composed of many separate instruments and players. The symphony can only play coherently and creatively as one when its individual instruments and players are attuned with one another.

Attunement in humans begins in the bonding experience between mother or caregiver and child, with the early exchange of smiles and the eruption of joy and trust that follows. This model of early play, which is beneficial for both mother and child, is one that underlies all subsequent human play.

As the child continues to grow and develop, his or her unique talents begin to emerge through the exploration of self-directed play. This self-organizing play mirrors the self-organizing emergent systems scientists are discovering, from the microcosm (subatomic particles) to the macrocosm (galaxies). Perhaps the heart-wisdom of artists, poet-saints and sages has correctly intuited the universe as inherently playful!

Research and collation of thousands of play histories, from murderers to Nobel Laureates and everyone in between, has revealed that the most successful and talented people in life are those who played. Their play interests were identified and supported early in life, and their unique play talents were encouraged.

The most successful adults don't experience a separation between work and play. Their work is their play!

The joy of play begins to break down as play becomes "coerced." This happens when we feel pressured to participate in activities that are considered playful or important by others, well-meaning parents for example, and we just don't experience the fun in it. Attunement is absent.

Freedom is an inherent component in authentic play. The power and joy of play are lost when it becomes corrupted by over-control or when it becomes "scripted." Unfortunately, the joy and benefits of play can be suppressed and contorted by parents more interested in living out their own needs through their child's performance than they are in encouraging their child's natural interests. These parents don't recognize the inherent potential of their child's unique play proclivities, but rather assert their own personal agendas, such as steering their child to become the star athlete or scholar that they never became.

Something similar can occur in adult work environments with a boss or corporate culture that doesn't see the talents in their employees or recognize the potential of their unique contributions. Such work environments lack the lightness, trust and flexibility of play, with its inherent ingenuity and creativity, and hinder the ability of the employee to "come into one's own."

Play Signatures

Play Scientists now know that play has certain "signatures."

Typically, *play is voluntary*; it is done for its own sake. If the goal of the activity is more important than the involvement in the activity itself, it usually is not playful.

Play often appears purposeless. This could be why many of us in our goal-oriented culture trivialize and consider play unproductive. Play Scientists know that although play *appears* purposeless, it is anything but. Play is in fact extremely necessary not only to our health and well-being, but to our survival. It has capacities to increase perseverance and progressive mastery. Yet, paradoxically, when we play, these are not our objectives.

"The opposite of play is not work, it is depression."

—*Brian Sutton-Smith*

Play is not pressured by time constraints. When we are in deep engagement and playing, time seems to fly out the window. In fact, neuroscience research suggests play is its own "state of being," similar to sleep and dreams, and perhaps just as important.

Play is fun! We delight in the deep involvement of play and are driven to it again and again because of its inherent joyfulness and benefits. Think of the squeals of the toddler being swung around by her father: "Do it again, Daddy, do it again!"

Finally, *play takes us out of our own limited self-consciousness.* Play is how we get out of our own way and open ourselves up to the exploration of the possible. Play provides us with a creative advantage and propels innovation.

Probably the biggest contribution of contemporary Play Science research is that we now know play is anything but trivial or optional. Play is a fundamental survival drive we must honor if we value our health and well-being. Play is as important to humans as adequate nutrition or sleep.

Like other basic survival drives such as caretaking, sex and hunger, play urges come from the deep survival centers of the brain. Like sleep, we can get along without play for a period of time. And like sleep, if we have not integrated this basic survival drive into our lives, we will feel negative consequences that will impact our health, well-being and ability to thrive and cope.

Innovative Advantage

In a rapidly changing world, both creativity and innovation are needed to achieve and maintain a competitive advantage. Companies such as Google and 3M know this and allow self-organized play within the workplace.

Global economic trends are leading the way for the emergence of the "creative economy." Assembly-line industrial-age linear thinking is obsolete.

It has been said that play is the greatest natural resource in a creative economy. We are now realizing that the future favors the survival of the most nimble and resilient. So when unexpected challenges occur, play helps us respond adaptively to a new situation with more robust resources and skills.

"Play is how humans learn to resolve conflict and build community."

Our global playground needs the power and joy of play to build intimacy and trust, both essential to healthy relationships.

Another way that play enhances our individual and collective lives is its crucial role in the development of empathy. The ability to put oneself in another person's shoes and feel for their experience is derived from shared playful interactions. These interactions foster the capacities for social attunement, the essence of social play. Play Science research into the lives of mass murderers and homicidal males revealed a deficiency in the ability to empathize, lack of self-regulation and a history of severe play deprivation. Combining a lack of empathy with an underdeveloped capacity to handle stress and a deficiency in resiliency—all qualities developed by play—comprises a toxic equation with devastating, often violent, real-world consequences we must begin to recognize and understand. Play is not trivial or optional.

Play is how humans learn to resolve conflict and build community. Play is the glue that holds us together while serving as the lubrication to help us through challenging times. If we lose a job or hit tough times, non-players typically respond in fear and simply "hunker down" or "dig in" hoping things go back to normal. They lack the emotional buoyancy needed for their own re-creation and personal growth.

From dogmatic religious fundamentalism and political fanaticism, to road rage and the US Congress, play is usually absent where extremism, rigidity and gridlock are found in individuals and organizations.

We now know that play is how humans develop the ability to manage their behavior. Any classroom teacher will agree that self-regulation is needed by all children to sit still, focus and learn. Those lacking in this ability are frequently impulsive and are unable to think before acting, which is typical of children labeled as having ADHD.

Yet another of play's rewards is that it prompts us to be continuously physically active, combating obesity and enhancing overall health and emotional well-being. By engaging fully in play, we can interrupt and reverse the smoldering damage of chronic stress. Play even gives the immune system a bounce!

We are built through play and built to play for a lifetime.

Reconnecting

Human beings are *neotenous,* which means we retain certain juvenile characteristics throughout the whole of our lives. We are the most playful of all animals on Earth!

Humans are presumably the most intelligent of all species. Play and intelligence are linked. Play literally feeds the brain's development of new connections and plasticity.

Unlike other animals that have adapted to specific environments, humans can inhabit all areas of the Earth, from the freezing far reaches of the Arctic to the scorching deserts of the Sahara. We spend extended time deep under the oceans and high in the stratosphere, and we can now explore the mysteries of outer space. No other animal has developed these capabilities and adaptations. Humans did not acquire such phenomenal resiliency and adaptive ability through the ages by simply sitting on a couch!

As human play has moved from its origins in natural settings to the urban parks and streets, and finally to the structured and omnipresent virtual screen play of today, some Play Scientists are concerned about what is now called "nature deficit."

Because the love of the natural world and a positive environmental ethic come from playing in nature, some Play Scientists feel that our nature deficit indicates trouble and may compromise our survival as a species. They question whether we are developing a biophobic generation, uninterested in preserving nature and her diversity.

Play is the way we become fully expressed human beings, healthy and sustainable individually and as a global community. We must play with Mother Nature, not bully, dominate and suppress her. How do we do this? Actually, it's quite simple. We just have to play more!

Critical Thinking

1. What do the authors mean by attunement and how can teachers best support this in an early childhood setting?
2. Write two paragraphs for a school newsletter on the benefits of young children engaging in play activities.

Create Central

www.mhhe.com/createcentral

Internet References

National Institute for Play
www.nifplay.org
The Exuberant Animal
www.exuberantanimal.com/index.php
The Early Learning Community
www.earlylearningcommunity.org/page/importance-of-play
Child Action, Incorporated
www.childaction.org/families/publications/docs/guidance/Handout13
-The_Importance_of_Play.pdf

STUART BROWN, MD, is founder and president of the National Institute for Play (*www.nifplay.org*) based in California. Dr. Brown coteaches "From Play to Innovation" at Stanford University's d.school. **KRISTEN COZAD** is the Institute's director of development and cofounder of PlayNovation, LLC. Through their work with the Institute they are dedicated to bringing the transformative power of play to public consciousness, policy and action. They also consult and present internationally on Play Science.

Article   Prepared by: Karen Menke Paciorek, *Eastern Michigan University*

Why Pre-K Is Critical to Closing the Achievement Gap

High-quality, universal pre-K can impact the nation's international ranking.

ELLEN FREDE AND W. STEVEN BARNETT

Learning Outcomes

After reading this article, you will be able to:

- List at least three strategies or action steps administrators could follow to help close the achievement gap.

- Choose one of the action steps and describe how implementation could bring about a change in student achievement.

- Discuss the achievement gap and explain programs showing success in closing the gap.

The recently released results of the 2009 Program for International Student Assessment (PISA) comparison of educational achievement across 65 countries has brought renewed attention to the achievement gap and recommended changes to improve U.S. performance. The U.S. was well down in the middle of the pack for reading, math, and science while Shanghai, a Chinese city with a population equal to that of New York, was at the top of the leader board. One might think recommendations on how the U.S. could gain ground might start with an analysis of education policy in Shanghai or the European nation with top scores: Finland. For example, we might consider emulating Finland's universal access to high-quality early care, education starting in infancy, and requirement that every public school teacher earn a master's degree. Or, we might replicate Shanghai's universal pre-kindergarten, in which all teachers must have at least a bachelor's degree, or China's 251-day school year.

Of course, not every policy followed by high-achieving countries is an effective strategy for the U.S. To identify those that are effective, we can look systematically at policies associated with higher scores internationally, and then look at the full body of education research to identify what works in the U.S. as well as abroad. Most of the recommendations for raising U.S. PISA scores we have seen so far ignore both international and U.S. research on the effects of policies. They often recommend policy changes that will do little to raise scores here, have not led

to success elsewhere, and neglect pre-K and its clear salience in the most successful countries. Yet, research supports the notion that high-quality pre-K should be one part of a broader reform strategy to help us emulate the success of systems in Shanghai, Singapore, Finland, and Norway. Although quality pre-K is just one arrow in the education reform quiver of school systems that are well-equipped to battle the achievement gap and compete at the highest level internationally, by itself, high-quality pre-K might eliminate 20 percent of the achievement gap. That's far from a panacea, but hardly trivial either.

The availability of preschool education is one strong predictor of differences in PISA scores across countries. In fact, institutionalized preschool education is found to increase school-appropriate behavior and cognitive abilities, both of which contribute to increased test scores. Studies also find that as preschool participation rates move toward universal coverage, average test scores rise *and* within-country inequality in eighth-grade math and science test scores falls. Other research finds that national achievement test scores rise with the level of public expenditure on preschool education and with the quality of preschool education, as measured, for example, by teacher qualifications. Note that all these studies focus on long-term impacts on achievement, and that preschool education also is found to increase earnings at the national level.

The international comparison results are consistent with U.S. research findings. A review of the literature makes clear that quality preschool education increases test scores, decreases school failure and dropout, and can produce even longer term benefits such as reductions in crime and increases in earnings. However, to result in real life-changing benefits, the initial impacts on early education must be quite substantial because initial improvements are only partially maintained over the long term.

Early Learning at a Glance

Adding to the complexity of this issue is the reality that all preschool programs are not created equal; some are much more effective than others. As a nation, we spend a considerable amount of money subsidizing what is often custodial child care that produces few, if any, benefits for child development. Head Start is better than typical child care, but it has not been nearly good enough to produce large long-term gains in either cognitive or social development. Fortunately, Congress and the Obama administration have both responded with reforms that will make Head Start more effective, including increasing Head Start teacher pay, which is half that of teachers in public schools. This discrepancy won't work in the U.S. or in any other country.

Turning to state and local preschool and pre-K, programs vary widely from place to place like the rest of public education. Some states have highly effective pre-K programs that are based on high standards and that are adequately funded. Others are barely better than subsidized child care—probably not harmful, but not likely to improve achievement.

Just how much could a commitment to quality preschool education do to improve U.S. test scores? The most effective programs might cut the achievement gap in primary and secondary education by half. Although that figure is probably too much to expect nationwide, even reducing the achievement gap between low-income and other students by 20 percent to 30 percent with this one reform would be a major accomplishment. To close the gap in primary and secondary education, preschool programs would have to produce immediate effects large enough to close half or more of the achievement gap at kindergarten entry. This is easy to do for simple literacy skills such as letter recognition and letter-sound correspondence. It is much more difficult for broad domains like language, mathematics, and social skills. However, these are the domains in which large gains are necessary if we are to have a strong, persistent impact on achievement and development more generally. Large gains are possible if we copy what has proved most effective in the past and learn not to repeat what has failed.

Action Steps for Principals

The answers reside right here in the U.S.—the difference between our performance on PISA and the performance by countries like Finland is that they do on a national basis what we do in only certain communities. The programs found to produce the largest gains have had well-educated, adequately paid teachers who exhibit high expectations for children's learning and development. These teachers worked with a well-defined curriculum under strong supervision. Our country, by dint of its cultural diversity, is less homogenous than Finland and Shanghai, so our challenge is greater. Yet some states and communities as different as Tulsa, Oklahoma; Union City, New Jersey; and Montgomery County, Maryland, have shown they know how to surmount those challenges. Other states and communities can learn from their successes. In fact, much could be accomplished if all school leaders would take the following 10 research-based, practice-tested action steps.

If you don't currently offer pre-K through your school:

1. **Reach out** to local preschool programs, child care centers, Head Start agencies, university experts, social service agencies, and parent groups to form an early childhood advisory council to develop transition plans, share professional development opportunities, and ensure that you are making the most of what is available through common planning and communication.

2. **Convert some, or all, of your pre-K special education classes into inclusion classes** by enrolling children without disabilities into the program. This is a low-cost way to increase preschool enrollment. You might need to adapt the curriculum to be appropriate for all children, but that will likely benefit the children with individualized education plans, too. The parents in your community will love it.

3. **Contract with local pre-K providers or offer pre-K yourself.** Some elementary schools with extra classroom space provide pre-K by making the space available to a local agency or Head Start, or the school district operates the preschool program, often offering tuition at a sliding scale. If your state regulations don't allow you to charge tuition, then form an education foundation to run the program.

If you do offer pre-K, do all of the above and in addition:

4. **Get educated** on what makes pre-K effective and different from the higher grades. If you try to impose the expectations you have for the higher grades for behavior, cleanliness, order, and curriculum scope and sequence on these classrooms, you won't be nearly as effective at closing the achievement gap. Children this age need intentional teaching that enables them to experiment, explore, learn to solve problems with others, and develop abstract thinking and self-regulation through make-believe play. This requires a large amount of self-initiated activity with teachers who know how to expand children's thinking and learning systematically during play and how to deliver instruction through play as well as through games, shared reading, planning and recall times, and other structured activities.

5. **Revise teacher evaluation and coaching tools** to include criteria that reflect effective, research-based teaching practices for pre-K. One size does not fit all when it comes to teaching. Focus on intentional teaching and effective use of small groups and other means of individualizing instruction.

6. **Hire only qualified preschool teachers.** Make sure that they have expertise in teaching 3- and 4-year olds. Former first-grade teachers with early childhood certification might not be adequately trained for pre-K teaching. Reassigning ineffective fourth-grade teachers definitely won't help you meet the promise of pre-K.

7. **Guarantee a diverse classroom composition.** Do everything you can to include mixed abilities and mixed incomes in the classroom. All children benefit from integration, and school failure is not isolated to those with a high number of low-income families. All children benefit from high-quality preschool, and even though the

most disadvantaged gain the most from pre-K, they also learn the most from more advantaged peers.

8. **Provide dual-language classrooms** where non-English speakers learn English but English speakers also become bilingual. This makes sense given our increasingly global economy and world languages goals for our schools, but it is also most effective educationally. Bilingualism is associated with more flexibility of thinking, higher achievement, and increased meta-linguistic ability. Moreover, children in dual-language classrooms learn just as much English as those in monolingual English classrooms, so there is no downside. Dual-language programs provide enough English-language experience so that children do not start kindergarten so far behind that they never catch up speaking English, while taking advantage of the child's developing home language base. Dual-language programs are most practical when there is a preponderance of one home language. When bilingual staff are lacking, schools can provide immersion in side-by-side home language and English-language classrooms where the children rotate weekly.

9. **Design professional development days expressly for the teachers in the pre-K program and other early grades.** It is clear that ongoing, classroom-specific, in-service education is critical to overall school success. However, professional development that consistently requires the pre-K teachers to "adapt this to the age of the children in your classroom" is not going to improve classroom practices. They don't need to just know where the children are going but how to get them there and where they came from developmentally. This is especially true for the domains that often are inadequately taught in teacher education programs: math, science, early literacy, oral-language development, bilingual acquisition, and inclusion of children with disabilities.

10. **Institute other schoolwide practices that meet the needs of young children.** For example, assemblies that are appropriate for fourth graders are almost never effective for 4-year-olds, cafeterias are not good places for young children to eat, and playground equipment is dangerous if not designed for younger children.

If American schools are going to close the achievement gap and move toward the top of the international achievement comparisons, widespread access to high-quality preschool will have to be one of the reforms that schools implement. If principals take the steps outlined here, they will shortly find test scores rising, grade retention falling, and special education loads might even decline. So to some extent, this is a self-financing reform. Beyond this, schools can use federal Title I funds and many states make funding available for pre-K. If adequate funds are not available, now is the time to make yourself heard at the local, state, and federal levels by telling the public and elected officials what you need to succeed in a global race to the top.

Critical Thinking

1. Suppose you are a kindergarten teacher in an elementary building that does not offer a pre-K program. Which one of the 10 recommendations listed in the article would you suggest your principal address first to help close the achievement gap?

2. Suppose you are a pre-K teacher in your community. Find out what the local elementary schools offer to help ease the transition into kindergarten for children leaving your program.

Create Central

www.mhhe.com/createcentral

Internet References

HighScope Educational Research Foundation
    www.highscope.org
Mid-Continent Research for Education and Learning
    www.mcrel.org
National Association for the Education of Young Children
    www.naeyc.org
Spark Action
    www.sparkaction.org
U.S. Department of Education
    www.ed.gov/teaching

ELLEN FREDE is co-director of the National Institute for Early Education Research (NIEER) and senior vice president of Acelero Learning Inc. **W. STEVEN BARNETT** is co-director of NIEER and a professor at Rutgers University.

Frede, Ellen; Barnett, W. Steven. From *Principal*, May/June 2011. Copyright © 2011 by National Association of Elementary School Principals. Reprinted by permission.

Article   Prepared by: Karen Menke Paciorek, *Eastern Michigan University*

The Hell of American Day Care

An Investigation into the Barely Regulated, Unsafe Business of Looking After Our Children

JONATHAN COHN

Learning Outcomes

After reading this article, you will be able to:

- Describe the economic importance of all children attending high-quality child care.

- Name three reasons why regulations for child care providers are so difficult to enforce.

- Share with parents points they should consider when looking for child care.

Trusting your child with someone else is one of the hardest things that a parent has to do—and in the United States, it's harder still, because American day care is a mess. About 8.2 million kids—about 40 percent of children under five—spend at least part of their week in the care of somebody other than a parent. Most of them are in centers, although a sizable minority attend home day cares. . . . In other countries, such services are subsidized and well-regulated. In the United States, despite the fact that work and family life has changed profoundly in recent decades, we lack anything resembling an actual child care system. Excellent day cares are available, of course, if you have the money to pay for them and the luck to secure a spot. But the overall quality is wildly uneven and barely monitored, and at the lower end, it's Dickensian.

This situation is especially disturbing because, over the past two decades, researchers have developed an entirely new understanding of the first few years of life. This period affects the architecture of a child's brain in ways that indelibly shape intellectual abilities and behavior. Kids who grow up in nurturing, interactive environments tend to develop the skills they need to thrive as adults—like learning how to calm down after a setback or how to focus on a problem long enough to solve it. Kids who grow up without that kind of attention tend to lack impulse control and have more emotional outbursts. Later on, they are more likely to struggle in school or with the law. They also have more physical health problems. Numerous studies show that all children, especially those from low-income

homes, benefit greatly from sound child care. The key ingredients are quite simple—starting with plenty of caregivers, who ideally have some expertise in child development.

By these metrics, American day care performs abysmally. A 2007 survey by the National Institute of Child Health Development deemed the majority of operations to be "fair" or "poor"—only 10 percent provided high-quality care. Experts recommend a ratio of one caregiver for every three infants between six and 18 months, but just one-third of children are in settings that meet that standard. Depending on the state, some providers may need only minimal or no training in safety, health, or child development. And because child care is so poorly paid, it doesn't attract the highly skilled. In 2011, the median annual salary for a child care worker was $19,430, less than a parking lot attendant or a janitor. Marcy Whitebook, the director of the Center for the Study of Child Care Employment at the University of California-Berkeley, told me, "We've got decades of research, and it suggests most child care and early childhood education in this country is mediocre at best."

At the same time, day care is a bruising financial burden for many families—more expensive than rent in 22 states. In the priciest, Massachusetts, it costs an average family $15,000 a year to place an infant full-time in a licensed center. In California, the cost is equivalent to 40 percent of the median income for a single mother.

Only minimal assistance is available to offset these expenses. The very poorest families receive a tax credit worth up to $1,050 a year per child. Some low-income families can also get subsidies or vouchers, but in most states the waiting lists for them are long. And so many parents put their kids in whatever they can find and whatever they can afford, hoping it will be good enough.

One indicator of the importance that the United States places on child care is how little official information the country bothers to collect about it. There are no regular surveys of quality and no national database of safety problems. One of the only serious studies, by Julia Wrigley and Joanna Dreby, appeared in the *American Sociological Review* in 2005. The researchers cobbled together a database of fatalities from state records, court documents, and media reports. On the surface, they said, day care appears "quite safe," but looking closer, they discovered "striking differences." The death rate for infants in home settings—whether in their own houses with a nanny or in home day cares—was seven times higher than in centers. The most common causes included drowning, violence—typically, caregivers shaking babies—and fire.

Statistics on Sudden Infant Death Syndrome (SIDS) are also revealing. ChildCare Aware of America, an advocacy group, calculated that, proportionally, about 9 percent of all reported SIDS deaths should take place in child care. The actual number is twice that. And while overall SIDS fatalities declined after a nationwide education campaign, the death rate in child care held steady.

Fatalities in child care remain relatively rare, but not as rare as they should be. In an investigation of Missouri day cares, *St. Louis Post-Dispatch* reporter Nancy Cambria documented 45 deaths between 2007 and 2010. One was three-month-old William Pratt, who died from blunt trauma after a caregiver threw him on a couch because she was frustrated with him. In 2012, a toddler named Juan Carlos Cardenas wandered off at an Indiana church day care. Nobody was watching him when he fell, face-first, into a baptismal pool and drowned.

Kenya Mire was an only child and hated it, and perhaps that's why she liked kids so much. After finishing high school, in 1999, she started training to be a medical assistant, hoping to work in a maternity ward. "I was just so interested in the idea of pregnancy," she says in her clear, measured way. "I always wanted to be that person where I was in the room with them from the time when they came in up through when they had the baby. I wanted to be the person that you told your story to."

When she was 22, however, Mire had to put her plans on hold, because she was pregnant herself. She and the father weren't together and her morning sickness got so bad she had to quit her job in a restaurant kitchen and move in with her mom. Despite all that, she felt "worry-free," she says. "I was just so excited to have a child." Eight years later, when she got pregnant again, it was different. This time, she knew how hard it would be.

When Mire went back to work, she put Kendyll in the same day care where she'd sent her son, Bryce: Grandma's Place—a bright, cheery operation with a professional staff. But Grandma's Place was expensive. Even with the subsidies Texas provides to low-income mothers, Mire had to pay $200 a week from her $12.50-an-hour job at a water utility company. Then the recession hit, and Mire lost the job. She had to pull Kendyll from the center.

Mire's dilemma was one that American parents, particularly single mothers, have struggled with for generations. The United States has always been profoundly uncomfortable with the idea of supporting child care outside the home, for reasons that inevitably trace back to beliefs over the proper role of women and mothers. At no point has a well-organized public day care system ever been considered the social ideal.

The first day cares were established during the Industrial Revolution, as increasing numbers of women in cities had to work. Jane Addams, the Progressive Era activist, was horrified to learn that all over Chicago, children were being left alone in tenement homes, morning till night. "The first three crippled children we encountered in the neighborhood had all been injured while their mothers were at work," she wrote in her 1910 memoir, *Twenty Years at Hull-House*. "One had fallen out of a third-story window, another had been burned, and the third had a curved spine due to the fact that for three years he had been tied all day long to the leg of the kitchen table, only released at noon by his older brother who hastily ran in from a neighboring factory to share his lunch with him."

Addams and other do-gooders created "day nurseries," although in many cities they were little more than baby farms. Geraldine Youcha writes in *Minding the Children* that a survey from that era by Chicago authorities "found children unclean and crowded into one small room without any playthings, and several nurseries in which the 'superintendent' did not even know the last names and addresses of some of the children."

The prevailing assumption at the time was that child care outside the home was deeply inferior to a mother's care. At best, it was regarded as a useful tool to "Americanize" the children of recent immigrants. Even Addams believed the optimal solution was government subsidies that would allow single mothers to look after their own children. ("With all of the efforts made by modern society to nurture and educate the young, how stupid it is to permit the mothers of young children to spend themselves in the coarser work of the world!" she wrote.) Toward that end, progressive states created widows' pensions, which were eventually expanded by the New Deal. Decades later, most people would know this kind of assistance simply as "welfare."

Arguably the best child care system America has ever had emerged during World War II, when women stepped in to fill the jobs of absent soldiers. For the first time, women were employed outside the home in a manner that society approved of, or at least tolerated. But many of these women had nowhere to leave their small children. They resorted to desperate measures—locking kids in the car in the factory parking lot, with the windows cracked open and blankets stretched across the back seats. This created the only moment in American politics when child care was ever a national priority. In 1940, Congress passed the Lanham Act, which created a system of government-run centers that served more than 100,000 children from families of all incomes.

After the war, children's advocates wanted to keep the centers open. But lawmakers saw them only as a wartime contingency—and if day care enabled women to keep their factory jobs, veterans would have a harder time finding work. The Lanham Act was allowed to lapse.

The federal government didn't get back into the child care business until the 1960s, with the creation of Head Start, which was narrowly targeted to support low-income children. A broader bill, designed to help working mothers by providing care to all kids who needed it, passed Congress a few years later. But President Nixon vetoed the legislation, saying he didn't want the government getting mixed up with "communal" child-rearing arrangements. Other than some increases in government funding for child tax credits and subsidies, federal child care policy has hardly changed in the last few decades.

But family life has changed immeasurably. In 1975, most American families had a male breadwinner and a female homemaker, compared with one in five today. Around two-thirds of mothers of young children now work outside the home.

Meanwhile, the idea that it is preferable to support low-income women to stay home with their children has become toxic in American politics. Since the passage of welfare reform in 1996, single mothers no longer get cash benefits unless they have a job or demonstrate progress toward getting one. Millions of women with meager resources who would have qualified under the old welfare regime must find somewhere for their young children to go while they're at work.

Day care, in other words, has become a permanent reality, although the public conversation barely reflects that fact. The issue of child care is either neglected as a "women's issue" or obsessed over in mommy-wars debates about the virtues of day care versus stay-at-home moms. Whether out of reluctance to acknowledge a fundamental change in the conception of parenthood—especially motherhood—or out of a fear of expanding the role of government in family life, we still haven't come to terms with the shift of women from the home to the workplace.

In many countries, day care is treated not as an afterthought, but as a priority. France, for instance, has a government-run system that experts consider exemplary. Infants and toddlers can attend *crèche,* which is part of the public health system, while preschoolers go to the *école maternelle,* which is part of the public education system. At every *crèche,* half the caregivers must have specialized collegiate degrees in child care or psychology; pediatricians and psychologists are available for consultation. Teachers in the *école maternelle* must have special post-college training and are paid the same as public school teachers. Neither program is mandatory, but nearly every preschooler goes to the *école maternelle.* Parents who stay at home to care for their children or hire their own caregivers receive generous tax breaks. It hardly seems a coincidence that 80 percent of French women work, compared with 60 percent of their American counterparts.

France spends more on care per child than the United States—a lot more, in the case of infants and toddlers. But most French families pay far less out of pocket, because the government subsidizes child care with tax dollars and sets fees according to a sliding scale based on income. Overall, the government devotes about 1 percent of France's gross domestic product to child care, more than twice as much as the United States does. As Steven Greenhouse once observed in *The New York Times,* "Comparing the French system with the American system . . . is like comparing a vintage bottle of Chateau Margaux with a $4 bottle of American wine."

There is one place in the United States where you can find a very similar arrangement: the military. In the 1980s, the Defense Department decided to address, rather than ignore, the same social changes that have transformed the wider economy. More women were entering the military, and many had children. Increasingly, the wives of male soldiers had jobs of their own. Believing that subsidized day care was essential for recruitment and morale, military leaders created a system

the National Women's Law Center has called a "model for the nation." More than 98 percent of military child care centers meet standards set by the National Association for the Education of Young Children, compared with only 10 percent of private-sector day cares.

A growing number of economists have become convinced that a comprehensive child care system is not only a worthwhile investment, but also an essential one. James Heckman, the Nobel-winning economist, has calculated that, in the best early childhood programs, every dollar that society invests yields between $7 and $12 in benefits. When children grow up to become productive members of the workforce, they feed more money into the economy and pay more taxes. They also cost the state less—for trips to the E.R., special education, incarceration, unemployment benefits, and other expenses that have been linked to inadequate nurturing in the earliest years of life. Two Fed economists concluded in a report that "the most efficient means to boost the productivity of the workforce 15 to 20 years down the road is to invest in today's youngest children" and that such spending would yield "a much higher return than most government-funded economic development initiatives."

In a July 2012 speech, Fed Chairman Ben Bernanke made the case that significant investment in early childhood would deliver even broader gains to the U.S. economy. "Notably, a portion of these economic returns accrues to the children themselves and their families," he said, "but studies show that the rest of society enjoys the majority of the benefits." Right now, too many Americans make major choices about work or finances based on the scarcity or cost of child care. Sometimes, this means women curtail their careers because it's cheaper to stay home or take a more flexible job than to pay for full-time care. Sometimes, a person of limited means pours a significant portion of their income into day care, which limits their ability to build a financial foundation for the future. When parents can find safe, affordable child care, they are more likely to realize their full economic potential. Their employers gain, too: Numerous studies show that access to quality day care increases productivity significantly.

This year, President Barack Obama has put forward what he calls a "universal pre-kindergarten" proposal. It would provide states with matching funds, so that they could set up their own programs for three- and four-year-olds, while modestly increasing subsidies for infant and toddler care. This plan would cost $75 billion over ten years, financed by higher cigarette taxes, which means it will meet serious political resistance. But the concept has support from key Democrats like House Minority Leader Nancy Pelosi, who has spoken of "doing for child care what we did for health care."

Since the 1930s, with the introduction of Social Security, the United States has constructed—slowly, haphazardly, often painfully—a welfare state. Pensions, public housing, health care—piece by piece, the government created protections for citizens that the market doesn't always provide. Child care is the major unfinished part of that project. The lack of quality, affordable day care is arguably the most significant barrier to full equality for women in the workplace. It makes it more likely that children born in poverty will remain there. That's why other developed countries made child care a collective responsibility long ago.

Critical Thinking

1. Ask three parents using child care how they chose that particular program for their child? What is most important for them to consider and why?

2. What are the challenges parents face when looking for child care?

3. Find the average cost for a week of child care for a three-year-old in your area.

Create Central

www.mhhe.com/createcentral

Internet References

Child Care Directory: Care Guide
www.care.com

Child Welfare League of America (CWLA)
www.cwla.org

Children's Defense Fund (CDF)
www.childrensdefense.org

Early Childhood Care and Development
www.ecdgroup.com

National Network for Child Care
www.nncc.org

National Resource Center for Health and Safety in Child Care and Early Education
http://nrckids.org

Article   Prepared by: Karen Menke Paciorek, *Eastern Michigan University*

Are We Paving Paradise?

In our rush to promote achievement, we've forgotten how 5-year-olds really learn.

ELIZABETH GRAUE

Learning Outcomes

After reading this article, you will be able to:

- Describe a hybrid kindergarten and name three observable qualities one might see in a hybrid kindergarten.

- Articulate the reasons for the change in kindergartens today from a generation ago and list some ways for kindergartens to become more child-centered.

Kindergarten teacher Celia Carlson passionately describes kindergarten in terms of transitions—it's the *only* first time that children will begin school, and it should be a place where both children and families adjust to a new, challenging context. She worries, though, that we've let go of what makes kindergarten a safe place for children to start. In our push to do more, sooner, faster, we fragment children into little pieces of assessment information and let go of the activities that enabled us to get to know them in more personal and integrated ways.

We've let go of the developmental piece that makes kindergarten a safe place for children to start school.

Across town, teacher Wendy Anderson feels like a rebel. Working in a high-poverty school, she struggles to maintain a semblance of a child-centered program. When she found a sensory table stacked with extra materials in another classroom, she asked whether she could have it. The kids flock to it, in need of kinesthetic experience and the joy of pouring, measuring, and comparing. "Where did you *get* that?" a colleague whispered, as though Wendy had brought in a unicorn or something illegal. Hers is also the only classroom that goes out for recess in the morning. Again, her colleagues ask, "How do you find the time?" Although she doesn't know why no one else goes out for recess, she wonders whether other classes lose precious time because of behavior issues associated with children who have not had a chance to play.

Teacher Pamela Gordon thinks that many people see her as old and eccentric. While everyone else uses worksheets, she continues to do projects with her students. They research together; and as they go, they integrate content required in the kindergarten curriculum. Currently, they're studying the lives of American Indians, figuring out how they obtained food and water and how the environment shaped their lives.

One reason so many of Pamela's colleagues favor worksheets is that they provide evidence for parents of what their children are doing. Instead of sending home worksheets, Pamela carefully writes a weekly letter to parents detailing activities and related learning, a great complement to children who answer the question, "What did you do at school today?" with a generic "We played."

These three teachers work hard to cultivate a children's garden within their classrooms. But just like in Joni Mitchell's well-known song, kindergarten seems threatened by developers who want to pave paradise and put up a parking lot. These teachers aren't mindlessly resisting new methods in favor of an outdated tradition; rather, they're fighting to keep children at the center of kindergarten.

The Evolution of Kindergarten
From a Focus on Children . . .

Kindergarten has always been a bit of an odd duck. It was a latecomer to the elementary school. Its teachers were educated in different programs, and its classrooms often looked like home, with gingham curtains and play kitchens. Teachers were left to craft a program that focused on the social and physical as well as on the academic. Guided by knowledge of human development, kindergarten teachers were interested in *children* rather than *curriculum content.*

To a Focus on Outcomes . . .

As kindergarten was incorporated into elementary school, programming slowly moved from half to full day in many areas and became governed by a desire for more academic content. Two movements prompted these shifts. First, as the number of women in the workforce increased, so did the number of children in child care. Kindergarten's traditional role of socializing children into group experiences seemed less relevant. Second, the notion of early intervention captured the interest of policymakers and the public. When Hart and Risley (1985) noted that middle-class children typically heard 8 million more words in a year than children living in poverty did, investing in preschool programs seemed just the right solution. Justified as a way to close the achievement gap; reduce special education referrals, teen pregnancy, and incarceration rates; and enhance earning power in adulthood, these early intervention programs evolved over time to be more literacy and mathematics focused. Child outcomes, rather than children's experiences, became the major element of program evaluation.

To a Focus on Literacy and Math

At the same time that preschool was changing, the elementary school was changing, too. States and districts developed grade-level standards, measurable and organized by content area. A key element in this process was research that stated that if students did not read at grade level by grade 3, they would never catch up (Stanovich, 1986). Districts mapped trajectories for students to hit the 3rd grade mark as well as interventions to nudge along the stragglers. Expectations were made explicit at each grade level, with a greater focus on literacy and mathematics.

For the first time, kindergarten was included in this map, with curriculum often designed by content-area specialists with limited experiences with 4-, 5-, and 6-year-olds. Although early learning standards covered kindergarten programs, the standards that counted—the content standards—were used to define a new kindergarten program. With the advent of pacing guides and high-pressure progress monitoring in literacy and math, attention to other elements of the kindergarten curriculum underwent a dramatic shift.

The Report Card: Then and Now

An easy way to see this shift is in the kindergarten report card. The report card I received as a kindergartner in 1960 was one page long; it focused on my ability to listen and play with others. In 1998—the year my oldest son started kindergarten—the progress report had sections on reading, speaking and listening, writing, science, social studies, social skills and work habits, and math, plus a large section for teacher comments. Each area included affective and behavioral information as well as skills. The social skills section was particularly informative, addressing issues of independence, flexibility, work habits, and peer interaction.

In contrast, the 2009 report card from that same school—note the name change from *progress report* to *report card*—reports on performance relative to expectations in language arts, mathematics, science, and social studies. It includes a lean section called the Child as Learner and Community Member. There's a single line for comments for each content area.

Unseen by families are thick grading guides that direct teacher ratings for each content area, requiring days of painstaking assessment—not to inform instructional practice but to make sure that students are meeting learning targets. For many kindergarten teachers, the report card obscures their ability to know students because as one teacher told me, "I don't have time to listen to children anymore." The report is more about tracking progress for administrative purposes than informing families about how their children are doing.

The Kindergarten Chimera

Thus, kindergarten has become a sort of *chimera*, a mash-up that has the genetic makeup of more than one species. Kindergarten has the genetic code of early childhood, with its attention to multiple dimensions of development and its focus on nurturing social relationships, along with the DNA of the content-focused elementary school. The current political, educational, and social context supports the elementary school elements of kindergarten's existence. However, the early childhood parts are losing ground; they should be on the endangered species list.

As someone who taught kindergarten for many years, I agree with standards-based teaching and the need to align expectations and practices across the education system. However, I worry that in the rush to promote content achievement we've forgotten that children are multidimensional beings who learn in complicated ways. Because the curriculum increasingly reflects the expertise of content specialists in the district office, the parts of kindergarten not explicitly listed on the report card are withering away or, at least, are not cultivated in a way that supports a balanced program and a balanced child. We do not attend, for example, to the future architect who builds with blocks, designing structures, managing materials, and testing the laws of physics. We also ignore the aesthetic child who paints, draws, sings, and dances.

This lack of focus on the early childhood part of kindergarten is especially important in the context of transition. A child who moves from a developmentally appropriate preschool program to a content-focused kindergarten experiences a kind of whiplash. We need a more ecological approach to kindergarten.

Making the Case
For Play

The growing allocation of kindergarten time to academic content has firmly pushed play to the edges. What counts as play in many classrooms are highly controlled centers that focus on particular content labeled as "choice" but that are really directed at capturing a specific content-based learning experience, such as number bingo or retelling a story exactly as the teacher told it on a flannel board. It's like calling the choices of doing the laundry, grocery shopping, or cleaning out your closet "playful." It also means that in-depth project work that involves research into child-initiated questions just takes too much time. If students become fascinated with the birds at the feeder outside the classroom window, for example, this cannot become a focus of learning because it's not listed in the standards.

What's lost with this shift? Attention to anything but clearly defined cognitive aspects of development. Although vitally important, learning content is inherently intertwined with other elements like motor skills, aesthetic experiences, and social-emotional development. In an increasingly sedentary, structured context, students have few opportunities for rich experiences of moving, creating, or interacting.

The early childhood community, which has traditionally valued play as a learning tool, has not been very articulate about play's importance in our evidence-based school economy. It's no longer enough to argue that play is the work of children;

we're now required to prove what children *get* from play. What they get must translate to increased achievement or reduced risk. So let's nail the evidence base.

Wendy Anderson takes her kindergartners out for recess and schedules free play because she recognizes that play is a complex activity that has many benefits beyond the pure joy it gives children. Learning to negotiate, share, and empathize are all key to playing; we deny children the opportunity to learn these skills in a kindergarten without play. Yes, Robert Fulghum (2004) was right: Everything you need to know, you learn in kindergarten. But the kindergarten he's talking about is one that values the social, the emotional, and the aesthetic; it's one that teaches through modeling, practice, and nurturing.

Rich play environments enable children to develop what psychologists call *executive function*. When children play, they learn to shift attention, remember, and inhibit impulses; as a result, they are able to plan, solve problems, and work toward a goal. These skills relate to later achievement in social areas and in academic content, such as mathematics and literacy (Bodrova & Leong, 2007; Diamond, Barnett, Thomas, & Munro, 2007). Doing away with play does away with opportunities to develop these skills.

In recent years, some have called for a kindergarten curriculum that once again includes attention to social and emotional competence (Raver, 2002), an important reminder that for children to succeed in school, a complex set of capacities must be carefully balanced.

For Relationships and Trust

Celia Carlson describes how students can no longer take the scenic route in kindergarten—her students are fast-tracked so they can get to the reading level mandated by the district by the end of the year. Although important, such reading supports often involve pulling students out of the classroom. Celia worries that she's not getting a chance to build the foundation that students need to be resilient learners who can handle frustration, work through problems, and focus on the essentials.

Relationships and trust take time—and time is in short supply in today's kindergarten. Celia sees students crumble when they hit any tiny bump—in the classroom, in the cafeteria, and on the playground. Her students dissolve into tears or pick fights in situations that challenge them. In the past, she would have better known their triggers and could have built opportunities for them to be resilient. The students have no reserves to draw from because teachers simply haven't had enough time to do this important work.

Relationships and trust take time—and time is in short supply in today's kindergarten.

The Cutoff Conundrum

Policymakers have addressed perennial concerns about readiness by requiring children to be older before they can enter school. The kindergarten entrance date has slowly but surely moved back from January so that most states now require

---

Elements of a Hybrid Kindergarten

- It addresses all areas of child development: social-emotional, physical, aesthetic, cognitive, linguistic.
- It's balanced, with time for whole-group, small-group, and independent activities. It provides opportunities for teacher-directed lessons and student choice. Some activities require physical activity; others focus on the mind.
- It's intellectually engaging, addressing issues of interest to 5-year-olds, respecting their curiosity and encouraging them to develop inquiry and problem-solving skills. It provides support for skills related to literacy and mathematics.
- It devotes *real* time to play, both indoors and out, and provides extended periods for children to choose activities.
- Its physical environment includes a dramatic play area, art supplies, unit blocks, equipment for sensory experiences, musical instruments, books, manipulatives, soft and hard surfaces, and a place to cuddle. Yes, cuddling is a requirement even in this touch-phobic society.
- It recognizes that kindergartners are eager learners who do not march lockstep through the curriculum. It toes a fine line between supporting students' current developmental levels and stretching them to attain standards.
- Its teacher has a background in early childhood education and knows the value of both guided reading and project inquiry, of both solving mathematics problems and exploring social issues. He or she advocates a balanced program and has support from colleagues, the principal, and the community.

---

children to be 5 in September. Some states have moved it even earlier, to a summer cutoff.

I lived through such a move when I taught kindergarten in Missouri in the mid-1980s. As the cutoff date moved from October 1 to July 1, my students got bigger and bigger—and the baseline for "typical" followed suit.

I have to wonder if this solution is, in fact, contributing to the problem it's meant to solve. With slightly older students, the expectations become a little more intense, which makes people worry about the kids who can't cope with the demands—which makes us once again try new strategies to ensure readiness. Is kindergarten caught in a recursive cycle where every fix induces more problems?

Kindergarten: A Hybrid Version

I recognize that today's children are different from those of even a decade ago and that kindergarten must evolve in the same way a garden does. But that evolution must support the very children that kindergarten should nurture. We need to step back and consider whether all the innovations and interventions, all the programs and progress monitoring, are actually getting us what we want. In our work to develop assessment-driven instruction, have we driven off without the child?

The assessment that kindergarten children deserve is broad-based, contextual, and inclusive of *all* dimensions of development—not just those few that feed the accountability machine. We need to reassess both the means and ends of kindergarten, remembering that under all the data we generate are real live children. Those children need us to create education experiences that are responsive, challenging, and nurturing of all the complexity that is a 5-year-old.

References

Bodrova, E., & Leong, D. J. (2007). *Tools of the mind: The Vygotskian approach to early childhood education.* Upper Saddle River, NJ: Prentice Hall.

Diamond, A., Barnett, W. S., Thomas, J., & Munro, S. (2007). Preschool program improves cognitive control. *Science, 318*(5855), 1387–1388.

Fulghum, R. (2004). *All I really need to know I learned in kindergarten.* New York: Ballantine Books.

Hart, B., & Risley, T. (1985). *Meaningful differences.* Baltimore: Brookes Publishing.

Raver, C. (2002). Emotions matter: Making the case for the role of young children's emotional development for early school readiness. *Social Policy Report, 16*(3), 3–18.

Stanovich, K. E. (1986). Matthew effects in reading: Some consequences of individual differences in the acquisition of literacy. *Reading Research Quarterly, 21*(4), 360–407.

Critical Thinking

1. Describe some of the characteristics of a hybrid kindergarten.
2. Why is play, both inside and outside, so important for kindergarten children?

Create Central

www.mhhe.com/createcentral

Internet References

Busy Teacher's Café
www.busyteacherscafe.com

Harvard Family Research Project
www.hfrp.org

National Association for the Education of Young Children
www.naeyc.org

National School Boards Association
www.nsba.org

Spark Action
www.sparkaction.org

ELIZABETH GRAUE is a professor of early childhood education in the Department of Curriculum and Instruction at the University of Wisconsin, Madison. She is also associate director of Faculty, Staff, and Graduate Development at the Wisconsin Center for Education Research; graue@education.wisc.edu.

Author's note— All teacher names are pseudonyms.

Graue, Elizabeth. From *Educational Leadership,* April 2011, pp. 12–17. Copyright © 2011 by ASCD. Reprinted by permission. The Association for Supervision and Curriculum Development is a worldwide community of educators advocating sound policies and sharing best practices to achieve the success of each learner. To learn more, visit ASCD at www.ascd.org.

Unit 2

UNIT

Prepared by: Karen Menke Paciorek, *Eastern Michigan University*

Young Children, Their Families, and Communities

Many different issues are addressed in this Unit titled Young Children, Their Families, and Communities and I invite you to reflect on your family, the types of experiences children today have as opposed to those you encountered, and the ways educators can help families as they navigate the ever-changing, fast-paced world while raising children. The role of fathers in the lives of their children has received renewed attention as parents work to find the many ways in which they can foster the development of their children. Mothers have traditionally taken on a significant role in rearing children but dads are increasingly taking on more responsibility and children fortunate enough to have a caring and invested father in their lives are so fortunate. As early childhood educators, our wish is for all young children to grow up in loving and supportive families with parents truly vested in providing what is best for their child.

Obesity and eating behaviors are very critical issues. Teachers working with young children and their families play a key role when it comes to educating parents and children about appropriate food choices and providing daily physical activity. First Lady Michelle Obama has taken on the issue of childhood obesity and healthy eating and is working hard to educate families, children, and school personnel about the importance of this topic. Childhood obesity is noticeable every time one enters a fast-food restaurant and hears a child order a meal by its number on the menu because they are so familiar with the selection at that particular restaurant. It is also evident on a playground where children just sit on the sideline not wanting to participate with their peers due to negative body image. Obese children miss more school, and obesity can affect students' performance on tests. As educators, it is our responsibility to encourage daily structured and unstructured physical activity, healthy food options, and education about the importance of leading a healthy lifestyle. While on the subject, it is important for teachers and caregivers to model appropriate eating habits and be involved in daily physical activity that will provide you with both the strength and endurance for your demanding job. A healthy and physically fit teacher is able to engage with the children and provide the support they need as they move throughout the classroom and school.

With technology being so readily accessible these days, 75 percent of mothers in a study at babycenter.com reported they have given their young children a phone to play with. It is time we examined any policies related to the use of technology by young children. The American Academy of Pediatrics recommends no screen time for children under the age of two, however many parents will report that recommendation is most often not followed in their home. There is a need to use the many strategies for introducing young children to technology in an age-appropriate way as technology will play a significant role in their lives. Already there are thousands of phone and computer applications for children three and under. An adult needs to supervise any use of technology by children so they don't become frustrated or, worse, get connected to an inappropriate site. There is a balance to using technology with young children and many experts recommend that when children can easily have access to the actual materials such as playing with blocks at home that should be the preferred method of learning but when it is not convenient, for instance when riding in a car, a computer app may fill in nicely.

When examining the partnerships between young children, their families, the communities in which they live, and the educational setting, one word keeps coming up again and again: relationships. While talking with two of my undergraduate students, Tyler and Kelly, we were laughing about the number of times the word "relationships" is used in our conversations about the work we do with young children and their families. Kelly and Tyler certainly understand the importance of developing healthy relationships between the adults in the early childhood setting and the young children and their families. These two future teachers are fully aware of the significant role they play in earning the trust of the children and families by developing strong relationships. My wish is for all children to have teachers like Tyler, Kelly, and the many other outstanding future teachers preparing to work all across our country. Think about how you can initiate relationships with young children and their families and also foster them throughout the year so that when challenging discussions are held, there will be some level of collaboration already in place. The chance to interact with families diminishes as the learner gets older until it is almost nonexistent at the secondary level.

Early childhood educators who recognize and fully embrace the rich contributions families can make as partners in the education process will benefit and so will the children. Sharing between the parents and teachers about the strengths and needs of the child become the path to student success. Families can provide a wealth of information about their child, and teachers who develop strong relationships with families are beneficiaries of this knowledge. Upon doing a check of web sites at a local school district, I came across a principal's page at one school. There the principal posted pictures of herself as an elementary student and shared some of her likes and skills when she was younger. Children and families form connections with those who take the time to get to know them. Share a bit about yourself and your interests, and you may be rewarded with information from families about the children in your class. Build on this information to provide learning experiences that are relevant and meaningful to your children.

Article   Prepared by: Karen Menke Paciorek, *Eastern Michigan University*

Why Dads Matter

A third of American children are growing up in homes without their biological fathers.

Lois M. Collins and Marjorie Cortez

Learning Outcomes

After reading this article, you will be able to:

- Describe the difference between a dad and a father figure in a child's life.

- Define the term "family churn" and how it affects young children.

- Discuss the effects on children, especially boys, growing up in a family without a dad.

Jordan Ott was the third of his mother's six children, born over the course of four marriages.

By age 8, he'd had two step-dads; his brothers and sisters had more or fewer based on birth order. Each child also had different numbers of siblings, depending on whether their own dads fathered other children. Ott has one full sister, four half-siblings and at one point had three step-siblings "that I know of," he said. His own father has mostly lived far away.

His story is not uncommon today. More than half of babies of mothers under 30 are born to unmarried parents. The divorce rate among those who do marry exceeds 40 percent, according to the 2012 State of Our Unions report.

These statistics play out most often in the form of absent fathers—or the arrival and departure of serial father figures involved in romantic relationships with a child's mother. (Moms still usually retain custody in a breakup or divorce.) Twenty-four million American children—one in three—are growing up in homes without their biological fathers, the 2011 Census says. Children in father-absent homes, it notes, are almost four times more likely to be poor.

Like Ott, now 25, children may grow up with lots of father figures, but no real dad. Or they can be like Arvie Burgos, 17 and in foster care in Utah, who grew up in a virtually man-free zone.

Ott said he learned not to pay attention to stepfathers, even one he had for years. "If I did something wrong and needed discipline, he was all over it. Otherwise, we didn't have too much to do with each other."

Meanwhile, Burgos' sole significant male role model was a young man he saw a few hours each month courtesy of a Big Brothers program. His father had never been part of his life and his mother was a drug addict. He could count on his grandmother, but she died when he was 15, about the time his mentor moved away.

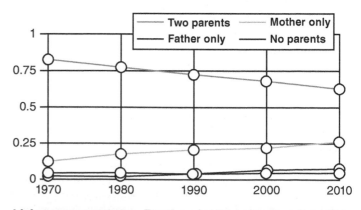

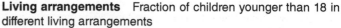

Living arrangements   Fraction of children younger than 18 in different living arrangements

Sources: Census IPUMS 1 percent sample for year 1970, and Census IPUM 5 percent samples for years 1980, 1990, and 2000, and Americans Community Survey (ACS) 2010.

"I think there's consensus that cultural and family factors are causing children's family lives to be more unstable than in the past," said Andrew J. Cherlin, author of *The Marriage-Go-Round* and director of the Hopkins Population Center at Johns Hopkins University. Experts debate whether recent cultural shifts or economic changes most undermine family stability, but, said Cherlin, "most who I respect believe both are at play."

"None of this implies men are better as dads than women are as moms."

Most children weather family turmoil and wind up OK, said Cherlin, who coined the term "family churn" to describe what happens to families as couples split, often moving dad out of the home and a new man in. A study in the *Journal of Marriage and Family* said children in such homes experience an average of more than 5.25 partnership transitions. That's tough for kids who are used to having their own fathers within reach.

"Dad also helps with impulse control and memory and enhances a child's ability to respond effectively to new or ambiguous situations, for boys and girls," said Warren Farrell, author of *Father and Child Reunion*. Children who are close to their fathers tend to achieve more academically, while kids with absent fathers are more likely to drop out. Fathers are the biggest factor in preventing drug use, Farrell said.

The time a dad spends with his children is a particularly strong predictor of how empathetic a child will become, according to commission of experts who wrote a proposal asking President Obama to create a White House Council on Boys and Men. The group, which Farrell helped assemble, compiled research showing infants with dads living at home were months ahead in personal and social development. Children who lack contact with fathers are more likely to be treated for emotional or behavioral problems. Girls with absent or indifferent fathers are more prone to hyperactivity. If dad is around, girls are less likely to become pregnant as teens.

As early as 1993, studies showed that dads also influenced whether their sons became teenage fathers. A Temple University study found no boys born to teen mothers became teen fathers if they had close relationships with their biological fathers, compared to 15 percent of those who didn't have that closeness.

"None of this implies men are better as dads than women are as moms," Farrell and the commission emphasized. Children need both.

But dad's place is not always secure. The commission report said, "The United States has done a better job of integrating women into the workplace than in integrating men into the family—especially into the lives of children in the non-intact family. We have valued men as wallets more than as dads." The result is "moms feeling deprived of resources and dads feeling deprived of purpose and children feeling deprived of the full range of parenting input."

Few have studied the relationship between children and sequential parent figures, said Paula Fomby, associate research scientist at University of Michigan. She said research suggests someone not biologically related is less likely to invest in a child for various hypothetical reasons, including unclear parental roles. Sometimes, father figures compete or are stretched thin by obligations to children fathered with other women.

The more transitions a child endures, the worse off he or she typically is, Cherlin said.

In Ott's case, not all the siblings growing up with him experienced the family's transitions the same way. Some of his younger half-siblings were actually living with both biological parents while he was dealing with a step-father. It was unequal and complicated as step-fathers treated him and his siblings each differently. He saw friends in intact families enjoy greater consistency, something he wants for his own future children.

"There is a great deal of evidence that children from single-parent homes have worse outcomes on both academic and economic measures than children from two-parent families," wrote scholar Elaine C. Kamarck and Third Way president Jonathan Cowan in the introduction to *Wayward Sons,* a report produced for Washington think tank Third Way. "There is a vast inequality of both financial resources and parental time and attention between one- and two-parent families."

The report also said absent fathers particularly impact the psychosocial and academic development of boys.

University of California-Berkeley's Philip A. Cowan and his wife, Carolyn Pape Cowan, study parent couples. Their research shows a couple's relationship is vital to their children, even if they are no longer intimate partners—whether they're divorced, separated or never married.

"The relationship between two biological parents determines a lot about how fathers are going to be involved, and that determines a lot how kids are going to be," he said.

Simply improving the job market for young adults, especially men, would do wonders to stabilize families.

If parents get along, their children tend to be more psychologically and emotionally healthy. Moms who feel their child's father backs them up are better mothers through all stages of the child's development, reports the U.S. Department of Health and Human Services—"more responsive, affectionate, and confident with their infants; more self-controlled in dealing with defiant toddlers; and better confidants for teenagers seeking advice and emotional support."

Ott's father lived too far away to be available physically or emotionally. Burgos "knew" his father through a single letter and a phone call. Neither of them gained the benefits the studies attribute to an involved, interactive dad.

The federal government is beginning to recognize how important fathers are to children after years of focusing almost exclusively on mothers. Government-funded programs to promote marriage for at-risk families now include money for paternal involvement, too, Cowan said. Social welfare programs have been told to include fathers in case management. The Obama, Bush and Clinton administrations all funded healthy-marriage initiatives. Cowan called attempts to include fathers "islands of hope," but concedes they're "fighting decades of prejudice."

The odds are still stacked against fathers in many government and nonprofit agencies designed to assist families, he said. Often, men's names are not included on case files, even when parents are married.

Simply improving the job market for young adults, especially men, would do wonders to stabilize families—particularly those just starting out, Cherlin said. Experts have been surprised by the real drop in divorce among the college-educated, who still can get good jobs. He said young people need more job training opportunities and apprenticeships, especially if they're not college-bound. Making sure tax policy doesn't discourage marriage and providing a modest earned income tax credit for disadvantaged childless young adults would also encourage formation of stable relationships, he added.

Stable relationships are something both Ott and Burgos long for, and each can picture one in his mind. But both admit to feeling somewhat unsure about how to make it happen in real life.

Burgos said he had some good teachers and a foster dad he liked a lot, but no confidants after his "big brother" Jacob

moved away. "I don't really have deep emotional conversations with anybody," he admits.

Ott recently married and hopes to have children and a stable family life. Burned more than once by the choices adults made when he was young, he keeps one eye on the past. It's a path he doesn't intend to travel.

"I've never had a family," Ott said. "I know what I'm not going to do."

Critical Thinking

1. Share with a father you know the benefits of him spending time developing a strong relationship with his child or children.

2. Plan ways you could involve fathers of children in your classroom who are not living in the same home. What activities would build a bond between the two?

Internet References

Father Involvement Research Alliance
http://www.fira.ca/

National Center for Fathering
http://www.fathers.com/

National Fatherhood Initiative
http://www.fatherhood.org/

Article

Prepared by: Karen Menke Paciorek, *Eastern Michigan University*

Building a Pedagogy of Engagement for Students in Poverty

The only surefire way to eliminate the achievement gap is to eradicate poverty. Since that's not going to happen anytime soon, educators can still take many research-proven steps to foster equality of opportunity in education.

PAUL C. GORSKI

Learning Outcomes

After reading this article, you will be able to:

- Explain the effects of the economic disparity found in schools today.

- List three strategies that have been found to be effective when working with children living in poverty.

- Advocate for services that benefit all children living in poverty.

I started kindergarten in 1976, a decade before personal computers were in vogue for people who could afford them. The image of largesse I remember from elementary school was the 64-count box of crayons—the one with the built-in sharpener. I didn't have language for it then, but I knew that box denoted privilege.

I also remember when poster board was the hot commodity. I watched some students tremble when teachers assigned projects requiring it. Russell, a classmate, was shamed into outing himself as poor when the teacher asked the class, "Who needs help getting poster board?" The teachers I most admired were subtler, dumping everybody's crayons into community bins and keeping a few sheets of poster board tucked behind a filing cabinet, distributing it discreetly to students whose families couldn't afford it. My family fell in-between. We could afford poster board, but I settled for boxes of 16-count crayons.

During a recent visit to a high-poverty school, I asked 8th graders how many of them had a working computer and Internet access at home; only a few of the 40 students raised their hands. Then I asked how many of them had been assigned homework that required access to computers and the Internet since the last grading period ended; everybody raised their hands.

Even before the e-revolution, Russell and other students who had no say in their families' financial conditions were at a disadvantage. That's when poster board was the commodity. Now it's computers. And the Internet. And printers.

It can be difficult to remember that many poor families simply cannot afford these technologies. It can be even more difficult to remember that the same families have reduced access to a bunch of other resources that influence learning, such as health care, recreational opportunities, and even clean air. And given shifting demographics and the recent recession, their numbers are growing, especially in suburban schools where many of us are unaccustomed to teaching low-income students.

Low-income youth learn best when pedagogy is driven by high academic expectations for all students—where standards aren't lowered based on socioeconomic status.

That's important because, as David Berliner (2009) reminds us, the only sure path to educational equity is eliminating poverty itself. As long as inequality abounds, so will those pesky achievement gaps. Unfortunately education practitioners can't eliminate poverty on their own. And we can't afford to wait, and poor families can't afford to wait, for poverty to be eliminated. Even as I work toward that bigger change, I have to commit to doing what I can to address the inequities that students are experiencing right now.

A study of 400 teachers in low-income schools found that those who rejected a deficit view of their students were happier with their jobs.

This is why I've spent much of the past five years reading every bit of research I can find on what works when it comes to mitigating the effects of economic inequality in schools. This is the question guiding my research: What can teachers and administrators do today, not to raise low-income students' test scores—as that obsession, itself, is a symptom of one of those bigger societal things that needs to change—but to improve educational opportunity?

Promising Practices and a Couple Caveats

Before considering my suggestions, remember that low-income people are infinitely diverse. No researcher knows your students better than you know them. So, no matter how tempting the easy solution may seem, there simply is no silver bullet, no nicely wrapped bundle of strategies that work for all low-income students everywhere. Aside from advocating for the social change necessary to eliminate poverty, the best thing we can do in the name of educational equity is honor the expertise of people in poor communities by teaming with them as partners in educational equity.

Second, more important than any strategy are the dispositions with which we relate to low-income families. Any strategy will be ineffective if I believe poverty is a marker of intellectual deficiency (Robinson, 2007). So I need to check my own biases even as I enact these strategies.

Classroom Strategies

Express high expectations through higher-order, engaging pedagogies. According to Lee and Burkam (2003), students labeled "at-risk" who attend schools that combine rigorous curricula with learner-centered teaching achieve at higher levels and are less likely to drop out than their peers who experience lower-order instruction. Like everyone else, low-income youth

learn best at schools in which pedagogy is driven by high academic expectations for all students—where standards aren't lowered based on socioeconomic status (Ramalho, Garza, & Merchant, 2010), and in classrooms where they have access to dialogic, inquiry-driven, collaborative pedagogies (Georges, 2009; Wenglinsky, 2002). Critical pedagogies and the development of critical literacies can be particularly helpful when it comes to school engagement among low-income students. Provide them with opportunities to tell stories about themselves that challenge the deficit-laden portrayals they often hear.

Enhance family involvement. Make sure opportunities for family involvement are accessible to parents and guardians who are likely to work multiple jobs, including evening jobs, who may not have access to paid leave, who may struggle to afford child care, and who may rely on public transportation. Start by providing transportation and on-site child care (Amatea & West-Olatunji, 2007; Van Galen, 2007).

Incorporate arts into instruction. Among the most instructionally illogical responses to the test score obsession is the elimination of arts programs—most commonly in lower-income schools—to carve out additional time for reading, writing, and math. Exposure to art, theater, and music education bolsters learning, engagement, and retention for all students and especially for low-income youth, whose families generally can't afford music lessons or art camp (Catterall, Chapleau, & Iwanaga, 1999; Pogrow, 2006). Take advantage of local artists and musicians, who might consider working with your students or helping you think about the arts in discipline-specific ways.

Incorporate movement into instruction. Low-income students also are losing access to recess and physical education. The lack of recreational facilities and green space in poor communities, costs associated with recreational sports, and work and family obligations, often means that recess or P.E. is the only opportunity for low-income youth to exercise. Students who are physically fit fare better in school, and childhood physical fitness is an indicator of how healthy a person will be as an adult (Fahlman, Hall, & Lock, 2006). Anything you can do to incorporate movement into learning will help mitigate these disparities.

Focus intently on student and family strengths. Having high expectations is not pretention. When teachers adopt a deficit view of students, performance declines. The opposite happens when teachers focus on student strengths (Haberman, 1995; Johns, Schmader, & Martens, 2005). It will be better for you, too. Robinson (2007) found in a study of 400 teachers in low-income schools that those who rejected a deficit view were happier with their jobs.

Analyze materials for class bias. Poor families often are depicted in stereotypical ways in picture books and other learning materials (Jones, 2008). A variety of useful tools exist to help us uncover these sorts of biases, such as the checklist of the National Association for the Teaching of English Working Party on Social Class and English Teaching (1982). Engage students in an analysis of the biases you uncover. And please retire that obnoxious picture of the "hobo" from your vocabulary wall. It's 2013.

Promote literacy enjoyment. According to Mary Kellett, "If we . . . acknowledge that literacy proficiency can be a route out of poverty . . . the most powerful strategy is to . . . promote reading enjoyment. This is likely to make the biggest impact on literacy proficiency" (2009, p. 399). This means literacy instruction should not focus solely on mechanics and should avoid practices that give students negative associations with literacy, such as forcing them to perform literacy skills publicly.

Reach out to families early and often. Many low-income parents and guardians experienced school as a hostile environment when they were students (Gorski, 2012). Any hesitance we experience when we reach out is not necessarily ambivalence about school. It might reflect reasonable distrust for the system we represent. It might be about long work hours or a lack of access to a telephone. Be persistent. Build trust. Most importantly, demonstrate trust by nurturing positive relationships. We can do this by facilitating ongoing communication rather than reaching out only when something is wrong, creating an equitable classroom environment across all dimensions of diversity, and refusing to invalidate concerns about inequalities that are raised by low-income families (Hamovitch, 1996).

A Few Higher-level Strategies

As we grow our spheres of influence, we might consider taking on some bigger battles for class equity.

Advocate universal preschool. Investment in early childhood education might be the most critical educational advocacy we can do, as disparities in access to early educational interventions compound throughout children's lifetimes (Bhattacharya, 2010).

Nurture relationships with community agencies, including health clinics and farms (for fresh food). Susan Neuman (2009) found that of all types of educational interventions for poor families, those based on coordinated efforts among educational, social, and health services were most effective.

Reduce class sizes. Despite the illusion of a debate, research shows that class size matters (Rouse & Barrow, 2006).

Increase health services in schools. Start by broadening vision screenings to include farsightedness, which relates to up close (book) reading (Gould & Gould, 2003). Other services and screenings should focus on risks that are elevated in low-income communities, such as asthma (Davis, Gordon, & Burns, 2011). Fight to keep nurses in low-income schools, where they are needed desperately (Telljohann, Dake, & Price, 2004).

Even as I work toward eliminating poverty, I have to commit to doing what I can do now to address the inequalities facing the people right in front of me.

Literacy instruction should not focus solely on mechanics but should promote the enjoyment of reading.

Conclusion

It bears repeating that teachers are not trained and schools are not equipped to make up for societal inequalities. This is why we should commit to doing all that we can in our spheres of influence toward class equity. And once we have done that, we can expand those spheres.

References

Amatea, E.S. & West-Olatunji, C.A. (2007). Joining the conversation about educating our poorest children: Emerging leadership roles for school counselors in high-poverty schools. *Professional School Counseling, 11* (2), 81–89.

Berliner, D. (2009). *Poverty and potential: Out-of-school factors and school success.* Tempe, AZ: Education and the Public Interest Center & Education Policy Research Unit.

Bhattacharya, A. (2010). Children and adolescents from poverty and reading development: A research review. *Reading & Writing Quarterly, 26,* 115–139.

Catterall, J., Chapleau, R., & Iwanaga, J. (1999). Involvement in the arts and human development: General involvement and intensive involvement in music and theater arts. In E.B. Fiske (Ed.), *Champions of change: The impact of the arts on learning* (pp. 1–18). Washington, DC: Arts Education Partnership, President's Committee on the Arts and the Humanities.

Davis, D.W., Gordon, M.K., & Burns, B.M. (2011). Educational interventions for childhood asthma: A review and integrative model for preschoolers from low-income families. *Pediatric Nursing, 37* (1), 31–38.

Fahlman, M.M., Hall, H.L., & Lock, R. (2006). Ethnic and socioeconomic comparisons of fitness, activity levels, and barriers to exercise in high school females. *Journal of School Health, 76* (1), 12–17.

Georges, A. (2009). Relation of instruction and poverty to mathematics achievement gains during kindergarten. *Teachers College Record, 111* (9), 2148–2178.

Gorski, P.C. (2012). Perceiving the problem of poverty and schooling: Deconstructing the class stereotypes that misshape education policy and practice. *Equity & Excellence in Education, 45* (2), 302–319.

Gould, M.C. & Gould, H. (2003). A clear vision for equity and opportunity. *Phi Delta Kappan, 85* (4), 324–328.

Haberman, M. (1995). *Star teachers of children in poverty.* Irvine, CA: Kappa Delta Pi.

Hamovitch, B. (1996). Socialization without voice: An ideology of hope for at-risk students. *Teachers College Record, 98* (2), 286–306.

Johns, M., Schmader, T., & Martens, A. (2005). Knowing is half the battle: Teaching stereotype threat as a means of improving women's math performance. *Psychological Science, 16,* 175–179.

Jones, S. (2008). Grass houses: Representations and reinventions of social class through children's literature. *Journal of Language and Literacy Education, 4* (2), 40–58.

Kellett, M. (2009). Children as researchers: What we can learn from them about the impact of poverty on literacy opportunities. *International Journal of Inclusive Education, 13* (4), 395–408.

Lee, V. & Burkam, D. (2003). Dropping out of high school: The role of school organization and structure. *American Educational Research Journal, 40,* 353–393.

National Association for the Teaching of English. (1982). Checklist for class bias and some recommended books. *English in Education, 16,* 34–37.

Neuman, S.B. (2009). Use the science of what works to change the odds for children at risk. *Phi Delta Kappan, 90* (8), 582–587.

Pogrow, S. (2006). Restructuring high-poverty elementary schools for success: A description of the Hi-Perform school design. *Phi Delta Kappan, 88* (3), 223–229.

Ramalho, E.M., Garza, E., & Merchant, B. (2010). Successful school leadership in socioeconomically challenging contexts: School principals creating and sustaining successful school improvement. *International Studies in Educational Administration, 38* (3), 35–56.

Robinson, J.G. (2007). Presence and persistence: Poverty ideology and inner-city teaching. *Urban Review, 39,* 541–565.

Rouse, C.E. & Barrow, L. (2006). U.S. elementary and secondary schools: Equalizing opportunity or replacing the status quo? *The Future of Children, 16* (2), 99–123.

Telljohann, S.K., Dake, J.A., & Price, J.H. (2004). Effect of full-time versus part-time school nurses on attendance of elementary students with asthma. *Journal of School Nursing, 20* (6), 331–334.

Van Galen, J. (2007). Late to class: Social class and schooling in the new economy. *Educational Horizons, 85,* 156–167.

Wenglinsky, H. (2002). *How teaching matters: Bringing the classroom back into discussions of teacher quality.* Princeton, NJ: Milken Family Foundation.

Critical Thinking

1. Why does the author list the incorporating of arts and movement into the curriculum for children living in poverty?

2. Does your state offer preschool for at-risk children or those living in poverty? If so, how accessible are the programs to children living in your area?

3. Reflect on practices you may have observed in the past or see happening today in schools that marginalize children living in poverty if they lack access to the required resources.

Internet References

Children's Defense Fund
http://www.childrensdefense.org/

National Center for Children in Poverty
http://www.nccp.org/?src=logo

The Urban Institute
http://www.urban.org/adolescents/index.cfm

Paul C. Gorski is an associate professor of integrative studies (education and social justice concentrations) at George Mason University, Fairfax, Va. He is author of *Reaching and Teaching Students in Poverty: Erasing the Opportunity Gap* (Teachers College Press, 2013) and coeditor of *The Poverty and Education Reader: A Call for Equity in Many Voices* (Stylus Press, 2013).

Article   Prepared by: Karen Menke Paciorek, *Eastern Michigan University*

Why Does Family Wealth Affect Learning?

How does the mind work—and especially how does it learn? Teachers' instructional decisions are based on a mix of theories learned in teacher education, trial and error, craft knowledge, and gut instinct. Such knowledge often serves us well, but is there anything sturdier to rely on?

Cognitive science is an interdisciplinary field of researchers from psychology, neuroscience, linguistics, philosophy, computer science, and anthropology who seek to understand the mind.

DANIEL T. WILLINGHAM

Learning Outcomes

After reading this article, you will be able to:

- Describe how stress due to low socioeconomic (SES) affects a family.

- Define a family investment model theory of child development.

Question: Why do wealthy kids usually do better in school than poor kids?

    Answer: Disadvantaged children face a host of challenges to academic success. These challenges fall into two broad categories. First, as one might expect, wealthier parents have the resources to provide more and better learning opportunities for their children. Second, children from poorer homes are subject to chronic stress, which research from the last 10 years has shown is more destructive to learning than was previously guessed. But research also shows it's not all about money.

"Common knowledge" does not always turn out to be true, especially in matters relating to schooling. But when it comes to wealth and educational outcomes, common knowledge has it right: on average, kids from wealthy families do significantly better than kids from poor families. Household wealth is associated with IQ[1] and school achievement,[2] and that phenomenon is observed to varying degrees throughout the world.[3] Household wealth is associated with the likelihood of a child graduating from high school[4] and attending college.[5] With a more fine-grained analysis, we see associations with wealth in more basic academic skills like reading achievement[6] and math achievement.[7] And the association with wealth is still observed if we examine even more basic cognitive processes such as phonological awareness,[8] or the amount of information the child can keep in working memory (which is the mental "space" in which thinking occurs),[9] or the extent to which the child can regulate his emotions and thought processes.[10]

But these effects are not due to household income alone. In fact, it's unlikely that they are *directly* due to income at all.[11] Imagine showering cash on a low-income family; there will not be a sudden boost to the children's cognition or academic achievement. The effects of wealth must be indirect and must accrue over time.

Indeed, researchers believe that a useful way to conceive of the impact of wealth is that it provides access to opportunities. Money is an obvious enabler of opportunities: cash buys books, and summer enrichment camps, and access to tutoring if it's needed. But in addition to financial capital, two other types of capital afford opportunities for children: *Human capital* refers to the skills or knowledge of individuals, usually based on their education and experience. Parents who have a good deal of human capital in the form of education will, in subtle and overt ways, impart their knowledge to their children. *Social capital* refers to beneficial connections in social networks, such as ties to people with financial or human capital. Parents with a lot of social capital might have friends or relatives who can provide helpful summer internships for their child, or they might be more likely to have well-placed friends who can advocate for their child if he has a problem at school.

Naturally, we'd expect financial, human, and social capital to be related. For example, someone who attends college is increasing her human capital through education, but she will also make friends in college and thus have connections (social capital) with other well-educated people.[12] That is why, rather than simply measuring family wealth, most researchers use a composite measure called *socioeconomic status* (SES) that includes measures of family income, parental education, and parental occupation.

How does SES affect educational outcomes? Most theories fall into one of two categories. *Family investment* models offer an intuitive mechanism: high-SES parents have more capital, and so can invest more in their children's development.[13] *Stress models* suggest that low SES is associated with long-term stress that has two consequences: it makes parents less effective, and it has direct, negative biological consequences for children's maturing brain systems.[14] These models are not mutually exclusive. Both could be right, and indeed, there is evidence that both factors contribute to the difficulty that low-SES students have in school. Indeed, much of the challenge in this research is separating the many factors that can have multiple effects and tend to occur together. For example, crowded housing conditions occur because of lack of financial capital and likely have direct effects on children's learning (it's hard to study in a crowded, noisy environment) as well as indirect effects (crowding makes health problems more likely and leads to greater stress). Despite these challenges, researchers have succeeded in identifying some of the many factors that contribute to the greater academic problems faced by students in low-SES families. Let's take a look at some of this evidence, bearing in mind that the studies cited here used methodologies that separate the effects of these co-occurring factors.

Family Investment Theories

Some factors associated with SES seem to be straightforward consequences of the amount of money available to the family. For example, low-income families cannot as readily afford books, computers, access to tutors, and other sources of academic support.[15] Indeed, these sources of intellectual stimulation are associated with better school outcomes,[16] and many poor families cannot afford them.[17]

There are other, more subtle consequences of SES, and these effects are present even before a child is born. Low-SES mothers tend to have less adequate access to health care, so their babies are at greater risk for low birth weight,[18] which is a risk factor for cognitive impairment[19] with consequences measurable at least into middle childhood.[20] There is also a high incidence of fetal alcohol syndrome in children born to low-SES mothers.[21] Fetal alcohol syndrome is caused by alcohol abuse by a woman when she's pregnant, and it results in a host of cognitive deficits for the infant. The greater incidence in low-SES pregnancies is thought to result not only from differences in mothers' drinking habits but, at least in part, from interactions with poor nutrition and possibly genetic factors.[22]

Once born, children in low-SES families have overall poorer health, which has a lasting impact on educational outcomes.[23] They are more likely to have a nutritionally inadequate diet[24] and poor access to health care,[25] which likely has wide-ranging

health consequences. They are more likely to develop serious chronic health problems,[26] which make low-SES kids miss more days of school than their peers,[27] which in turn is associated with negative school outcomes.[28] Missing school is particularly destructive for low-SES kids; they benefit *more* from school than their wealthier counterparts,[29] presumably because their homes and neighborhoods do not provide the same cognitive richness and challenge.

Poor children are also exposed to a number of risks in their physical environment.[30] They are more likely to live in substandard housing with greater exposure to lead, and subsequently show higher blood lead levels than wealthier children.[31] Even a trace amount of lead is known to have serious negative effects on cognition.[32] Kids in low-SES families are also more likely to share a room and generally to live in more crowded conditions,[33] which is known to affect academic performance.[34] This effect may be due to the simple fact that a more crowded home is noisier, making it more difficult to concentrate, but crowding also likely makes it harder for parents to maintain a calm, orderly home, which also impacts cognition.[35]

Perhaps the best-known effect of financial capital on schooling is that wealthier families often seek housing in what they believe to be superior school districts. But even before children start school, kids from higher-SES families are likely to have daycare providers who are less harsh and more sensitive than daycare providers of lower-SES kids; higher-quality daycare is associated with better math and reading scores through elementary school.[36] And once kids start school, poor children are more likely to have teachers who are less experienced or have marginal qualifications.[37] There is also evidence that, when teaching mathematics, teachers of poor children are more likely to emphasize basic computations rather than more advanced procedures and their conceptual underpinnings. The teachers of low-SES students also spend less classroom time on instruction. These data indicate that teachers are not emphasizing basic instruction because the kids are less capable; rather, low-SES kids are more likely to be assigned to teachers who emphasize basic instruction.[38]

All of the foregoing effects are consequences of reduced financial capital. Human capital—the knowledge and skills of the parents that can be imparted to their children—is also important. For example, a great deal of evidence shows that low-SES parents speak less often to their children, and with a more limited vocabulary and simpler syntax, than their high-SES counterparts,[39] a phenomenon that begins when children are still infants.[40] Mother's speech in particular is tightly linked to toddler vocabulary growth.[41] There is some evidence that this effect is partly due to differences in parents' knowledge about child development. Parents who know more about how children learn and grow talk to their children in more complex ways and more often solicit ideas from their children, and high-SES parents more often have this knowledge.[42] There is also evidence that the crowded homes of low-SES families contribute: when the home is crowded, parents are more likely to talk to children briefly and in directives.[43]

Children in low-SES families are read to by their parents less often,[44] and they watch more television than their high-SES counterparts.[45] Their parents are less likely to buy toys that teach shapes or colors or the names of letters.[46] All of these sources of cognitive stimulation that low-SES kids miss are known to have positive impacts on reading and math scores at school.[47]

Finally, more-educated parents are more concerned about imparting human capital to their children, or at least, they are more concerned about spending time with their children. Although one might suppose that parents who work more (either for extra income or out of necessity) will spend less time with their children, this effect is actually rather small.[48] Parents who work more hours tend to sacrifice other activities in order to spend time with their children. Income is also a weak predictor of time spent with children, but there is a robust effect of education, with better-educated parents spending more time with their children.[49]

What about social capital? There too, low-SES kids are at a disadvantage. Parental feeling of connectedness and involvement in their child's school is associated with student achievement,[50] and low-SES parents are less involved in their children's schools.[51] At least part of this effect seems to be due to race and class differences that contribute to a lack of trust between parents and teachers or administrators.[52] Low-SES kids also tend to befriend students who are themselves not engaged at school.[53]

Stress Theories

There appears to be ample evidence supporting family investment theories: families with more financial, human, or social capital invest more of it in their children and their children benefit. Still, the support for family investment theories does not mean that other factors cannot contribute to the effect of SES on education, and indeed, there are also data supporting stress theories.

The basic idea behind stress theories was well captured by a policy statement from the American Academy of Pediatrics published in January [2012].[54] Low SES is associated with chronic stress that, if not buffered by supportive relationships, has longterm, negative consequences on brain development, which are expressed in cognitive performance. There are several steps, which I show in Figure 1, in the logic behind this theory, and there is at least some supporting evidence for each.

First, SES and stress are inversely correlated: that is, low-SES families suffer greater stress than mid- or high-SES families.[55] The reasons that stress is associated with SES likely seem self-evident. Among other factors, low-SES families more often go hungry (or are uncertain whether they'll have enough food in the coming month),[56] have greater worries about job insecurity and financial problems,[57] and are more likely to live in neighborhoods with high crime rates.[58] Indeed, levels of hormones associated with stress—cortisol and catecholamines—are inversely correlated with SES.[59]

Second, there is evidence that these stressors affect parenting. Most parents know that they are not at their best with their kids when they feel under stress. Low-SES parents are more often harsh and inconsistent in parenting practices.[60] These practices are at least partly mediated by chronic stress; stress makes it more likely that parents will suffer behavioral and emotional problems,[61] and stress, along with some differences in beliefs about discipline, accounts for much of the differences between low-, mid-, and high-SES parenting practices.[62] Parental depression and stress have been linked with behavioral problems in children and with difficulties regulating emotions.[63]

Third, there is evidence of a direct effect of stress on children's brains.[64] Mothers under chronic stress during pregnancy have babies who develop more slowly during the first year, and who show lower mental development at 12 months.[65] As a child, chronic stress affects how the body responds to stress—the longer a child lives under stressful conditions (crowding, noise, substandard housing, exposure to violence, etc.), the higher his or her basal levels of cortisol (a stress hormone) and the more muted his or her reaction to a standard stressor such as being asked to work math problems in one's head.[66] In addition to changing the way the brain responds to stressful events, chronic stress changes the anatomy of the brain. For example, young adults who report high levels of verbal abuse as children show abnormalities in white matter tracts (which are like cables that connect different parts of the brain).[67] The effect of stress on the brain is most profound when children are young and the brain is still quite plastic.[68] All in all, the impact of stress on brain anatomy is wide-ranging, but not equivalent throughout. Five regions seem particularly vulnerable to its effects. These are parts of the brain that support working memory, long-term memory, spatial processing, and pattern recognition.[69] These findings showing brain changes associated with chronic stress are important because they suggest a possible mechanism by which stress may lead to differences in cognition. But they should not be interpreted as showing that kids subjected to chronic stress have brain damage or can't learn. They surely can learn, but these data give us some idea of the challenges they face.

Fourth, there is evidence that stress directly affects children's cognitive abilities. A large research literature from laboratory studies shows that short-term stress interferes with the formation of new memories,[70] especially when the stress is unrelated to the event to be remembered and occurs at a different time.[71] For example, the child who is bullied on the bus on his way to school will remember the bullying episode well, but there will be a cost to everything he encounters at school that day. Remarkably, the same is true if he's bullied *on the bus ride home*. The stress exacts a cost to memories formed hours earlier. There is also direct evidence that the sort of stressors low-SES kids experience affect cognition. For example, when there has been a homicide in the neighborhood less than one week prior to testing, students score significantly lower on reading and vocabulary assessments.[72] In the longer term, there is evidence that suffering chronic stress as a child leads to reduced working-memory capacity in adulthood.[73]

Fifth, there is evidence of the buffering effect of warm parenting. Even in the face of life stress, nurturing parents make a child feel safe, and so the negative consequences of chronic stress will be lessened.[74] In one study, having nurturing parents at age 4 was related to the volume of the hippocampus (a crucial memory structure) at age 14.[75] In another study,[76] foster children aged 3 to 5 were shown to have atypical activity in

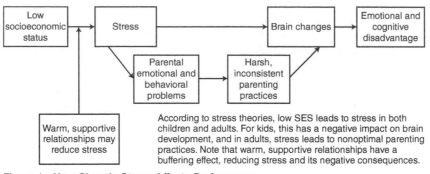

Figure 1   How Chronic Stress Affects Performance

the hypothalamic-pituitary-adrenal (HPA) axis, a set of structures that responds to stress. This atypical activity was associated with adverse events in the child's past. But the children responded well to an intervention in which adults were taught to better recognize signs of distress in the child, and to respond in a sensitive way. Nine months after the training, the atypical activity in the HPA axis was reduced for these children.

What Are the Implications?

What sort of intervention would help low-SES kids fulfill their educational potential? Reading the foregoing analysis of the broad impact of SES might lead one to conclude that an equally broad array of social services targeting home and family life, as well as school interventions, would be necessary—the sort of thing that the Harlem Children's Zone is famous for and the Coalition for Community Schools has long advocated. At the least, something like the Perry Preschool seems necessary. It emphasized high-quality preschool for children living in poverty, as well as weekly home visits to involve parents and encourage them to extend the preschool curriculum to the home.[77] But what can be done by an individual teacher?

We should keep in the forefront of our minds that the trends discussed here are exactly that—trends. There are harsh, inconsistent parents with stressed-out children in high-SES homes, and sensitive, consistent parents with well-prepared children in low-SES homes. Obviously, making assumptions about kids and their home lives based on parents' income or occupation is nothing more than stereotyping. Still, it is well to keep in the back of your mind that these trends exist: a child from a poor family is more likely to be under chronic stress than a child from a middle-class family, for example.

The difficult balance is to recognize the challenges each individual child faces, but not use them as a reason to lower expectations for achievement or appropriate behavior. High expectations need not be an additional source of stress—students thrive when high expectations are coupled with high levels of support.[78] Many low-SES kids are not getting the cognitive challenge they need from their homes and neighborhoods, but neither are they getting the support they need.

To compensate, teachers should offer in the classroom what these children are missing at home. Much of this is what we've

called human capital—academic knowledge and skills—which is the teacher's bread and butter. It's also well to remember that some of this knowledge, though important for long-term success, is not academic knowledge. It's knowledge of how to interact with peers and adults, how to interact with large institutions like a school or a government agency, how to interact with authority figures, how to schedule one's time, strategies to regulate one's emotions, and so on. Some of this information is taught implicitly, by example, but much of it can be taught explicitly.

The research reviewed here also highlights the importance of a calm atmosphere in the classroom and in the school. This is obviously a goal that virtually every teacher shares—no one wants a chaotic classroom—but knowing that a child's neighborhood and home might be noisy, crowded, and threatening makes the creation of a serene, joyful classroom all the more important. Kids in more chaotic classrooms show higher levels of stress hormones.[79] Knowing the consequences of stress for cognition, and the potential long-term consequences to the brain, makes the matter more urgent.

The research literature on the impact of SES on children's learning is sobering, and it's easy to see why an individual teacher might feel helpless in the face of these effects. Teachers should not be alone in confronting the impact of poverty on children's learning. One hopes that the advances in our understanding of the terrible consequences of poverty for the mind and brain will spur policymakers to serious action. But still, teachers should not despair. All children can learn, whatever their backgrounds, and whatever challenges they face.

Notes

1. Greg J. Duncan, Jeanne Brooks-Gunn, and Pamela Kato Klebanov, "Economic Deprivation and Early Childhood Development," *Child Development* 65, no. 2 (1994): 296–318.

2. See, for example, Selcuk R. Sirin, "Socioeconomic Status and Academic Achievement: A Meta-Analytic Review of Research," *Review of Educational Research* 75, no. 3 (2005): 417–453.

3. Organization for Economic Cooperation and Development, PISA 2009 Results: Overcoming Social Background *Equity in Learning Opportunities and Outcomes*, vol. 2 (Paris: OECD, 2010), http://dx.doi.org/10.1787/9789264091504-en.

4. National Center for Education Statistics, Digest of Education Statistics, "Percentage of High School Dropouts among Persons 16 through 24 Years Old (Status Dropout Rate), by Income Level, and Percentage Distribution of Status Dropouts, by Labor Force Status and Educational Attainment: 1970 through 2007" (U.S. Department of Education, 2008), accessed January 6, 2012, www.nces.ed.gov.programs/digest/d08/tables/dt08_110.asp.

5. Dalton Conley, Capital for College: Parental Assets and Post-secondary Schooling, *Sociology of Education* 74, no. 1 (2001): 59–72.

6. See, for example, Nikki L. Aikens and Oscar Barbarin, Socioeconomic Differences in Reading Trajectories: The Contribution of Family, Neighborhood, and School Contexts, *Journal of Educational Psychology* 100, no. 2 (2008): 235–251.

7. See, for example, Chuansheng Chen, Shin-Ying Lee, and Harold W. Stevenson, "Long-Term Prediction of Academic Achievement of American, Chinese, and Japanese" Adolescents, *Journal of Educational Psychology* 88, no. 4 (1996): 750–759.

8. Grover J. Whitehurst, "Language Processes in Context: Language Learning in Children Reared in Poverty," in *Research on Communication and Language Disorders: Contribution to Theories of Language Development,* ed. Lauren B. Adamson and Mary Ann Romski (Baltimore: Paul H. Brookes, 1997), 233–266.

9. Kimberly G. Noble, M. Frank Norman, and Martha J. Farah, "Neurocognitive Correlates of Socioeconomic Status in Kindergarten Children," *Developmental Science* 8, no. 1 (2005): 74–87.

10. Gary W. Evans and Jennifer Rosenbaum, "Self-Regulation and the Income-Achievement Gap," *Early Childhood Research Quarterly* 23, no. 4 (2008): 504–514.

11. David M. Blau, "The Effect of Income on Child Development," *Review of Economics and Statistics* 81, no. 2 (1999): 261–276.

12. For a discussion, see Robert H. Bradley and Robert F. Corwyn, "Socioeconomic Status and Child Development," *Annual Review of Psychology* 53 (2002): 371–399.

13. See, for example, Lorraine V. Klerman, *Alive and Well? A Research and Policies Review of Health Programs for Poor Young Children* (New York: Columbia University Press, 1991).

14. Rand D. Conger, Xiaojia Ge, Glen H. Eider Jr., Frederick O. Lorenz, and Ronald L. Simons, "Economic Stress, Coercive Family Process, and Development Problems of Adolescents," *Child Development* 65, no. 2 (1994): 541–561.

15. Bradley and Corwyn, "Socioeconomic Status and Child Development."

16. Aikens and Barbarin, "Socioeconomic Differences in Reading Trajectories."

17. Amy J. Orr, "Black-White Differences in Achievement: The Importance of Wealth," *Sociology of Education* 76, no. 4 (2003): 281–304.

18. Michael S. Kramer, Louise Seguin, John Lydon, and Lise Goulet, "Socio-Economic Disparities in Pregnancy Outcome: Why Do the Poor Fare So Poorly?" *Paediatric and Perinatal Epidemiology* 14, no. 3 (2000): 194–210.

19. Maureen Hack, H. Gerry Taylor, Nancy Klein, Robert Eiben, Christopher Schatschneider, and Nori Mercuri-Minich, "School-Age Outcomes in Children with Birth Weights under 750 g," *New England Journal of Medicine* 331, no. 12 (1994): 753–759.

20. H. Gerry Taylor, Nancy Klein, Nori M. Minich, and Maureen Hack, "Middle-School-Age Outcomes in Children with Very Low Birthweight," *Child Development* 71, no. 6 (2000): 1495–1511.

21. Barbara Cone-Wesson, "Prenatal Alcohol and Cocaine Exposure: Influences on Cognition, Speech, Language, and Hearing," *Journal of Communication Disorders* 38, no. 4 (2005): 279–302.

22. Colleen M. O'Leary, "Fetal Alcohol Syndrome: Diagnosis, Epidemiology, and Developmental Outcomes," *Journal of Paediatrics and Child Health* 40, no. 1–2 (2004): 2–7.

23. Anne Case, Angela Fertig, and Christina Paxson, "The Lasting Impact of Childhood Health and Circumstance," *Journal of Health Economics* 24, no. 2 (2005): 365–389.

24. Ernesto Pollitt, Kathleen S. Gorman, Patrice L. Engle, Juan A. Rivera, and Reynaldo Martorell, "Nutrition in Early Life and the Fulfillment of Intellectual Potential," *Journal of Nutrition* 125, no. 4 Supplement (1995): 1111S–1118S.

25. Katherine E. Heck and Jennifer D. Parker, "Family Structure, Socioeconomic Status, and Access to Health Care for Children," *Health Services Research* 37, no. 1 (2002): 171–184.

26. Edith Chen, Andrew D. Martin, and Karen A. Matthews, "Understanding Health Disparities: The Role of Race and Socioeconomic Status in Children's Health," *American Journal of Public Health* 96, no. 4 (2006): 702–708.

27. Mariajosé–Romero and Young-Sun Lee, *A National Portrait of Chronic Absenteeism in the Early Grades* (New York: National Center for Children in Poverty, 2007).

28. Lennart S. Ohlund and Kerstin B. Ericsson, "Elementary School Achievement and Absence Due to Illness," *Journal of Genetic Psychology* 155, no. 4 (1994): 409–421.

29. Douglas D. Ready, "Socioeconomic Disadvantage, School Attendance, and Early Cognitive Development: The Differential Effects of School Exposure," *Sociology of Education* 83, no. 4 (2010): 271–286.

30. For a review, see Gary W. Evans, "Child Development and the Physical Environment," *Annual Review of Psychology* 57 (2006): 423–451.

31. Robert L. Jones, David M. Homa, Pamela A. Meyer, Debra J. Brody, Kathleen L. Caldwell, James L. Pirkle, and Mary Jean Brown, "Trends in Blood Lead Levels and Blood Lead Testing among US Children Aged 1 to 5 Years, 1988–2004," *Pediatrics* 123, no. 3 (2009): e376–e385.

32. Latha Chandramouli, Colin D. Steer, Matthew Ellis, and Alan M. Emond, "Effects of Early Childhood Lead Exposure on Academic Performance and Behaviour of School Age Children," *Archives of Disease in Childhood* 94, no. 11 (2009): 844–848.

33. Dowell Myers, William C. Baer, and Seong-Youn Choi, "The Changing Problem of Overcrowded Housing," *Journal of the American Planning Association* 62 (Winter 1996): 66–84.

34. Dominique Goux and Eric Maurin, "The Effect of Overcrowded Housing on Children's Performance at School," *Journal of Public Economics* 89, no. 5–6 (2005): 797–819.

35. Jean E. Dumas, Jenelle Nissley, Alicia Nordstrom, Emilie Phillips Smith, Ronald J. Prinz, and Douglas W. Levine, "Home Chaos Sociodemographic, Parenting, Interactional, and

Child Correlates," *Journal of Clinical Child and Adolescent Psychology* 34, no. 1 (2005): 93–104.

36. Eric Dearing, Kathleen McCartney, and Beck A. Taylor, Change in Family Income-to-Needs Matters More for Children with Less, *Child Development* 72, no. 6 (2001): 1779–1793.

37. Richard Ingersoll, The Problem of Underqualified Teachers in American Secondary Schools, *Educational Researcher* 28, no. 2 (1999): 26–37.

38. Laura M. Desimone and Daniel A. Long, Teacher Effects and the Achievement Gap: Do Teacher and Teaching Quality Influence the Achievement Gap between Black and White and High- and Low-SES Students in the Early Grades? *Teachers College Record* 112, no. 12 (2010): 3024–3073.

39. Betty Hart and Todd R. Risley, Meaningful Differences in the Everyday Experience of Young American Children (Baltimore: Paul H. Brookes, 1995); and Dale Walker, Charles Greenwood, Betty Hart, and Judith Carta, "Prediction of School Outcomes Based on Early Language Production and Socioeconomic Factors," *Child Development* 65, no. 2 (1994): 606–621.

40. Jerome Kagan and Steven R. Tulkin, "Social Class Differences in Child Rearing During the First Year," in *The Origins of Human Social Relations,* ed. H. Rudolph Schaffer (London: Academic Press, 1971), 165–185.

41. Erika Hoff, "The Specificity of Environmental Influence: Socioeconomic Status Affects Early Vocabulary Development via Maternal Speech," *Child Development* 74, no. 5 (2003): 1368–1378.

42. Meredith L. Rowe, "Child-Directed Speech: Relation to Socioeconomic Status, Knowledge of Child Development and Child Vocabulary Skill," *Journal of Child Language* 35, no. 1 (2008): 185–205.

43. Gary W. Evans, Lorraine E. Maxwell, and Betty Hart, "Parental Language and Verbal Responsiveness to Children in Crowded Homes," *Developmental Psychology* 35, no. 4 (1999): 1020–1023.

44. Helen Raikes, Barbara Alexander Pan, Gayle Luze, Catherine S. Tamis-LeMonda, Jeanne Brooks-Gunn, Jill Constantine, Louisa Banks Tarullo, H. Abigail Raikes, and Eileen T. Rodriguez, "Mother-Child Bookreading in Low-Income Families Correlates and Outcomes during the First Three Years of Life," *Child Development* 77, no. 4 (2006): 924–953.

45. Reed W. Larson and Suman Verma, "How Children and Adolescents Spend Time Across the World: Work, Play, and Developmental Opportunities," *Psychological Bulletin* 125, no. 6 (1999): 701–736.

46. Duncan, Brooks-Gunn, and Klebanov, "Economic Deprivation and Early Childhood Development," and Judith R. Smith, Jeanne Brooks-Gunn, and Pamela M. Klebanov, "Consequences of Living in Poverty for Young Children's Cognitive and Verbal Ability and Early School Achievement," in *Consequences of Growing Up Poor,* ed. Greg J. Duncan and Jeanne Brooks-Gunn (New York: Russell Sage Foundation, 1997), 132–189.

47. Robert Crosnoe, Tama Leventhal, R. J. Wirth, Kim M. Pierce, Robert C. Pianta, and the NICHD Early Child Care Research Network, "Family Socioeconomic Status and Consistent Environmental Stimulation in Early Childhood," *Child Development* 81, no. 3 (2010): 972–987.

48. Cathleen D. Zick and W. Keith Bryant, "A New Look at Parents' Time Spent in Child Care: Primary and Secondary Time Use," *Social Science Research* 25, no. 3 (1996): 260–280.

49. Liana C. Sayer, Anne H. Gauthier, and Frank F. Furstenberg Jr., "Educational Differences in Parents' Time with Children: Cross-National Variations," *Journal of Marriage and Family* 66, no. 5 (2004): 1152–1169.

50. Christopher Spera, "A Review of the Relationship among Parenting Practices, Parenting Styles, and Adolescent School Achievement," *Educational Psychology Review* 17, no. 2 (2005): 125–146.

51. Kathleen Herrold and Kevin O'Donnell, Parent and Family Involvement in Education, 2006–07 School Year, from the National Household Education Surveys Program of 2007 (Washington, DC: National Center for Education Statistics, 2008).

52. Clea A. McNeely, James M. Nonnemaker, and Robert W. Blum, "Promoting School Connectedness: Evidence from the National Longitudinal Study of Adolescent Health," *Journal of School Health* 72, no. 4 (2002): 138–146.

53. Robert K. Ream and Russell W. Rumberger, "Student Engagement, Peer Social Capital, and School Dropout among Mexican American and Non-Latino White Students," *Sociology of Education* 81, no. 2 (2008): 109–139.

54. Jack P. Shonkoff, Benjamin S. Siegel, Mary I. Dobbins, Marian F. Earls, Andrew S. Garner, Laura McGuinn, John Pascoe, and David L. Wood, "Early Childhood Adversity, Toxic Stress, and the Role of the Pediatrician: Translating Developmental Science into Lifelong Health," *Pediatrics* 129, no. 1 (2012): e224–e231.

55. R. Jay Turner and William R. Avison, "Status Variations in Stress Exposure: Implications for the Interpretation of Research on Race, Socioeconomic Status, and Gender," *Journal of Health and Social Behavior* 44, no. 4 (2003): 488–505.

56. John T. Cook and Deborah A. Frank. "Food Security, Poverty, and Human Development in the United States," *Annals of the New York Academy of Sciences* 1136 (2008): 193–209.

57. Rand D. Conger, Katherine J. Conger, and Monica J. Martin, "Socioeconomic Status, Family Processes, and Individual Development," *Journal of Marriage and Family* 72, no. 3 (2010): 685–704.

58. Dafna E. Kohen, Jeanne Brooks-Gunn, Tama Leventhal, and Clyde Hertzman, "Neighborhood Income and Physical and Social Disorder in Canada: Associations with Young Children's Competencies," *Child Development* 73, no. 6 (2002): 1844–1860.

59. Sheldon Cohen, William J. Doyle, and Andrew Baum, "Socioeconomic Status Is Associated with Stress Hormones," *Psychosomatic Medicine* 68, no. 3 (2006): 414–420; and Andrew Steptoe, Sabine Kunz-Ebrecht, Natalie Owen, Pamela J. Feldman, Gonneke Willemsen, Clemens Kirschbaum, and Michael Marmot, "Socioeconomic Status and Stress-Related Biological Responses Over the Working Day," *Psychosomatic Medicine* 65, no. 3 (2003): 461–470.

60. Conger, Conger, and Martin, "Socioeconomic Status, Family Processes, and Individual Development."

61. Rand D. Conger and M. Brent Donnellan, "An Interactionist Perspective on the Socioeconomic Context of Human Development," *Annual Review of Psychology* 58 (2007): 175–199; and Dafna E. Kohen, Tama Leventhal, V. Susan Dahinten, and Cameron N. McIntosh, "Neighborhood Disadvantage: Pathways of Effects for Young Children," *Child Development* 79, no. 1 (2008): 156–169.

62. See, for example, Ellen E. Pinderhughes, Kenneth A. Dodge, John E. Bates, Gregory S. Pettit, and Arnaldo Zelli, "Discipline Responses: Influences of Parents' Socioeconomic Status, Ethnicity, Beliefs about Parenting, Stress, and Cognitive-Emotional Processes," *Journal of Family Psychology* 14, no. 3 (2000): 380–400.

63. Rachel Chazan-Cohen, Helen Raikes, Jeanne Brooks-Gunn, Catherine Ayoub, Barbara Alexander Pan, Ellen E. Kisker, Lori Roggman, and Allison Sidle Fuligni, "Low-Income Children's School Readiness: Parent Contributions Over the First Five Years," *Early Education and Development* 20, no. 6 (2009): 958–977.

64. Bruce S. McEwen, "The Neurobiology of Stress: From Serendipity to Clinical Relevance," *Brain Research* 886, no. 1–2 (2000): 172–189.

65. Elysia P. Davis and Curt A. Sandman, "The Timing of Prenatal Exposure to Maternal Cortisol and Psychosocial Stress Is Associated with Human Infant Cognitive Development," *Child Development* 81, no. 1 (2010): 131–148.

66. Gary W. Evans and Pilyoung Kim, "Childhood Poverty and Health: Cumulative Risk Exposure and Stress Dysregulation," *Psychological Science* 18, no. 11 (2007): 953–957.

67. Jeewook Choi, Bumseok Jeong, Michael L. Rohan, Ann M. Polcari, and Martin H. Teicher, "Preliminary Evidence for White Matter Tract Abnormalities in Young Adults Exposed to Parental Verbal Abuse," *Biological Psychiatry* 65, no. 3 (2009): 227–234.

68. Michelle M. Loman and Megan R. Gunnar, "Early Experience and the Development of Stress Reactivity and Regulation in Children," *Neuroscience and Biobehavioral Reviews* 34, no. 6 (2010): 867–876.

69. Daniel A. Hackman and Martha J. Farah, "Socioeconomic Status and the Developing Brain," *Trends in Cognitive Sciences* 13, no. 2 (2009): 65–73.

70. Marie D. Sauro, Randall S. Jorgensen, and C. Teal Pedlow, "Stress, Glucocorticoids, and Memory: A Meta-Analytic Review," *Stress* 6, no. 4 (2003): 235–245.

71. Marian Joëls, Zhenwei Pu, Olof Wiegert, Melly S. Oitzl, and Harm J. Krugers, "Learning Under Stress: How Does it Work?" *Trends in Cognitive Sciences* 10, no. 4 (2006): 152–158.

72. Patrick Sharkey, "The Acute Effect of Local Homicides on Children's Cognitive Performance," *Proceedings of the National Academy of Sciences* 107, no. 26 (2010): 11733–11738.

73. Gary W. Evans and Michelle A. Schamberg, "Childhood Poverty, Chronic Stress, and Adult Working Memory," *Proceedings of the National Academy of Sciences* 106, no. 16 (2009): 6545–6549.

74. For a review, see Megan R. Gunnar and Carol L. Cheatham, "Brain and Behavior Interface: Stress and the Developing Brain," *Infant Mental Health Journal* 24, no. 3 (2003): 195–211.

75. Hengyi Rao, Laura Betancourt, Joan M. Giannetta, Nancy L. Brodsky, Marc Korczykowski, Brian B. Avants, James C. Gee, Jiongjiong Wang, Hallam Hurt, John A. Detre, and Martha J. Farah, "Early Parental Care Is Important for Hippocampal Maturation: Evidence from Brain Morphology in Humans," *Neuroimage* 49, no. 1 (2010): 1144–1150.

76. Philip A. Fisher, Megan R. Gunnar, Mary Dozier, Jacqueline Bruce, and Katherine C. Pears, "Effects of Therapeutic Interventions for Foster Children on Behavioral Problems, Caregiver Attachment, and Stress Regulatory Neural Systems," *Annals of the New York Academy of Sciences* 1094, no. 1 (2006): 215–225.

77. Clive R. Belfield, Milagros Nores, Steve Barnett, and Lawrence Schweinhart, "The High/Scope Perry Preschool Program: Cost Benefit Analysis Using Data from the Age-40 Followup," *Journal of Human Resources* 41, no. 1 (2006): 162–190.

78. Valerie E. Lee, Julia B. Smith, Tamara E. Perry, and Mark A. Smylie, *Social Support, Academic Press, and Student Achievement: A View from the Middle Grades in Chicago* (Chicago: Consortium on Chicago School Research, 1999).

79. See, for example, Marie-Claude Geoffroy, Sylvana M. Côté, Sophie Parent, and Jean Richard Séguin, "Daycare Attendance, Stress, and Mental Health," *Canadian Journal of Psychiatry* 51, no. 9 (August 2006): 607–615.

Critical Thinking

1. Why won't money alone improve the academic performance of young children living in poverty?

2. What interventions or investments would best help low-SES children succeed in school?

Create Central

www.mhhe.com/createcentral

Internet References

Children's Defense Fund (CDF)
www.childrensdefense.org

Harvard Family Research Project
www.hfrp.org

HighScope Educational Research Foundation
www.highscope.org

Zero to Three
www.zerotothree.org

DANIEL T. WILLINGHAM is a professor of cognitive psychology at the University of Virginia. His most recent book, *Why Don't Students Like School?* is designed to help teachers apply research on the mind to the classroom setting. For his articles on education, go to www.danielwillingham.com. Readers can pose specific questions to "Ask the Cognitive Scientist" by sending an e-mail to amered@aft.org. Future columns will try to address readers' questions.

Willingham, Daniel T. From *American Educator*, Spring 2012, pp. 33–39. Copyright © 2012 by Daniel T. Willingham. Reprinted by permission.

Article   Prepared by: Karen Menke Paciorek, *Eastern Michigan University*

Increasing Family Engagement in Early Childhood Programs

JAMILAH R. JOR'DAN, KATHY GOETZ WOLF, AND ANNE DOUGLASS

Learning Outcomes

After reading this article, you will be able to:

- Develop a list of ways ideas used in Illinois could be applied in many different programs and places.

- Articulate the importance of relationships between the adults caring for young children.

S trengthening Families is a relationship-based child abuse and neglect prevention initiative started nationally in 2001 through a partnership between the Doris Duke Charitable Foundation and the Center for the Study of Social Policy (CSSP) in Washington, DC. Thirty-five states and several thousand early childhood programs nationwide implement Strengthening Families in early care and education settings. The states and programs build research-based protective factors into early childhood systems and programs to prevent child abuse and neglect.

Protective factors are positive attributes that strengthen all families, not just those at risk for child abuse and neglect (see "Strengthening Families—Protective Factors"). The factors incorporate principles and practices regarding relationships, families, and community engagement from the NAEYC Early Childhood Program Standards, Head Start Program Performance Standards, and other measures of quality in early childhood education.

In the Strengthening Families approach, early childhood teachers and child welfare professionals work intentionally through relationships with families to build protective factors. The approach is based on what early childhood professionals have known for years:

- Early childhood programs are places to foster supportive relationships that help build stronger families.
- There is a close relationship between teachers and families of very young children.
- Early childhood programs offer daily opportunities for observation and learning with families.

- Families interact with early childhood programs as empowered consumers rather than as clients or recipients of a service.

The key to implementing Strengthening Families is increasing meaningful family engagement in programs and communities. Emotional and behavioral characteristics related to healthy relationships include empathy, warmth, genuineness, respect, self-disclosure, and energized feelings (feeling liked and welcome). These characteristics need to be part of the relationships between families and program staff in order for families to feel cared about by, part of, and engaged in an early care and education program (Hanna 1991).

Strengthening Families Illinois

Illinois became a pilot state for implementing Strengthening Families in early 2005. The Strengthening Families Illinois (SFI) leadership team includes early childhood professionals and parent leaders representing more than 40 partners—early childhood programs, agencies, community organizations—committed to embedding protective factors in their services for children and families. SFI engages families, bridges the gap between early childhood programs and the child welfare system, and develops early childhood learning networks.

Participating Programs

- Develop an action plan, based on a self-assessment, to improve an aspect of programming related to building the protective factors
- Participate in training and staff development on protective factors, communicating with families, and more (see the section "Professional Development Makes the Implicit Explicit," for a full list of topics)
- Participate in monthly network meetings to reinforce what staff learn in the trainings
- Participate in evaluation efforts that include annual parent and staff surveys

Strengthening Families—Protective Factors

1. **Parental Resilience: Parents need to be strong and flexible.**
   What it is: Having problem-solving skills; being able to rebound; being flexible; experiencing emotional well-being.
   How early childhood programs build it: Being welcoming and supportive; building relationships with families; meeting one-on-one with families; working with families to develop family goals and identify resources; involving families in decisions about their children and the program.

2. **Social Connections: Parents need friends.**
   What it is: Having a positive peer network, mutual support systems, and community connections.
   How early childhood programs build it: Making space available for families to meet informally; supporting parents in planning events for parents and children; arranging family field trips and family activities outside the center; providing volunteer opportunities; working closely with parent advisory groups.

3. **Knowledge of Parenting and Child Development: Being a great parent is part natural and part learned.**
   What it is: Understanding what children are learning—and what they are capable of learning—at different ages and stages; having appropriate approaches to teaching and guiding children.
   How early childhood programs build it: Making parenting information available in families' home languages; sharing classroom observations with parents; telling parents something positive about what their children did during the day; conducting home visits; offering parenting classes; sending home newsletters; setting up lending libraries for parents; holding parent-teacher conferences.

4. **Concrete Support in Times of Need: We all need help sometimes.**
   What it is: Being able to meet basic needs; having access to program services, informal support, and resources to deal with a crisis.

   How early childhood programs build it: Building relationships with families so they feel comfortable sharing the challenges they face; making space available for staff to meet privately with families; responding to signs of parent and family distress; being connected to and familiar with community services and organizations (e.g., food programs, clothing closets).

5. **Social and Emotional Competence of Children: Parents need to help their children communicate.**
   What it is: Helping children identify and express feelings in positive ways and helping them understand that other people have feelings and needs; teaching ways to resolve conflicts; encouraging friendships.
   How early childhood programs build it: Using social and emotional curricula (e.g., Second Step, Center on the Social and Emotional Foundations for Early Learning (CSEFEL), I Can Problem Solve); offering parenting education opportunities; providing individualized support to parents; helping families understand age-appropriate social and emotional skills and behaviors; encouraging children to express their feelings through words, artwork, and expressive play.

6. **Healthy Parent–Child Relationships: Give your children the love and respect they need.**
   What it is: Bonding with the child; nurturing the child; fostering secure attachment; having a loving, reciprocal parent–child relationship; setting healthy boundaries.
   How early childhood programs build it: Offering parent–child activities and parenting education opportunities.

Protective factors are adapted, with the authors' permission, for the Center for the Study of Social Policy's second edition of *Strengthening Families—A Guidebook for Early Childhood Programs* (Washington, DC: CCSP, 2008) and from K.G. Wolf's *Living the Protective Factors—How Parents Keep Their Children Safe and Families Strong* (Chicago: Strengthening Families Illinois, Be Strong Families, 2012). The factors are available at www.strengtheningfamilies.org.

Making a Difference

In spring 2011 Strengthening Families Illinois evaluated early childhood programs that had been participating in the Illinois initiative for more than two years (Douglass 2011). The evaluation included review of parent and staff surveys, programs' completion of a survey instrument, interviews, and site visits. The evaluation asked what difference participation in SFI made. Respondents stated overwhelmingly that participation in Strengthening Families resulted in more and better-quality family involvement. Ninety-two percent found that being part of SFI helped them define and articulate their family engagement and family support efforts.

Program staff described the following ways SFI helped them to be more effective in their family engagement efforts: increased parent involvement and attendance at family events and meetings; increased parent-to-parent interactions and relationships; increased parent leadership; and improved parent–staff formal and informal communication.

Elements of Success

What is it about Strengthening Families Illinois that is responsible for these successes? Evaluation results suggest explanations in five main areas.

1. **Protective factors and Parent Cafés.** First and foremost are the protective factors. Initially, Strengthening Families based its national efforts on early childhood providers and child welfare professionals working intentionally with families to build protective factors. In 2005 an Illinois parent challenged the SFI leadership team: "You've got important information [the protective factors] that families need, and you're planning

to give it to us by going through early childhood programs. Why not give it to families directly?"

With assistance from parent leaders, SFI rewrote the protective factors in more accessible language in order to deliver them directly to parents through parent-to-parent learning rather than program-to-parent learning. Strengthening Families Illinois developed Parent Cafés, based on the World Café model (Brown & Isaacs 2005) (see "What Is the World Café?"). SFI adapted the process for peer-to-peer parent learning about the six protective factors and self-reflection, with parent leaders leading parents in small group discussions.

What Is the World Café?

The World Café is a small group conversation process that facilitates consensus building and strategic planning. A "host" welcomes participants to a café-like environment. Participants and a "table host" sit four or five to a table and discuss a question, with the table host facilitating. After 15 or 20 minutes, the table host stays at the table and the participants move to other tables and discuss a different question.

SFI Parent Cafés take place in early childhood settings. Parents, grandparents, and others who are responsible for children's care are participants, and parent leaders are hosts. The secret of the cafés' effectiveness is that parents lead, learn from, and assist parents. They discuss questions related to the protective factors, such as "What do you do to help your child control her strong emotions?", and issues that matter to participants as individuals, families, and community members, such as resourcefulness during tough economic times or violence in the community. After three rounds of discussion, there is a large group debriefing, or "harvest," that assists participants in bringing together what they have learned.

More than 8,000 parents have participated in Parent Cafés in Illinois since they began in 2007, and the results are overwhelmingly positive. Parent Cafés support diversity because SFI organizes them in different languages and around different groups (teen moms, fathers, foster parents, and others). Early childhood programs involved in SFI hold the cafés. They reach out to their families and the community through invitations, newsletters, parent boards, and social media. They are led by parents, for parents, which is what makes them meaningful.

2. A welcoming community and culture in the program. Ninety parents took part in a focus group café to discuss what makes them want to participate in their child's program (see "Inviting Parent Participation"). The consensus was that parents participate when they feel welcome. To make parents feel welcome, program staff need to build relationships with them before expecting them to come to events or serve on committees.

Developing relationships with families is an intentional commitment of all program staff. Discussion of parent involvement should be part of the hiring, supervision, and performance

---

Inviting Parent Participation

Parents say, I will come if . . .

- I helped plan the activity.
- Someone I know or care about asks me to attend (more than once).
- I feel positive about the content.
- I feel it's important that I be there.
- I have transportation.
- I promised to go with someone.
- My contributions are valued.
- My children can come with me.
- There's dinner!

Reprinted, with permission, from Strengthening Families Illinois's *You're Welcome: Parent Leaders Speak Out on What It Takes to Promote Real Parent Engagement* (Chicago: Author, 2011), at www.strengtheningfamiliesillinois.org/mirror/downloads/Youre_Welcome_web1.pdf.

---

evaluation process. In addition, parent–staff relationships need to be supported through team building, professional development opportunities, and discussions at program staff meetings. Research conducted on behalf of Strengthening Families Illinois (Douglass 2009; Douglass & Klerman 2012) raised the point that an early childhood program is unlikely to be successful in engaging parents effectively and positively if the program climate is not supportive of staff. What happens between staff is reflected in the relationships between staff and parents.

3. Professional development makes the implicit explicit. In Illinois, a group from the state's Strengthening Families leadership team identified seven training topics for programs adopting the approach: (1) protective factors, (2) communicating with families, (3) recognizing and responding to signs of family stress, (4) building strong relationships with families, (5) collaborating with child welfare, (6) social and emotional foundations for learning, and (7) helping children heal from trauma. SFI partners developed the curriculum, and child care resource and referral agencies and Illinois hub coordinators provided training for participants in their local learning networks.

4. Commitment to the Strengthening Families program strategies. Including family members in the CSSP program self-assessment process, completed every three years, strengthens early childhood program–family relationships. Based on the results of a self-assessment, program representatives, family members, coaches, accreditation facilitation staff, and others develop an action plan to identify areas that can be strengthened. The plan is their commitment to strengthening components of their programming by embedding the protective factors and a family-strengthening approach in their work with children and families.

5. Tools to assist with implementation. SFI supports participating programs with tools and resources. Programs create and share resources with each other as well. The resources vary from sample lesson plans and staff meeting agendas to posters (e.g., "Protective Factors," "101 Ways to Nurture Your Spirit"), perennial calendars (365 ways to engage parents), and Café Talk (25 questions on each protective factor). These resources keep front and center the protective factors, programs' Strengthening Families commitment, and the messages staff receive during professional development.

Conclusion

What makes the difference when Illinois early childhood programs build successful, collaborative relationships with families? The difference is staff's desire to shift and deepen their practice and to change practices that may be subtle barriers to closer staff–family connections. The shift from being child centered to family centered is difficult. It requires professional development, new practices, reinforcement, tools, and new ways of interacting with families and colleagues. But the benefits are profound. Describing how Strengthening Families Illinois had made a difference, one program director said, "When a parent was chronically late, we used to look at our watches at pick-up time and complain to each other about how inconsiderate she was. Now, we say to each other, 'I wonder what's going on with her and how we could help.'" Changes like this are at the heart of Strengthening Families Illinois's success in strengthening relationships with families.

For more information about Strengthening Families nationally and Strengthening Families Illinois, visit www.strengtheningfamilies.net and www.strengtheningfamiliesillinois.org, respectively.

References

Brown, J., & D. Isaacs. 2005. *The World Café—Shaping Our Futures through Conversations that Matter.* San Francisco: Berrett-Koehler.

Douglass, A. 2009. *Early Care and Education Partnerships That Keep Children Safe: How Strengthening Families Illinois Influenced Change in Child Care Programs.* Chicago: Strengthening Families Illinois.

Douglass, A. 2011. *Strengthening Families Illinois Learning Network Program Evaluation Report.* Chicago: Strengthening Families Illinois.

Douglass, A., & L. Klerman. 2012. "The Strengthening Families Initiative and Child Care Quality Improvement: How Strengthening Families Influenced Change in Child Care Programs in One State." *Early Education and Development* 23: 1–20.

Hanna, S.L. 1991. *Person to Person: Positive Relationships Don't Just Happen.* Englewood Cliffs, NJ: Prentice Hall.

Critical Thinking

1. What support could be offered to parents of young children to help them with the challenges of parenting?
2. Choose one of the outcomes of the program described in the article and indicate how that could be applied in a program with which you are familiar.

Create Central

www.mhhe.com/createcentral

Internet References

The AARP Grandparent Information Center
www.aarp.org/relationships/friends-family

Administration for Children and Families
www.hhs.gov/children/index.html

Children, Youth and Families Education and Research Network
www.cyfernet.org

Children's Defense Fund (CDF)
www.childrensdefense.org

Harvard Family Research Project
www.hfrp.org

Jamilah R. Jor'dan, PhD, is an assistant professor in the Department of Early Childhood and Bilingual Education at Chicago State University, and a senior consultant for Strengthening Families Illinois. Jor'dan was vice president of the NAEYC Governing Board and an advisor to NAEYC's Supporting Teachers, Strengthening Families initiative. Her research focuses on community violence, family child care, program quality, and family-strengthening practices. jjordan@csu.edu **Kathy Goetz Wolf** is founder and CEO of Be Strong Families, a national resource on strengthening families, engaging parents, building protective factors, and developing parent–provider partnerships. She has served as project director of Strengthening Families Illinois for the past eight years. kathy@bestrongfamilies.net **Anne Douglass**, PhD, is assistant professor of early childhood education at the University of Massachusetts Boston. Her work focuses on early childhood policy, professional development, strengthening families, ethics, and the preservation and promotion of caring in organizations. anne.douglass@umb.edu

Jor'dan, Jamilah R.; Goetz Wolf, Kathy; Douglass, Anne. From *Young Children*, November 2012, pp. 18–23. Copyright © 2012 by National Association for the Education of Young Children. Reprinted by permission. www.naeyc.org.

Article Prepared by: Karen Menke Paciorek, *Eastern Michigan University*

Connecting with Families

Tips for Those Difficult Conversations

Jodi Whiteman

Learning Outcomes

After reading this article, you will be able to:

- Name one strategy described by the author that you could use in a conversation with families.

- Describe the role teachers of young children have in supporting families of young children.

K im arrives for her first day as a teacher in a mixed-age infant/toddler classroom at an Early Head Start program. She is excited about this new adventure. She immediately finds that she enjoys working with the babies very much but has trouble communicating with some of their parents, especially when a sensitive concern arises.

On Thursday, her third day on the job, she notices in the morning that 6-month-old Fernando has a terrible diaper rash. When Fernando's mother picks him up that evening, Kim mentions the rash. Fernando's mother says, "That happened at the center. He was fine all weekend and this morning." Kim is confused and worried by this. "Now what do I do?" she asks herself.

The next day 2-year-old Alicia bites another child. Kim later shares with Alicia's father what had happened. He angrily tells her that she obviously is not a good teacher since she could not watch the children to make sure this didn't happen. Kim feels intimidated and tells him she is sorry. That night Kim questions if she has made the right career choice. She knows she loves children, but she never thought working with families would be so hard. She decides to talk to her supervisor, Heath, and get some help from him.

What the Research Tells Us

Many teachers have experiences and feelings like Kim's. Few early childhood professionals enter the field with a strong interest in working with families (Powell 2003). Often early care and education teachers begin their careers without realizing that their work means that they need to partner with families. Teachers may feel unsure and uncomfortable when discussing difficult topics with them (Powell 2003). Both new and seasoned early care and education professionals are eager for help and need a chance to learn strategies and skills, along with practical tools, for holding difficult conversations.

When Kim spoke with Heath, he told her that NAEYC conducted a parent survey to understand parents' perceptions of both center-based child care programs and family child care home providers. The survey asked families whether they turn to program staff for child-related guidance, information, and support (Olson & Hyson 2005). Heath shared two findings from the parent survey that he thought were important for Kim to think about. First, "parents regarded advice giving as intrusive. They preferred to receive information in a cooperative, respectful manner, in the context of a relationship based on a sharing of information. Secondly, parents thought teachers needed more training in parent communication, specifically around communicating about difficult topics".

Heath shared information from another survey that he thought might help Kim. ZERO TO THREE, working with MetLife Foundation and Hart Research Associates, conducted a nationwide parent survey. In the survey, 80 percent of families noted that professionals, including early childhood teachers, either powerfully or moderately influence their decisions regarding their children (Hart Research Associates 2009). Teachers of young children have a significant role in helping and supporting families, yet the teachers themselves need help and support to do so effectively. Talking to Heath, who listened carefully, and getting useful information from him helped Kim realize that she was not alone with her questions and struggles about working with families. Kim felt relieved, supported, and ready to learn more about how to effectively partner with families.

Getting Started

Approaching parents or family members with something they might not want to hear is never easy, especially with the limited time available during drop-off and pickup times. It helps to get to know families well before there is a need to bring up a sensitive topic. That builds a sense of trust and caring that makes it much easier to ask for some time to talk together about a question or concern. Here are some strategies that can help build provider–family relationships. These same strategies can be useful when there is a difficult topic to bring up.

Asking questions and wondering is a strategy that helps providers connect with families. By asking thoughtful questions, teachers honor parents' knowledge of their child. Wondering together with families demonstrates curiosity on the teacher's part, puts the teacher and family member on an equal footing, and demonstrates respect for the family member.

Regarding Fernando's situation, Kim acknowledged to his mother that she might have made a mistake, saying, "I think my question about Fernando's diaper rash got us off to a difficult start. I didn't mean to do that. I just wanted to make sure that you knew about the rash. I thought about what happened and realized that while I was well meaning, I am new here, and we don't even know each other. I hope we can start over. I am wondering if you are available at the end of the day to discuss how to best treat Fernando's diaper rash." Kim might then ask questions such as, "I wonder, has Fernando had a rash like this before?" After listening to his mother's response, she could ask other questions such as, "How did you handle it then?" and "What would you like us to do here?" Kim's asking questions and wondering may help Fernando's mother feel open to participating in the conversation and can go a long way toward building a positive relationship.

Two other strategies that help build relationships with families are active listening and showing empathy. Active listening is listening carefully to what the other person is saying and stating back to them what you understood. This process allows the other person to hear, think about, and clarify her own words. Active listening also involves paying attention to nonverbal messages, such as body language and facial expressions, which help you understand the speaker's meaning. Empathizing involves expressing your understanding and acceptance of another person's experiences and feelings. Teachers can do this by reflecting back what they are seeing and hearing from families; for example, "It can be tough to figure out what to do when your child is acting out. It sounds like this is taking a lot out of you."

Kim decided to use these two strategies to begin building a relationship with Alicia's father. Kim acknowledged to him that she might have gotten off on the wrong foot the day before. Then she expressed empathy for his feelings and used active listening. Kim said, "It sounds like you are really upset about this. I'm sorry this is difficult to hear, and I can understand why it would be! I can imagine that you don't want to hear about Alicia hurting another child. You might even worry if she is somehow in trouble with me. It is typical for children her age to show some aggression when they are frustrated, so I am not upset with her at all. Can I share with you a little bit more about the situation? That way maybe we can better understand what is going on. Then maybe we can find ways to help her so she doesn't end up getting frustrated and biting."

These strategies can help build a foundation of trust, caring, and connection that allows both families and providers to give and receive help, support, and information that benefits young children.

Think About It

- How do you feel when you are challenged in a relationship with a family member? How can you identify your feelings, and can you understand why you may be feeling those emotions?
- Consider a time when someone really listened to you. What did they do to show you they were listening? How did this make you feel? How can you use this experience during difficult conversations that may arise in your work with families?

Try It

- Explore some of the strategies listed in this column, and role-play with your co-worker or supervisor.
- Commit to taking a workshop on establishing relationships with families. Contact your NAEYC Affiliate, www.naeyc.org/affiliates/offices, the local child care resource and referral network (CCR&R), or a community college for professional development opportunities and information about establishing relationships with families.

References

Hart Research Associates. 2009. *Parenting Infants and Toddlers Today: Research Findings.* www.zerotothree.org/about-us/funded-projects/parenting-resources/final_survey_report_3-11-2010.pdf.

Olson, M., & M. Hyson. 2005. "Professional Development. NAEYC Explores Parental Perspectives on Early Childhood Education." *Young Children* 60 (3): 66–68. www.naeyc.org/files/naeyc/file/ecprofessional/STSF_parentsandchildren.pdf.

Powell, D.R. 2003. "Relations between Families and Early Childhood Programs." In *Connecting with Parents in the Early Years,* eds. J. Mendoza, L.G. Katz, A.S. Robertson, & D. Rothenberg, 141–54. Champaign, IL: Early Childhood and Parenting Collaborative, University of Illinois at Urbana–Champaign. http://ecap.crc.uiuc.edu/pubs/connecting.html.

Critical Thinking

1. What are some barriers to having difficult conversations with families?
2. Share two strategies that would be helpful to teachers as they build relationships with families.

Create Central

www.mhhe.com/createcentral

Internet References

American Academy of Pediatrics
www.aap.org

Child Welfare League of America (CWLA)
www.cwla.org

Children, Youth and Families Education and Research Network
www.cyfernet.org

Harvard Family Research Project
www.hfrp.org

Teachers Helping Teachers
www.pacificnet.net/~mandel

JODI WHITEMAN, MEd, is the director of the Center for Training Services and Special Projects at ZERO TO THREE. Jodi has worked in the infant/family field for 15 years. jwhiteman@zerotothree.org.

Whiteman, Jodi. From *Young Children*, March 2013, pp. 94–95. Copyright © 2013 by National Association for the Education of Young Children. Reprinted by permission. www.naeyc.org.

Article   Prepared by: Karen Menke Paciorek, *Eastern Michigan University*

Stopping Childhood Obesity Before It Begins

DEBORAH MAZZEO ET AL.

Learning Outcomes

After reading this article, you will be able to:

- Describe some of the long term health concerns due to childhood obesity.

- Name some of the strategies that can be implemented for daily physical activity for preschool children.

Attention to exercise during preschool years gives children a healthier start and a better chance to avoid obesity later.

"I wish I had half their energy." If you're a parent or teacher of young children, you undoubtedly utter this phrase often. The energy of preschoolers seems so boundless it may not occur to parents, teachers, or even pediatricians that some children between ages two and five aren't getting enough or the right kind of exercise—and that it can lead to a lifelong struggle with obesity. Requiring physical activity as early as preschool may be the only way to keep children from developing the poor habits that contribute to obesity and are much harder to change as they get older.

A barrage of public service announcements and campaigns such as First Lady Michelle Obama's Let's Move! program have made us aware that obesity is a major health concern, affecting one-third of adults and 17% of children and adolescents (Centers for Disease Control and Prevention, 2007; White House Task Force on Childhood Obesity, 2010). Perhaps more surprising is the rise in obesity rates for children under age five. The number of obese children between two and five has doubled over the past 30 years (Story, Kaphingst, & French, 2006) and almost tripled over the past 40 years (Skelton, 2009). Obese children are more likely to be obese adults and are at much greater risk for developing diabetes, hypertension, and high blood cholesterol. In addition to the negative health consequences, cognitive and affective consequences are also evident: Overweight children miss four times as much school as their normal-weight peers

(Satcher, 2005), and obese children, especially girls, are more likely to maintain a poor body image (Strauss, 2000).

Despite heightened awareness, we haven't gotten better at preventing obesity. When children start preschool, many already are not meeting recommended guidelines for physical activity (National Association for Sport and Physical Education [NASPE], 2010). Perhaps it's because parents and teachers don't take it seriously until children are older—when the consequences are more apparent. Or perhaps many of us focus on one factor, like diet and nutrition, and not on others, like exercise. Indeed, although most primary care physicians rate lack of exercise as an important barrier to obesity prevention and treatment, in first-year appointments with babies and their parents, 55% report they never discuss it (Spivack, Swietlik, Alessandrini, & Faith, 2010).

Most parents and teachers believe young children are very active, and they may simply not know how much exercise children should be getting—or even recognize when they're overweight or obese (Baughcum, Chamberlin, Deeks, Powers, & Whitaker, 2000; Parry, Netuveli, Parry, & Saxena, 2008). Each day, preschoolers should accumulate *two hours* of exercise, including 60 minutes of structured physical activity and 60 minutes of unstructured physical activity (Pica, 2006). Further, Pica notes, 10- to 15-minute increments over the course of the day that yield 120 minutes is preferable; 30 minutes of continuous exercise could be developmentally inappropriate. Preschoolers shouldn't be sedentary for more than 60 minutes at a time (except when sleeping) and should develop competence in movement skills that are building blocks for more complex movement tasks, such as rolling, kicking, throwing, and catching (NASPE, 2010).

Early Intervention

Preschool is a crucial time for obesity prevention, as children are developing eating and physical activity habits. A lack of physical activity at preschool may contribute more to overweight children than parental influences such as modeling and supporting physical activity or providing fitness equipment in the home (Trost, Sirard, Dowda, Pfeiffer, & Pate, 2003). Some 80% to 85% of children's time at preschool is sedentary (Cardon & De Bourdeaudhuij, 2008). The amount of physical activity this age group gets is highly contingent upon the preschool they attend (Trost, Ward, & Senso, 2010).

With over half of preschool-aged children spending eight or more hours per day in childcare settings, early childhood day care centers are an obvious place to implement policies and programs to address the health needs of this age group (Finn, Johannsen, & Specker, 2002).

While there are many guidelines related to health and physical activity for preschool centers, policies at the local or program level for ensuring that preschools meet the criteria are virtually nonexistent. The onus, therefore, is on individual early childhood day care centers and preschools to make physical activity a priority in their programs by making programmatic changes and providing adequate staff training. The amount of physical activity children participate in may be driven by a lack of space, equipment, and outdoor playtime. Despite motor development being the area of human development that is best understood and most documented (Bredekamp, 1992), there also is a clear lack of knowledgeable staff with respect to movement education. Movement education is exactly that—learning about the best and most developmentally appropriate ways to be physically active. Research suggests that workshops, reflective conversations, and one-on-one meetings with consultants can lead to changes in early childhood educators' attitudes and skills relative to physical activity (Helm & Boos, 1996).

> **Preschool is a crucial time for obesity prevention, as children are developing eating and physical activity habits.**

Developing Healthy Habits

At a time when the increased focus on academic content is overshadowing the need for physical activity at all levels of education, parents and preschool teachers can't overlook the importance of proper physical development for toddlers and young children. By making the necessary changes to their programs and training their staff adequately, preschools can ensure that children engage in the right amount and kind of physical activity, reaping not only long-term learning and developmental benefits but also getting an early start on developing healthy habits that last a lifetime.

References

Baughcum, A., Chamberlin, L., Deeks, C., Powers, S., & Whitaker, R. (2000). Maternal perceptions of overweight preschool children. *Pediatrics, 106,* 1380–1386.

Bredekamp, S. (1992). What is "developmentally appropriate" and why is it important? *Journal of Physical Education, Recreation, and Dance, 63* (6), 31–32.

Cardon, G. & De Bourdeaudhuij, I. (2008). Are preschool children active enough? Objectively measured physical activity levels. *Research Quarterly for Exercise and Sport, 79* (3), 326–332.

Centers for Disease Control and Prevention. (2007). *State-level school health policies and practices: A state-by-state summary from the School Health Policies and Programs Study 2006.* Atlanta, GA: U.S. Department of Health and Human Services.

Finn, K., Johannsen, N., & Specker, B. (2002). Factors associated with physical activity in preschool children. *The Journal of Pediatrics, 140* (1), 81–85.

Helm, J. & Boos, S. (1996). Increasing the physical educator's impact: Consulting, collaborating, and teacher training in early childhood programs. *Journal of Physical Education, Recreation, and Dance, 67* (3), 26–32.

Mid-continent Research for Education and Learning. (2009). *Let Me Play Head Start: Draft report for program evaluation.* Denver, CO: Author.

National Association for Sport and Physical Education. (2010). *Active start: A statement of physical activity guidelines for children from birth to age 5* (2nd ed.). Reston, VA: Author.

Parry, L., Netuveli, G., Parry, J., & Saxena, S. (2008). A systematic review of parental perception of overweight status in children. *Journal of Ambulatory Care Management, 31,* 253–268.

Pica, R. (2006). Physical fitness and the early childhood curriculum. *Young Children, 61* (3), 12–19.

Satcher, D. (2005). Healthy and ready to learn. *Educational Leadership, 63* (1), 26–30.

Skelton, J.A. (2009). Prevalence and trends of severe obesity among U.S. children and adolescents. *Academic Pediatrics, 9* (5), 322–329.

Spivack, J., Swietlik, M., Alessandrini, E., & Faith, M. (2010). Primary care providers' knowledge, practices, and perceived barriers to the treatment and prevention of childhood obesity. *Obesity, 18* (7), 1341–1347.

Stork, S. & Sanders, S. (1996). Developmentally appropriate physical education: A rating scale. *Journal of Physical Education, Recreation, and Dance, 67* (6), 52–58.

Story, M., Kaphingst, K., & French, S. (2006). The role of child care settings in obesity prevention. *Future Child, 16* (1), 143–168.

Strauss, R.S. (2000). Childhood obesity and self-esteem. *Pediatrics, 105* (1), 15–20.

Trost, S., Sirard, J., Dowda, M., Pfeiffer, K., & Pate, R. (2003). Physical activity in overweight and nonoverweight preschool children. *International Journal of Obesity, 27,* 834–839.

Trost, S., Ward, D., & Senso, M. (2010). Effects of child care policy and environment on physical activity. *Medicine in Science and Sports Exercise, 42* (3), 520–525.

White House Task Force on Childhood Obesity. (2010). *Solving the problem of childhood obesity within a generation.* Washington, DC: Author.

Critical Thinking

1. In examining the cause of childhood obesity the Centers for Disease Control (2009) recommended all students in grades P–12 be actively engaged in daily physical education. This conflicts with the current push for more seat time learning and academics. This focus as been called "obesogenic," which is described as the school environment actually encouraging obesity by focusing on sedentary work, limited physical education and recess, and cafeteria food containing high fat, many calories, and limited nutrition. Think about this and share your thoughts.

2. The authors indicate that preschoolers should have an hour of structured and unstructured physical activity every day. Interview two pre-kindergarten teachers and see how their program schedule accommodates this need. What amount of time would they estimate their children receive in each category?

Create Central

www.mhhe.com/createcentral

Internet References

Action for Healthy Kids
www.actionforhealthykids.org

American Academy of Pediatrics
www.aap.org

American Alliance of Health Physical Education Recreation and Dance
www.aahperd.org

American Diabetes Association
www.diabetes.org

Kid Fit
http://kid-fit.com

National Association for the Education of Young Children
www.naeyc.org

Article   Prepared by: Karen Menke Paciorek, *Eastern Michigan University*

The Impact of Teachers and Families on Young Children's Eating Behaviors

Erin K. Eliassen

Learning Outcomes

After reading this article, you will be able to:

- Write a list of at least five steps that will assist in the development of positive eating behaviors.

- Share ways in which our society places pressure on children related to food and eating.

Young children depend on their families and teachers to support their well-being and promote positive development, including eating behaviors. Children's food preferences and willingness to try new foods are influenced by the people around them (Bellows & Anderson 2006).

The eating behaviors children practice early in life affect their health and nutrition—significant factors in childhood overweight and obesity (Clark et al. 2007)—and may continue to shape food attitudes and eating patterns through adulthood (Birch 1999; Campbell & Crawford 2001; Westenhoefer 2002). Eating environments—mealtime and snack—that make food fun, offer new foods and a variety, and encourage children to taste and choose the foods they want let children develop food attitudes and dietary practices that ultimately support good health (Campbell & Crawford 2001).

Developing Eating Behaviors

The development of eating behaviors is a dynamic process that begins in infancy and continues throughout life. In this article, *eating behaviors* refers to food preferences, patterns of food acceptance and rejection, and the types and amounts of food a person eats. Genetics and the contexts in which foods are presented are two key factors that underpin the development of eating behaviors. Although parents provide a child's biological predisposition, which may affect factors like taste perception, they are not the only adults influencing the development of a child's eating behaviors. Every family member and caregiver interacting with a child at meals or snacks has the potential to do so.

In center- and home-based child care settings, teachers and family child care providers influence children's eating behaviors by the foods they offer, the behaviors they model, and their social interactions with children at snack and mealtimes (Savage, Fisher, & Birch 2007). Here are a few examples of how these factors influence eating behaviors.

Repeated exposure to a new food reduces a child's fear of the food and helps increase acceptance. Observing families and teachers eating and enjoying a variety of foods makes these foods more appealing to children. In contrast, children who are pressured to eat specific foods learn to dislike them. Restricted access to some foods, such as cookies or potato chips, often results in overconsumption of those foods when children are free to choose them (Savage, Fisher, & Birch 2007).

Educators and Families are Role Models

Based on research, the following six subsections discuss food fears, care environments, food behavior models, food restriction, pressures to eat, and food as a reward or celebration. Each area offers suggestions for educators and families to help children develop positive, early eating behaviors.

Food Fears

Most children naturally demonstrate fears of new foods. Neophobia, or fear of the new, is a protective behavior observed in omnivores, including humans, that helps prevent consumption of harmful substances (Birch 1999). Teachers help decrease children's fears by creating supportive environments with enjoyable, nutritious, and fun early food experiences.

For example, teachers could involve families by encouraging each family to bring every child a tasting sample of a unique food their child enjoys (or the teacher may offer suggestions of foods to taste). The teacher can arrange a tasting schedule, with a different family sharing a food tasting each week. Once every family has had an opportunity to share, host a classroom tasting party with all of the foods and invite parents to enjoy the event with their children. Although experiments vary, researchers tell us that offering a food 10 to 15 times appears necessary to increase a child's food acceptance (Savage, Fisher, & Birch 2007). Activities like tasting parties expose children to foods from different cultures and provide opportunities to learn more about their friends.

The acceptance of new foods is a slow process. Particularly through the ages 2 to 5, persistence is essential (Birch 1999; Satter 2008). A teacher/caregiver may think it is best to hold off on introducing food variety until children's fearful responses decrease. Instead, it is important to continue introducing a variety of foods throughout early childhood. Although children are skeptical of many foods during these early years, the variety of foods they accept is greater in this developmental phase than it is in later childhood (Skinner et al. 2002).

Enjoyable or satisfying experiences with a food highly influence a child's subsequent selection of the food on given occasions or its adoption into his or her regular diet. These experiences are as simple as frequent family meals during which the television is off and parents or caregivers are tuned in to the mealtime experience by talking and enjoying the foods themselves. Positive exposure to multiple foods helps children develop a taste for more foods, choose them as regular mealtime selections, and have needed dietary variety—whole grains, fruits, and vegetables. Many children lack opportunities to taste a variety of healthful foods, compared to the numerous chances our culture makes available for tasting high-fat, calorie-dense foods (Savage, Fisher, & Birch 2007).

Care Environments

Child care settings foster positive development of eating behaviors for 2- to 5-year-olds. Caregivers introduce variety in the foods served at meals and snacks and encourage families to do the same when they send lunches from home. Programs can guide parents by sharing comprehensive lists of foods that present a variety of grains, fruits, vegetables, nuts and seeds, and meats and beans, and an illustration of their nutritional value. For instance, using MyPyramid (www.mypyramid.gov) food groups helps families categorize foods and prepare lunches with variety and nutritional balance. Teachers can share examples of simple, creative lunches with variety in color, texture, and taste to appeal to young children.

Being persistent and providing repeated exposures to foods is important for both teachers and families. Avoid temptations to remove healthy foods from the program's meal or snack menus just because children reject them. Support families in continuing to offer lunch items even if their child does not consume the food on a given day. When serving a new item such as snap peas at snack time, include it two or three times a month and encourage children to look, smell, touch, and taste the new food. It is perfectly acceptable for a child to avoid a new vegetable the first several times it is offered. Inviting children to touch and smell the food helps them take small steps toward tasting. Encouraging rather than requiring children to eat a food is the key objective.

Food Behavior Models

Families are typically children's first significant models of eating behavior (Golan & Weizman 2001). Child care providers also are early role models. Positive role modeling correlates

Ten Steps to Positive Eating Behaviors

1. Provide a variety of foods at meals and snacks, especially whole grains, vegetables, and fruits.
2. Offer repeated opportunities to taste new foods.
3. Share with families nutrition resources, such as lists of foods (by category) to guide their food selections and offer new ideas for meals sent from home.
4. Apply the same guidelines to food selections in teachers' lunches brought from home.
5. Sit with children at meals, and enjoy conversation. Talk about the taste, texture, appearance, and healthful aspects of foods.
6. Plan adequate time for all children to finish eating.
7. Respect a child's expression of satiety or sense of being full.
8. Develop a routine for serving snacks, applying the same rules whether offering carrots, crackers, or cookies.
9. Wash hands before snack and mealtime; encourage touching and smelling a food as a step toward tasting.
10. Find alternatives to using food as a reward or serving foods high in fat, sugar, or salt as part of a celebration.

with an increased interest in food and less food fussiness among children (Gregory, Paxton, & Borzovic 2010). Poor role models influence children's perceptions of foods and mealtimes (Matheson, Spranger, & Saxe 2002). For example, negative comments about the taste or texture of a food will make a child less willing to try it. On the other hand, a child is more likely to try a food if he or she observes an adult enjoying it.

Teachers and caregivers become role models by engaging with children at mealtime and sitting down and eating with them. This practice is often called family-style dining. When early childhood programs provide meals, teachers and staff can model healthy eating behaviors by eating the same foods the children eat.

Staff who bring their lunches can model the same kinds of healthy eating as described in the guidelines the program suggests for families who send lunches with their children. For example, if parents send a fruit and a vegetable item, then teachers can include both of these items in their lunches. If children have milk, water, or 100 percent fruit juice as a beverage, teachers should drink these same beverages.

Interesting and engaging mealtime conversations create greater food enjoyment (Hughes et al. 2007). Adults can talk positively about the foods they are eating and also invite the children to describe colors, tastes (sweet, sour, salty), and textures (crunchy, smooth, stringy). However, the conversation should not be about the food alone. Also engage children in conversation about other appropriate topics, such as animals or family activities. Too much emphasis on the foods may decrease the children's interest.

Food Restriction

Many well-meaning adults try to control the way children eat. They may believe that restricting or forbidding unhealthy foods will decrease children's preference for them, but the opposite is true (Satter 2008). Pressuring a child to eat one type of food (such as fruit or vegetables) leads to resistance. When an adult restricts access to certain foods (such as sweets or french fries), a child may become preoccupied with the restricted food.

A study on the effect of restricted access to foods among a population of 3- to 6-year-olds (Fisher & Birch 1999) found that the children focused great attention on the visible but inaccessible food through spontaneous clapping and chanting. In a similar study (Fisher & Birch 1999), restricting a desired, palatable snack food substantially increased children's selection of that food compared to times when both it and similar foods were freely available.

Avoid making comments about children's frequency or quantity consumption of a given food. For example, when serving cookies for snack, offer them as all other snacks are served. Their quantity should not be restricted unless the quantity of all snack foods is restricted. Early childhood educators can develop routines for offering all snacks, both unfamiliar and favorite foods, in the same unbiased way.

Pressure to Eat

When families or teachers pressure children to eat at mealtimes, the practice negatively influences a child's food intake as well as attitude toward food (Galloway et al. 2006). Gregory, Paxton, and Brozovic (2010) report that children pressured to eat were less interested in food over time; whereas, when parents modeled healthy eating, the children expressed greater interest in food and less food fussiness. Coercion to eat specific quantities or types of foods may mean that children eat more at the given meal, but over time they will likely avoid the targeted food (Satter 2008).

In a study involving adults, Batsell and colleagues (2002) traced common food dislikes to the adults' childhood experiences in being pressured to consume certain foods. Galloway and colleagues (2006) learned that refraining from the use of pressure and simply eating with and talking to the children had a more positive impact on children's attitude toward the food offered.

While pressure to eat contributes to a dislike of certain foods, emphasis on having a "clean plate" may hinder children's recognition of the internal cues of hunger and satiety and contribute to overeating (Satter 2008). It is important for adults to respect the child's expression of food preference and fullness (particularly if the child tastes a food) and to follow a schedule that gives children enough time to eat.

Food as a Reward or Celebration

Food as reward or celebration is common in some early childhood settings. Such practices may be well intentioned but can have negative consequences and impact long-term eating behaviors (Birch 1999; Brown & Ogden 2004). Food rewards or party treats are often sweets or other "desired" snack items. Giving a desired food as a reward enhances a child's preference for the food (Puhl & Schwartz 2003).

By establishing guidelines for the use of food in the classroom, early childhood programs encourage families to provide alternatives to fast-food lunch parties or cupcake celebrations and to bring instead, for example, fruits or muffins. Class celebrations or everyday activities also give young children opportunities to prepare their own foods in the classroom. Children enjoy making edible art fruit or vegetable skewers, or snacks resembling animals.

Alternative practices for recognition and celebration are growing in variety in early childhood settings. Instead of food, teachers recognize children by giving them special opportunities, such as selecting a song for the group to listen or dance to, choosing a game to play with friends, or having first choice of equipment for gross motor play. Non-food-related activities, like bringing a favorite book or game to class to read or share with friends, are other ways to acknowledge individuals.

Conclusion

Early childhood educators who understand the importance of their role in the development of children's healthful eating behaviors can help improve the lifelong health of the children they serve. They can offer meaningful, positive experiences with food, including growing, preparing, and eating foods with children. Regardless of the foods offered at home, the early childhood educator has the opportunity to model selection and enjoyment of a variety of foods. Food in the program should be associated with opportunities and fun experiences rather than rules and restrictions. Tasting activities help children learn about foods, manners, and even other cultures.

Everyone caring for children needs to be aware that some food strategies have negative effects on the development of eating behaviors. Food practices involving pressure and restriction may not only affect childhood health but also have long-lasting implications, such as problematic behaviors of binge eating and dietary restraint among adults (Puhl & Schwartz 2003).

A supportive, caring early childhood environment offers guidance through adult modeling, serving a variety of nutritious foods at meals and snacks, and exposing children to new foods in the classroom. These practices encourage children's development of healthy eating attitudes and behaviors and promote positive long-term health outcomes.

References

Batsell, R., A. Brown, M. Ansfield, & G. Paschall. 2002. "You Will Eat All of That! A Retrospective Analysis of Forced Consumption Episodes." *Appetite* 38 (3): 211–19.

Bellows, L., & J. Anderson. 2006. "The Food Friends: Encouraging Preschoolers to Try New Foods." *Young Children* 61 (3): 37–39. www.naeyc.org/yc/pastissues/2006/may.

Birch, L. 1999. "Development of Food Preferences." *Annual Reviews of Nutrition* 19 (1): 41–62.

Brown, R., & J. Ogden. 2004. "Children's Eating Attitudes and Behaviour: A Study of the Modeling and Control Theories of Parental Influence." *Health Education Research* 19 (3): 261–71.

Campbell, K., & D. Crawford 2001. "Family Food Environments as Determinants of Preschool-Aged Children's Eating Behaviors: Implications for Obesity Prevention Policy. A Review." *Australian Journal of Nutrition and Dietetics* 58 (1): 19–25.

Clark, H., E. Goyder, P. Bissel, L. Blank, & J. Peters. 2007. "How Do Parents' Child-Feeding Behaviours Influence Child Weight? Implications for Childhood Obesity Policy." *Journal of Public Health* 29 (2): 132–41.

Fisher, J., & L. Birch. 1999. "Restricting Access to Palatable Foods Affects Children's Behavioral Response, Food Selection, and Intake." *American Journal of Clinical Nutrition* 69 (6): 1264–72.

Galloway, A., L. Fiorito, L. Francis, & L. Birch. 2006. "'Finish Your Soup': Counterproductive Effects of Pressuring Children to Eat on Intake and Affect." *Appetite* 46 (3): 318–23.

Golan, M., & A. Weizman. 2001. "Familial Approach to the Treatment of Childhood Obesity." *Journal of Nutrition Education* 33 (2): 102–07.

Gregory, J., S. Paxton, & A. Brozovic. 2010. "Maternal Feeding Practices, Child Eating Behavior and Body Mass Index in Preschool-Aged Children: A Prospective Analysis." *The International Journal of Behavioral Nutrition and Physical Activity* 7: 55–65.

Hughes, S., H. Patrick, T. Power, J. Fisher, C. Anderson, & T. Nicklas. 2007. "The Impact of Child Care Providers' Feeding on Children's Food Consumption." *Journal of Development & Behavioral Pediatrics* 28 (2): 100–07.

Matheson, D., K. Spranger, & A. Saxe. 2002. "Preschool Children's Perceptions of Food and Their Food Experiences." *Journal of Nutrition Education and Behavior* 34 (2): 85–92.

Puhl, R., & M. Schwartz. 2003. "If You Are Good You Can Have a Cookie: How Memories of Childhood Food Rules Link to Adult Eating Behaviors." *Eating Behaviors* 4 (3): 283–93. www.faeriefilms.com/images/Schwartz_-_If_You_Are_Good.pdf.

Satter, E. 2008. *Secrets of Feeding a Healthy Family.* Madison, WI: Kelcy Press.

Savage, J., J. O. Fisher, & L. Birch. 2007. "Parental Influence on Eating Behavior: Conception to Adolescence." *Journal of Law, Medicine & Ethics* 35 (1): 22–34.

Skinner, J., B. Carruth, W. Bounds, & P. Ziegler. 2002. "Children's Food Preferences: A Longitudinal Analysis." *Journal of the American Dietetic Association* 102 (11): 1638–47.

Westenhoefer, J. 2002. "Establishing Dietary Habits During Childhood for Long-Term Weight Control." *Annals of Nutrition & Metabolism* 46 (supplement): 18–23.

Critical Thinking

1. How many times does a young child need to be exposed to a food prior to accepting it into their diet? What early food experiences affected your eating habits today?

2. What steps can early childhood educators take to assist young children in developing healthy eating habits?

Create Central

www.mhhe.com/createcentral

Internet References

Administration for Children and Families
www.hhs.gov/children/index.html

Action for Healthy Kids
www.actionforhealthykids.org

American Academy of Pediatrics
www.aap.org

American Alliance of Health Physical Education Recreation and Dance
www.aahperd.org

American Diabetes Association
www.diabetes.org

Kid Fit
http://kid-fit.com

Teacher Quick Source
www.teacherquicksource.com

Teachers Helping Teachers
www.pacificnet.net/~mandel

Article   Prepared by: Karen Menke Paciorek, *Eastern Michigan University*

Caring for Rosie the Riveter's Children

BILL MACKENZIE

Learning Outcomes

After reading this article, you will be able to:

- Name three specific program services available in the Kaiser programs that were a part of what was called the best day care there ever was.

- Describe why the services offered at the Kaiser Shipyards are in demand today.

During the Second World War. women in the United States who worked in the war industries in such jobs as welders, riveters, heavy machinery operators, and parachute riggers were heralded in the media as "Rosie the Riveter." From 1943 to 1945 a fortunate few of these workplace pioneers participated in a memorable experiment in child care at Kaiser shipyards. Here, two of the most ambitious, business-run, on-site child care centers in the United States were established to meet family needs. The centers operated 24 hours a day, 364 days a year. They were called "a new [employer-employee] development in industrial relations" (Kaiser, n.d.) and "a model for child care in the post-war world" (*The New York Times* 1944).

Lisa Gilbert, Southwest Washington Medical Center in Vancouver, Washington, recalls that her mother, a welder, and her father, a machinist, both worked at one of the two Kaiser Portland, Oregon, shipyards. She remembers the child care center she attended as a child: "My mother said care at the shipyard was a whole lot better an environment than leaving me at home" (Gilbert, pers. interview).

Eleanor Roosevelt Urged On-site Child Care

The war escalated, and by early 1943 the Kaiser Company employed twelve thousand women at its Portland-area shipyards. Four thousand were mothers, and many had preschool-age children. Accessible, affordable child care on site meant that Kaiser could reduce worker lateness, absenteeism to care for a sick child, and early departures to meet family needs (Kaiser, n.d.).

Eleanor Roosevelt encouraged Henry Kaiser to build modern, model centers for child care at his two Oregon shipyards to encourage other businesses around the country to follow his lead (Goodwin 1994). The centers were a rarity of excellent care, with innovative features—an on-site infirmary, multiple outdoor play yards enclosed by the building, and the added service of prepared food that war workers could buy as a take-home family meal (Hymes 1978).

Today's Working Mothers and Their Children

- The number of working mothers with young children has significantly increased over the past 30 years— from 39 percent of the workforce in 1975 to more than 63 percent in 2009 (BLS 2010).
- 5.5 million children younger than age 5 and 2.3 million children ages 5 to 14 are in child care while their mothers work (US Census Bureau, n.d.).
- Half of all 9-month-old infants are enrolled in care outside the home (Halle et al. 2009).
- Less than 10 percent of employers across the country offer child care at or near the work site (Galinksy et al. 2008).

Kaiser Child Care Faces Some Protests

Initially not everyone embraced the concept of group child care, including the Federal Security Agency and the Children's Bureau. The then US Office of Education asserted that group child care outside the home was "a danger to parental authority, particularly the mother-child relationship" (Tuttle 1995). Despite the opposition, Kaiser proposed that two centers be built, each with 15 rooms and serving 375 children on each of the three work shifts (Kaiser, n.d.).

Kaiser's son, Edgar, guided the project, and the centers took shape at two massive Portland shipyards, Swan Island and Oregonship. He won over his opponents, turning to them for names of the best person to act as consultant and overall director of the centers. Lois Meek Stoltz, child development educator, a researcher at the Institute for Child Welfare, University of

California–Berkeley, and past president of the National Association for Nursery Education (NANE [NAEYC's precursor]) was named on every list. "Right at the shipyard," Stoltz said, ". . . children will play and eat and sleep in an environment especially planned for them, while not far away, their mothers— welders, clerks, timekeepers, and secretaries—put in a full eight-hour shift" (*The New York Times* 1943).

Because the centers were designed to accommodate the 24-hour-a-day shipyard schedule, children were accepted around-the-clock in a three-part schedule. Parents' fees were $5.00 a child, additional children $3.75 each, for a 6-day week. Operating costs not covered by fees were written into Kaiser's cost-plus-fixed-fee contracts with the federal government (Tuttle 1995).

Attention to the Whole Child and the Family

The Kaiser Centers were built with both the child and the family in mind. The centers' cutting-edge design incorporated 15 classrooms that radiated out from a center core of 15 separate playgrounds, like spokes on a wheel. Covered porch areas allowed children to play outdoors even during frequent Oregon rains.

A typical 24-hour day at the center started at 6:15 a.m. with day shift breakfast followed by indoor and outdoor play, a break for fruit/juice and cod liver oil, lunch, nap, and snack, with pick-up time at 4:00 p.m. (Kaiser, n.d.). Shifts varied. Stoltz describes how some children "arrived about 4:30 p.m. . . .played, had supper, played some more, and then slept until their mothers called for them sometime after 1:30 a.m." (Hymes 1978, 48).

The Kaiser Centers were initially intended to serve children from ages 2 to 6 years. After finding that many mothers needed care for younger children, they lowered the age level to 18 months. The age range widened as the center identified other needs. School-age children ages 6 to 12, for example, were enrolled during their parents' swing and graveyard shifts and on weekends and school holidays when parents worked. In the summer vacation months, 6- and 7-year-old children were accepted by both centers as a separate play group. Center directors also created Special Service Rooms for parents who needed only short-term child care for a day or two.

Quality Staffing and Support

Center staff included one hundred trained nursery and kindergarten teachers from 25 major colleges (Hurwitz 1998). They worked a 48-hour week, 50 weeks a year. Kaiser insisted on raising teachers' salaries to match those of workers in his yards. "They made us feel like treasured members of the profession," recalled teacher Ruth Berkman (Zinsser 1984, 78).

On the health front, 10 registered nurses staffed infirmaries in each center, along with a medical consultant and five child nutritionists. Nutritionists prepared food for the children and prepackaged meals for a fee for the busy women workers (Kaiser, n.d.).

The Kaiser centers did just about everything for the parents and children. "The notion of thinking not only of children, [but of] their parents, was for many of us a relatively new idea," wrote James L. Hymes Jr., manager of the Child Service Department of the two centers (1995, 29).

Kaiser's Legacy

The Kaiser Child Service Centers paid attention to the whole child, including social, emotional, mental, and physical needs. Equipment and materials for children in the centers were state of the art, models for the future. At the war's end, servicemen came home, and most women left their industry jobs to return to their families and homemaking. Kaiser's shipyard Child Service Centers were dismantled.

Today, however, as families depend on two salaries to meet higher costs of living, even more American women are working, but on-site child care tied to workplaces remains limited. Kaiser's legacy provides a model not only for superior child care, but for care in a setting supportive of the *whole* family.

References

BLS (US Bureau of Labor Statistics). 2010. *Women in the Labor Force: A Databook.* 2010 ed. www.bls.gov/cps/wlf tablc7 -2010.pdf.

Galinksy, E., J.T. Bond, & K. Sakai, with S.S. Kim & N. Giuntoli. 2008. *National Study of Employers.* http://familiesandwork.org/ site/research/reports/2008nse.pdf.

Goodwin, D.K. 1994. *No Ordinary Time—Franklin and Eleanor Roosevelt: The Home Front in World War II.* New York: Simon & Schuster.

Halle, T., E. Hair, M. Nuenning, D. Weinstein, J. Vick, N. Forry, & A. Kinukawa. 2009. *Primary Child Care Arrangements of U.S. Infants: Patterns of Utilization by Poverty Status, Family Structure, Maternal Work Status, Maternal Work Schedule, and Child Care Assistance.* Executive summary. Office of Planning, Research and Evaluation Research Brief #1 (May). www.researchconnections.org/files/childcare/pdf/ OPREResearchBrief1Exec_FINAL.pdf.

Hurwitz, S.C. 1998. "War Nurseries—Lessons in Quality." *Young Children* 53 (5): 37–39.

Hymes, J.L., Jr. 1978. "The Kaiser Child Service Centers: Lois Meek Stolz." In *Early Childhood Education on Living History Interviews: Book 2—Care of the Children of Working Mothers,* 27–56. Carmel, CA: Hacienda Press.

Hymes, J.L., Jr. 1995. "The Kaiser Child Service Centers—50 Years Later: Some Memories and Lessons." *Journal of Education* 177(3): 23–38.

Kaiser Company Inc. n.d. *Child Service Centers. Oregon Shipbuilding Corporation.* Portland, OR: Author.

The New York Times. 1943. "The Nursery Comes to the Shipyard." November 7.

The New York Times. 1944. "Nurseries Solve Big Problem for Mothers in Kaiser Shipyards." November 17.

Tuttle, W.M., Jr. 1995. "Rosie the Riveter and Her Latchkey Children: What Americans Can Learn about Child Day Care from the Second World War." *Child Welfare* 74(1): 92–114.

US Census Bureau. n.d. *Housing and Household Economic Statistics Division, Fertility and Family Statistics. Who's Minding the Kids? Child Care Arrangements: Summer 2006.* www.census .gov/population/www/socdemo/child/tables-2006.html.

Zinsser, C. 1984. "The Best Day Care There Ever Was." *Working Mother* (Oct.): 76–78.

Critical Thinking

1. How do the child care services available for families today differ from those available 70 years ago?

2. Interview two parents whose children attend child care today and ask them what services do they wish their child's program provided that they don't currently.

Create Central

www.mhhe.com/createcentral

Internet References

Association for Childhood Education International (ACEI)
www.acei.org

Administration for Children and Families
www.hhs.gov/children/index.html

Child Care and Early Education Research Connections
www.researchconnections.org

Child Care Services Association
www.childcareservices.org/fs/finding.html

National Association for the Education of Young Children
www.naeyc.org

BILL MACKENZIE is a communications manager with Intel Corporation's Northwest Region, in Oregon. Prior to joining Intel 14 years ago, he worked as a business and politics reporter with *The Oregonian* newspaper, on the professional staff of a US House of Representatives committee, and as a high school teacher of American history. bill.mackenzie@intel.com. **Our Proud Heritage** is published in the March and November issues of *Young Children* and features contributing writers who offer insights on past practice, knowledge, and leadership in early childhood education. For submission guidelines, go to www.naeyc.org/yc/columns/ourproudheritage or contact one of the coordinators: Edna Runnels Ranck at edna.ranck@verizon.net, or Charlotte Anderson at charli@charlottephd.com. An archive of Our Proud Heritage columns is available online at www.naeyc.org/yc/columns.

MacKenzie, Bill. From *Young Children,* November 2011, pp. 68–70. Copyright © 2011 by National Association for the Education of Young Children. Reprinted by permission. www.naeyc.org.

Unit 3

UNIT

Prepared by: Karen Menke Paciorek, *Eastern Michigan University*

Diverse Learners

This unit focuses on the many diverse learners who attend our early childhood programs and schools. In the graduate early childhood seminar I teach for students earning their Master's degree in ECE, we have many lengthy discussions about the number of children they encounter on a daily basis with a Sensory Processing Disorder (SPD) or an Obsessive-Compulsive Disorder (OCD) as well as those receiving a diagnosis of Autism Spectrum Disorder (ASD). The students, all teaching young children from the ages of birth to eight, were seeking help from the professional literature, each other, and other professionals to assist them as they learned about the effects these disorders can have on a child's ability to learn and function as a contributing member of the classroom community. Educators of young are increasingly being called on to assist families as they help navigate the choppy waters they face with a child who is displaying behaviors not found in typically developing children. We must continue to educate ourselves about the services available and strategies that can help the child become a part of the home and school environment in ways that will lead to a productive life.

If we want students to perform at a high level we must have high expectations for behavior, academic achievement, and future goals. When educators fail to provide the support to students that will allow them to achieve both now and in the future we fail in our job. Who are we to determine after a brief assessment or one test the fate of a child's educational experience for the rest of his or her time in school? We must not underestimate ability and should hold all teachers and students to high standards and constantly encourage everyone to succeed. An educated population is better for us all and ensuring from the very beginning that all children have the necessary tools to be successful learners benefits all of society. It is less expensive to provide children early with the skills they will need and the resources to be successful learners than to provide remedial help for 13 years of education.

Another issue with deep implications for the early childhood profession is how we care for and educate children in inclusive environments. Nationwide, college and university programs are adapting to new standards from the National Association for the Education of Young Children (NAEYC) and the Council for Exceptional Children (CEC) which require programs educating teachers at two and four year institutions to include much more content and field experiences working with children, especially children with disabilities in inclusive environments. As teacher

preparation institutions adapt to meet the new standards, there will be more teachers out in the field better equipped to meet the needs of special needs children and their families. The new standards are all-encompassing in their focus on the diversity and richness in the children and families we serve. Secretary of Education Arne Duncan has stated that inclusive education is the responsibility of all educators and the adults who work with children are significant contributors to their learning and education. Recruiting and retaining qualified teachers who are well prepared to work with all children in environments that are established to be inclusive and differentiated is the new norm in schools. Preservice teachers need many experiences in settings serving diverse learners. This can be challenging for teacher-preparation institutions located in communities lacking diversity. Education students with limited experience of other cultures or interacting with children and families who are different from themselves must supplement their own experiences to be successful teachers able to meet the needs of all children and families. Assess your prior experiences with children and families and see if you need to volunteer or work in settings different from your past work to better equip yourself with skills needed to work with all families and children. We tend to gravitate to familiar and comfortable experiences, but good teachers stretch themselves to become familiar with the life experiences children in their class bring to the learning environment. Spend some time with a family who has a child with a disability. Get to know the stresses that child as well as the parents and other siblings may deal with on a day-to-day basis. If you own a car and many of your families depend on public transportation, take the bus one day to more fully understand the frustrations that can come from depending on a fixed schedule. Shop for groceries in the local markets used by the families in your classroom. In short, really get to know the many different life experiences the families you work with face in their daily lives.

The ongoing need for learning experiences to be differentiated is a recurring theme in teacher preparation programs as well as in staff development sessions all across the country. All teachers must remember that individualizing learning can be accomplished through a thoughtful and intentional approach. All educators, but especially those who work with young children, need familiarity with Response to Intervention (RTI) and the steps educators can take to, as my Great Aunt Nene used to say, "do a stitch in time to save nine." Early prevention is one of the cornerstones of our profession. The strong foundation we build early in a child's life will serve him or her well into the future. We know that if we can intervene early and work with the child and family we can help that child get on track and compete with peers.

There are more and more examples of teachers adjusting their image of diverse learners and families. Only when all educators are accepting of the wide diversity that exists in family structures and among individual children will all children feel welcomed and comfortable at school. The collaboration of families, the community, and school personnel will enable children to benefit from the partnership these three groups bring to the educational setting. The articles in this unit represent many diverse families and children and the issues surrounding young children today. An open mind and tolerance for families that may not be of the same composition as your own will allow educators to support all learners.

Article   Prepared by: Karen Menke Paciorek, *Eastern Michigan University*

1 in 68 Children Now Has a Diagnosis of Autism Spectrum Disorder—Why?

With rates of the disorder yet again rising according to new CDC numbers, a look at how doctors are diagnosing autism spectrum disorder in children, and what might be done better.

ENRICO GNAULATI

Learning Outcomes

After reading this article, you will be able to:

- Discuss some theories for the startling increase in numbers of children diagnosed with autism.

- List behaviors physicians are using as possible indicators a child may have an autism spectrum disorder.

- Name differences researchers have observed in boys and girls related to autism spectrum disorders.

Rates of autism spectrum disorder (ASD) are not creeping up so much as leaping up. New numbers just released by the Centers for Disease Control and Prevention reveal that one in 68 children now has a diagnosis of ASD—a 30 percent increase in just two years. In 2002, about one in 150 children was considered autistic and in 1991 the figure was one in 500.

The staggering increase in cases of ASD should raise more suspicion in the medical community about its misdiagnosis and overdiagnosis than it does. Promoting early screening for autism is imperative. But, is it possible that the younger in age a child is when professionals screen for ASD—especially its milder cases—the greater the risk that a slow-to-mature child will be misperceived as autistic, thus driving the numbers up?

The science stacks up in favor of catching and treating ASD earlier because it leads to better outcomes. Dr. Laura Schreibman, who directs the Autism Intervention Research Program at the University of California, San Diego embodies the perspective of most experts when she says, "Psychologists need to advise parents that the 'wait-and-see' approach is not appropriate when ASD is expected. Delaying a diagnosis can mean giving up significant gains of intervention that have been demonstrated before age 6."

The younger in age we assess for problems, the greater the potential a slow-to-mature kid will be given a false diagnosis.

There is a universal push to screen for ASD at as young an age as possible and growing confidence that the early signs are clear and convincing. Dr. Jose Cordero, the founding director of the National Center on Birth Defects and Developmental Disabilities conveys this fervor.

"For healthcare providers, we have a message that's pretty direct about ASD. And the message is: The 4-year-old with autism was once a 3-year-old with autism, which was once a 2-year-old with autism."

Many researchers are now on the hunt for atypical behaviors cropping up in infancy that could be telltale signs of ASD. For instance, a team of experts led by Dr. Karen Pierce at the Autism Center of Excellence at the University of California, San Diego, has used eye-tracking technology to determine that infants as young as 14 months who later were diagnosed as autistic showed a preference for looking at movies of geometric shapes over movies of children dancing and doing yoga. This predilection for being engaged by objects rather than "social" images is thought to be a marker for autism.

Even the quality of infants' crying has come under scientific scrutiny as a possible sign of the disorder. Dr. Stephen Sheinkopf and some colleagues at Brown University compared the cries of a group of babies at risk for autism (due to having an autistic sibling) to typically developing babies using cutting-edge acoustic technology. They discovered that the at-risk babies emit higher-pitched cries that are "low in voicing," which is a term for cries that are sharper and reflect tense vocal chords. Dr. Sheinkopf, however, cautioned parents against over-scrutinizing their babies' cries since the distinctions were picked up by sophisticated acoustic technology, not by careful human listening.

"We definitely don't want parents to be anxiously listening to their babies' cries. It's unclear if the human ear is sensitive enough to detect this."

What gets lost in the debate is an awareness of how the younger in age we assess for problems, the greater the potential a slow-to-mature kid will be given a false diagnosis. In fact, as we venture into more tender years to screen for autism, we need to be reminded that the period of greatest diagnostic uncertainty is probably toddlerhood. A 2007 study out of the University of North Carolina at Chapel Hill found that over 30 percent of children diagnosed as autistic at age two no longer fit the diagnosis at age 4. Since ASD is still generally considered to be a life-long neuropsychiatric condition that is not shed as childhood unfolds, we have to wonder if a large percentage of toddlers get a diagnosis that is of questionable applicability in the first place.

Expanding autistic phenomena to include picky eating and tantrums can create more befuddlement when applied to small children.

The parallels between a slow-to-mature toddler and a would-be-mildly-autistic one are so striking that the prospect of a false diagnosis is great. Let's start with late talkers. Almost one in five 2-year-olds are late talkers. They fall below the expected 50-word expressive vocabulary threshold and appear incapable of stringing together two- and three-word phrases.

Data out of the famed Yale Study Center have demonstrated that toddlers with delayed language development are almost identical to their autistic spectrum disordered counterparts in their use of eye contact to gauge social interactions, the range of sounds and words they produce, and the emotional give-and-take they are capable of. Many tots are in an ASD red-zone who simply don't meet standard benchmarks for how quickly language should be acquired and social interactions mastered.

Expanding autistic phenomena to include picky eating and tantrums can create more befuddlement when applied to small children. Several years ago a study published in the *Journal of the American Dietetic Association* tracking over 3,000 families found that 50 percent of toddlers are considered picky eaters

by their caregivers. The percentage of young children in the United States who are picky eaters and have poor appetites is so high that experts writing in the journal *Pediatrics* in 2007 remarked, " . . . it could reasonably be said that eating-behavior problems are a normal feature of toddler life."

Tantrums also are surprisingly frequent and intense during the toddler years. Dr. Gina Mireault, a behavioral scientist at Johnson State College in Vermont, studied kids from three separate local preschools. She discerned that toddlers tantrumed, on average, once every few days. Almost a third of the parents surveyed experienced their offsprings' tantrums as distressing or disturbing.

Too much isolated play, manipulating objects in concrete ways, can also elicit autism concerns. But, relative to young girls, young boys are slower to gravitate toward pretend play that is socially oriented. In a French study of preschoolers' outdoor nursery play published in *PLoS One* in 2011, the lead investigator Stéphanie Barbu concluded, " . . . preschool boys played alone more frequently than preschool girls. This difference was especially marked at 3–4 years."

This is significant, since there is a strong movement to detect autistic spectrum disorder earlier, with the median age of diagnosis now falling between ages 3 and 4. Boys' more solitary style of play during these tender years, without gender-informed observation, can make them appear disordered, rather than different.

Parents and educators shouldn't assume the worst when male toddlers play alone. Many little boys are satisfied engaging in solitary play, or playing quietly alongside someone else, lining up toy trains, stacking blocks, or pursuing any range of sensorimotor activities, more mesmerized by objects than fellow flesh-and-blood kids. According to Dr. Barbu, it's not until about age 4 or 5 that boys are involved in associative play to the same extent as girls. That's the kind of play where there's verbal interaction, and give-and-take exchanges of toys and ideas—or, non-autistic-like play.

One in 42 boys are now affected by autism, a ratio that calls into question whether boys' differences get abnormalized.

It is commonly believed that autism spectrum kids lack a "theory of mind." I'll provide a layman's definition of this term first, by a layman. Josh Clark, a senior writer at HowStuffWorks.com, provides a fine, no-frills definition: "It refers to a person's ability to create theories about others' minds—what they may be thinking, how they may be feeling, what they may do next. We are able to make these assumptions easily, without even recognizing that we are doing something fundamentally amazing."

It's this very ability to "mind read," or understand that others have thoughts, feelings, and intentions different from our own, and use this feedback to be socially tuned in, that is considered

Related Story

Letting Go of Asperger's

Roy Richard Grinker, in his acclaimed book *Unstrange Minds,* masterfully documents the challenges he faced raising Isabel, his daughter with pronounced autism. At age 2, she only made passing eye contact, rarely initiated interactions, and had trouble responding to her name in a consistent fashion.

Her play often took the form of rote activities such as drawing the same picture repeatedly, or rewinding a DVD to watch identical film clips over and over. Unless awakened each morning with the same greeting, "Get up! Get up!," Isabel became quite agitated. She also tended to be very literal and concrete in her language comprehension: expressions like "I'm so tired I could die" left her apprehensive about actual death. By age 5, Isabel remained almost completely nonverbal.

When the signs of autism spectrum disorder are indisputable, as in Isabel's case, early detection and intervention are crucial to bolster verbal communication and social skills. The brain is simply more malleable when children are young. Isabel's story in *Unstrange Minds* is a heroic testament to the strides a child can make when afforded the right interventions at the right time.

Diagnostic conundrums enter the picture when we frame autism as a spectrum disorder, (as it is now officially designated in the newly minted *Diagnostic and Statistical Manual 5th Edition,* the psychiatric handbook used to diagnose it) and try to draw a bold line between a slow-to-mature toddler and one on the mild end of the spectrum. What is a doctor to make of a chatty, intellectually advanced, three-year-old patient presenting with a hodgepodge of issues, such as: poor eye contact, clumsiness, difficulties transitioning, overactivity or underactivity, tantruming, picky eating, quirky interests, and social awkwardness? Does this presentation indicate mild ASD? Or, does it speak to a combination of off-beat developmental events that result in a toddler experiencing transitory stress, who is otherwise normal, in the broad sense?

We entrust our children to professionals like psychiatrists and psychologists to tease apart the delicate distinctions between mild ASD and a slower pace of development. The trained professionals are supposed to know best. But, do they? A pediatrician is the professional who is most likely to be consulted when a child is suspected of having ASD. While most pediatricians are adequately educated and trained to assess for ASD, a good many of them aren't. How many pediatricians who actually call themselves pediatricians have specialized training in pediatric medicine and/or pediatric mental health?

Several years ago, Gary L. Freed, MD, chief of the Division of General Pediatrics at the University of Michigan, initiated a survey of physicians listed as pediatricians on state licensure files in eight states across the United States: Ohio, Wisconsin, Texas, Mississippi, Massachusetts, Maryland, Oregon, and Arizona. According to the survey, 39 percent of state-identified pediatricians hadn't completed a residency in pediatrics. And even for those who had, their training in pediatric mental health was minimal.

Currently, the American Academy of Pediatrics estimates that less than a quarter of pediatricians around the country have specialized training in child mental health beyond what they receive in a general pediatric residency. The latest data examining pediatricians who have launched themselves into practice reveals that 62 percent of them feel that mental health issues were not adequately covered in medical school. These figures hardly inspire widespread confidence as regards relying on pediatricians to accurately diagnose ASD.

In a 2010 study, 45 percent of graduate students in child psychology had little exposure to coursework in child/adolescent lifespan development.

This brings me to my own cherished profession: child psychology. What does survey data tell us about the current training of child psychologists that speaks directly to their ability to separate out abnormalcy from normalcy?

Poring over the numbers of a 2010 study out of the University of Hartford in Connecticut, I discovered that 45 percent of graduate students in child psychology had either no exposure to, or had just an introductory-level exposure to, coursework in child/adolescent lifespan development. It is in these classes that emerging child psychologists learn about what is developmentally normal to expect in children.

It would appear that the education and training of a sizable percentage of pediatricians and child psychologists leaves them ill-equipped to tease apart the fine distinction between mild ASD and behaviors that fall within the broad swath of normal childhood development.

When the uptick in ASD numbers was made public by the Centers for Disease Control and Prevention the week before last, Dr. Marshalyn Yeargin-Allsopp, chief of their Developmental Disabilities Branch, said in a press release, "The most important thing for parents to do is to act early when there is a concern about a child's development. If you have a concern about how your child plays, learns, speaks, acts, or moves, take action. Don't wait."

On the one hand, a clarion call of this nature is the push the parents of a child with an unmistakable case of moderate-to severe-ASD (like Isabel above) absolutely

(continued)

Related Story   *(continued)*

need. On the other hand, Dr. Yeargin-Alsopp's remark seems to stoke the very anxiety that haunts the average parent of a slow-to-mature, but otherwise normal kid, edging that parent to transport the kid to a doctor, where there's a good chance that doctor will lack a solid knowledge-template as to what constitutes normal.

Early screening and treatment for ASD must remain a top public health priority, but the numbers make it clear that professionals would benefit from familiarizing and re-familiarizing themselves with the broad range of what is considered normal early childhood development, and with how young boys and girls differ in behaviors that resemble autistic phenomena. Otherwise the ASD numbers will rise, yet again, with a pool of slow-to-mature children being falsely diagnosed.

---

a hallmark sign of autism. However, between the ages of 3 and 4 the average girl is roughly twice as capable as the average boy at reading minds, and the gap doesn't markedly close until they reach about age 5 or older.

That was the conclusion arrived at by Sue Walker, a professor at Queensland University of Technology, Brisbane, Australia, in her 2005 *Journal of Genetic Psychology* study looking at gender differences in "theory of mind" development in groups of preschoolers. Being mindful of boys' less mindfulness during the early toddler years needs to be considered to prevent an inappropriate diagnosis of mild ASD.

Faulty fine-motor skills are often seen as part of an autistic profile. Yet, preschool aged boys have been shown to lag behind their female classmates in this domain. A classic study of preschoolers by Drs. Allen Burton and Michael Dancisak out of the University of Minnesota discovered that females in the 3- to 5-year-old range significantly outperform boys at this age in their acquisition of the "tripod" pencil grip. The so-called "tripod" pencil grip, where the thumb is used to stabilize a pencil pressed firmly against the third and fourth digits, with the wrist slightly extended, is generally considered by teachers and occupational therapists as the most effective display of fine-motor dexterity when it comes to writing and drawing.

Finger pointing is one of the fundamental ways that young children express and share their interests, as well as manifest curiosity in the outside world. It's scant use is seen as a warning sign of autism. However, researchers at the University of Sussex in England conducted tests at monthly intervals on 8-month-old infants as they emerged into toddlerhood and found that girls learn to point earlier than boys.

Which is all to say that young boys' social-communication approaches, play styles, and pace of fine-motor development leave them living closer to the autistic spectrum than girls. This confound may explain why boys are five times more likely than girls to be ascribed the diagnosis. One in 42 boys are now affected by autism, a ratio that calls into question whether boys' different pace at acquiring social, emotional, and fine-motor skills gets abnormalized.

It's important to not overstate the case. The possibility that a slow-to-mature toddler will be confused as moderately or severely autistic is slim. On the extreme end, autism is, more often than not, a conspicuous, lifelong, disabling neurological condition.

Critical Thinking

1. What should parents do if they notice more than a few of the behaviors listed in the article in their child?

2. How would you respond to teachers who indicate they don't feel prepared to have a child or children who may have an autism-spectrum disorder in their classroom?

Internet References

American Academy of Pediatrics
   http://www.aap.org/en-us/Pages/Default.aspx
Autism Speaks
   http://www.autismspeaks.org
Centers for Disease Control and Prevention
   http://www.cdc.gov/ncbddd/autism/index.html/

Article   Prepared by: Karen Menke Paciorek, *Eastern Michigan University*

Inclusion in Infant/Toddler Child Development Settings

More Than Just Including

REBECCA PARLAKIAN

Learning Outcomes

After reading this article, you will be able to:

- Develop a list of effective teaching strategies for differentiating daily routines to include all children.

- Implement practices to develop strong working relationships with all adults who are involved in the lives of children.

Thomas, who is 2 years old, was diagnosed at birth with a genetic disorder that impacts his ability to walk and talk. His teacher, Marisa, sits him near several other children playing with cars and trucks, an activity she knows he enjoys from talking with his mother. Marisa carefully places a bolster behind Thomas to support him in the seated position. She then offers him the choice of two different trucks. He reaches for one and she says, "*Dump truck.* You want the *dump truck.* Here you go." Marisa then sits down as well and asks the children, "Would you like to push your trucks down a ramp? We can set it up." She leans a long block against a shelf and watches as each child pushes a car down the ramp. When it is Thomas's turn, she helps him to a standing position so he can send his car careening down the ramp as well. Then she says, "Hmmm, what do you think will happen if we make the ramp even higher?"

Thomas's child development program experience is typical for his age group: his teachers provide developmentally appropriate learning opportunities embedded in play, and they encourage parallel play, in which children play near—and next to—one another. Early childhood professionals also use language to label the objects and experiences children encounter. In this center, teachers facilitate inclusion by making minor adaptations to include Thomas in the same learning and play opportunities as his peers. *Inclusion* has long been a term used to describe the practice of including a child with special needs in age-appropriate general education classes in their home schools (FSU Center for Prevention and Early Intervention Policy 2002).

Increasingly, the term is being used to describe the process of including very young children—infants and toddlers—with special needs in a setting comprised mostly of children without disabilities. Although most early care and education professionals support inclusion for infants and toddlers, they frequently have questions about how best to meet the needs of children with special needs while continuing to apply developmentally appropriate practice with the rest of the group.

Today, most child development programs include children with a range of skills and abilities, some without special needs and some whose development may be either delayed or advanced for their age. Often, inclusion describes what a high-quality early care and education setting is already doing—adapting curricula and approaches to meet the unique needs of each child. This article offers concrete developmentally appropriate strategies that infant/toddler programs can use to support the ongoing development of children with a range of skills and needs.

Promoting Partnerships with Families

Partnering with the family of a child with special needs is much like partnering with any family. Collaboration requires mutual respect, open communication, and trust. Of course, parents must be viewed as the experts on their children. This is especially the case when teachers work closely with parents of children with disabilities or developmental delays. Parents, for example, are expert in positioning their child with cerebral palsy or understanding which toys are most appealing to their baby with a visual impairment. Parents have begun to learn which sensory information is most difficult to manage for their toddler with autism spectrum disorder (ASD) or what floor play activities will help their baby (born 10 weeks prematurely) develop the ability to roll and crawl.

Teachers can develop closer partnerships with families using these strategies:

Ask families to provide information about the child's strengths and needs to teachers and staff. Information about the child's disability or delay and ideas for adapting caregiving approaches to meet the child's needs can help teachers individualize their approach to caring for the child. It also increases the continuity of care between home and the early childhood setting, which contributes to a sense of safety and security in very young children.

Keep the lines of communication open. As children master new skills, you may develop new questions. For example, you may want to ask a parent how to help a child transition into his walker or how a family is approaching toilet learning with their toddler with autism.

Develop trust over time. It is frequently during the infant and toddler years that parents first learn their child is not meeting developmental milestones and may have a delay or disability. This can be an especially difficult time for parents, as they begin to accept that their child has special needs for either the short- or long-term. As a result, parents may vary in how open and willing they are to discussing their child's unique needs. It helps to phrase questions in terms of "wondering," as in: "I'm wondering what play positions work best for Trevor" or "I'm wondering what you've found is most comforting to Samantha when she gets overwhelmed."

Remember that a child with special needs is a child first. Families can help teachers understand their child's individual strengths and unique cues, the activities their child prefers, and the family's hopes and goals for the child.

Promoting Partnerships with Early Intervention Providers

Early intervention is the practice of identifying developmental delays or disabilities as early as possible and then providing therapeutic services to build on the child's strengths and address the child's developmental needs. Infants and toddlers who have been diagnosed with a disability or developmental delay may already be receiving early intervention services from a community provider.

Communities are legally required to evaluate children and provide early intervention services to eligible children ages birth to 3 through Part C of the Individuals with Disabilities in Education Act (IDEA). Early intervention services may include (but are not limited to) special instruction; occupational, physical, and speech and language therapies; and/or psychological services. The IDEA requires that these services be provided in the infant or toddler's home or other "natural environments"—places where young children spend their time, such as a child development program.

Early intervention professionals may regularly, or on occasion, visit an early childhood program to provide services to a particular child. These visits do not require any additional work on the part of the teacher. Typically, the early intervention provider works one-on-one with the child to assist with play, problem solving, language, motor, sensory, or social skills in the context of daily routines.

Teachers and staff can partner with early intervention professionals by requesting and discussing strategies and ideas about adaptations that can help a child with special needs participate more fully in the program. Tips for partnering with early intervention professionals who visit your site include the following:

Have an open-door policy. With a family's consent, welcome early intervention professionals to your site. Provide information about the program's daily routines and the best times to visit a particular child.

Share your observations and experiences. Early childhood professionals have important information to share with early intervention providers. Provide details about the child's typical day, the ways in which the child communicates (for example, gestures, pictures, or speech), the child's social skills and preferred activities, and any challenges the child is facing in the setting (Woods 2008). Teachers can also share information about the child's strengths and interests—for example, that a child's favorite activity is making music or that the child is a great helper at clean-up time. The early interventionist can then use these moments as learning opportunities during the therapeutic visit.

Feel free to ask questions about the child receiving services. For example, a head teacher may wonder how to position an infant with spina bifida on the floor during playtime. Or she may struggle with how to help a toddler with autism cope more effectively with daily transitions. Early intervention providers can offer some ideas and strategies, or connect staff with health care professionals who can help.

Learn more about goals for the child's development. These goals are outlined in the child's Individualized Family Service Plan (IFSP), which also includes information about the early intervention services the child receives and his developmental strengths and needs. If parents have signed a consent form allowing the early intervention provider to share information about their child with you, ask what goals the child is working toward accomplishing. This can help teachers better understand what learning experiences and caregiving strategies will best meet the child's needs and support learning.

Strategies for Adapting Daily Routines and Activities

The time frame for the development of any skill is defined by a range of weeks or months—with some children showing mastery early in the range and others much later. Because development occurs at a different pace for every child, the strategies discussed below are useful for *all* infants and toddlers, regardless of whether they have a diagnosed disability or delay. In a sense, these strategies embrace the dual ideas of individualization (modifying curricula and caregiving approaches to the needs and strengths of each child) and universal design for learning (designing curriculum in such a way as to give all children equal opportunities to learn) (Center for Applied Special Technology, n.d.).

Modifying Daily Routines and Activities

Some children with disabilities—and many children without—have difficulty understanding daily routines and coping with transitions. While daily schedules are found in most toddler classrooms, the additional strategies that follow may provide enhanced support to young children who have challenges in this area:

Create Individualized Schedules

Make a mini version of your daily schedule, with small photos or pictures of each activity affixed to a Velcro strip in the order they occur. Have toddlers move each activity to a *Done* pocket when it is complete, and use this as an opportunity to point out what will happen next. This helps children prepare for transitions.

Make "First, Then" Charts

Some toddlers have a hard time coping with activities they dislike or have difficulty with. Help toddlers understand that their "nonpreferred" activity won't last forever by creating a laminated page with the word *First* on one side and the word *Then* on the other side. Velcro a picture of the nonpreferred activity under First and a preferred activity under Then. After lunch, use language and the chart to show and tell the child, "**First** we will wash our hands and faces, and **then** we will use playdough."

Offer Visual Instructions

For simple daily routines, such as throwing out one's snack plate or washing hands, snap photos of each step in the process. Laminate the photos and post them in order at the children's level. Show and tell children the different steps of the routine to promote their initial success and to support their longer-term mastery of the routine—this is called "error-free learning" (Hodgdon 2011, 80).

Providing Positioning Support

Low muscle tone is part of many different disabilities. Low muscle tone can make it difficult for children to sit for long periods, suck a bottle, drink, eat by mouth, speak, and play in the same ways other children do. These tips may help these children better access the opportunities in your setting:

Consult with the Child's Occupational Therapist

(If possible) for ideas about positioning and seating. Check with the family to discuss what seated and floor-play positions work best at home.

Provide a Range of Seating Options

Include chairs, beanbags, and wedges for circle time and floor play. Experiment and see which provides the best support for children. Keep circle time brief, and allow children to move around or change position as needed.

Encourage Play with Both Hands

Many times children with low muscle tone sit to play, but continue to support themselves with one hand on the floor. This means they do not use both hands in play, an important skill to help children develop bilateral (two-handed) coordination and midline skills (left–right movement across the middle of the body). These children may benefit from positional support—such as a stool, chair, or wedge—when playing on the floor.

Offer Regular Tummy Time for Babies

Babies with low muscle tone may have an especially difficult time holding their heads up when on their stomach. Offer tummy time by placing a bolster under their chests to provide a little support. Another option is sitting on the floor and placing babies on their tummies across your thigh.

Supporting Back-and-Forth Interactions

Communication skills are a common area of developmental delay in the first three years. Research finds, however, that for many children with disabilities in inclusive settings, social engagement, social acceptance, and friendships are realistic and meaningful outcomes (Odom, Buysse, & Soukakou 2011). Inclusive settings offer enhanced access to available playmates, which may serve as an important precursor to establishing friendships (Buysse, Goldman, & Skinner 2002).

Early childhood professionals can support a young child's early communication efforts with peers and others by using responsive caregiving practices, including these:

Give Meaning to the Message

(Weizman & Greenberg 2002). If you see an infant gazing at a toy, explain this behavior by saying, "You like the bumpy ball!" and then giving it to her to play with. If a baby is protesting during a diaper change, narrate his experience by saying, "You are uncomfortable. You want to get up. You don't like diaper changes!" Even though infants do not yet understand all of what adults are saying, by responding to these behaviors (sounds, gestures, and expressions), parents and teachers show children that their behaviors have meaning. Over time, babies discover that their behavior can make things happen, which is the foundation of communication.

Arrange the Environment to Promote Requests

Children are most often motivated to communicate their wants, needs, and interests. Placing some toys in clear plastic bins or on a shelf just slightly out of reach encourages a child to request through eye gaze, pointing, or vocalization. For example, you might see an 18-month-old toddler gazing at some nesting cups in a clear bin. You can then model the language that would be used to make a simple request: "You *want* the cups? '*Want that.*' Here you go." (Of course, many toys should remain available at children's level and within their reach.) This strategy can also be used at mealtimes. For example, offer children three crackers, instead of a handful, which creates the opportunity for them to request more.

Create Unexpected Moments That Encourage Communication

Imagine rolling a ball back and forth with a 2-year-old. All of a sudden you hold the ball and don't roll it back. This unexpected moment creates an opportunity for the child to communicate "more" or "ball" through words, sounds, gestures, or gaze (Warren, Yoder, & Leew 2002). You can also use this strategy during songs or other familiar turn-taking games ("Row, row, row your . . ." [pause]) or on the playground (pausing while pushing the child on a swing, for example).

Build on Children's Interests

The "usefulness of any activity is determined . . . by its appeal to children" (Cook, Klein, & Tessier 2008, 160). Cook, Klein, and Tessier believe activities should reflect children's interests, offer opportunities for repetition (especially important for children with cognitive delays), and support the development of specific skills. Most early childhood teachers do this spontaneously, after much experience. However, when the program includes children with special needs, "this important emphasis on specific skills cannot be left to chance . . . these children require explicit examples, meaningful repetition, and a variety of related experiences".

Curriculum planning is necessary to ensure that (1) skills are introduced within engaging routines, (2) there are opportunities for children to explore materials and interact with others, and (3) skills are repeated in new contexts across the day. For example, you might plan an activity in which children can wash toy dishes outside on the playground. In this activity, children can practice skills as diverse as one-to-one correspondence (for example, rote-counting to three using child-sized plates) and understanding prepositions and following one-step requests ("Take the plate **out** of the water" or "Put the sponge **on** the table"). Children can repeat these skills at circle time by counting three felt bears and three "porridge bowls." You can then give children turns to "take the bear **out** of the bag" or "put the bear **on** the felt board."

Conclusion

Inclusion is, ultimately, about individualizing the early childhood setting and developmentally appropriate practices to maximize the possibility that a child is able to learn and grow to her fullest potential. Inclusion strategies, thus, support *all* children while offering thoughtfully designed supports and interventions to individual children based on their needs. As a result, inclusion settings offer more than just a foundation in preliteracy and prenumeracy skills. Inclusion provides all children with a model for the world as a place of acceptance and ability, where every member of the group has much to offer and much to learn.

References

Buysse, V., B.D. Goldman, & M.L. Skinner. 2002. "Setting Effects on Friendship Formation among Young Children with and without Disabilities." *Exceptional Children* 68 (4): 503–17.

Center for Applied Special Technology, n.d. "About Universal Design for Learning." www.cast.org/udl.

Cook, R.E., M.D. Klein, & A. Tessier. 2008. *Adapting Early Childhood Curricula for Children with Special Needs.* 7th ed. Upper Saddle River, NJ: Pearson.

FSU (Florida State University) Center for Prevention & Early Intervention Policy. 2002. "What Is Inclusion? Including School-Age Students with Developmental Disabilities in the Regular Education Setting." White paper. www.cpeip.fsu.edu/resourceFiles/resourceFile_18.pdf.

Hodgdon, L.A. 2011. *Visual Strategies for Improving Communication: Practical Supports for Autism Spectrum Disorders.* Rev. ed. Troy, MI: QuirkRoberts.

Odom, S.L., V. Buysse, & E. Soukakou. 2011. "Inclusion for Young Children with Disabilities: A Quarter Century of Research Perspectives." *Journal of Early Intervention* 33 (4): 344–56.

Warren, S.F., P.J. Yoder, & S.V. Leew. 2002. "Promoting Social-Communicative Development in Infants and Toddlers." In *Promoting Social Communication: Children with Developmental Disabilities from Birth to Adolescence,* eds. H. Goldstein, L.A. Kaczmarek, & K.M. English, 121–50. Baltimore, MD: Brookes.

Weizman, E., & J. Greenberg. 2002. *Learning Language and Loving It.* 2nd ed. Toronto, ON: The Hanen Centre.

Woods, J. 2008. "Providing Early Intervention Services in Natural Environments." *The ASHA Leader.* www.asha.org/Publications/leader/2008/080325/f080325b.htm.

Critical Thinking

1. What can families do to support your work with their child? What support would be most important to you?

2. How would you describe inclusion to someone not familiar with the term as it applies to programs serving young children?

Create Central

www.mhhe.com/createcentral

Internet References

Association for Childhood Education International (ACEI)
www.acei.org

The Council for Exceptional Children (CEC)
www.cec.sped.org

First Signs
http://firstsigns.org

Harvard Family Research Project
www.hfrp.org

Zero to Three
www.zerotothree.org

REBECCA PARLAKIAN, MEd, of ZERO TO THREE, has developed a range of resources and curricula for parents and professionals. She recently coproduced a podcast series for parents, "Little Kids, Big Questions." Rebecca's professional interests include early childhood special education and infant/toddler assessment. rparlakian@zerotothree.org.

Article   Prepared by: Karen Menke Paciorek, *Eastern Michigan University*

Kids Who Feel Too Much

Children with sensory processing disorder sometimes overreact or underreact to touch, sounds, and food textures. Doctors debate the condition, but parents say it's real, and therapists say it's treatable.

BETSY STEPHENS

Learning Outcomes

After reading this article, you will be able to:

- Name some of the most common symptoms for a child with a sensory processing disorder.

- Describe some of the strategies used by occupational therapists to assist children with a sensory processing disorder.

Playdates, parties, meals at kid-friendly restaurants are the types of activities you'd expect to fill the days of a typical 3-year-old boy. But that's not the case for Charlie Phelps of Raleigh, North Carolina.

"We usually avoid restaurants," says Charlie's mother, Katie Phelps. "I don't do playdates because he could pitch a fit—it's not unusual for him to throw himself into walls—or wander off by himself. I don't want something to go wrong and for people to start seeing him in a different light."

She is thinking specifically of a Christmas party that ended in tears—both Charlie's and hers. Her son, then 2, couldn't keep his eyes off the Polar Express train chugging around a miniature track. He had no interest in decorating cookies, playing with other kids, or doing anything that involved leaving the train. After about an hour, Phelps thought that stopping the train might encourage Charlie to join the party.

"All hell broke loose," she remembers. Charlie screamed with an intensity that most kids save for shots at the doctor's. Phelps tried explaining that the train was tired and needed a nap. She tried distracting her distraught son by telling him about the other fun activities. She took him outside, hoping the cool air would help. When Phelps was out of options and Charlie couldn't settle down, she decided it was time to leave. "He screamed and kicked like a bucking bull all the way home," remembers Phelps. He was still crying as she carried him into the house, but he managed to look up at her and say, "Mommy, you rock baby," referring to a calming ritual she'd created. Phelps brought her son to the recliner, held him tight and whispered "Rock, baby" in his ear repeatedly as they settled into the comforting motion of the chair.

"We did that for 45 minutes, and then he put his hand on my face and said, 'I so sorry, Mommy,'" says Phelps. "I put him to bed, went to the front porch, and bawled my eyes out."

Of course, every mom of a toddler could tell similar tales, but for Phelps this particular story is not an isolated incident. Charlie has these kinds of outbursts often: when the wheel he's watching on the grocery store cart comes to a stop, when another child gets near the toy he's playing with, or when Phelps tries to trim his fingernails or take him for a haircut.

Though frustrated by his behavior, Phelps hadn't wanted to make too much of it. "We just thought he was a difficult 2-year-old," she says. Friends and family seemed to shrug off these behaviors too, with comments like, "He is such a boy." But some of Phelps's relatives quietly questioned whether Charlie might have autism, and when he went to preschool, his teacher immediately noticed how strongly he objected when he was asked to transition from one activity to another. She suggested Charlie be observed by the county's early-childhood-education intervention services so that she could learn ways to help him. This led to a more formalized evaluation to test for suspected language delays.

As it turns out, Charlie was not diagnosed with autism, though he did have a language delay. An occupational therapist determined that his inability to go from one activity to the next and his penchant for ramming into walls was a result of sensory processing disorder (SPD), a condition that is common in children who have autism but also affects a surprising number of young kids who do not. Though recent studies show the condition impacts as many as 5 to 10 percent of kids, the mainstream medical community still has not officially endorsed SPD as a diagnosis—which means that insurance won't cover therapy for it.

Mixed Messages

SPD affects the way a child processes messages sent to his brain from any of the five main senses—sight, hearing, taste, smell, and touch. He might have mild sensory intolerances or he might find it extremely difficult to handle sensory stimulation (such as when he's at a busy grocery store or a loud sports event). Normally, if a child is tapped on the shoulder, his nervous system informs his brain that he received a light touch. For a child with SPD, the message can get misinterpreted and the child may feel that he was hit hard. Or the message may get completely lost, leaving him unaware that he's been touched at all, explains Lucy Jane Miller, Ph.D., founder of STAR Center, an SPD therapy and research facility in Greenwood Village, Colorado. Most kids with SPD are a mixture of both over- and under-sensitive, which explains why inconsistent behavior is a hallmark of the disorder, adds Lindsey Biel, an occupational therapist (OT) in New York City and coauthor of *Raising a Sensory Smart Child.*

Two lesser-known senses that can be affected by SPD are the vestibular and proprioceptive systems. They detect incoming sensory information, which is then delivered to the brain. Vestibular refers to movement sensations such as swinging or going down a slide. The proprioceptive system provides information to the muscles and joints, like telling the legs to apply more pressure when walking up stairs than when walking on flat ground, for example. If messages from the proprioceptive system get confused in the brain, a child might appear to be excessively clumsy or aggressive because he's not aware of how much force he's applying.

Continuously receiving jumbled messages can be frustrating for a child, and his inexplicable reactions to everyday happenings can be confusing to his parents. His behavior can become even more unpredictable when he's asked to transition from one activity to another, as was the case with Charlie. When a child's nervous system is working so poorly, it can take him a long time to focus and settle into what he's doing, explains Biel. Asking him to turn his attention to something new could be just too much for him.

Every child can have trouble shifting gears sometimes, but it's the number of senses affected and the severity of symptoms that will determine whether a child is considered to have SPD. Much as with autism, these symptoms occur on a spectrum. If a child's sensory needs are intense and persistent, everyday activities that are necessary for social, emotional, and educational growth might be difficult for him. This has repercussions down the line. For example, your child might not like the sensation of Play-Doh in his hands. This may not seem important, but manipulating squishy objects is one way kids develop the muscles and coordination to accomplish skills that will be necessary later, says Dr. Miller. A child who avoids using his hands in these developmental years may later have difficulty holding or maneuvering a pencil.

Rewiring the Brain

More than 40 years ago, occupational therapist and neuroscientist A. Jean Ayres, Ph.D., developed therapeutic treatments to address what she called "sensory integration dysfunction." Though the term for the disorder has changed to SPD, the basic principles of Dr. Ayres's therapy are still being used as the foundation for the methods many OTs use to treat SPD. Treatment consists of carefully designed, multisensory activities that challenge one or more sensory systems simultaneously—such as swinging while throwing beanbags at a target, which presents both a vestibular and a visual challenge. The goal: to help build neural pathways that can lead to appropriate responses to information that comes into a child's brain through the senses. This is time-consuming and requires frequent repetition, but it's necessary. "Nerves that fire together wire together," explains Biel. "So each time you practice something, you strengthen the neural connections so that it eventually becomes automatic."

Since Charlie began working with an OT, Phelps and her husband have learned to recognize when Charlie needs extra stimulation, often by using the mini trampoline their therapist recommended. "We'll say, 'Okay, it's time to jump!' He holds on to the handle and jumps, and it really calms him." A treatment like "brushing" is another technique used with children who react too strongly to stimuli. A specially trained therapist uses a soft plastic-bristled surgical brush to apply deep pressure to a child's skin and make her feel more relaxed. It's a widely used method but also controversial: There's no scientific evidence to prove its effectiveness.

A Disputed Diagnosis

In the past year, SPD has taken some big hits from the medical community. Last June, the American Academy of Pediatrics (AAP) released an updated policy statement on SPD, saying it should generally not be diagnosed because studies have yet to prove that it's completely separate from other developmental disabilities, such as autism and ADHD. "We can see kids have problems, but are they related to another disorder or are they from their own disorder?" asks pediatrician Larry Desch, M.D., a lead author of the statement and member of the autism subcommittee of the AAP's Council on Children with Disabilities.

Equally problematic for the SPD community was the fact that the disorder was excluded from the new edition of the American Psychiatric Association's *Diagnostic and Statistical Manual of Mental Disorders* (*DSM-5*, being released this month), which is what doctors and therapists use for diagnosis and treatment guidelines. Clinical psychologist Matthew M. Cruger, Ph.D., is among those who believe SPD is not a separate condition. "Parents describe sensory symptoms, which are clearly distressing for the child *and* the parents. I don't minimize that what they see looks like sensory struggles. But the children I work with often end up being described as having autism or ADHD," says Dr. Cruger, senior director of the Learning and Development Center at the Child Mind Institute, in New York City.

"It's not an obvious diagnosis," says Dr. Miller, who adds that the behavior of a child with SPD can be confused with that of a kid who may have overlapping behaviors and a different diagnosis, such as ADHD. A child who doesn't get enough proprioception will seek ways to stimulate his muscles and joints—continuously moving, or chewing constantly on non-food items such as straws and pen caps, she says. What's more, roughly 40 percent of the time kids have both SPD and ADHD, found a study by Dr. Miller and her colleagues.

The American Psychiatric Association has not ruled out making note of SPD in a possible online version of the *DSM-5*, where it, along with other proposed disorders, will be mentioned, says David Shaffer, M.D., former chair of the division of child psychiatry at Columbia University, in New York City. This can encourage further research on the disorder, which will help determine whether to include SPD in the future, says Dr. Shaffer, who was on the committee that determined what was included in the manual.

Spotting the Symptoms

A child with SPD regularly exhibits many of these behaviors:

- Finds any of the following intolerable: loud noises; dirt on her hands; having hair, fingernails or toenails cut; receiving an unexpected hug; walking barefoot on grass or sand
- Doesn't notice when touched; almost always prefers sedentary activities to active ones; seems unaware of bodily sensations such as heat, cold, or hunger
- Uses either too much or too little force when, say, holding a pencil, or tapping someone's arm
- Is passive, quiet, slow to respond to directions
- Is excessively cautious and afraid to try new things; upset by transitions or unexpected changes; avoids group activities
- Wants to spin or swing excessively; takes many risks during play and is constantly moving
- Is accident-prone and has difficulty with physical skills such as riding a bicycle or catching a ball

If you're worried about your child, it's best to have a comprehensive evaluation by a multidisciplinary team that includes your child's pediatrician, as well as a psychologist and an occupational therapist who specializes in sensory issues. To find a therapist, go to spdfoundation.net, click on "Find Services," check the box for occupational therapist, and add your state. Those with the "SPDF" icon next to their listing have advanced training in SPD.

Occupational therapists say that SPD treatment should complement therapy for other issues, potentially making it easier to improve a child's overall behavior and development. "When a child is more sensitive to touch, he may avoid close contact with other kids during free play," explains Rachel Rudman, an occupational therapist in Lawrence, New York, with a specialty in pediatrics. "If that issue is addressed and he begins to participate in group play, he'll also have more opportunities to practice and improve his language skills."

Pediatrician and *Parents* advisor Ari Brown, M.D., has seen sensory therapy work in her own patients. "There's value in it for kids who are struggling socially and in school," she says. Although she believes "a child doesn't need to have a diagnosis to need help," she also recognizes that this presents a real challenge for families who can't afford to pay out of pocket

for occupational therapy sessions that can cost $130 an hour or more. For them, she has this advice: "Your child might qualify for services under a different diagnosis code. For example, kids often have motor problems and OT will be covered for that," explains Dr. Brown. Children can also be treated through the school system; many children receive therapy because they qualify for special-ed services.

Seeing Is Believing

As the medical world sorts it out, parents like Lori Kennedy say they don't need a manual to tell them whether SPD is real or whether it can be treated with occupational therapy. Without OT, her 7-year-old son, Davis, might still have problems with his coordination, and a diet consisting of nothing more than Cream of Wheat, Malt-O-Meal, and vanilla ice cream.

When Davis was 6 months old, Kennedy offered him a spoonful of baby food. "He had the most violent reaction," she recalls. She got lots of "picky eater" advice from doctors and therapists, but it wasn't until Kennedy took her then 2-year-old to a pediatric clinic specializing in occupational, speech, and physical therapy that she finally heard something different: Her son's eating issues stemmed from SPD. The diagnosis made sense to Kennedy. "He also wouldn't wear any kind of enclosed shoes, so he wore flip-flops everywhere," says Kennedy, of Austin, Texas. "We took him to the beach in Florida and as soon as we put him on the sand he'd cry hysterically." An OT explained to her that for Davis, the sensation of walking on the sand felt more like walking on broken glass.

During weekly sessions at the clinic and at home, Davis would chew on a rubber straw to help him strengthen the muscles in his jaw and get used to sensations in the back of his mouth. Davis had quick success in most areas; his coordination improved immensely and he mastered the playground obstacle course he'd had no success with before. But progress with food was slow to come. Finally, when Davis was 3, the therapist was able to feed him oatmeal and peanut butter.

He received help because his SPD involved a developmental issue (feeding) that was covered by insurance. His second-grade teacher helped him get services in school, citing Section 504 of the Rehabilitation Act of 1973, which protects kids with disabilities from being discriminated against at school. Davis is excused from class on Friday mornings to attend therapy provided by the school, his desk is near the teacher's desk, he's given extra time to complete tasks, he's allowed to sit on an exercise ball rather than a hard chair, and Velcro is attached to the underside of his desk so he can access it when he feels the need for sensory input. "He's getting everything he needs," says Kennedy.

Charlie, on the other hand, only gets therapy nine months out of the year because his school system stops services in the summer. Last year, Charlie's parents borrowed close to $4,000 so their son could continue his therapy. "He's been working so hard," says Phelps. "I didn't want him to lose everything over the summer and have to start all over again when the school year started." Charlie is on target to meet early learning and cognitive goals for his age, but this is the result of a lot of hard work.

"If he could rock in his dad's recliner and drink chocolate milk out of a straw all day, he would," Phelps adds. "But he needs to do other things, a little bit at a time. So we're doing everything we can to get him ready before he goes to kindergarten."

Critical Thinking

1. Why is it important for a child with a SPD to receive intervention early on instead of waiting until the child is in elementary school?

2. What is the role of the classroom teacher with a student with a SPD and how can the teacher best support the child and his or her family?

Create Central

www.mhhe.com/createcentral

Internet References

American Academy of Pediatrics
www.aap.org

The Council for Exceptional Children (CEC)
www.cec.sped.org

First Signs
http://firstsigns.org

Meet Me at the Corner
www.meetmeatthecorner.org

You Can Handle Them
www.disciplinehelp.com

Zero to Three
www.zerotothree.org

Article Prepared by: Karen Menke Paciorek, *Eastern Michigan University*

Teach Up for Excellence

All students deserve equitable access to an engaging and rigorous curriculum.

CAROL ANN TOMLINSON AND EDWIN LOU JAVIUS

Learning Outcomes

After reading this article, you will be able to:

- Choose one of the principles of teaching up the authors describe in the article and describe how that would look if implemented in your future classroom.

- Describe what the authors call "peacock" moments of success.

Within the lifetime of a significant segment of the population, schools in the United States operated under the banner of "separate but equal" opportunity. In time, and at considerable cost, we came to grips with the reality that separate is seldom equal. But half a century later, and with integration a given, many of our students still have separate and drastically unequal learning experiences (Darling-Hammond, 2010).

Many of our schools are overwhelmingly attended by low-income and racially and linguistically diverse students, whereas nearby schools are largely attended by students from more affluent and privileged backgrounds (Kozol, 2005). Another kind of separateness exists *within* schools. It's frequently the case that students attend classes that correlate highly with learners' race and socioeconomic status, with less privileged students in lower learning groups or tracks and more privileged students in more advanced ones (Darling-Hammond, 2010).

The logic behind separating students by what educators perceive to be their ability is that it enables teachers to provide students with the kind of instruction they need. Teachers can remediate students who perform at a lower level of proficiency and accelerate those who perform at a higher level. All too often, however, students in lower-level classrooms receive a level of education that ensures they will remain at the tail end of the learning spectrum. High-end students may (or may not) experience rich and challenging learning opportunities, and students in the middle too often encounter uninspired learning experiences that may not be crippling but are seldom energizing. No group comes to know, understand, and value the others. Schools in which this arrangement is the norm often display an "us versus them" attitude that either defines the school environment or dwells just below the surface of daily exchanges.

Difficult to Defend

Research finds that sorting, this 21st century version of school segregation, correlates strongly with student race and economic status and predicts and contributes to student outcomes, with students in higher-level classes typically experiencing better teachers, curriculum, and achievement levels than peers in lower-level classes (Carbonaro & Gamoran, 2003). Further, when lower-performing students experience curriculum and instruction focused on meaning and understanding, they increase their skills at least as much as their higher-achieving peers do (Educational Research Service, 1992).

These findings are even more problematic when combined with our current understanding that the human brain is incredibly malleable and that individuals can nearly always outperform our expectations for them. The sorting mechanisms often used in school are not only poor predictors of success in life, but also poor measures of what a young person can accomplish, given the right context (Dweck, 2007). Virtually all students would benefit from the kind of curriculum and instruction we have often reserved for advanced learners—that is, curriculum and instruction designed to engage students, with a focus on meaning making, problem solving, logical thinking, and transfer of learning (National Research Council, 1999).

In addition, the demographic reality is that low-income students of color and English language learners will soon become the majority of students in our schools (Center for Public Education, 2007; Gray & Fleischman, 2004). Given that low-level classes are largely made up of students from these groups and that students in such classes fare poorly in terms of academic achievement, the societal cost of continuing to support sorting students is likely to be high (Darling-Hammond, 2006).

Finally, Americans tend to be justly proud of the democratic ideals that represent this nation. We nourish those ideals when we invest in systems that enable each individual to achieve his or her best (Gardner, 1961). In contrast, we undercut those ideals when the systems we create contribute to a widening gap between those who have privilege and those who do not (Fullan, 2001).

Too few students—including those who excel academically—regularly have education experiences that stimulate and stretch them. *Teaching up* is one key approach that teachers can use to regularly make such experiences available to all students, regardless of their backgrounds and starting points.

Seven Principles of Teaching Up

To create classrooms that give students equal access to excellence, educators at all levels need to focus on seven interrelated principles.

1. *Accept that human differences are not only normal but also desirable.* Each person has something of value to contribute to the group, and the group is diminished without that contribution. Teachers who teach up create a community of learners in which everyone works together to benefit both individuals and the group. These teachers know that the power of learning is magnified when the classroom functions effectively as a microcosm of a world in which we want to live. They craft culturally and economically inclusive classrooms that take into account the power of race, culture, and economic status in how students construct meaning; and they support students in making meaning in multiple ways (Gay, 2000).

2. *Develop a growth mind-set.* Providing equity of access to excellence through teaching up has its roots in a teacher's mind-set about the capacity of each learner to succeed (Dweck, 2007). It requires doggedly challenging the preconception that high ability dwells largely in more privileged students. The greatest barrier to learning is often not what the student knows, but what the teacher expects of the student (Good, 1987).

    A teacher with a growth mind-set creates learning experiences that reinforce the principle that effort rather than background is the greatest determinant of success, a notion that can dramatically help students who experience institutional and instructional racism. A growth mind-set also creates classrooms that persistently demonstrate to students and teachers alike that when a student works hard and intelligently, the result is consistent growth that enables people to accomplish their goals.

    Teachers who teach up provide students with clear learning targets, guidelines, and feedback as well as a safe learning environment that supports them as they take their next steps in growth, no matter what their current level of performance is. Through words, actions, and caring, the teacher conveys to students "I know you have the capacity to do what's required for success; therefore, I expect much of you. Because I expect much, I'll support your success in every way I can. I'm here to be your partner in achievement."

3. *Work to understand students' cultures, interests, needs, and perspectives.* People are shaped by their backgrounds, and respecting students means respecting their backgrounds—including their race and culture. Teaching any student well means striving to understand how that student approaches learning and creating an environment that is respectful of and responsive to what each student brings to the classroom.

The sorting mechanisms used in school are not only poor predictors of success in life, but also poor measures of what a young person can accomplish.

Many of us know the Golden Rule: Treat others as you would want to be treated. In classrooms that work for a wide spectrum of people, the Platinum Rule works better: Treat others as *they* want to be treated. This principle relates not only to teacher and student interactions, but also to teacher choices about curriculum and instruction.

For teachers who teach up, understanding students' learning profiles is the driving force behind instructional planning and delivery. A learning profile refers to how individuals learn most efficiently and effectively. How we learn is shaped by a variety of factors, including culture, gender, environmental preferences, and personal strengths or weaknesses. Teachers can talk with their students about preferred approaches to learning, offer varied routes to accomplishing required goals, and observe which options students select and how those options support learning (or don't). Teachers who teach up select instructional strategies and approaches in response to what they know of their students' interests and learning preferences, rather than beginning with a strategy and hoping it works. Teaching up is not about hope. It's about purposeful instructional planning that aims at ensuring high-level success for each student.

4. *Create a base of rigorous learning opportunities.* Teachers who teach up help students form a conceptual understanding of the disciplines, connect what they learn to their own lives, address significant problems using essential knowledge and skills, collaborate with peers, examine varied perspectives, and create authentic products for meaningful audiences. These teachers develop classrooms that are literacy-rich and that incorporate a wide range of resources that attend to student interests and support student learning.

    Teachers who teach up also ensure that students develop the skills of independence, self-direction, collaboration, and production that are necessary for success. They commend excellence as a way of life and demonstrate to learners the satisfaction that comes from accepting a challenge and investing one's best effort in achieving it. They know that when tasks help students make sense of important ideas, are highly relevant to students' life experiences, and are designed at a moderate level of challenge, students are willing to do the hard work that is the hallmark of excellence. These teachers scaffold each student as he or she takes the next step toward excellence.

For example, a high school teacher began a study of *Romeo and Juliet* by having students think of instances in books, movies, TV shows, or their own lives when people's perceptions of others made it difficult to have certain friends, be in love with a particular person, or feel supported in their marriage. In this culturally diverse class, every student offered examples. They were fascinated with how often this theme played out across cultures, and they eagerly talked about what the examples had in common. As the teacher continued to guide them in relating the play to their own examples, the students remained highly engaged with a classic that might otherwise have seemed remote to them. When students make cultural and linguistic connections with content, they display more sophisticated thinking about essential learning goals (Gibbons, 2002).

5. *Understand that students come to the classroom with varied points of entry into a curriculum and move through it at different rates.* For intellectual risk-taking to occur, classrooms need to feel safe to students from a full range of cultural, racial, and economic backgrounds. Teachers who teach up understand that some students may feel racially and culturally isolated in their classes. Therefore, they find multiple ways for students to display their insights for the group. These teachers understand that every student needs "peacock" moments of success so classmates accept them as intellectual contributors.

For instance, a teacher might observe a student in a small-group setting who is questioning his peers about the solution to a math problem they are pursuing because it does not seem correct to him. A teacher who overhears the exchange might simply say to the group, "It seems important to me that Anthony raised the question he posed to you. His thinking brought to your attention the need to think further about your solution. The ability to ask a challenging question at the right time is a good talent to have." Elizabeth Cohen (1994) calls that *attribution of status.*

Teaching up means monitoring student growth so that when students fall behind, misunderstand, or move beyond expectations, teachers are primed to take appropriate instructional action. They guide all students in working with the "melody line" of the curriculum— the essential knowledge, understanding, and skills— while ensuring ample opportunity for individuals and small groups to work with "accompaniments"—that is, scaffolding for students who need additional work with prerequisites and extending depth for students who need to move ahead. For example, some students might need additional work with academic vocabulary, the cornerstone skills of literacy and numeracy, or self-awareness and self-direction. Other students will explore and apply understandings at more expert levels.

Teaching up also calls on teachers to use formative assessment data to guide instructional planning, scaffold the learning of struggling students, and extend learning for advanced students. In other words, teaching up requires both high expectations and high personalization.

For instance, in a middle school science study of simple machines, the teacher made certain to preteach key vocabulary to students who found academic vocabulary challenging. Students then examined and analyzed several Rube Goldberg contraptions, watched and discussed a video, and read designated sections from a text. This multimodal approach ensured that everyone had a solid baseline of experience with concepts they would then explore.

Following a formative assessment on the topic, students worked on one of two tasks. Students who needed additional reinforcement of how simple machines worked went on a guided tour of the school and speculated which simple machines were involved in mechanisms they came across in their tour, such as an elevator. Later, they used print and web sources to confirm or revise their projections. Students who had already demonstrated solid mastery of the topic worked in teams to identify a problem at school or in their lives that three or more simple machines working together could solve; they also used web and text sources to confirm or revise their projections.

6. *Create flexible classroom routines and procedures that attend to learner needs.* Teachers who teach up realize that only classrooms that operate flexibly enough to make room for a range of student needs can effectively address the differences that are inevitable in any group of learners. They see that such flexibility is also a prerequisite for complex student thinking and student application of content (Darling-Hammond, Bransford, LePage, & Hammerness, 2007). Teachers who teach up carefully select times when the class works as a whole, when students work independently, and when students work in groups. They teach their students when and how to help one another as well as how to guide their own work effectively. This kind of flexibility is commonly found in kindergarten classrooms—a strong indication that it's within reach of all grade levels.

An elementary math teacher in one such classroom regularly used formative assessment to chart students' progress. On the basis of what she learned, she built into her instructional plans opportunities for small-group instruction in which she could teach in new ways concepts that some students found difficult, extend the thinking of students who had mastered the concepts, and help students connect what they were learning to various interest areas. Occasionally, she modified the daily schedule so she could work with a portion of the class more intensively. In those instances, some students might work on writing assignments or with longer-term projects in the morning while the teacher met with a given group on a math topic and guided their work. In the afternoon, students would reverse assignments so that she could work with the morning's writers on math. She found that working with the small groups at key times in the learning cycle significantly increased the achievement of virtually all the students in the class.

In the same vein, a team of high school teachers took turns hosting a study room after school on Monday through Thursday. They expected students who hadn't completed their homework to attend. They also invited students who were having difficulty with course requirements and encouraged all students to come if they wanted additional support. Many students did. The sessions, which were less formal than class, also promoted sound relationships between the teachers and their students and among the students themselves.

7. *Be an analytical practitioner.* Teachers who teach up consistently reflect on classroom procedures, practices, and pedagogies for evidence that they are working for each student—and modify them when they're not. They are the students of their students. They are vigilant about noticing when students "do right," and they provide positive descriptive feedback so students can successfully recall or replicate the skill, knowledge, or behaviors in question. They empower students to teach them, as teachers, what makes students most successful. They share with students their aspirations for student success. They talk with students about what is and isn't working in the classroom, and they enlist students' partnership in crafting a classroom that maximizes the growth of each individual and of the group as a whole.

Consider a group of primary teachers who conducted individual assessments of kindergartners' understanding of symmetrical and asymmetrical figures and then discussed what they observed. They realized that vocabulary played a large role in the success of students who mastered the concept. As a result, they were better positioned to support the growth of students who were initially less successful by adding vocabulary practice to math instruction.

Or, consider a middle school teacher who talked often with his students about his confidence that they were engineers of their own success. To reinforce that point, he carefully observed students during whole-class, small-group, and independent work. He'd make comments privately to students as he moved among them or as he stood at the door when they entered or left the room: "Josh, you provided leadership today when your group got off task. I wanted you to know it made a difference." "Ariela, you stuck with the work today when it was tough. Good job!" "Logan, are you still on track to bring in a draft of your paper tomorrow so you'll have a chance to polish it before it's due next week?"

A Challenge Worth Taking

In her provocative book, *Wounded by School*, Kirsten Olson (2009) concludes that perhaps the deepest wounds schools inflict

on students are wounds of underestimation. We underestimate students when they come to us with skills and experiences that differ from the ones we expected and we conclude they're incapable of complex work. We underestimate students when they fall short of expectations because they don't understand the school game and we determine that they lack motivation. We underestimate them when we allow them to shrink silently into the background of the action in the classroom. We underestimate them, too, when we assume they're doing well in school because they earn high grades, and we praise them for reaching a performance level that required no risk or struggle.

Classrooms that teach up function from the premise that student potential is like an iceberg—most of it is obscured from view—and that high trust, high expectations, and a high-support environment will reveal in time what's hidden.

Martin Luther King Jr. (1965) reminded us that human beings are

> caught in an inescapable network of mutuality, tied in a single garment of destiny. Whatever affects one directly affects all indirectly. I can never be what I ought to be until you are what you ought to be, and you can never be what you ought to be until I am what I ought to be. This is the interrelated structure of reality.

That truth has never been more evident than it is today. Schools have the still-untapped possibility of helping all kinds of learners become what they ought to be by developing the skill—and will—to proliferate classrooms in which equal access to excellence is a reality for all learners.

Every student needs "peacock" moments of success so classmates accept them as intellectual contributors.

References

Carbonaro, W., & Gamoran, A. (2003). The production of achievement inequality in high school English. *American Educational Research Journal, 39*(4), 801–827.

Center for Public Education. (2007). The United States of education: The changing demographics of the United States and their schools. Alexandria, VA: Author.

Cohen, E. (1994). *Designing groupwork: Strategies for the heterogeneous classroom.* New York: Teachers College Press.

Darling-Hammond, L. (2006). Interview with Linda Darling-Hammond. *PBS Nightly Business Report.* Retrieved from www.pbs.org/nbr/site/features/special/WIP_hammondl.

Darling-Hammond, L. (2010). *The flat world and education: How America's commitment to equity will determine our future.* New York: Teachers College Press.

Darling-Hammond, L., Bransford, J., LePage, P., & Hammerness, K. (2007). *Preparing teachers for a changing world: What teachers should learn and be able to do.* San Francisco: Jossey-Bass.

Dweck, C. (2007). *Mindset: The new psychology of success.* New York: Ballantine.

Educational Research Service. (1992). *Academic challenge for the children of poverty: The summary report* (ERS Item #171). Arlington, VA: Author.

Fullan, M. (2001). *The new meaning of educational change* (3rd ed.). New York: Teachers College Press.

Gay, G. (2000). *Culturally responsive teaching: Theory, research and practice.* New York: Teachers College Press.

Gardner, J. (1961). *Excellence: Can we be equal and excellent too?* New York: Harper and Row.

Gibbons, P. (2002). *Scaffolding language and scaffolding learning: Teaching second language learners in mainstream classrooms.* Portsmouth, NH: Heinemann.

Good, T. L. (1987). Two decades of research on teacher expectations: Findings and future directions. *Journal of Teacher Education, 38*(4), 32–47.

Gray, T., & Fleischman, (2004/2005). Successful strategies for English language learners. *Educational Leadership, 62*(4), 84–85.

King, M. L., Jr. (1965). Commencement address for Oberlin College, Oberlin, Ohio.

Kozol, J. (2005). *The shame of the nation: The restoration of apartheid schooling in America.* New York: Crown.

National Research Council. (1999). *How people learn: Brain, mind, school, and experience.* Washington, DC: National Academies Press.

Olson, K. (2009) *Wounded by school.* New York: Teachers College Press.

Critical Thinking

1. Write your response to a job interview question which asked you why all students should have a rigorous curriculum that challenged and engaged them in the learning process.

2. Currently many schools implement a so called tracking or sorting approach to teaching where students with similar abilities are grouped together in one class. Discuss this approach to teaching from the viewpoint of both the teacher and student.

Create Central

www.mhhe.com/createcentral

Internet References

Association for Childhood Education International (ACEI)
www.acei.org

Awesome Library for Teachers
www.awesomelibrary.org/teacher.html

Child Care and Early Education Research Connections
www.researchconnections.org

Donors Choose
www.donorschoose.org

Free Resources for Educational Excellence
http://free.ed.gov

Global SchoolNet Foundation
www.gsn.org

Make Your Own Webpage
www.teacherweb.com

Meet Me at the Corner
www.meetmeatthecorner.org

Mid-Continent Research for Education and Learning
www2.mcrel.org/compendium

National Association for the Education of Young Children
www.naeyc.org

CAROL ANN TOMLINSON is William Clay Parrish Jr. Professor at the Curry School of Education, University of Virginia. Her work with differentiated instruction focuses on developing classrooms that provide equity of access to high-quality learning opportunities for all students; cat3y@virginia.edu. EDWIN LOU JAVIUS is founder of EDEquity, an organization that works to help educators develop an equity mind-set as a means of eliminating the achievement gap.

Tomlinson, Carol Ann; Javius, Edwin Lou. From *Educational Leadership*, February 2012, pp. 28–33. Copyright © 2012 by ASCD. Reprinted by permission. The Association for Supervision and Curriculum Development is a worldwide community of educators advocating sound policies and sharing best practices to achieve the success of each learner. To learn more, visit ASCD at www.ascd.org.

Article   Prepared by: Karen Menke Paciorek, *Eastern Michigan University*

The Wonder Years

Children's success in public schools begins at birth, and it's time our attitudes and funding reflect the importance of education in the early years.

ANNIE PAPERO

Learning Outcomes

After reading this article, you will be able to:

- Articulate the importance of children entering kindergarten with skills that will enable them to maximize the learning opportunities.

- Describe the role of high quality preschool programs for young children.

What if every child entered kindergarten ready to learn? What a difference it would make to school leaders, families, and our society if all children received high-quality care during their first three years of life. Evidence continues to grow that school success begins at birth. Our children will never achieve at their highest levels until we change our attitudes—and commit money and resources—to reflect the importance of the first three years of life.

As education leaders, we need to be aware of the established links between very early childhood experiences and later achievement. School leaders—who shoulder the responsibility of raising achievement—are in an extraordinary position to advocate for high-quality care for infants and toddlers. They can make a strong argument that early childhood education is a crucial part of any plan for student achievement and success.

The Risks of Growing Up Poor

Research overwhelmingly confirms the role of early childhood education in later school success. In spite of this, many in public education pay little attention to it, perhaps because teacher and school leaders believe it's out of their sphere of influence.

Although we typically view kindergarten as the beginning of formal schooling, it actually is a continuation of all the learning that has come before. For some children, the early years provide a wealth of developmental riches. In stark contrast, some children face a paucity of opportunity and start out far behind.

One well-recognized risk factor for young children is growing up poor. Children make up a quarter of the U.S. population. However, they are disproportionately represented in poverty, accounting for 35 percent of the nation's poor. Children under age 6 are the poorest demographic group in our country—important to note because, not surprisingly, poverty is more detrimental to the development of young children than to that of older children.

Poverty is associated with lower levels of school achievement and higher levels of behavioral problems. Early poverty shapes later school achievement in many ways. One factor is how language is used in each child's environment. Both parents and children from more affluent, professional backgrounds possess vocabularies that are twice the size of those used by parents and children on welfare. Research shows that these differences in language noted in children when they were 3 were found to be predictors of vocabulary and language development when they were 9 and 10.

Another risk factor faced by infants and toddlers is having a depressed or severely stressed primary caregiver. When a caregiver is unable, for any reason, to establish a warm, responsive relationship with a very young child, development can be affected. The risks include poorer regulation of negative emotion, higher levels of insecure attachment, lower rates of compliance, cognitive and language delays, and lower levels of social competence.

Many of these risks have the potential to alter children's future development paths. For example, the quality of an infant's attachment to a caregiver predicts later social competence, empathy, self-esteem, flexibility, and problem-solving abilities.

Interestingly, the ages of 6 months to 18 months appear to be particularly sensitive to the effects of the quality of caregiving. Many researchers have found that impairments in caregiving during this window of development lead to persistent developmental problems including cognitive impairment, difficulty with peers, hyperactivity, and difficulty regulating attention and emotion—even if conditions subsequently improve for these children.

Children learn to successfully express and regulate emotion through caring, ongoing interactions with significant others in their lives. This self-regulation is a skill that any educator recognizes as important for academic and social success in school.

That Ship Has Sailed

Public schools face significant challenges when children arrive for kindergarten with vastly different levels of development. Metaphorically, a majority of children are on a ship that departs at birth, sailing at a strong clip toward higher developmental levels, fueled by rich environments and quality interactions. Unfortunately, some children are left on shore, lacking the responsive interactions and enriched environments that would carry them along.

We expect those left on shore to catch up and perform at the same levels academically as those who have been on the ship for five years already. It would be quite the feat for a young child with few resources to swim fast enough to climb aboard that ship.

Both sets of children may sit in the same classroom with the same teacher at age 5. But some children have an easier time surrounded by familiar knowledge and skills, while others must simultaneously learn academics and stay afloat in a world where they have no prior experience and far fewer applicable skills. Some very capable and resilient children manage to excel under these difficult circumstances, while many more do not.

It is our responsibility to make sure all children have a chance at academic success. With such unequal starting points, we face a very difficult task. One child may be ready for advanced math, while another child is struggling to focus and learn in the classroom.

It is time for all of us, especially education leaders who are in the position to advocate nationwide, to declare that all children should be on that ship before it sails.

The Role of a High-Quality Program

Early high-quality programs for infants, toddlers, and preschoolers that are accessible and affordable to all families have the greatest potential to help with this goal. Early high-quality care has been found to improve the cognitive, language, and social development of children, particularly those who are low-income, with effects that stretch into the early school years.

Group size, caregiver/child ratio, adult responsiveness, and continuity are some of the factors that determine the quality of care. Infants need to form trusting relationships with a primary care provider. Frequent changes in caregiving have been found to be related to insecure attachment and more problematic behaviors. Many low-income parents are more likely to seek out informal arrangements with relatives or other community members. This type of care has the potential to be less stable than center-based care. Frequent daycare changes are associated with insecure attachment and lower levels of social competence.

In fact, children's relationships with trusted teachers appear to provide children with some of the same benefits as a secure attachment to a parent. In addition, research has found that stability of early care also appears to enhance school adjustment in first grade.

A low child-to-adult ratio is also an important factor in high-quality care. Higher child-to-adult ratios have been found to result in elevated stress levels in children. Sustained, elevated levels of cortisol production in children have been linked to chronic illness and to difficulties concentrating and controlling anger.

Economic Benefits

High-quality early childhood programs can produce significant economic benefits to our society. Research studies that have followed children for more than 40 years are now showing savings of $13 or more for every dollar spent 40 years ago on intervention for 3- and 4-year-old children at risk.

The children who received half-day preschool paired with weekly home visits by their teachers when they were 3 and 4 have been found longitudinally to have higher levels of school achievement, reduced pregnancy and delinquency rates in adolescence, higher high school graduation rates, higher levels of college attendance, increased employment, and lower rates of single parenthood.

Would even earlier intervention, before the age of 3, lead to even greater economic savings and a higher level of student achievement? A 1995 review of model intervention programs showed that IQ effects produced persisted for the longest amount of time among the children who were participants in the two experimental studies that enrolled them as infants in full-day programs.

The Carolina Abecedarian Project, which provided full-day care for low-income children beginning during the first three months of life, has produced evidence that the children who received intervention sustained an IQ advantage over their peers through adulthood, achieved higher levels in reading and math, completed more years of schooling, had lower rates of drug use and early parenthood, and had higher rates of college enrollment and employment.

In a subsequent experiment, researchers provided intervention beginning in kindergarten instead of infancy. Although the school-age intervention aided children's academic achievement, it did not impact their IQs and its effects were significantly weaker than they were for the children who received services as infants.

Often, people object to early childhood programs because they believe that society should not pay for the failure of individuals to provide for themselves and their children. To reframe that argument, consider that it may be preferable to invest in early, high-quality programs that improve student achievement than to pay a much greater sum for remedial education, juvenile detention, adult incarceration, and welfare payments. Research suggests that financial investment in the first few years of life would simultaneously save money and improve the conditions of poverty.

Advocate for Early Childhood

As school leaders, we serve all children, from the poorest of the poor to those who come from the wealthiest families. We exist in every community, and we have a voice that needs to be heard. The issue of early care affects us directly.

We can bring all individuals involved in the care and education of children from birth through adulthood to the same table to talk about what is working or not working for our children. We can each learn more about the resources and gaps in our communities for the families with young children, and we can advocate for improvements that include better care for infants and toddlers.

We can advocate in our own communities and at the national level, drawing attention to the early years, giving voice to a community of educators and children who receive very little of society's attention or resources. We are in the position to spread the word that K–12 public schools alone cannot make up for the deficiencies experienced by so many children during the first five years of life. We can demand a more equal starting line for all children when they reach our schools.

From Diapers to Decimals

Any serious discussion of closing the achievement gap, almost by definition, must include a discussion of the provisions being made for infants and toddlers. For those children who arrive without adequate experiences, we are in the position to advocate for interventions that make sense from a developmental perspective, providing our most challenged children with the opportunities to form strong relationships with reliable adults, and not just provide for the practice of rote facts and measurable academic skills.

Understanding the research is the first step for us as leaders in education and for those who advocate for the children in this country. Research strongly suggests that we would experience higher levels of achievement in our public schools if we as a society ensure that all of our infants and toddlers are provided with the opportunity to relate to adults who provide responsive, sensitive care.

Prekindergarten is not the starting line. The journey began at birth, leaving many children behind. From diapers to decimals,

development is a continuum, and we cannot as a society continue to view the first five years of life as a "private domain." Children's success in our public schools begins at birth, and both our attitudes and our funding structures should reflect that knowledge.

Critical Thinking

1. What are some risk factors children bring with them when they enter K–12 schools?

2. How can school administrators help combat how these risks affect young children entering their schools?

Create Central

www.mhhe.com/createcentral

Internet References

Child Welfare League of America (CWLA)
www.cwla.org

Children, Youth and Families Education and Research Network
www.cyfernet.org

Children's Defense Fund (CDF)
www.childrensdefense.org

Meet Me at the Corner
www.meetmeatthecorner.org

Mid-Continent Research for Education and Learning
www2.mcrel.org/compendium

National Association for the Education of Young Children
www.naeyc.org

National School Boards Association
www.nsba.org

Teachers Helping Teachers
www.pacificnet.net/~mandel

ANNIE PAPERO (alpapero@ship.edu) is an assistant professor of early childhood teacher education at Pennsylvania's Shippensburg University.

Article

Prepared by: Karen Menke Paciorek, *Eastern Michigan University*

Individualizing Instruction in Preschool Classrooms

Increasing numbers of young children with diagnosed disabilities and unique learning needs are enrolled in early childhood programs. Individualizing learning opportunities is one widely accepted practice for successful inclusion.

MARY B. BOAT, LAURIE A. DINNEBEIL, AND YOULMI BAE

Learning Outcomes

After reading this article, you will be able to:

- List strategies that will be helpful when differentiating experiences to meet the needs of all children.

- Describe how scaffolding strategies can be effective in the classroom.

In 2003, 34 percent of young children with disabilities received special education services in community-based early childhood programs such as child care centers, Head Start classrooms, and nursery schools (U.S. Department of Education, 2005). These services are provided by early childhood special educators.

However, these special education professionals usually spend just a few hours each week with the children. If early childhood inclusion is to be a successful educational approach, it is imperative that ALL early childhood teachers understand and are able to provide individualized instruction to young children with special needs. This article describes teaching techniques that preschool teachers can use to support the learning needs of all children with whom they work, including young children with disabilities and special needs.

The term *instruction* refers to the methods used to teach a curriculum (Bredekamp & Rosegrant, 1992). In early childhood education, instruction encompasses many different types of learning experiences ranging from non-directive to directive (Wolery, 2005; Wolery & Wilbers, 1994).

Just as children's learning falls along a continuum from passive to active, so does the process of instruction. Instruction may be as basic as modeling how to put on a coat, or it can be as complex as helping children learn to read. The degree to which teacher direction or guidance is used depends on the objective of the experience and the children's individual needs. Thus, for teaching to be *instruction*, it must be intentional. The result of appropriately individualized instruction is meaningful learning for all young children.

What Is Instruction?

Instruction refers to intentional teaching methods.

When is something teachers do or say considered to be *instruction*? When a teacher draws a young child into a conversation about a picture or experience, is that teacher providing instruction? Perhaps it is, if the teacher is creating an opportunity for the child to express herself verbally or practice turn-taking skills. Teaching is instructive if it is done *intentionally* to provide support or opportunities for children's learning.

Teachers who are aware of children's learning needs continuously look for ways to support their learning.

How to Individualize Instruction

The process of individualizing instruction consists of four primary steps (Pretti-Frontczak & Bricker, 2004):

- **Get to know each child's** interests, needs, and abilities
- **Create opportunities for learning** that build on children's interests
- **Scaffold children's learning** through supportive interactions
- **Monitor children's progress** toward achieving important goals

These components are interrelated and form the framework for decision making around individualization.

To successfully create engaging learning opportunities for children, teachers must know

- what children enjoy and value,
- what children are capable of doing, and
- what adults can and should expect from each child (skills as well as appropriate content standards)

Teachers who know about the children can then create learning opportunities based on that information and support their learning through instructional strategies that promote growth.

Skilled teachers determine whether children are making appropriate progress toward achieving goals by monitoring progress (assessment) *and* using that information to change instructional strategies and intensity as appropriate.

Get to Know Each Child

Most children are naturally curious about their surroundings and eagerly participate in learning activities. For some children, however, it is difficult to identify what motivates them to be more fully engaged. Teachers who pay attention to what children do and say can usually find out what motivates them. This is true for all children, but even more so for children with disabilities because they may not exhibit the same kinds of behaviors as their typically developing peers.

Teachers who successfully work with children who have special needs are diligent in identifying child interests by collaborating with families and other service providers who know the child. This knowledge, coupled with teaching skills, is essential to determine how to use individual information about children to work toward desired outcomes for them.

For example, identifying familiar, common objects is a skill mastered by most preschool children and is a goal on many individualized education plans (IEPs). Some young children, however, have little interest in typical objects in early childhood classrooms. This does not mean that these children are not interested in objects, but rather that their interests fall outside the spectrum of items that appeal to most young children.

Teachers certainly want to encourage young children to be able to identify and name common objects. This skill is necessary for language and literacy development, and provides a common frame of reference for interactions with peers. Teachers who know children well can identify what is likely to motivate them to develop an interest in everyday early childhood learning materials.

Create Opportunities for Learning

The ability to generate and sustain children's interest in learning is a critical skill for effective early childhood teachers. Teachers who can pique children's curiosity and then use appropriate instructional strategies to convey information and skills provide children with rich learning environments (Sandall &Schwartz, 2008).

Maya, a 4-year-old, was diagnosed with a language delay. Maya's teacher, Mr. Flores, is working with her on using words for common objects and activities in the classroom rather than gestures such as pointing or grabbing objects. Mr. Flores seeks a way to motivate Maya's use of vocabulary. He carefully observes what interests Maya and uses this information to set up learning opportunities.

Mr. Flores notes that Maya enjoys working in the art center and especially painting and cutting paper. To provide her with an opportunity to practice using words for common objects, he places crayons and scissors just out of her reach, creating a situation in which Maya must ask for the items. He does not hand the objects to her until she names or attempts to name them.

Mr. Flores may further support Maya's learning by modeling the correct words and asking Maya to repeat them. She is then rewarded by receiving the objects she desires.

This scenario may be repeated, but should be utilized only to help Maya use her vocabulary to obtain what she desires or get her needs met. Mr. Flores actively reinforces Maya's independent attempts to use her vocabulary, because independence is the ultimate goal.

The strategy described here works well for Maya, but effective teachers know that it will not work for every child. Thus, it is imperative that teachers know individual children's interests, cultures, and values before determining the best way to create learning opportunities (Copple & Bredekamp, 2009). For example, a Native American child whose family culture teaches that it is not polite to ask for objects may not respond to the strategy that worked for Maya.

Early childhood teachers use a variety of strategies to facilitate learning opportunities for children. The seven techniques in Table 1 vary in level of teacher direction as well as in the degree to which a child must respond (Ostrosky & Kaiser, 1991). The first several strategies do not require a child's response for an activity to continue. The later strategies are much more directive.

When creating opportunities for learning, make sure that children are ultimately in control of the situation. Even though the intent is to entice a child into the interaction, the child may or may not respond. Teachers try to create opportunities that interest and engage children in learning, but there is no way to make them be interested.

All of the strategies mentioned here are effective ways to engage all children, not just those who have disabilities. Instructional strategies are intended to provide the minimal assistance necessary for the child to successfully attempt the skill (Wolery, 2005; Wolery, Ault, & Doyle, 1992). When using these strategies, do not single out children or foster their dependence. Drawing attention to differences in how children are supported may decrease the likelihood the target children will participate in the opportunity. When planning an intervention, always ask if the strategy is appropriate for the individual child, necessary, and sufficient to promote success.

Scaffold to Support Learning

When teachers support learning, the key is to determine what type and intensity of support will be most helpful to individual children. A teacher's simple glance may draw one child's attention to an inappropriate behavior. Another child may need a verbal reminder. Yet another may benefit from specific guidelines or examples of positive behavior. One child may follow when the teacher demonstrates how to properly hold scissors to cut paper, while another may need hand-over-hand support for the same activity.

In all likelihood, children only need support temporarily, so savvy teachers know that fading their support is critical to children's independence. Effective teachers know how to

Table 1 Teaching Strategies That Pique Children's Interest

1. **Comment** about an event that appears to interest the child. This technique prompts the child to repeat, respond to, or expand on the comment. A teacher looking at a child's painting might say, "Look at all of the bright colors you used! I see pink, green, and purple."

2. **Expand** on a child's statement. Elaborate with one or two key words that are likely to build the child's expressive vocabulary. A child may say, "I have truck," and the teacher may elaborate by saying, "Yes, you have a red fire truck."

3. Introduce an **unexpected event**. Set up situations that capture a child's attention through novelty and create cognitive dissonance. A teacher might do something that is inconsistent with the daily routine or the way children typically perceive their environment. For example, hold a child's name card upside down or start to dress a doll by putting a shoe on its hand.

4. Initially provide **inadequate portions or insufficient materials**. Without sufficient quantity to complete a task, the child is likely to ask for more. If only a small ball of modeling compound is available, the child may ask for more to roll out and use a cookie cutter to make shapes.

5. **Block access**. When a teacher subtly denies a child access to a preferred object or event, the child is likely to request the object or ask for assistance. The teacher might set out bright balls in a plastic container with a tight lid. A child who is interested in playing with the balls will request help to open the container.

6. Create **opportunities to choose**. When children are given choices among objects, events, or activities, they are more likely to actively participate. Choices provide children with opportunities to develop expressive language and cognitive skills. Some choices may be routine, such as offering either crackers or cereal at snack time. Other choices capitalize on children's interests by building on their activities: "Would you like the letter you wrote to go in the mailbox? Or do you want to take it home with you?"

7. Make a **direct request** to say or do something that requires more than a yes or no answer. For example, insist that a child state the name of an object before it is available for play: "Please say 'ball' if you want the orange ball."

Table 2 Match Support to Children's Needs

Support	Child Needs	Examples of Teaching Strategies
Time	Time to process information and to act on a request.	Ask a child to begin cleaning up. Provide plenty of wait time after the request to see if the child complies before making a further intervention.
		Ask a child to share something he enjoyed about a field trip. Provide enough wait time for the child to reflect and respond.
Gesture	A reminder to perform a skill.	Point to the trash can as child gets up from snack and leaves her milk carton.
		Make a "shh" sign to remind children to be quiet during a story.
Verbal Prompt	More explicit information to successfully perform a skill.	Verbally remind a child to put away the toys she used in one center before moving to another.
		Verbally remind a child to put on a smock before waterplay.
Model or Demonstration	How to do a challenging skill or help remembering how to perform a skill.	Demonstrate how to put on a glove. Show how to spread fingers and pull on the glove one finger at a time.
		Suggest that a child watch how a peer holds a pitcher to pour a beverage.
Physical Prompt	When acquiring a skill, child needs physical guidance to be successful.	Use a hand-over-hand techniques to help a child figure out how to balance table blocks.
		Physically help a child grasp and hold a coat zipper.

individualize support to be just the right amount of help. What criteria facilitate this decision-making? Beyond knowing children's individual interests and preferences, there are indicators that may help teachers think about individual situations. Table 2 provides examples of how support from teachers or families may be matched to children's needs.

Scaffolding Strategies

Response-prompting strategies (Wolery, 2005; Wolery, et al., 1992) is a phrase used to describe the process of providing help (or prompts) in order for the learner to make a desired response. Levels of prompting can be ordered from most-to-least or least-to-most.

- **A most-to-least strategy** can be implemented if the child is learning a complex motor skill such as dressing. At first, adults provide children with a great deal of help and gradually reduce the amount of assistance as the child acquires the skill.

- **Least-to-most prompting** can be used when the child knows how to do something, but must be supported to use the skill. For example, children often need help to generalize the skill of turn taking to new situations. While they might be proficient at taking turns when playing Peek-a-Boo with an adult, they might not be comfortable taking turns when they play with a stacking toy. The teacher provides the least amount of help necessary for the child to successfully take turns, providing more help as needed in order for the child to be successful.

The amount of help provided is planned and structured to match the child's skill level and desired outcome.

Peer-mediated strategies are another type of technique that can be used to support individual child learning (DiSalvo & Oswald, 2002; Kohler & Strain, 1999; Robertson, Green, Alpers, Schloss, & Kohler, 2003). These strategies are implemented when a more accomplished peer is paired with one who needs to develop or hone skills.

Peer mediation often occurs naturally in preschool settings. Children typically observe and interact with others in ways that scaffold development. An important aspect of designing curriculum and the learning environment is to make sure that young children have ample opportunities to interact with and learn from one another.

Formal peer-mediated strategies go a step further, when a teacher intentionally pairs children. A teacher typically identifies a peer who possesses a desired (target) skill and works with that child to show him or her how to support a child who has yet to develop the skill.

- First, the teacher coaches the more accomplished peer on how to interact with the target child in a supportive manner, typically through role playing.
- The teacher then structures situations in which the peer "mentor" and the child developing the skill can play or work together utilizing the target skill.

For example, Matthew may have difficulty entering peer group play situations. He often resorts to disrupting the group or aggressive behavior when his attempts to join are rebuffed. The teacher may coach Tarin, a socially-skilled child who is frequently a part of the group Matthew tries to join, to prompt Matthew to use appropriate words to request participation or materials. The teacher role-plays (practices) with Tarin the specific prompts he might use. In turn, Matthew is prompted to use more appropriate interaction strategies. The teacher provides Tarin with statements he can use with Matthew to positively reinforce his use of the target skill(s).

Pay attention to what children do and say.

Just as learners have choices about whether or not to engage in an instructional interaction, more accomplished peers must also be given choices about their involvement as mentors with other children.

Monitor Children's Progress

Effectively individualizing instruction is a cycle that involves knowing individual children, knowing effective instructional strategies, and determining whether or not the choices made resulted in child learning. The final step in this cycle of individualized instruction—monitoring and documenting children's progress—is just as important as knowing the best strategy to use (Pretti-Frontczak & Bricker, 2004).

Without this step, the capacity of teachers to meaningfully affect children's learning is minimized and time is wasted. Determining whether or not instruction is effective must be an evidence-based process in which children's learning is documented. To accomplish this:

- First give a strategy time to work—most meaningful learning does not occur overnight.
- Then, determine the best way to collect and use evidence of children's learning.

Identify the target skill or behavior in order to keep track of children's developmental or academic progress. Choose a method of recording observations that can be incorporated into daily routines and activities.

Focused observation helps teachers plan and implement meaningful curriculum and teaching strategies. Table 3 outlines some ways to document observations that can fit into a busy classroom schedule.

Make Sound Decisions Based on Data

The information that teachers collect as they observe and document children's learning is critically important to inform curricular decisions. Understanding when to introduce new content or increase support for a difficult skill depends on using the information collected as part of the observation process. Teachers must analyze and use the data they gather to determine if their teaching strategies are effective and make changes when the data suggests that they are not (Luze & Peterson, 2004).

The Role of IEPs

Individualization is the foundation of IEP development. IEP annual goals and objectives or benchmarks are target skills for the child to reach. While the annual goals provide a framework for a minimum level of accountability for individual children, they do not reflect the total of what children with disabilities learn in a given year, nor are they the curriculum.

IEP annual goals provide outcomes and direction that help young children access the general curriculum and developmentally typical environments. Although IEPs may include information that supports identifying appropriate instructional strategies, often it is up to the classroom teacher to determine the best way to help a child achieve his or her goals.

Appropriately individualized instruction leads to meaningful learning.

Fortunately, all of the strategies discussed here can help teachers implement instructional strategies that support the

Table 3 Observation Techniques to Document Children's Learning

1. **Observe and record children's behavior at specific times of the day or week.** Choose a time during which the target child is likely to use a skill or behavior AND when enough adults are present.

2. **Make quick checks throughout the day.** If the skill or behavior is something that occurs fairly often, a relatively easy way to monitor progress is to pick a standard time (perhaps every hour) and record whether or not the behavior occurred at that time. While this does not yield detailed information, it indicates how often the behavior occurred.

3. **Use found objects to help keep track.** Use objects (in multiple pockets of an apron, for example) to help keep track of children's behavior. Claire is trying to keep track of how often Shoshanna initiates an interaction with a peer during 90-minute center time. Every time she sees Shoshanna initiate an interaction, she moves a small block (or other object) from one pocket to another. At the end of the day, she counts the number of blocks and records the number of initiations observed.

4. **Record the level of help a child requires.** For some children who have disabilities or special needs, it takes a long time to achieve a goal. Break down a task into smaller steps and document those steps to check for progress. Or track the amount of help a child needs to be successful. With Shoshanna, at first she might need very direct verbal prompts to approach another child (Claire asks Shoshanna to say, "Ashley will you play with me?"). After a while though, the teacher might just have to say "Shoshanna, what do you want Ashley to do?" in order to help Shoshanna approach Ashley. Finally, Claire might just need to gesture (point a finger at Ashley) in order to help Shoshanna know what to do. While Shoshanna still is not initiating interactions independently, she is certainly learning and making important progress toward that goal.

diverse learning needs of all children in a classroom. Effective teachers understand that, although IEPs may specify annual goals, these goals will be achieved when the skills to be learned are embedded in the classroom routine with strategies that facilitate children's development.

Individualizing instruction enables skilled teachers to provide meaningful learning experiences to all young children, including those with special needs (McWilliam, Wolery, & Odom, 2001). In order to provide effective instruction, teachers must

- be knowledgeable about the learners, including their abilities, interests, and needs
- create learning opportunities that are embedded in daily routines, activities, or experiences that capture children's interest and draw them into an instructional interaction
- implement a planned and structured approach for curriculum content
- make thoughtful decisions about the right kind and amount of support for children to be successful
- monitor the success of instruction to make sound decisions to support children's learning and development

Teaching is a reflective and intentional process. When scaffolding children's learning, teachers can choose from a variety of tools in their instructional toolbox!

References

Bredekamp, S., & Rosegrant, T. (1992). Reaching potentials through appropriate curriculum: Conceptual framework for applying the guidelines. In S. Bredekamp & T. Rosegrant (Eds.), *Reaching potentials: Appropriate curriculum and assessment for young children,* (vol. 1.), (pp. 9–25). Washington, DC: National Association for the Education of Young Children.

Copple, C., & Bredekamp, S. (2009). *Developmentally appropriate practice in early childhood programs* (3rd ed.). Washington, DC: National Association for the Education of Young Children.

DiSalvo, C.A., & Oswald, D.P. (2002). Peer-mediated interventions to increase social interaction of children with autism. *Focus on Autism and Other Developmental Disabilities, 17*(4), 198–207.

Kohler, F.W., & Strain, P.S. (1999). Maximizing peer-mediated resources in integrated preschool classrooms. *Topics in Early Childhood Special Education, 19,* 92–102.

Luze, G.J., & Peterson, C.A. (2004). Improving outcomes for young children by assessing intervention integrity and monitoring progress: "Am I doing it right and is it working?" *Young Exceptional Children, 7*(2), 20–29.

McWilliam, R.A., Wolery, M., & Odom, S.L. (2001). Instructional perspectives in inclusive preschool classrooms. In M.J. Guralnick (Ed.), *Early childhood inclusion: Focus on change* (pp. 503–527). Baltimore, MD: Brookes.

Ostrosky, M.M., & Kaiser, A.P. (1991). Preschool classroom environments that promote communication. *Teaching Exceptional Children, 23,* 6–10.

Pretti-Frontczak, K., & Bricker, D. (2004). *An activity-based approach to early intervention* (3rd ed.). Baltimore, MD: Brookes.

Robertson, J., Green, K., Alpers, S., Schloss, P.J., & Kohler, F. (2003). Using a peer-mediated intervention to facilitate children's participation in inclusive childcare activities. *Education and Treatment of Children, 26,* 182–197.

Sandall, S.R., & Schwartz, I.S. (2008). *Building blocks for teaching preschoolers with special needs* (2nd ed.). Baltimore, MD: Brookes.

U.S. Department of Education, Office of Special Education Programs. (2005). *Twenty-fifth annual report to Congress on the implementation of the Individuals With Disabilities Education Act.* Washington, DC: Author.

Wolery, M. (2005). DEC recommended practices: Child-focused practices. In S. Sandall, M.L. Hemmeter, B.J. Smith, & M.E. McLean (Eds.), *DEC recommended practices: A comprehensive guide for practical application* (pp. 71–106). Longmont, CO: Sopris West.

Wolery, M., Ault, M.J., & Doyle, P.M. (1992). *Teaching students with moderate and severe disabilities: Use of response prompting strategies.* White Plains, NY: Longman.

Wolery, M., & Wilbers, J. (1994). *Including children with special needs in early childhood programs.* Washington, DC: National Association for the Education of Young Children.

Critical Thinking

1. Reflect back to a previous experience with young children when you observed another adult or implemented yourself one of the teaching supports listed in Table 2 in the article. Describe the behavior and what happened after you implemented the specific support.

2. Ask a teacher of young children to describe strategies they implement to get children's interest in a learning experience.

Create Central

www.mhhe.com/createcentral

Internet References

Association for Childhood Education International (ACEI)
www.acei.org

Awesome Library for Teachers
www.awesomelibrary.org/teacher.html

The Council for Exceptional Children (CEC)
www.cec.sped.org

Free Resources for Educational Excellence
http://free.ed.gov

Global SchoolNet Foundation
www.gsn.org

National Association for the Education of Young Children
www.naeyc.org

MARY B. BOAT, PhD, is Associate Professor and Program Coordinator, Early Childhood Education, University of Cincinnati, Ohio. She has worked directly and conducted research with young children with, or at risk for, disabilities. **LAURIE A. DINNEBEIL,** PhD, is the Judith Daso Herb Chair in Inclusive Early Childhood Education at the University of Cincinnati. She is a former preschool special education teacher and has worked extensively in the fields of early intervention and early childhood special education. **YOULMI BAE,** MEd, is a doctoral student and research assistant in Early Childhood Special Education at the University of Toledo, Ohio. She was an early childhood teacher in Korea and has worked with preschool Korean American children in a Korean Academy in Toledo.

Article   Prepared by: Karen Menke Paciorek, *Eastern Michigan University*

Response to Intervention and Early Childhood Best Practices

Working Hand in Hand So All Children Can Learn

Kurt is struggling in your universal prekindergarten classroom. After several meetings with you and your supervisor, Kurt's parents ask for a formal evaluation. Before scheduling the full evaluation, the director of special education requests your response-to-intervention (RTI) plan. You might think you do not have one in place—but wait! Early childhood best practices are closer to RTI than you might think.

KAREN WISE LINDEMAN

Learning Outcomes

After reading this article, you will be able to:

- Describe the three tiers in RTI.

- Share why preschool teachers are especially important when it comes to implementing RTI.

In addition to the No Child Left Behind Act of 2001 (Pub. L. No. 107–110, 115 Stat. 1425) and the 2004 reauthorization of the Individuals with Disabilities Education Improvement Act (Pub. L. No. 108–446, 118 Stat. 2647), educators working with school-age children are using response to intervention (RTI) to address special education services in grades K–12 (Coleman, Roth, & West 2009). Before the implementation of RTI, children typically received special education services only after they "failed" or had already developed problems. Children with early signs of delays—in child care settings or preschool programs—would eventually need services later in school once they met the requirement for placement (McCabe 2006).

But why wait for children to need special education services? Why wait for children to fail or for them to fall behind? Educators want to catch delayed skills *before* children fall through the cracks. RTI is different from the traditional screen, evaluate, and referral path to early intervention services. It provides tiered interventions for young children in authentic settings, allowing teachers to intervene early. RTI is a systematic and intentional teaching practice that can help prevent nondiagnosed children from needing special education services and from receiving unnecessary labels (McCabe

2006). It does so by encouraging teachers to clearly and explicitly differentiate the level and intensity of support to match the needs of individual children. RTI is proactive and can help all children, not just those at risk (Coleman, Buysse, & Neitzel 2006).

However, it is important to note that a specific medical diagnosis at birth or later (e.g., deafness or Down syndrome) can lead a child *directly* to early intervention without using RTI as the prerequisite for services. The RTI process should never delay a child's access to needed special education services.

Since RTI has found some success in K–12 classrooms for children with learning disabilities and for addressing literacy difficulties early in cost-effective and flexible ways (e.g., Barton & Stepanek 2009; Callender 2012), it makes sense to implement RTI in preschool settings. The Division for Early Childhood (DEC), NAEYC, and the National Head Start Association (NHSA) have written a joint paper defining RTI and articulating its use in preschool settings (DEC, NAEYC, & NHSA 2013). The paper outlines how RTI uses data-driven instruction as well as assessments to improve learning for all children, but with great focus and concern to keep instruction, assessments, and curricula developmentally, culturally, and individually appropriate.

RTI is an efficient framework for systematically addressing children's needs. However, when using RTI in preschool, teachers must remember to look at the whole child, her natural setting, and her family, and to use authentic evaluations that focus not only on challenges but on strengths as well. For example, instead of a school psychologist taking a preschooler into the hall for a letter-identification screening, the classroom teacher can use data from authentic classroom observations and take into account the child's home language as well as design interventions based on her strengths.

Early childhood educators want every child to succeed; however, each child is unique. Everyone does not learn in the same way, so teachers must change their instruction, teaching style, or even curriculum to meet children's needs. Home visits, family interviews, and parent involvement are essential throughout the teaching and learning process. Educators collect baseline data in all developmental domains at the beginning of the year, keep portfolios, use early learning standards, document, assess, and use data to drive instruction. When these practices are not successful, teachers call in other colleagues, differentiate their instruction, create small groups of children, reflect, reassess, and try again. Early childhood educators meet children where they are. This is the very nature of early childhood best practices and RTI (Barnett, VanDerHeyden, & Witt 2007; Coleman, Roth, & West 2009; Copple & Bredekamp 2009).

It is important to note that, unlike in K–12 classrooms, RTI in the preschool setting is new, and only a few studies support its design or success (Greenwood et al. 2011). However, individual pieces are already in place in most developmentally appropriate early childhood classrooms, which implement clear, explicit, and systematic teaching practices. This article outlines the steps of RTI and illustrates what it can look like in a preschool classroom. Keep in mind that the tiers represent the types of services or interventions teachers use; they are not for labeling children. Additionally the examples given throughout are only suggestions. RTI and early childhood best practices advocate authentic and engaging activities. The main goal of this article is to empower preschool educators to continue to provide developmentally appropriate practices while working within the RTI framework.

Tier 1: Everyone Gets High-Quality Instruction

In Tier 1 of RTI—the base of the triangle (see diagram below)—teachers conduct universal developmental screenings for children and provide high-quality instruction for everyone. Teaching practices are child centered and grounded in research (NCLB 2001). This weeds out lessons that are "cute" or the temptation to teach the letter *K* every March. Instruction and curriculum—that is, a teacher's plan to get the children from point A to point B—must be evidence based. This means educators need to be sure the curricula and programs they use have research studies supporting their effectiveness. This may be the hardest part of RTI for preschool, since very few studies have large-scale research supporting them (Greenwood et al. 2011).

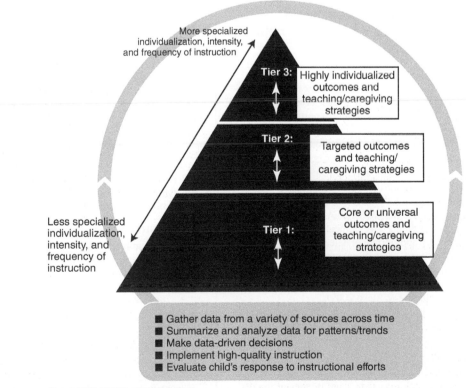

Source: DEC, NAEYC, and NHSA (2013).

Ensuring the Curriculum Is Based on Research

So how do you know if a curriculum is research based? The US Department of Education, along with the Institute of Education Sciences, has created the What Works Clearinghouse at www.ies.ed.gov/ncee/wwc. Use the drop-down menus to see current research on early childhood curricula. Resources are mainly prepackaged curricula for purchase (e.g., Creative Curriculum and Building Blocks for Math). As more large-scale research studies on early childhood curricula are conducted and posted, more information will be available.

NAEYC's recommendations for developmentally appropriate practices are based on child development research and learning theories (McCabe 2006; Copple & Bredekamp 2009). It is important to use the most effective means to reach children. If children are not learning, it should not be because of ineffective teaching practices (Elliott 2008; Walker-Dalhouse & Risko 2009). First and foremost, RTI in preschool is grounded in developmentally appropriate practice for all children.

Did They Learn?

Collecting and using data to guide instruction is an important component of both early childhood best practices and RTI (Elliott 2008). Since every child is unique, some children will not meet their goals through Tier 1 strategies.

First and foremost, RTI in preschool is grounded in developmentally appropriate practice for all children.

After instruction, educators assess to see what was learned and by whom. Assessments can take many forms. Teachers monitor children's progress through continuous and ongoing assessment, which they can maintain by having children complete tasks and then comparing the children's efforts against other children of a similar age or against norms. Assessment tools often come with the curriculum, but all may not be developmentally appropriate. Some curricula, however, do provide naturalistic and authentic forms of assessing children's development (e.g., Creative Curriculum GOLD and HighScope COR), allowing teachers to use observation to align children's development with a standard or norm. Developmentally appropriate practice encourages teachers to use authentic forms of assessment for progress monitoring, such as running records, checklists, anecdotal records, photos, and even video, as well as children's work samples and portfolios (Walker-Dalhouse & Risko 2009).

The first tier in RTI is high-quality, evidenced-based instruction for all, and universal developmental screenings with continued progress monitoring for each child. If a child is not making progress with the current instruction or curriculum used in Tier 1, the teacher will consider Tier 2 interventions.

This morning you observe, take notes, and document the dialogue of two 4-year-olds completing a number order puzzle, while the teaching assistant asks them questions.

Ms. McKeever: What are you looking for?

Tariq: We need the one that fits here *(points to 11; they are looking for 12)*.

Kurt: Nope *(tries 18)*.

Tariq: Doesn't work.

Kurt: *(Both boys try 14 and then 12.)* Got it! It's this one!

Ms. McKeever: What number did you find?

Tariq: *(Tariq and Kurt count in unison from the beginning: 1, 2, 3 . . .)* 14!

Kurt: That is not 14. *(Counts again on his own, missing a piece as he counts)* 11!

Tariq: 11!

Kurt: 12! It is 12. *(They finish the puzzle to 20 using trial and error.)* Later in the day you review your notes and create a math lesson to help the boys work on the numerals 12 and 13, while preparing another lesson for Kurt to work on one-to-one correspondence. The data, observation, and children's dialogue drive your instruction and lesson planning.

RTI Resources

What Works Clearinghouse. A review of the research used to determine evidence-based curricula. www.ies.ed.gov/ncee/wwc

Recognition and Response: Pathways to School Success for Young Children. An outline of how RTI looks when implemented with preschoolers. www.recognitionandresponse.org

Center for Response to Intervention in Early Childhood. A tool for developing and researching evidenced-based interventions specifically used for preschool. www.crtiec.org

"Frameworks for Response to Intervention in Early Childhood: Description and Implication." This joint paper by DEC, NAEYC, and NHSA outlines how RTI uses data-driven instruction and assessments to improve learning for all children. www.naeyc.org/content/frameworks-response-intervention

Assessment Resources

These resources are available through NAEYC.

- *Developmental Screening in Early Childhood: A Guide*, 5th ed., by Samuel J. Meisels and Sally Atkins-Burnett (2005)
- *The Power of Observation: Birth to Age 8*, 2nd ed., by Judy R. Jablon, Amy Laura Dombro, and Margo L. Dichtelmiller (2007)
- *Windows on Learning: Documenting Young Children's Work*, 2nd ed., by Judy Harris Helm, Sallee Beneke, and Kathy Steinheimer (2007)
- *Understanding RTI in Mathematics: Proven Methods and Applications*, edited by Russell Gersten and Rebecca Newman-Gonchar (2011)

Response to Intervention and Early Childhood Best Practices: Working Hand in Hand So All Children Can Learn by Karen Wise Lindeman

97

Tier 2: They Haven't All Mastered the Skill

Each child learns at his own developmental pace, so it is important for teachers to modify and differentiate instruction for the children who do not learn in Tier 1. Providing interventions is Tier 2 in RTI, and many of these interventions can be embedded throughout the day (Barnett, VanDerHeyden, & Witt 2007). For example, a teacher can work on improved pencil grip with Sha-Shan in the writing center by providing large crayons, and on one-to-one correspondence during block building with Miguel by modeling counting during his play. RTI includes ability grouping and separate interventions in the elementary setting, but these are not appropriate or necessary for the early childhood classroom due to the great range of children's skills and the need for young children to learn with peers in authentic and meaningful ways, not in isolation.

This support is not considered special education services, but it does intentionally help a child who simply needs more time or instruction, or needs the topic or skill presented in a different way. Once the child masters the skill or meets the milestone, the teacher responds by moving her instruction back to Tier 1. Tiers are fluid and allow teachers' interventions to move in and out and back in again, helping them respond to constant progress monitoring, documentation, and the advice from other professionals (Elliott 2008). For example, a speech/language therapist, a school psychologist, an occupational or physical therapist, or even another classroom teacher can help by conducting additional observations and offering feedback (Walker-Dalhouse & Risko 2009).

It is important for teachers to document why, how, and how often they intervene, and for the interventions to be research based. For more ideas on how to implement Tier 2 interventions, and to learn about the Recognition and Response Observation and Rating Scale (RRORS) currently being developed, visit the Recognition and Response website, www.recognitionandresponse.org.

Tier 3: Some More, But Not All

Most children master skills with Tier 2 interventions; however, a small percentage might not "respond to your interventions" (Barnett, VanDerHeyden, & Witt 2007). For example, even after providing Kurt with numerous opportunities and consulting with his family to provide additional experiences at home, Kurt has not yet made progress.

Here instruction moves to Tier 3, the top of the triangle in RTI, where teachers and a team of related professionals implement intense, individualized interventions with varied instructional practices focusing on the whole child, his environment, and his family.

As always, these interventions include families. Family members are an integral part of the team, offering insights into the child's interests and behaviors, and giving children unique experiences and opportunities at home. Tier 3 does not mean special education services, labels, or a diagnosis. Tier 3 interventions in preschool may be opportunities for a child to work

one-on-one with a teacher or to have more exposure to meaningful learning experiences. The intervention implemented in Tier 2 may need to be offered more often or with more intensity. Since not all interventions are related to cognitive skills, the setting and environment can be factors in supporting social-emotional or gross motor development. By reviewing the data (e.g., observations, work samples) collected throughout the year, the team can begin to problem solve child-specific interventions. If an instructional accommodation or teaching approach has helped the child, these interventions do not need to be removed.

> **RTI is a systematic and intentional framework for ensuring all children learn. When combined with early childhood best practices, it has the potential to increase children's learning and catch delays early.**

Also, teachers can use several different levels of interventions for different domains. A child can receive Tier 2 interventions for an academic skill and Tier 3 interventions for behavior (Greenwood et al. 2011). For example, Luke is making progress with the teacher's small group (Tier 2) literacy interventions but still needs direct, intense, one-on-one (Tier 3) interventions to help control his strong emotional reactions when taking turns with other children. If he does not make progress with Tier 3 interventions, the team can decide if a full evaluation is necessary. RTI is not the only path to special education services (McCabe 2006; CRTIEC 2009), and RTI should not delay a child from receiving such services.

So tell Kurt's school district about the accommodations you have already tried with the struggling preschooler—show them your portfolios, checklists, observations, and progress-monitoring results—and continue to keep his parents and other professionals involved in the discussion, as needed. Early childhood best practices require educators to *respond to* young children and provide high-quality, developmentally appropriate *interventions*.

Conclusion

RTI is a systematic and intentional framework for ensuring all children learn. When combined with early childhood best practices, RTI has the potential to increase children's learning and catch delays early. Each tier allows teachers to respond in developmentally appropriate ways to young children, in partnership with families and other professionals. Educators need to be empowered to develop quality early childhood practices at each tier. RTI can improve intentional and explicit early interventions and help to meet individual children's needs. If a child does not respond to these interventions, preschool teachers, other professionals, and families can problem solve strategies to ensure success. RTI and early childhood best practices can go hand in hand so all children can learn.

References

Barnett, D.W., A.M. VanDerHeyden, & J.C. Witt. 2007. "Achieving Science-Based Practice Through Response to Intervention: What It Might Look Like in Preschools." *Journal of Educational and Psychological Consultation* 17(1): 31–54.

Barton, R., & J. Stepanek. 2009. "Three Tiers to Success." *Principal Leadership* 9(8): 16–20.

Callender, W.A. 2012. "Why Principals Should Adopt Schoolwide RTI." *Principal* 91(4): 8–12.

Coleman, M.R., V. Buysse, & J. Neitzel. 2006. *Recognition and Response: An Early Intervening System for Young Children At-Risk for Learning Disabilities.* Chapel Hill: The University of North Carolina at Chapel Hill, FPG Child Development Institute. www.readingrockets.org/article/11394/.

Coleman, M.R., F.P. Roth, & T. West. 2009. *Roadmap to Pre-K RtI: Applying Response to Intervention in Preschool Settings.* New York: The National Center for Learning Disabilities. www .sde.idaho.gov/site/rti/resourcesDocs/Early%20Childhood/ roadmaptoprekrti.pdf.

Copple, C., & S. Bredekamp, eds. 2009. *Developmentally Appropriate Practice in Early Childhood Programs: Serving Children From Birth Through Age 8.* 3rd ed. Washington, DC: NAEYC.

CRTIEC (Center for Response to Intervention in Early Childhood). 2009. "Myths About Response to Intervention in Early Childhood." www.cde.state.co.us/early/downloads/CFCoorMtgs/Multi%20 Tier%20System/MythsaboutRtIinEarlyChildhood-Final9-1-09.pdf.

DEC (Division for Early Childhood of the Council for Exceptional Children), NAEYC, & NHSA (National Head Start Association). 2013. "Frameworks for Response to Intervention in Early Childhood: Description and Implications." Arlington, VA: DEC; Washington, DC: NAEYC; Alexandria, VA: NHSA. www.naeyc .org/content/frameworks-response-intervention.

Elliott, J. 2008. "Response to Intervention: What & Why?" *The School Administrator* 65(8): 10–18. www.aasa.org/ SchoolAdministratorArticle.aspx?id=4932.

Greenwood, C.R., T. Bradfield, R. Kaminski, M. Linas, J.J. Carta, & D. Nylander. 2011. "The Response to Intervention (RTI) Approach in Early Childhood." *Focus on Exceptional Children* 43(9): 1–22. www.milcleaders.org/media/cms/files/Content/ Pages/Focus%20on%20Exceptional%20Children.pdf.

McCabe, P.C. 2006. "Responsiveness to Intervention (RTI) in Early Childhood: Challenges and Practical Guidelines." *Journal of Early Childhood and Infant Psychology* 2: 157–180.

NCLB (No Child Left Behind Act of 2001). Pub. L. No. 107–110, 115 Stat. 1425.

Walker-Dalhouse, D., & V.J. Risko. 2009. "Crossing Boundaries and Initiating Conversations About RTI: Understanding and Applying Differentiated Classroom Instruction." *The Reading Teacher* 63(1): 84–87.

Critical Thinking

1. Why are families an integral part of the team, especially when it comes to Tier 3 interventions?

2. Explain how intentional teaching and RTI work together to provide optimal learning experiences for all children.

Create Central

www.mhhe.com/createcentral

Internet References

The Council for Exceptional Children (CEC)
www.cec.sped.org

Intervention Central
www.interventioncentral.org

National Center on Response to Intervention
www.rti4success.org

National Association for the Education of Young Children
www.naeyc.org

National School Boards Association
www.nsba.org

KAREN WISE LINDEMAN, PhD, is an assistant professor and early childhood program coordinator at State University of New York (SUNY) at Fredonia. Karen's past roles include prekindergarten and kindergarten teacher, early intervention service provider, and teacher of the deaf. karen.lindeman@fredonia.edu.

Unit 4

UNIT

Prepared by: Karen Menke Paciorek, *Eastern Michigan University*

Supporting Young Children's Development

Teaching children in their early childhood years certainly involves much more than teaching academic content. The development of the whole child must be thoughtfully addressed through the activities available for each child. Anecdotal reports from teachers of young children point to increasingly aggressive behaviors displayed in classrooms with children as young as two years of age. Kicking, hitting, yelling, and a whole host of other aggressive behaviors that are dangerous, destructive to materials, or disturbing the learning environment are occurring with increasing frequency. Teachers can help children engaging in these behaviors by implementing a focused and consistent approach to guiding behavior. Again, the word relationships plays a key role in helping seriously disruptive children learn to be socially acceptable members of the classroom, their families, and society. I see helping young children acquire appropriate behavioral control as the most challenging part of teaching. There are many concrete strategies for meeting standards, planning learning experiences, and assessing young children; however, addressing individual needs that impact a child's behavior requires an intentional and very individualized approach. Beginning teachers can learn from more seasoned teachers who can share strategies that have proven successful in the past.

There is such discord going on in our profession when it comes to play, a core principle of our field. Early childhood researchers, professionals, and teachers speak constantly about the need for children to engage in freely-chosen exploration and manipulation of a variety of materials yet giving children the opportunity to do so often results in criticism from administrators who are focused on raising test scores. It is similar to the volumes of research on the importance of eating a healthy diet and exercising as obesity is quickly becoming our major health issues. We read the research but choose to follow another path. It's time for early childhood educators to arm themselves with the data to speak with conviction about the need for children to interact with materials that engage their minds and cause them to ponder, think, create, and explore.

Recently, I conducted a professional development in-service session for all of the kindergarten and first grade teachers in a school district located in the suburbs of a large Midwest city. The one issue about which the teachers were most concerned was the lack of time for play for their children. The administration even went so far as to cancel recess and require teachers to have a detailed lesson plan if children were to be away from their desks for more than five minutes. The lack of play and the steady increase in required formal testing, even for kindergarteners, is causing many educators to strongly criticize, and in some cases leave the field, due to frustration over the forcing of developmentally inappropriate practices. The articles in this unit serve as resources for any staff looking for research that supports the need for play in programs and schools serving children in the early childhood years. The development of important social and emotional skills during the early childhood years will serve the children well as they move through childhood and into adulthood. Social and emotional skills are best learned in natural settings where children have to rely on skills they have previously developed as they navigate the challenge of making friends, figuring out how they fit into society and begin to develop an idea of how others see them as an individuals. Educators receive many questions from parents about what is called rough and tumble or big body play among young children. The need for children to engage in appropriate large muscle play is strong and the development of gross motor skills and the ability to control those muscles is a valuable skill to learn. As educators, we constantly straddle that line between what is developmentally appropriate for children's development and legal restrictions placed on educators from school administrators and insurance companies. A balance can be found and there is no need to eliminate playgrounds or recess for legal issues if there is proper supervision and appropriate and well-maintained equipment. Many insurance companies serving educational institutions have developed outstanding resource materials which provide appropriate guidelines.

The title of this unit, once again, must be stressed: Supporting Young Children's Development. Teachers who see their job of working with young children as finding the approach that best supports each child's individual development will be most successful. We are not to change children to meet some idealistic model, but we should become investigators whose job it is to ferret out the individual strengths and learning styles of each child in our care. Enjoy each day and the many different experiences awaiting you when you work with young children and their families.

Article   Prepared by: Karen Menke Paciorek, *Eastern Michigan University*

Making the Right Choice Simple

Selecting Materials for Infants and Toddlers

ANI N. SHABAZIAN AND CAROLINE LI SOGA

Learning Outcomes

After reading this article, you will be able to:

- Share with teachers and children's families the importance of choosing appropriate materials for infants and toddlers.

- List the criteria for safe toys.

- Describe what constitutes a developmentally appropriate material.

It is always the children who give shape to things and not the things that shape the children. The various materials are seen in terms of their many different possibilities and transformations.

—Mirella Ruozzi

As the opening quotation illustrates, infants and toddlers are not passive recipients of the world around them but rather are active participants continuously engaging with their environment. Thus, young children need a world that is safe to explore, one where they are encouraged to venture and discover. An infant's world should be replete with opportunities to see, hear, feel, touch, taste, smell, and move. This article explores ways to optimize the various possibilities and transformations materials provide for infants and toddlers (Ruozzi 2010). For our purposes we define *materials* as objects that children interact with, and we particularly value those that encourage physical exploration. We address two questions: (1) What criteria should teachers use to select infant and toddler materials? (2) How should materials look, feel, and sound?

Criteria for Selecting Play Materials

A thoughtful, intentional selection of materials ensures a dynamic and evolving environment that promotes learning. The following considerations apply when choosing materials for infants (birth to 18 months) and toddlers (18 months to 3 years): Are the materials developmentally appropriate and do they encourage active participation? Are they open-ended, healthy and safe, and neutral and nonbiased?

Developmentally Appropriate Materials

NAEYC states that developmentally appropriate practices take into account what is known about the individual child, what is known about child development and learning, and what is known about the child's culture (NAEYC 2009a). First, in selecting developmentally appropriate materials, it is important to use knowledge about children's individual interests and approaches to learning. This helps ensure that teachers meet and cultivate children's interests and needs. For example, asking 14-month-old Clara to throw a ball forward into a basket five feet away is outside of Clara's zone of proximal development—what she knows and is able to do. This sets her up for failure and may negatively impact her sense of self-competence. However, Clara enjoys sorting balls into different-size containers. To recognize their own abilities and build their social-emotional development, infants and toddlers need to feel a sense of competence and satisfaction with the materials they engage with on a regular basis (Copple & Bredekamp 2009).

Second, teachers can use their knowledge about children's development to make general predictions about a particular age group and their capabilities and provide materials appropriate for the children's developmental stages (Copple & Bredekamp 2009).

For example, group developmental needs dictate placement of materials. For mobile babies, teachers can place similar items, such as assorted jar lids and board books, in small baskets and arrange them in different infant-accessible areas of the room. Low, sturdy, shallow shelves allow mobile infants to pull themselves up and independently get objects. This is an empowering experience. Teachers can help children develop a sense of predictablity in their environment and confidently navigate the space by limiting the rotation of materials.

Finally, infants' and toddlers' previous experiences influence how they interact with materials. It is critical for teachers to consider children's social and cultural backgrounds when choosing play materials so they can match and expand children's zone of proximal development (Vygotsky 1978). For example, 26-month-old Lucas's primary home language is Japanese, so the teachers ask his parents to bring in Japanese cookbooks and empty boxes from Japanese foods they eat at home to incorporate into the dramatic play area. Knowing young children's backgrounds helps teachers select materials that reflect children's cultures.

Materials That Encourage Participation

Eighteen-month-old Shea takes a basket of Duplos from the shelf and puts it on the floor. As she holds one block, she stacks another on top of it, then another, until she has connected three pieces. When she tries to add a fourth piece, the stack falls apart. She tries again and again to add another block, but the stack always falls. Shea exclaims, "Coming apart!"

Infants and toddlers need materials that they can manipulate—try, perhaps fail, rethink, try again, and succeed. Materials that encourage exploration provide feedback and help them learn that they can make things happen. The cause-and-effect relationship they learn fosters a more in-depth understanding of the world, helping them realize the relationships between actions and reactions. For example, when the Duplos stay up, Shea knows she successfully stacked them. When 8-month-old Robby shakes a rattle, he hears a sound that he made happen. Gerson (2008) found that hands-on experiences provide a framework for infants' understanding of their own actions as well as others that observational experiences do not.

It is critical for teachers to consider children's social and cultural backgrounds when choosing play materials.

When including technology, teachers should do so in developmentally appropriate ways. One study demonstrates that children 15–21 months old learned more words through a live presentation than from watching a children's television program (Krcmar, Grela, & Lin 2007). This illustrates the importance of actively engaging children instead of relying on electronic or televised materials for children's learning. However, teachers can use some technology with infants and toddlers. Shared intentional technology time can encourage conversations with children and introduce new vocabulary. It can also offer children access to images of friends, family, animals, and objects that they would not otherwise see (NAEYC 2012).

> Two-year-old Ben presses the image of a harp on a tablet and a short melody plays. Sonique, 22 months old, joins him. They use an app together to explore sounds different instruments make. Sonique presses the image of the tuba and they both laugh at the sound it makes. Ben squeals and says, "Tuba make funny noise!"

Exploring the tablet with another child encourages Ben to learn about musical instruments and actively engage with a peer—supporting both his language and social skills.

Open-Ended Materials

Brain growth happens most rapidly from birth to age 3 (Toga, Thompson, & Sowell 2006). Therefore infants and toddlers need to play with objects that stimulate and enhance brain development. To encourage young children's curiosity, exploration, and learning, effective teachers provide open-ended materials. These types of materials do not have predetermined purposes but instead offer many possibilities. Jack Petrash (2002) writes, "Children who are encouraged to play with the same object in a number of different ways develop . . . flexible thinking that can consider a problem from a number of different perspectives" (42). The ability to view a problem from different perspectives is called *divergent thinking* and is a learned process that requires practice (Scott, Leritz, & Mumford 2004). Divergent thinking is a crucial initial step in developing problem-solving skills. Open-ended materials foster divergent thinking skills because children can use them flexibly and with multiple outcomes. Examples of open-ended materials are cardboard tubes, boxes, paper, blocks, and leaves. While it is important that the majority of materials for infants and toddlers be open-ended, not every item needs to be. For example, puzzles or shape sorters have only one outcome but provide immense, age-appropriate feedback to children regarding spatial awareness—how things fit in space and in relation to each other.

Healthy and Safe Materials

It is important that materials for infants and toddlers be safe and sturdy. Items should be made of durable, resilient, and nontoxic materials such as stainless steel and bamboo. Many products infants and toddlers play with, such as toys, household items, and containers, are made from plastics. A report released by Environment and Human Health, Incorporated (Wargo, Cullen, & Taylor) in 2008 states that some plastics may be harmful to children. Two harmful chemicals found in plastics, bisphenol A (BPA) and the phthalate DEHP, were present in the tissues of most people tested, with the highest concentrations in children. BPA and DEHP were detected in blood, urine, and breast milk. Both compounds cross the blood-brain barrier, which may negatively affect brain formation—particularly in infants' developing brains and other organs. To limit exposure to these toxins, teachers can use BPA-free plastics and alternatives, such as bamboo baskets, stainless steel bowls and buckets, and wooden cars, trucks, and blocks.

Infants and toddlers can learn a lot by exploring natural materials (Curtis et al. 2013). For example, bark and shells provide wonderful textures for young children to explore. These simple, open-ended, natural materials inspire imaginative play while instilling a connection with nature. This also encourages infants' and toddlers' curiosity of the natural world. However, for younger infants whose primary mode of material exploration is through mouthing, it is important for adults to observe children closely to reduce the risk of choking. Also, teachers may wish to consider the durability of natural materials. For example, thicker, larger shells are more suitable than small, delicate ones.

Conversely, not all manufactured materials are poor choices. Plastics tend to be easier to clean and disinfect than natural materials, and for materials in large volumes, such as Duplos, this may be crucial for appropriate sanitation. Choose fabric items such as cloth teethers or cloth dolls for toys that are frequently mouthed so that they can be laundered.

Neutral, Nonbiased Materials

Two-year-old Alyssa frequently plays with boy and girl baby dolls. She swaddles the dolls and uses sign language to sign *up* to each of them. She then picks up the dolls and pats them on the back, saying "Sh, sh, sh."

Alyssa's representational play shows her same care and interactions with each doll, regardless of the dolls' gender or race. However, Todd and Thommessen (2010) found that infants as young as 9 months old showed strong preferences for gender-typical toys. For example, boys were drawn to vehicles and girls were drawn to dolls. It is important for teachers to be cognizant of the messages items relay. Presenting dramatic play materials in pink hues and vehicles in blue hues may suggest that these materials are meant for particular genders. Materials should convey equality and acceptance and not reinforce social or cultural prejudices. As the above anecdote illustrates, teachers can offer baby dolls of both genders, and a balance of different races and ethnicities. Teachers can also provide multicultural books in many languages and hang pictures that reflect the children's families—traditional and nontraditional—and different cultures and ethnicities.

Materials That Support Different Domains

Effective teachers offer a variety of materials to support differing developmental needs, interests, and abilities of infants and toddlers. For example, to further infants' physical development, teachers provide materials such as balls and risers to address gross motor skills. To foster toddlers' social development, they provide child-size props that mimic common objects in daily life, such as a telephone or a play kitchen. Teachers can provide soft spaces where toddlers can go to be alone, promoting their self-regulation. To expand infants' cognitive development, such as their understanding of object permanence, teachers provide fabrics for peekaboo. In sum, there should be enough varied materials to address all developmental domains equally.

How Materials Should Look, Sound, and Feel

Children have a predisposition toward beauty, and we try to give visibility to this within their learning processes.

—Mirella Ruozzi

The presentation of materials and the importance of beauty in children's lives is often undervalued or overlooked. Karen Heid states, "Aesthetics enables students to engage deeply in both their personal and interactive learning" (2005, 48). Materials should have simple designs, clean lines, and subtle features. Display items so they are orderly, appealing, and inviting to young children. For example, teachers can put materials in transparent containers or shallow woven baskets so children can easily see what is inside. Containers should have subtle hues—preferably neutral shades—so as not to distract from the materials. NAEYC Physical Environment Accreditation criterion 9A.09 explains that "a welcoming and accessible environment contains elements such as features that moderate visual and auditory stimulation" (NAEYC 2009b).

Effective teachers offer a variety of materials to support differing developmental needs.

In addition to esthetics, the amount of material can also affect children's use of items. Offering too many options at once can overwhelm an infant or toddler and compromise the depth of exploration of materials (Knopf & Welsh 2010). For example, a young infant surrounded by a tube, rattle, soft toy, and a piece of fabric may quickly explore each object by mouthing, touching, or moving it. If a teacher offers the infant only the tube and fabric, she is likely to spend a longer time exploring each item and possibly seeing how the two objects interact with each other.

> Four-month-old Lila grasps fabric with her fingers, balls it up, and brings the fabric close to her mouth. She pulls the fabric away from her mouth and then moves it back toward her. Her eyes blink as the fabric moves across her face. She repeats these actions several times with what appears to be clear intention.

Materials' sounds also impact how infant and toddlers explore them. Infants enjoy producing an effect with materials, such as rattles. However, they tend to not like loud or sudden noises. Wooden materials, fabrics, and soft toys can absorb sound and minimize ambient noise (Curtis & Carter 2003).

Finally, since children from birth to age 2 are in the sensorimotor stage, a material's feel also matters (Piaget 1952). According to Piaget, during the sensorimotor stage infants and toddlers use their senses to learn about the world around them. Materials should be light and easy to grasp and offer a variety of textures and temperatures. For example, wood is warm and inviting, while plastics tend to be cold. Tactile experiences include opportunities to explore sand, water, mud, and ice.

Conclusion

As infants and toddlers explore their environments, they select and process information, construct hypotheses, and make decisions about the world around them. Materials can invite them to be active learners and participants in their environments. Materials help infants and toddlers learn to solve problems and independently make choices based on their developmental abilities and their individual interests. By making thoughtful, intentional choices, care-givers can offer children materials that create a safe, healthy, engaging, and developmentally appropriate environment.

References

Copple, C., & S. Bredekamp, eds. 2009. *Developmentally Appropriate Practice in Early Childhood Programs Serving Children From Birth Through Age 8.* 3rd ed. Washington, DC: NAEYC.

Curtis, D., K.L. Brown, L. Baird, & A. Coughlin. 2013. "Planning Environments and Materials That Respond to Young Children's Lively Minds." *Young Children* 68 (4): 26–31. www.naeyc. org/yc/files/yc/file/201309/YC0913_Curtis_Planning_Environments.pdf

Curtis, D., & M. Carter. 2003. *Designs for Living and Learning: Transforming Early Childhood Environments.* St Paul, MN: Redleaf.

Gerson, S.A. 2008. "What's in a Mitten? The Effects of Active Versus Passive Experience on Action Understanding." Master of science thesis, University of Maryland. http://drum.lib.umd.edu/bitstream/1903/8474/1/umi-umd-5517.pdf

Heid, K. 2005. "Aesthetic Development: A Cognitive Experience." *Art Education* 58 (5): 48–53.

Knopf. H.T., & K.L. Welsh. 2010. "Infant/Toddler Materials Guide." Columbia, SC: Yvonne & Schuyler Moore Child Development Research Center, University of South Carolina. http://scpitc.org/wp-content/uploads/2012/04/SC-Infant-Toddler-Materials-Guide.pdf

Krcmar, M., B. Grela, & K. Lin. 2007. "Can Toddlers Learn Vocabulary From Television? An Experimental Approach." *Media Psychology* 10 (1): 41–63.

NAEYC. 2009a. "Developmentally Appropriate Practice in Early Childhood Programs Serving Children From Birth Through Age 8." Position statement. Washington, DC: NAEYC. www.naeyc. org/positionstatements/dap

Critical Thinking

1. Develop a list of 6 appropriate materials for infants and 10 for toddlers based on the reading.

2. What impact does the social and cultural background of infants and toddlers play in the selection of appropriate materials?

3. Explain to parents what they should consider when choosing toys for their children.

Internet References

Baby Center
http://www.babycenter.com/0_toy-safety-guidelines_423.bc

Choosing Appropriate Toys and Equipment
http://www.earlychildhoodnews.com/earlychildhood/article_view.aspx?ArticleID=222

Good Toys for Young Children by Age and Stage
http://www.naeyc.org/toys

Infant and Toddler Materials Guide

http://scpitc.org/wp-content/uploads/2012/04/SC-Infant-Toddler-Materials-Guide.pdf

Parents Guide to Appropriate Toys

http://www.parents.com/fun/toys/baby-toys/your-guide-to-age-appropriate-toys

Zero to Three

http://zerotothree.org

ANI N. SHABAZIAN earned her BA from UCLA and her MA in human developmental psychology from Harvard University. She completed her MA/PhD in urban schooling at UCLA. Dr. Shabazian holds a dual appointment at Loyola Marymount University (LMU), serving as assistant professor in the LMU School of Education and as director of the LMU Children's Center. ani.shabazian@lmu.edu

CAROLINE LI SOGA earned her MA in early childhood education from Loyola Marymount University. She is currently associate director of Loyola Marymount University Children's Center, providing high-quality care for children ages birth to 5 years. csoga@lmu.edu

Article   Prepared by: Karen Menke Paciorek, *Eastern Michigan University*

Which Toys Promote High-Quality Play? Reflections on the Five-Year Anniversary of the TIMPANI Study

Jeffrey Trawick-Smith, et al.

Learning Outcomes

After reading this article, you will be able to:

- Discuss the impact the quality of children's preschool play has on later development.

- Indicate what constitutes quality in children's toys.

- Share with parents the important findings of the TIMPANI study.

L ealem looks over a new set of toys she will introduce in her preschool classroom. Rainbow people—two dozen multicolored wooden people with no features—stand at attention on a table. "I wonder what kinds of play these toys will inspire," she says to Jeffrey as he prepares to study how children will use them during choice time. "What will the children do with them?"

During choice time many children use them and do so in different ways. Two 4-year-old boys, Jim and Emir, approach the table where these toys are displayed and engage in a pretend-play theme. Jim selects a yellow figure and explains that it is the creature who will capture all the other figures. Emir manipulates the other pieces, pretending that they are running away. "Let's say he eats up all of these guys," announces Jim, the child doing the chasing. He then growls frighteningly. Emir cries, "Run, run, as fast as you can!" He herds all of the other wooden people to a corner of the table and says, "He can't get them here, all right? They're in the apartment and the doors are locked." The play continues for several minutes.

Later, 5-year-old Melly goes to the table by herself. She pulls all four chairs away from the table and lines them up in a row. She then places the wooden people in lines on each of the chairs. "They're watching a movie," Melly says to Lealem as she passes by. The teacher notices that all the red people are lined up on one chair, all the blue on another, and so on. The activity is brief, but the child is completely engaged in the play.

On the same day, 4-year-old Amy and 5-year-old Hana discover that they can stack the colorful people on top of each other. For a few minutes they build tall and precarious towers with the toys. Then they stand back, admiring their work. Amy claps with delight and calls a teacher over: "Look what we made! Please take a picture!"

Near the end of choice time, two 3-year-old boys wander by the table, briefly look at the toys, handle them, then move on to another area of the classroom, seemingly uninterested.

Observing these different interactions, Lealem and Jeffrey ask themselves, "What exactly is the impact of these toys on play? Some children pretend with them, while others use them to sort or build. Some children interact with peers while using them; others play alone. Some don't play with the toys at all."

W ith such a diversity of children's responses to a single play material, can we really say that this or any other toy is beneficial for *all* children in preschool classrooms? For five years, the Center for Early Childhood Education at Eastern Connecticut State University has been struggling with this question. Students and I conduct an annual toy study called TIMPANI (Toys That Inspire Mindful

Play and Nurture the Imagination) for several reasons. Such research is important and provides practical information for teachers. The quality of children's play in preschool predicts later social and intellectual development (Vygotsky 1976), and a large percentage of classroom play includes toys. However, toys have received little research attention. Preschool teachers need empirical evidence to guide the decisions they make about which toys to provide in their classrooms.

In this article we reflect on toys on the fifth anniversary of our project. We summarize some of the big ideas drawn from our findings that may be useful to preschool teachers as they choose new play materials for their classrooms.

What Are Toys and Why Do We Study Them?

We consider toys to be any concrete object that children can manipulate to carry out self-directed and meaningful play activities that are enjoyable for the process and not because they result in a product. A toy could be a pretend-play prop, a building material, an art medium, a set of natural objects to explore scientifically, or even a stick. For the purposes of our research, we do not consider computer applications, videos, or books to be toys. Further, we do not study outdoor play equipment because our recording equipment is available only indoors.

We consider toys to be any concrete object that children can manipulate to carry out self-directed and meaningful play activities that are enjoyable for the process and not because they result in a product.

Sometimes teachers ask us why we call the things we study *toys*. To some, the term sounds dated. The trend is to use more education-related names when referring to what children play with in classrooms. For example, we have heard puzzles and blocks referred to as *instructional materials*. This may stem from a misconception among some administrators or policy makers that play and all things used in play are unimportant for learning. Some teachers try to assuage these concerns by changing their vocabulary. A kindergarten teacher summarized the problem this way: "I avoid using the *P*-word—*play*. It's just not appreciated anymore. We talk about *learning* centers and *learning* materials and *learning* time. That seems to satisfy everyone." We use the words *toys* and *play* in our research to communicate that they are fundamental aspects of childhood.

Why do we study toys? Toys influence various aspects of children's play. For example, some toys, such as pretend-play props and blocks, prompt more social interaction than other materials (Ivory & McCollum 1999; Elmore & Vail 2011). Toddlers and young preschoolers engage in more symbolic make-believe with realistic props, whereas older preschoolers perform more make-believe with nonrealistic objects such as blocks, nondescript rubber shapes, or paper towel rolls (Trawick-Smith 1993). A number of studies show that boys and girls often choose different, and sometimes gender-stereotyped, toys to play with (Cherney & Dempsey 2010; Francis 2010). These intriguing findings have led us to conduct our TIMPANI studies on a broad range of toys and to examine their impact on many different aspects of play.

How We Study Toys

Each year we ask parents, teachers, university faculty, and college students to nominate toys they would like us to study. We ask them to identify toys they believe are developmentally beneficial and enjoyable. Because types of toys vary depending on the manufacturer, we ask people to identify the specific brands of the toys they nominate. We screen the toys to eliminate any that are inappropriate for preschoolers—for example, board games that are too difficult for young children, war toys, or commercial action figures related to popular television programs or movies.

We then place each toy in four different preschool classrooms serving children and families of diverse cultural and socioeconomic backgrounds. We video record children's natural play with each toy for three days in each classroom, for a total of 240 hours of video. Two of us independently view the videos and rate each toy according to the quality of children's play, using a rating system developed in a previous research project (Trawick-Smith, Russell, & Swaminathan 2011). (See "Determining Quality of Play.") The two raters always have a high level of agreement in rating the toys. We then use a series of statistical analyses to determine whether differences in scores among the toys we studied are significant—that is, whether they are beyond what we would expect by chance.

TIMPANI Findings: Five Years of Toy Research

After studying toys for five years, we have identified toys that score high and low on our rating system. We have rarely found a toy that inspires high-quality play for all children all the time. Our most important finding, however, is that the impact of a particular toy on children's play is varied and complex. This is

Determining Quality of Play

What do we look for when we rate a toy? We assign the toy a score for each of the following dimensions of play:

- Does a child using the toy demonstrate **thinking and learning behaviors,** such as exploring objects, displaying facial expressions of deep concentration, and commenting on new concepts or discoveries?
- Does the child engage in **problem solving** with the toy, such as trying to overcome challenging obstacles and completing difficult tasks?
- Does the child show **curiosity** when playing with the toy, such as asking questions about its properties and uses or showing facial expressions of puzzlement or fascination?
- Does the child show **sustained interest,** such as persisting in play with the toy with minimal distraction?
- Does the child engage in **creative expression,** such as using the toy in a novel way or conveying unique ideas?
- Does the child enact **symbolic transformations,** such as using the toy to represent something completely different and engaging in pretend play?
- Does the child **collaborate and communicate** with peers when playing with the toy?
- Can the child **use the toy independently** without expressions of frustration or the need for adult assistance?

illustrated by the play with the rainbow people in the opening vignette. The children played with these figures in many different ways. The effect of the figures on the quality of children's play varied according to children's backgrounds and characteristics. From our studies we have drawn five important conclusions about toys that have implications for teachers of young children.

1. Children don't always choose to play with toys that inspire the highest quality play

A teacher we interviewed explained that she included certain toys in her classroom because "children absolutely love them." Although this is an important dimension of a toy, children's toy preferences and a toy's impact on play are two different things. Every year we identify toys that have positive effects on the quality of play but are rarely chosen by children during choice time. Alternatively we always find toys that are less likely to promote high-quality play but are very popular. The rainbow people exemplify this finding. They were one of the highest-scoring

toys for quality of play in the year we studied them, but children chose them less frequently than any other toy.

Implications for teachers. Careful observation of what children do with toys reveals their impact on play. Through observation, teachers can identify toys that children choose often and that also inspire high-quality play. In our research, large interlocking construction blocks and a wooden train set are examples of such toys. Many children were drawn to these toys and engaged in very high-quality play when using them.

Teachers might also learn that popular toys may have a less positive impact on play. However, through asking questions, modeling, and scaffolding play activities, teachers might enrich play with such toys. Some toys may promote high-quality play but are rarely used. Teachers might encourage more frequent play with such toys by introducing them with enthusiasm at group time, placing them in more prominent locations in the classroom, and modeling their use during choice time.

One other possible outcome of toy observation is that a toy may be neither used often nor supportive of quality play. Our research suggests that such toys exist—including some that are commonly found in preschools. Teachers can remove these toys from the classroom altogether or reintroduce them later in the year as children grow older and develop new skills and interests that are matches for those toys. Teachers can also try them again with another group in another year. Giving up on toys that have long been included in one's classroom can be difficult, but it may be necessary for some toys and some groups of preschoolers.

2. Children of different genders and from diverse backgrounds play with toys in different ways

One of the most important TIMPANI research findings is that how children play with toys is influenced by age, gender, culture, and socioeconomic status. As shown in the opening vignette, variations in play with rainbow people were highly related to gender and age. One year we found that a Play-Doh set with cutting, shaping, and rolling tools received higher scores on play quality when girls played with it, as compared to boys. In contrast, a marble run—a set of tracks and marbles—received higher scores when used by boys. Two collections of miniature toy vehicles—a set of wooden cars, trucks, and road signs and a wooden train set—received particularly high scores on play quality when Latino children and children from families with low incomes played with them.

A toy that is novel and engaging to a child with one set of experiences may be less inspiring to a child with different experiences.

Children of different genders and of diverse cultural and socioeconomic backgrounds may play with fewer or different kinds of toys in their homes. Their play styles and toy preferences may be shaped by their families' cultural beliefs. For example, some families highly value collective, collaborative interactions. Their children might be drawn to toys that inspire higher levels of social participation, such as toy vehicles and pretend-play sets that allow active interactions among many peers. A toy that is novel and engaging to a child with one set of experiences may be less inspiring to a child with different experiences. For example, a child who has played with many different types of construction materials since age 2 may be less excited about a new building set. A child who has had few opportunities to build with construction materials may be especially inspired by these toys.

Implications for teachers. In observing play with toys, teachers may find that some toys inspire higher quality play for girls than for boys or for children of particular cultural backgrounds. When teachers provide a balance of these toys, children of all cultures and both genders can have access to materials that prompt high levels of play quality. Teacher observations may also reveal a few toys that engender high-quality play for all children in the classroom. Examples from our studies of these universally effective toys include magnetic construction shapes and plastic tools. Identifying and providing such toys for preschoolers not only elevates play quality for all children, but may also promote richer cross-gender and cross-cultural play.

Our findings on the effects of toys on the play of children of diverse backgrounds also suggest a need to collaborate with families when choosing materials for the classroom. Teachers might ask families about which toys hold cultural meaning for them. Are there toys that reflect the family's cultural beliefs or practices? What toys did the adults play with when they were children? What toys did older siblings or cousins enjoy playing with? What family experiences do children enjoy? Teachers can then build on these experiences through the classroom play materials. A study conducted in Puerto Rico revealed that families have keen insights into the kinds of toys that inspire their children's play (Trawick-Smith 2010). In this investigation, families indicated that their children often engaged in elaborate family-oriented play with dolls, vehicles, and miniature people—toys not unlike the rainbow people described in the opening vignette. These family insights were borne out in later classroom observations.

3. Simple, open-ended toys promote higher quality play than realistic ones with only one use

Nearly all of the highest-scoring toys in our rating system have a simple design and can be used in many different ways. For example, children used Tinkertoys—one of our highest-scoring toys one year—to engage in a remarkable number of play activities. Children built various structures, used them as pretend-play props (magic wands and helicopters were particularly prevalent), and made rolling creations for block ramps. We observed one

group of children use large interlocking construction blocks—another high-scoring toy—to first build a house and then a cell phone, so the mother in the house could call her children. The uses of such toys are limited only by children's imaginations.

Open-ended toys that lead to high-quality play contribute more to academic outcomes than many educational toys.

Compare these examples to the way children used a talking telephone. This electronic toy carries on conversations with children and selects a theme for them by asking questions such as, "Do you want to go to the zoo?" It prompted the lowest levels of quality and popular play of any toy in our project.

We also found that so-called educational toys, such as a toy telephone that is supposed to teach language and numbers, do not often inspire high-quality play. These toys often have only one use, whether it is counting, recognizing letters, or naming animals. While children may find them interesting initially, they quickly abandon these toys during choice time. We have concluded that open-ended toys that lead to high-quality play contribute more to academic outcomes than many educational toys.

One simple open-ended toy scored higher than all others across all five years of our study: hardwood unit blocks. This will not surprise experienced preschool teachers. There is a good reason blocks have been a fixture in early childhood classrooms since Caroline Pratt designed them in 1913 (Tunks 2013). Blocks inspire construction, make-believe, artistic expression, motor play, and sorting and categorizing. We also found that children's language and social interactions improved more when playing with unit blocks than with any other toy.

Implications for teachers. These findings suggest that teachers can rely on *simple* and *open-ended* as criteria for selecting toys for the classroom. Teachers might ask, "How many different ways can children play with these toys?" "Will they inspire divergent and imaginative play themes as well as problem-solving activities? Or, will they restrict play to a narrow range of behaviors?"

4. Some effective toys inspire only one dimension of play; balance across toys is important

Over the course of the study we have identified toys that were exceptional in inspiring one or several aspects of play, but were far less effective in enhancing play in other areas. For example, wooden puzzles received high scores on three dimensions of our rating system (thinking/learning, problem solving, and sustaining attention) but low scores on creative expression, imagination, and social interaction. In contrast, collage materials received remarkably high ratings on creativity and imagination but relatively low scores on problem solving and social interaction. Teachers may choose to include these materials in their classrooms because they have powerful, if narrower, effects on play. Not all toys inspire play in all areas.

Implications for teachers. We recommend balance across toys so that children are inspired to engage in all critical dimensions of play. When equipping a classroom, teachers might provide a core group of toys that meets most or all play quality criteria and appeals to children of multiple backgrounds and characteristics. These could include, for example, blocks and other construction toys, toy vehicles, and plastic tools. Teachers might then add toys that are effective in enhancing one or more dimensions of play—art materials to promote creative expression; sorting and ordering materials, such as Montessori cylinder blocks, that enhance thinking and problem solving; and dramatic play props to encourage social interaction and language skills.

5. **Educators can offer families support in selecting toys for their children**

Many families possess good instincts about which toys their children will play with in meaningful ways (Trawick-Smith 2010); however, families sometimes ask for help in choosing toys. They may be misled by advertisements that make claims about a toy's learning value, uncertain about toys related to movies or television shows, or hesitant about action figures that come with special meals at fast food restaurants. Teachers can provide checklists, post articles, and lead workshops for families about choosing toys that benefit children's development. Teachers might think about holidays and birthdays when they share information. They can also share with individual families their observations of their child's classroom toy use.

Implications for teachers. When talking about toys, teachers should consider costs and guide families to less expensive but equally beneficial options. Many toys that effectively support high-quality play are expensive. However, we have found online relatively inexpensive facsimiles of most of our highest-scoring toys: train sets, wooden vehicles and road signs, smaller sets of interlocking blocks (without elaborate accessories), wooden blocks, and plastic tool sets. As long as the less expensive versions are safe, the toys will work well for play at home where there is less wear on them than in a classroom.

Final Thoughts: The Importance of Being Responsive

Our research has provided insights into the effects of toys on young children's play. It has also raised new questions. Ultimately our study shows that it is important for teachers to consider individual children's needs, skills, and interests when they select toys for their classrooms, just as they respond to individual children's

---

Memo to: Infant and Toddler Teachers Everywhere
From: Linda Gillespie and Rebecca Parlakian
Date: May 2014
Subject: Play—The True Work of Childhood

Play is often referred to as a child's work. As infant and toddler teachers know well, play is a profoundly important medium for learning and development for very young children. Beginning at birth, play unfolds in the context of a responsive, caring adult—that's you—who sets the stage for exploration by creating a safe base from which babies can explore. Through playful back-and-forth interaction with their important adults, including both family members and teachers, babies learn they are loved, important, and fun to be with. Discoveries made by infants and toddlers lay the foundation for critical social-emotional qualities such as self-confidence, self-esteem, a sense of identity, and the desire to relate to and connect with others—including their peers and favorite adults (like you and your colleagues). Children use these early social-emotional skills to establish and maintain reciprocal relationships all their lives.

Within a loving and supportive relationship, baby's play unfolds. During play, babies lift, drop, look, pour, bounce, hide, build, knock down, and more. They test key scientific concepts, such as the sounds various objects make when tossed off a high chair tray, and discover the function of objects (to roll, to pop up, or to be stacked). Between birth and age 3, children are developing mathematical concepts, including the concepts *all gone, more,* and *less,* and the meaning of *one* and *two.* Spatially, babies are experimenting by using shape sorters, nesting cups, and stacking blocks, and trying to fit their bodies into various spaces. They master language and literacy skills as they learn the sounds of their parents' and teachers' voices, discover the rules of conversation, and act out stories in dramatic play. All this learning during play is because you and other important adults take the time to respond, set up the environment, plan, and carefully observe babies' play.

Play is, indeed, the true work of childhood. When we observe carefully, it tells us what children know and what they are thinking about; what they are wondering, testing, and predicting; and, most importantly, what skills they are ready to master. And then we, as caring teachers, can plan and support their development and learning. Play is a joyful process of testing, learning, and discovery within supportive relationships with parents, teachers, providers, and peers. Play offers a path through which infants and toddlers gain the skills, knowledge, and joy in learning that prove essential to success in school and beyond.

Which Toys Promote High-Quality Play? Reflections on the Five-Year Anniversary of the TIMPANI Study by Jeffrey Trawick-Smith, et al.

111

needs in all other aspects of teaching. A single set of toys cannot meet the needs of all children in a classroom year after year. A child with specific interests, a unique temperament, or developmental disabilities, or who is from a particular culture, may require a unique collection of toys to inspire high-quality play. Observations of toy use, experimentation with new materials, and interviews with families help teachers find optimal combinations of toys that support all dimensions of play for all children.

Critical Thinking

1. Why is it important for teachers to consider individual children when selecting toys for their classroom?

2. Based on what you read in the article, choose three toys that you feel would be appropriate for a young child in your life. Why did you make those choices?

Internet References

Choosing Appropriate Toys and Equipment
   http://www.earlychildhoodnews.com/earlychildhood/article_view.aspx?ArticleID=222

Eastern Connecticut State University
   http://www.easternct.edu/cece/timpani.html

Good Toys for Young Children by Age and Stage
   http://www.naeyc.org/toys

TIMPANI Study on You Tube
   https://www.youtube.com/watch?v=PvTxz__-7qw

JEFFREY TRAWICK-SMITH, EdD, holds the Phyllis Waite Endowed Chair in Early Childhood Education at Eastern Connecticut State University. He has conducted numerous studies on young children's play and cultural diversity in early childhood development. trawick@easternct.edu

JENNIFER WOLFF, BS, served as a research assistant at Eastern and is a preschool teacher in the New Britain, Connecticut, public school system.

MARLEY KOSCHEL, BS, was a research assistant at Eastern and is a graduate assistant and master's degree student at Wheelock College in Boston.

JAMIE VALLARELLI, BS, was a research assistant at Eastern and is a kindergarten teacher in the Windham, Connecticut, public school system.

LINDA GILLESPIE, MS, at ZERO TO THREE, focuses on babies and families, and **REBECCA PARLAKIAN,** MA, promotes the healthy development of infants and toddlers as director of parenting resources at ZERO TO THREE.

Article   Prepared by: Karen Menke Paciorek, *Eastern Michigan University*

Bringing Boys and Girls Together

Supporting Preschoolers' Positive Peer Relationships

In Arizona, the weather allows children to enjoy outdoor play year-round. No matter what outdoor activities attract children's attention, I often notice the same pattern—boys play with boys, and girls play with girls. One morning, most of the boys gather around the large toy dump trucks, and a group of girls prepares for a birthday party in the sandbox. As the girls make cakes out of wet sand, a boy drives his truck over and stops to watch. Observing his interest, I wonder what I can do to help bring these preschoolers together.

HILLARY MANASTER AND MAUREEN JOBE

Learning Outcomes

After reading this article, you will be able to:

- Plan appropriate classroom experiences that will enable both sexes to play with peers of the same sex as well as the opposite.

- Share with colleagues suggestions for encouraging boys and girls playing together.

Children thrive in inclusive settings where each child is an important part of the community. When differences are celebrated and similarities discovered, children learn to value themselves, appreciate their peers, and develop meaningful and significant relationships with one another. A sizeable body of research indicates that promoting positive contact and cooperation between people of different groups (e.g., different ethnicity, race, developmental ability, or gender) can improve intergroup attitudes and relationships (Cameron & Rutland 2008; Gaertner et al. 2008).

Often the preschool years mark a child's introduction to the world of peers and peer relationships. Research supports the notion that children benefit in many ways from positive peer interactions. In early childhood programs, friendships foster a sense of connection and security and build self-esteem and self-confidence, helping young children adapt more readily to the preschool setting (Dunn 2004; Ladd 2009). Friendships provide important opportunities for children to learn and develop.

During the early years, friendships might appear to be constantly changing. We see 3-year-olds show preferences for playing with particular classmates, but at this age a friend is pretty much anyone with whom a child spends time. Three-year-olds might seek out a peer who is playing with something of interest or be attracted to outward appearances. Sometimes a friendship is motivated simply by physical proximity. We notice children bonding as they sit together at snack time or even when they find a classmate wearing similar clothing. Four- or five-year-olds tend to select friends with common interests and spend time together absorbed in an activity. Older preschoolers are curious about others and make efforts to connect and engage. During this stage, children participate in complex peer play more frequently and for longer stretches of time (Vandell, Nenide, & Van Winkle 2006).

Best practice emphasizes the importance of respecting and promoting diversity in children's play experiences and friendships (Derman-Sparks & Edwards 2010). A broad range of playmates exposes children to variety in their play experiences. When children try different activities and ways of communicating and interacting, they are better poised to develop the flexibility to interact successfully in a range of social groups and situations. The benefits of diversity in peer relationships are clear. So what can educators do when many children spend their time with only half of their peers—those of their own sex?

Friendships foster a sense of connection and security and build self-esteem and self-confidence, helping young children adapt more readily to the preschool setting.

Gender and Early Peer Relationships

As early as the preschool years, children tend to play with and befriend same-sex companions (Mehta & Strough 2009). This is a well-documented phenomenon known as *gender segregation,* which becomes even more prevalent across the elementary years and generally persists throughout life (Vandell, Nenide, & Van Winkle 2006; Mehta & Strough 2009). Although adults often dismiss gender segregation as part of childhood, one concern is that boys and girls may be socializing in different ways, learning and practicing relationship skills in isolation from one another. During preschool, the gender composition of peer groups impacts group size, proximity to (and supervision by) adults, and the types of activities in which children engage (Fabes, Martin, & Hanish 2003; Fabes et al. 2003). For example, groups of preschool boys tend to be larger, and they often play farther from adults and engage in more active play than girls' groups.

Acceptable or effective behaviors in one group may not be the same in a different peer group, and this could impact the success of interactions when children do come together. To illustrate, using an indirect request ("I need a crayon.") may be more successful with peers who have developed similar communication styles than with those who favor more direct means ("Give me a crayon."). With time and continual modeling and reinforcement by their same-sex peers, girls and boys in preschool seem to grow progressively different in their styles of behaving and relating—and even in their emerging cognitive and academic interests and skills (Fabes, Hanish, & Martin 2007; Martin & Dinella 2002). Researchers find that preschoolers who spend the most time in same-sex play are the most gender-stereotypical in their behaviors (e.g., in aggression and activity levels, in play with sex-typed toys, and in sex-typed activities) by the end of the school year (Martin & Fabes 2001).

Why Do Children Segregate?

Children are natural sorters—they tend to group people and things into simple categories in order to make sense of their world. Gender is a particularly salient category for grouping people because it is visual, concrete, and simple (Bigler & Liben 2007). It is also meaningful to preschoolers as they identify with and grow in their understanding of their own gender.

The ability to discriminate social categories such as gender is apparent from infancy, and children often view people perceived to be in the same category as being more similar to one another than they actually are. In fact, preschoolers commonly have *essentialist thinking,* meaning that they believe there is some innate characteristic that ties members of a group together and makes them similar (Gelman 2004). This leads them to exaggerate differences between people who are in the group and those who are not, making it hard for them to see what they have in common. For example, they may make overgeneralized assumptions that "boys are loud" rather than recognizing that there are some boys *and* girls who are louder and, conversely, some boys *and* girls who are more soft-spoken. Presumed

similarity to particular peers of the same sex plays a role in preschoolers' playmate choices (Martin et al. 2011).

Gender is a particularly salient category for grouping people because it is visual, concrete, and simple.

From infancy, children begin to develop gender schemas—cognitive representations of "maleness" and "femaleness" (Martin & Ruble 2004). These schemas grow, in large part, from children's observations of the world and the frequent associations they notice among particular people, behaviors, objects, and roles. Children also create schemas based on the direct or perceived messages they receive from adults, siblings, peers, the media, and others (Martin & Ruble 2004; Blaise & Taylor 2012). They develop a sense of what is "for me" and what is "not for me," and this can shape their choices and behaviors from the early preschool years (Zosuls, Lurye, & Ruble 2008). Gender schemas motivate behaviors that conform to these ideas, as well as guide assumptions, interpretations, and expectations about the people and experiences that children encounter (Blakemore, Berenbaum, & Liben 2009; Blaise & Taylor 2012).

> **"Pink is for girls, blue is for boys. That ball is pink, so it's for girls."**
> **"Boys like to play with cars. He must also like cars."**
> **"The girls always play games together in the playhouse. They probably won't let me play too."**

With this kind of thinking, it is no surprise that girls and boys often form inaccurate ideas about the other sex that can translate into less interest or even reluctance to engage with other-sex peers.

Bringing Boys and Girls Together

Teachers are in a unique position to cultivate children's cross-gender interactions and friendships. By intentionally planning and supporting certain experiences, educators can encourage children to build a social world characterized by meaningful relationships with peers of both sexes.

Tune In to Social Patterns

To purposefully increase engagement and interactions between boys and girls, teachers must tune in to the social patterns in the classroom. Systematic observation methods are useful, such as scanning the room or playground periodically and jotting down which children are playing together and where. Or teachers might pay attention to the dramatic play area or the sensory table and observe which children move in and out of these spaces and how they engage with one another. Or they might focus on one or two children for a day, noting with whom they interact and how.

Processing classroom observations using prior knowledge of the children and the classroom community guides the teachers' next approaches. For example, knowing that 4-year-old Madeline tends to play with just a few girls and is easily overwhelmed by noise and activity, the teacher should be thoughtful in deciding when and how to encourage Madeline to interact with peers with whom she might not normally engage, including boys. The teacher might choose a quiet, calm activity such as puzzles, and set up a buddy center for collaborative play. This may gently encourage Madeline to join in play with new classmates. When teachers intentionally use observation and reflection skills over time, the skills become effortless and raise awareness of gender issues when organizing children's experiences with classmates.

Take Action

Teachers can create opportunities that bring boys and girls together—to communicate, cooperate, play, and learn with one another. After noticing a boy and a girl building quietly with blocks next to each other, the teacher might introduce a stuffed dog and wonder aloud if it needs a home. If it becomes apparent through classroom observation that the playhouse and the tool bench tend to polarize children by sex, a teacher could move these materials closer together. She could create an opportunity to combine interests by asking if the playhouse needs repairs. When used in an intentional but flexible manner, simple strategies such as reorganizing the classroom environment, introducing a small change to an activity, or simply commenting when children appear to be enjoying time spent working or playing together (with the emphasis on *together*) can increase engagement between boys and girls.

Address Exclusion

At choice time in the 4s classroom, Trayvon races to the top of the loft and announces, "I'm a doctor!" "Me too!" exclaims Matthew, who joins him in gathering the doctor tools scattered around the "office." As Reanna climbs the stairs announcing, "I am a doctor too!" the boys respond in unison, "No girls allowed in the loft!"

Although it's okay to choose to play alone or with just a few friends, it is not okay to exclude others because they are different. Exclusion also happens when children take on the role of gender police ("We're playing with our babies, and boys can't be mommies."). It is important to address these occurrences. Gender exclusion is just as hurtful and unfair as exclusion based on any other characteristic, leaving children feeling rejected and potentially perpetuating gender stereotypes.

We might even create girl/boy divisions ourselves—by declaring, for example, that it is the "girls' turn in the block area" in an effort to encourage girls to expand their play. Such well-intentioned practices serve to separate boys and girls and reinforce the notion that they are different. In fact, just using gendered language in the classroom can send this message as well.

"Boys, please line up at the door."
"Girls at the square table and boys at the round table for center time."
"Good morning, boys and girls!"

Tips for Bringing Boys and Girls Together

Create an inclusive setting.
Communicate the expectation that boys and girls can and should be friends.

Explain your zero tolerance for gender-based (or other) teasing, exclusion, and bullying.

Be mindful of your words and actions about cross-sex friendships around children.

Be aware of the information and messages children receive from other sources. For example, eliminate books, posters, and other classroom materials that polarize boys and girls.

Increase contact, cooperation, and collaboration.
Intentionally plan boy/girl work and play opportunities, including those with a common goal.

Pair other-sex peers as partners without calling attention to gender.

Guide and assist children in discovering ways to integrate each others' ideas.

Model blending of interests. For example, a group of children engaging in superhero play could be brought together with children playing restaurant to create a superhero restaurant where everyone could be challenged to invent superhero food.

Adjust the environment.
Adjust activities to promote engagement between other-sex peers. For example, provide opportunities for cross-gender, small-group work focusing on one goal, such as completing a puzzle.

Organize the classroom to encourage children with different interests to play in closer proximity.

Provide positive examples of cross-gender relationships through children's literature and classroom materials.

We wouldn't use characteristics such as race or religion to label children in such a manner (Blaise & Taylor 2012), so why use gender?

Ensuring that all children feel accepted and welcomed—by everyone—supports a positive classroom environment. In an inclusive classroom, children and teachers celebrate diversity and discover similarities and common interests. When we take action to help children focus on their common interests, we create opportunities for girls and boys to share positive experiences with one another—and this may encourage them to seek each other out in the future.

I hear the boys' remark to Reanna, then see her begin to climb down. I ask the doctors, "What are those stickers for?" Trayvon answers, "You give them out when you give shots!" I comment that Reanna has

stickers too. "We're all doctors!" they say together. When I tell them that I am a patient ready for my appointment, they all begin working together to care for me. Later at circle time, we talk about how nice it is to include others in our play and how good it feels when we're included.

Together but Apart

At small group time, six preschool children hurry over to the table, excited to juice oranges. I have placed six hand squeezers and cups around the table, along with a large bowl of orange halves. The children each take a seat in front of a squeezer and begin earnestly examining their tool.

When preschool children are together but not engaged with each other and appear to be content in their play, it may be tempting to leave well enough alone. However, we can take action by making simple changes in an activity to orient children to one another and provide opportunities for interaction and collaboration. When girls and boys work and play together in positive ways, they discover common ground and practice negotiation, cooperation, and communication skills with one another.

I wonder how to make the orange squeezer activity more collaborative. After a few minutes, I gather the squeezers and pull out a cup of colored sticks. I hand out the sticks to intentionally form mixed-sex partnerships, and I ask everyone to find the person with the matching color. The children are excited! To encourage teamwork and cooperation, I give one squeezer to each pair of children. The partners immediately start talking and figuring out how to take turns squeezing the oranges and holding the cup.

Friendships

Since the beginning of the school year, 4-year-olds Juan and Rachel have become best friends over dump truck racing and falling down to make each other laugh. One morning Rachel's father tells me that a play date with Juan is planned for that afternoon. I am surprised to see that Rachel's face has fallen. She tugs on her father's sleeve and whispers, "I don't want to go to Juan's house." As Rachel runs off to the swing set, I mention that she seems reluctant about the play date. Her father explains that she protested during the entire ride to school. He suspects this is due to another child's teasing Rachel and Juan about loving each other and getting married.

Being aware of and reflecting on the messages children hear—whether from the media, peers, parents, or teachers—helps us understand the meaning children make about friendships with the other sex. Clearly, 4-year-olds are not in romantic relationships with one another. However, well-meaning but teasing comments that suggest this ("Oh, look how cute they

are together! They're boyfriend and girlfriend.") can confuse and embarrass children or even end a friendship. It is important to take action and help children focus on what it means to be a friend (especially if they themselves are the ones declaring the romance). Additionally, children benefit from seeing examples of girls and boys in healthy, balanced (equal roles), nonromantic relationships. Children's literature, personal stories, videos, and photographs are wonderful tools for this.

During circle time we talk about friendship—who can be a friend, what makes a good friend, and what you do to be a good friend. I share a story about my daughter Megan's best friend in kindergarten, David. The children are fascinated, so I promise to bring in a picture of the duo the next day. Although the play date gets cancelled, Rachel and Juan are back dump truck racing together on the playground that afternoon.

Concluding Thoughts

Although the long-term consequences of sex segregation and integration remain areas for research, it is clear children benefit from different-gender peer interactions. Such experiences give children opportunities to learn from and about others, to develop attitudes of respect and acceptance, and to broaden their social competence. With intentional planning, attention to classroom environment, activities, and routine practices, and with support for children in their interactions and relationships, teachers can create and foster opportunities for peer experiences between boys and girls. This helps build relationships that are meaningful, positive, and successful for all children.

References

Bigler, R.S., & L.S. Liben. 2007. "Developmental Intergroup Theory: Explaining and Reducing Children's Social Stereotyping and Prejudice." *Current Directions in Psychological Science* 16(3): 162–66.

Blaise, M., & A. Taylor. 2012. "Using Queer Theory to Rethink Gender Equity in Early Childhood Education." *Young Children* 67(1): 88–98.

Blakemore, J.E.O., S.A. Berenbaum, & L.S. Liben. 2009. *Gender Development*. Clifton, NJ: Psychological Press.

Cameron, L., & A. Rutland. 2008. "An Integrative Approach to Changing Children's Intergroup Attitudes." Chap. 12 in *Intergroup Attitudes and Relations in Childhood through Adulthood*, eds. S.R. Levy & M. Killen, 191–203. New York: Oxford University Press.

Derman-Sparks, L., & J.O. Edwards. 2010. *Anti-Bias Education for Young Children and Ourselves*. Washington, DC: NAEYC.

Dunn, J. 2004. *Children's Friendships: The Beginnings of Intimacy*. Malden, MA: Blackwell.

Fabes, R.A., L.D. Hanish, & C.L. Martin. 2007. "Peer Interactions and the Gendered Social Ecology of Preparing Young Children for School." *Early Childhood Services* 1(3): 205–18.

Fabes, R.A., C.L. Martin, & L.D. Hanish. 2003. "Young Children's Play Qualities in Same-, Other-, and Mixed-Sex Peer Groups." *Child Development* 74(3): 921–32.

Fabes, R.A., C.L. Martin, L.D. Hanish, M.C. Anders, & D.A. Madden-Derdich. 2003. "Early School Competence: The Roles of Sex-Segregated Play and Effortful Control." *Developmental Psychology* 39(5): 848–59.

Gaertner, S.L., J.F. Dovidio, R. Guerra, M. Rebelo, M.B. Monteiro, B.M. Rick, & M.A. Houlette. 2008. "The Common In-Group Identity Model: Applications to Children and Adults." Chap. 13 in *Intergroup Attitudes and Relations in Childhood through Adulthood,* eds. S.R. Levy & M. Killen, 204–219. New York: Oxford University Press.

Gelman, S.A. 2004. "Psychological Essentialism in Children." *Trends in Cognitive Science* 8(9): 404–409. www.wjh.harvard.edu/~lds/readinggroup/Gelman2004tics.pdf.

Ladd, G.W. 2009. "Trends, Travails, and Turning Points in Early Research on Children's Peer Relationships: Legacies and Lessons for Our Time?" Chap. 2 in *Handbook of Peer Interactions, Relationships, and Groups,* eds. K.H. Rubin, W.M. Bukowski, & B. Laursen, 20–41. New York: Guilford.

Martin, C.L., & L. Dinella. 2002. "Children's Gender Cognitions, the Social Environment, and Sex Differences in Cognitive Domains." Chap. 8 in *Biology, Society, and Behavior: The Development of Gender Differences in Cognition,* eds. A.V. McGillicuddy-De Lisi & R. De Lisi, 207–39. Westport, CT: Ablex.

Martin, C.L. & R.A. Fabes. 2001. "The Stability and Consequences of Young Children's Same-Sex Peer Interactions." *Developmental Psychology* 37(3): 431–46. www.apa.org/pubs/journals/releases/dev-373431.pdf.

Martin, C.L., R.A. Fabes, L. Hanish, S. Leonard, & L.M. Dinella. 2011. "Experienced and Expected Similarity to Same-Gender Peers: Moving Toward a Comprehensive Model of Gender Segregation." *Sex Roles* 65(5): 421–434.

Martin, C.L. & D. Ruble. 2004. "Children's Search for Gender Cues: Cognitive Perspectives on Gender Development." *Current Directions in Psychological Science* 13(2): 67–70.

Mehta, C.M., & J. Strough. 2009. "Sex Segregation in Friendships and Normative Contexts Across the Lifespan." *Developmental Review* 29(3): 201–20.

Vandell, D.L., L. Nenide, & S.J. Van Winkle. 2006. "Peer Relationships in Early Childhood." Chap. 22 in *The Blackwell Handbook of Early Childhood Development,* eds. K. McCartney & D. Phillips, 455–70. New York: Blackwell.

Wanerman, T., L. Roffman, & C. Britton. 2011. *Including One, Including All: A Guide to Relationship-Based Inclusion.* St. Paul, MN: Redleaf.

Zosuls, K.M., L.E. Lurye, & D.N. Ruble. 2008. "Gender: Awareness, Identity, and Stereotyping." In *Encyclopedia of Infant and Early Childhood Development,* eds. M.M. Haith & J.B. Benson, vol. 2, 1–13. Oxford, UK: Elsevier.

Critical Thinking

1. Observe in a classroom serving three- and four-year-old children. What do you see that indicates the sexes are playing separately? Does the classroom teacher make any efforts to encourage the children to play together?

2. Develop a list of some of your favorite childhood memories of playing with friends. Write the names of the friends down. Did you have friends of mostly the same sex as yourself or did you have friends from both sexes?

Create Central

www.mhhe.com/createcentral

Internet References

Association for Childhood Education International (ACEI)
www.acei.org

Awesome Library for Teachers
www.awesomelibrary.org/teacher.html

Busy Teacher's Café
www.busyteacherscafe.com

National Association for the Education of Young Children
www.naeyc.org

Teacher Planet
http://teacherplanet.com

Teacher Quick Source
www.teacherquicksource.com

Teachers Helping Teachers
www.pacificnet.net/~mandel

You Can Handle Them
www.disciplinehelp.com

HILLARY MANASTER, MEd, is a program manager at the Sanford Harmony Program at Arizona State University in Tempe. Hillary worked as an early elementary school teacher for 10 years and has spent the past five years focusing on supporting early social and emotional development. hillary.manaster@asu.edu. **MAUREEN JOBE**, MEd, is a second grade teacher at the Arizona State University Preparatory Academy in Phoenix. Maureen has taught young children for 19 years in inclusive preschool and elementary settings. maureen.jobe@asu.edu.

Manaster, Hillary; Jobe, Maureen. From *Young Children,* November 2012, pp. 12–17. Copyright © 2012 by National Association for the Education of Young Children. Reprinted by permission. www.naeyc.org.

Article   Prepared by: Karen Menke Paciorek, *Eastern Michigan University*

CHAOS in Kindergarten?

JENNA BILMES

Learning Outcomes

After reading this article, you will be able to:

- Explain why social and emotional skills are so important for children to develop as a tool to assist them in adjusting to kindergarten.

- Name effective strategies for developing relationships and connections with young children.

Let's consider two children any kindergarten teacher will recognize:

Alejandro is a bundle of energy as he enters the classroom. After a quick "Hi" to his teacher, he tosses his things into his cubby and joins a group of friends who've discovered the new magnets. Hearing the teacher's signal for circle time, Alejandro says to his buddies, "Put them back in the box. We gotta go!" In a moment, he's on his sit-upon, singing the Good Morning Song.

Emma enters the classroom, ignoring the teacher's friendly greeting. As she jams her belongings into her overstuffed cubby, she steps over her lunch box, which has tumbled to the floor. Just after Emma joins the children in the writing center, a child in the group calls for help because Emma is grabbing her things. Ignoring the teacher's redirection to come to another area, Emma slaps at a girl and pushes a basket of markers to the floor. "It's going to be another one of those days," the teacher sighs.

We all know these two children. Alejandro is typical of many kindergarten students. He demonstrates self-regulation, plays well with others, contributes to the classroom community, and follows rules. On the other hand, children like Emma struggle through the day, leaving behind them a trail of chaos and bad feelings.

Although most kindergartners are more like Alejandro, the Emmas aren't a tiny minority. Ten percent of kindergartners show behavior problems or disrupt their class.[1] This number triples for at-risk children. And children with self-control problems rarely succeed academically.

It's not only the Emmas who suffer. With all a teacher has to accomplish during the kindergarten year, having students who lack the skills to "do school" is a real challenge. Other students are also hampered by the frequent drama. But once teachers stop thinking of disruptive children as naughty and instead think of them as lacking social and emotional skills, we can see the situation as no more challenging than teaching the basics of reading and mathematics.

Just as educators have identified key language and literacy skills—like phonological awareness—that underlie children's ability to learn to read, researchers have identified key social and emotional skills that underlie children's ability to succeed in school. And just as we've learned how to strengthen students' foundational skills in cognitive domains, we can help students like Emma build the interpersonal skills they need to move successfully through the school day.

Teaching social and emotional skills—taking students from where they are to where they need to be—is similar to teaching skills in any domain. To become increasingly competent, children need to feel both capable of and excited about learning. They need a supportive environment, multiple activities, and sufficient practice to internalize skills like how to develop relationships and how to resist the urge to grab something they want. Let's consider how teachers can help early elementary students develop four key skills: building adult-child relationships, belonging to a group, regulating themselves, and adapting "home" behaviors to fit classroom expectations.

Relationships with Teachers

Jacob has no use for adults at school. He runs away from the playground monitor, frequently reminds the music teacher "you're not the boss of me," and pulls away when his classroom teacher tries to give him an affectionate pat.

Students tend to behave well for teachers they like and who like them. Unfortunately, children like Jacob have a knack for behaving in very unlikeable ways. They make it difficult for adults to like them, which exacerbates their defiance over time. And a history of unpleasant interactions with adults gets in the way of a child's ability to see adults as valuable resources to support learning. The teacher's task, then, is twofold: to build relationships with kids who pull away and to help these children see teachers as valuable resources.

The way we build mutually affectionate, respectful relationships with kids isn't much different from the way we'd build relationships with a new friend or coworker. Intentionally weave opportunities to build personal connections into the school day.

Invite your Jacob to help you carry the crate of balls back from the playground, using those minutes together to talk about last weekend's activities. As your class walks to the library, walk beside him and ask about favorite books, or whether he has any pets at home, or where the sticker on his shirt came from. Send a message to the student that you truly enjoy these chats—and his company. This is one of the most effective ways to improve a student's cooperation.

Once you develop a mutually caring relationship with a young child, you'll find she has a vested interest in living up to your expectations. So when she behaves inappropriately, you'll be in a position to help her reflect on what happened and work alongside her to plan alternative ways to handle the situation next time. Before responding punitively, think about the kind of response you'd appreciate from your supervisor if you made an error at work. Say things like, "It's OK. We all make mistakes. Let's talk about what went wrong." End with a message of trust: "I know you can learn how to do this."

Belonging

Madison does well when she can work side by side with one other child in the classroom. However, whenever she's assigned to a work station with three or four other children, she hoards materials, gets into spats, and causes enough ruckus that the teacher sends her away from the area to work by herself.

Children enter the classroom community at different levels of social competence. Some can easily navigate working in groups; others are still mastering working in pairs. Set up areas in the classroom where students can work alone, in pairs, or in small groups. Allow your Madison to work at a smaller table. Help her learn large-group skills by inviting her to join you at a table with a big group from time to time, so you can model and facilitate successful interactions.

Sherry has a different belonging issue: When the class works together to clean up the classroom, Sherry inevitably responds to the teacher's request to throw away a stray paper towel or wash out the paint cups with, "Why do I have to do that? I didn't use it." Working cooperatively for the good of the classroom community is foreign to her.

When we facilitate children's attachment to trusted adults, we help them become more amenable to adult guidance. And when we help children identify themselves as belonging to the classroom family, we create in them a desire to work and play cooperatively with others in the community and to conform to classroom expectations.

Most young children are naturally drawn to exclusive clubs. Build on this attraction. Work together to create a name for your class and a community symbol, such as a class flag, that you hang on the wall. Write a class pledge that students will recite each day, such as, "The Sunshine Bears are kind. The Sunshine Bears are helpful. The Sunshine Bears stay safe." As your Sherry begins to identify herself as a member of the classroom community, she'll be more likely to look out for others and work cooperatively—and wash out paint cups she didn't use.

Self-regulation

Demarco is a tangle of energy with his hands on everyone and everything. He rocks his chair back and forth, often tipping it over to the delight of the other children. He pokes his neighbors during group time, disrupting everyone's learning.

Most young children are not programmed to stay still for extended periods of time. Pushing against a child's nature to be in motion invites disruptive behavior. Unfortunately, teachers often instinctively react to their Demarcos by making them lose outdoor time or sitting them down to "think about" their behavior. Research indicates that the reverse might be a better strategy; getting kids active leads to improved concentration and learning.[2]

Get all students out of their seats for frequent "brain breaks" before doing concentrated cognitive tasks. Have kids march around the room to upbeat music, do a quick round of freeze dancing, or play Simon Says.

Add extra physical tasks for your Demarco. Have him fetch the storybook from your desk, erase the whiteboard, or pick up all the carpet squares. Look for "heavy work" like helping to move a table or carrying a box of books.

Demarco also acts before he thinks. If somebody bumps him, he strikes out; if he sees something he wants, he takes it. He gets angry and uses profanity.

Impulsive children like Demarco seem to thrive in a physically well-ordered environment, with clearly labeled boxes, baskets, and shelves and lots of white space on the walls. Rituals and predictable routines, along with a daily schedule posted at students' eye level, help impulsive kids organize their days without feeling anxious. Use masking tape or adhesive dots to assign an impulsive student a specific place in line or in the circle at group time.

Transitions can be particularly challenging for impulsive kids. Help them stay organized and out of trouble by giving them specific tasks, like pushing in all the chairs or wiping down the tables. When you see a student bouncing around the room, get down to her level and ask, "What's your plan?" A plan can be as simple as "I'm getting a drink." One quick question and response is often enough to get an impulsive student back on track.

When a student's impulsive action has resulted in damage, help him or her do an instant replay. Together, reconstruct how the problem began and walk through what *did* happen and what might have happened if the student had made a different choice. Many children benefit from physically reenacting an event, this time making a better behavior choice.

Adaptability

"I feel like I spend half of my time reminding children of the rules," Ms. Benson complained. Pointing to a group in the corner, she added, "Especially those three. How many times do I have to repeat myself?"

It's frustrating when children fail to adapt their "home" behaviors to meet classroom expectations. Sooner or later, most students conform to expectations. But for others, adaptation is much more difficult. We can help these children by letting all students participate in creating classroom guidelines, helping them understand what those guidelines look like in practice, and enforcing guidelines consistently.

For kindergartners, it's best to begin with three or so guiding principles of behavior, or "big rules." Big rules should be overarching ideas that reflect a life compass. They should be rules that apply not only to young children, but also to everyone. Three big rules you might start with are "We take care of ourselves. We take care of one another. We take care of our world."

Introduce these rules to students one at a time over a series of days. Write, "We take care of ourselves" on a piece of chart paper and invite children to give examples of what that looks like. You might ask, "How can we keep ourselves safe?" or "How might we help ourselves learn new things?" Record students' ideas on the chart and add to the list during the school year.

Many children benefit from reenacting an event, this time making a better behavior choice.

Students will suggest things like washing hands, brushing teeth, or paying attention. These examples might be called little rules. When redirecting children, use a little rule/big rule format: "Adrian, give the paper back to Marcella. Remember, we take care of each other" or "Let's all pick up papers from the playground. We need to take care of our world."

Be careful about giving children three warnings ("You have until the count of three. . .."). We might think giving a grace period is kind, but for some children it leads to a misunderstanding. Most children will hear "This is your first warning: Stop splashing water on the floor" as "Stop splashing water on the floor."

However, if you consistently give three warnings before you act, a few children will think, "I can keep splashing until she gives her final warning." It's not that they're defiant. Rather, they understand your real rule—that you'll allow the action to go on for a while longer. Help students understand your rules by always saying what you mean and meaning what you say.

Why Take Time?

Some may argue that with all that teachers have to teach, we have no time to spend on these strategies. In reality, when we don't invest time to teach students social and emotional skills, we opt to be interrupted month after month with defiance, bickering, and worse. We can spend our time reacting to disruptive

behaviors, or we can invest our time in helping students gain social and emotional competencies so they can manage their own behavior. The choice is ours.

Notes

1. West, J., Denton, K., & Reaney, L. M. (2001). *The kindergarten year: Findings from the Early Childhood Longitudinal Study, kindergarten class of 1998–1999* (NCES 2001-023). Washington, DC: U.S. Department of Education. As cited in Raver, C. C., & Knitze, J. (2002). *Ready to enter: What research tells policymakers about strategies to promote social and emotional school readiness among three- and four-year-olds.* New York: National Center for Children in Poverty.

2. Ratey, J. J. (2008). *Spark: The revolutionary new science of exercise and the brain.* New York: Hachette.

Critical Thinking

1. What are three effective teaching techniques teachers could use in their classroom to help children self-regulate?

2. Ask a few teachers of young children for a list of their classroom rules. Ask how the rules were developed and are they effective in guiding behavior? What would you consider when developing rules for your own classroom?

Create Central

www.mhhe.com/createcentral

Internet References

Preventing Challenging Behaviors
  http://challengingbehavior.org/do/resources/documents/rph_preventing_challenging_behavior.pdf
Child Welfare League of America (CWLA)
  www.cwla.org
Children, Youth and Families Education and Research Network
  www.cyfernct.org
Early Childhood Care and Development
  www.ecdgroup.com
First Signs
  http://firstsigns.org
National Association for the Education of Young Children
  www.naeyc.org
National Center on Response to Intervention
  www.rti4success.org

JENNA BILMES (jbilmes@gmail.com) is a program associate with WestEd Child and Family Services and an early childhood consultant. She is the author of *Beyond Behavior Management: The Six Life Skills Children Need* (Redleaf, 2012).

Article

Prepared by: Karen Menke Paciorek, *Eastern Michigan University*

Assessing Young Children's Learning and Development

The process of assessment is different from the common perception of testing.

JACQUELINE JONES

Learning Outcomes

After reading this article, you will be able to:

- Describe the role of the school administrator and teachers in ensuring all assessment procedures will provide the information needed to differentiate the learning for each child.

- Share with someone not in education the way standards, curriculum, and assessment work together.

A new class of young children enters kindergarten. They are wide-eyed, curious, and energetic. Yet, teachers, administrators, and parents are grappling with a host of questions: Are all the children ready for school? Do they have the skills necessary to be successful in school and in life? What do the teachers and parents need to do so that each child is prepared to succeed in kindergarten and beyond? How will each child perform when he or she reaches third grade and starts taking tests used for accountability decisions?

To answer these questions, teachers need to understand how young children are developing, as well as what children should know and are able to do on an ongoing basis. However, getting meaningful answers to these questions is a complex process that requires strong and informed administrative leadership. It is the principal who sets the tone for teachers, parents, and children; allocates resources; and guides the assessment process to ensure that assessment results lead to implementation of appropriate instructional programs that ultimately result in stronger health, social-emotional, and cognitive outcomes for young children.

Assessment and Testing

Understanding the rapid and episodic learning and development of young children is a complex undertaking. In the early years, each child experiences the most dramatic developmental and learning period in his or her lifetime. In addition, there is marked variability among children in the rate and pattern of typical development. Motor, social-emotional, and cognitive development can follow different trajectories among young children. Yet, effective teaching and learning depends on the teacher's power of observation, the ability to document those observations, and the ability to implement an extensive repertoire of assessment strategies in a developmentally appropriate manner.

Assessment has become an intensely debated issue in educational discourse. There are those who believe that assessment of any kind is antithetical to good early childhood practice. This perspective lies in opposition to the notion that test results are the primary window into understanding young children's learning and program effectiveness.

In the early childhood context, assessment is the ongoing process of collecting information about young children's learning in order to make informed instructional and programmatic decisions. According to this definition, some form of assessment is happening most of the time in early learning environments. When adults observe children's social interactions, engage in conversations with children, and scrutinize drawings and constructions, they are looking for indications of how children are making sense of the world and how they are expressing that understanding. Each day as teachers and families interact with young children, they are assessing, either formally or informally, how language skills are developing, whether motor coordination seems on track, and if social interactions are appropriate. Without continuous observations of children and the products of their work and play, adults have no way of knowing when to provide the correct pronunciation or definition of a word; when to provide a set of experiences that will support the child's understanding of an emerging concept; or when to model appropriate social interactions.

The process of assessment is different from the common perception of testing, which is a more formal method of collecting information about learning and development that is sometimes norm-referenced and strictly administered. The challenge lies in determining which method of assessment should be used and what is the most accurate interpretation and use of the results.

Standards Lead the Process

Regardless of the type of instrument used, the assessment process should not exist in isolation. It must be firmly grounded in an agreed-upon set of standards, guidelines, or expectations about what young children should know and are able to do at certain phases in their lives. Early learning standards must guide the assessment questions—not the reverse. What young children should know and do and what dispositions toward learning are important for success in school and in life constitute the developmental and educational questions that must be answered before assessment strategies are selected.

All states and the District of Columbia have preschool early learning standards, and about half have developed standards for infants and toddlers. These standards should cover a range of domains. The 1995 National Education Goals Panel report outlines domains such as physical well-being and motor development, social-emotional development, approaches toward learning, language development, cognition, and general knowledge. Also, these standards should be developmentally appropriate, reflect the most current early childhood research, and be clear and understandable to early childhood professionals, school administrators, families, the community, and policymakers.

Think Assessment Systems

Once developmentally appropriate standards have been established, the assessment question can be posed: How will we know that children are learning what we want them to learn? However, the answer to this question does not rest on the results of any single assessment instrument. Rather, a carefully considered set of questions, a comprehensive set of assessment strategies, and a systematic approach are required. The first and perhaps the most important task is to clearly define the purpose of the assessment in order to select the best instrument available for that use and for the target group. The intent of the assessment process might be to answer additional questions such as:

- What is the health, social-emotional, and cognitive status of children as they enter kindergarten?
- Do all children have the basic visual, auditory, and cognitive skills to be successful in school?
- Are all children entering kindergarten with the skills they need to be successful in school?
- Do any individual children require modifications to the teacher's instructional plan?
- How do all children, including sub-groups of children, compare with similar groups of children in other states, nationwide, and internationally?
- What resources are in place to support program quality as cohorts of children navigate through the system?

Answers to these and other questions require the design and implementation of comprehensive early learning assessment systems that are aligned to high-quality early learning standards, reflect a broad range of domains, and can assist teachers and administrators in monitoring and improving the learning and development for young children.

Based on early learning standards, a comprehensive assessment system contains information about the process and context of young children's learning and development. These systems include a range of assessment tools that can answer multiple questions in order to promote learning and development. Components of a comprehensive early learning assessment system follow.

Screening and Referral Measures

High-quality tools used to determine whether all children in the program have adequate physical, cognitive, visional, and auditory functioning to be successful.

Kindergarten Entry Assessments

An evaluation of the status of children's learning and development conducted upon kindergarten entry to provide a benchmark of how children are progressing across a broad range of domains. The results of kindergarten entry assessments are used to guide the teacher's planning for individual children and to improve program effectiveness.

Ongoing Formative Assessments

Ongoing developmentally appropriate assessments to monitor children's progress and guide and improve instructional practice. These assessments are typically linked directly to the classroom instructional program.

Measures of Environmental Quality and Adult-Child Interaction

Indicators of the overall quality of early learning environments and of the quality of interactions between teachers and children.

Standardized Norm-Referenced Assessments

Well-designed, valid, and reliable measures that provide information on how a specific group of children is progressing compared with a comparable group of children.

Overall, the repertoire of assessment tools should have a clear purpose, define the use of the assessment results, and reflect the standards of quality outlined in the 1999 *Standards for Educational and Psychological Testing* developed by the American Educational Research Association, American Psychological Association, and National Council on Measurement in Education. Data from assessment results should be used to inform continuous program improvement, including decisions regarding the effectiveness of the instructional program, the allocation of resources, and the nature and scope of professional development. The process itself should yield the maximum amount of information with minimal intrusion on instructional time. Strong leadership is needed to guarantee that assessment results are viewed by teachers, families, and children as indicators of progress in meeting the standards.

Leadership Matters

The design and implementation of a successful, comprehensive, early learning assessment system depends on strong administrative leadership. Teachers need professional development, support, and encouragement as the school culture adopts an attitude of inquiry around children's learning and development. The traditional fear of assessment must be replaced with a realistic understanding of the strengths and limitations of assessment instruments and a focus on appropriate interpretation and use of the results.

A comprehensive assessment system will not rely on the findings of a single measure. Rather, if teachers are engaged in continuous observation and documentation of how children are meeting the standards, any standardized measure should be viewed as verification of the ongoing formative assessment process. Any surprises should be carefully examined and understood to determine where misalignment with the standards might have occurred. Young children should never feel pressure to achieve a particular test score; they should be comfortable demonstrating what they know in both informal and formal settings.

The power of leadership was outlined by Joesph Murphy in his 2001 presentation on *Leadership for Literacy,* where he listed leaders' responsibilities:

- Establishing clearly defined, challenging, and public standards that are the focus of all activities;
- Creating a shared belief that all children can learn and that educators have the knowledge, skill, and resources to effectively teach;
- Guiding the assessment system;
- Providing the expertise to ensure that teachers are implementing programs that can help children meet the standards;
- Providing, honoring, and protecting the time teachers and staff need to carry out their work;
- Creating a system of monitoring progress toward the specified goals and ensuring that this information is used and understood;
- Providing for a coherent system of professional development activities;
- Maintaining a district administration that minimizes rapid staff turnover; and
- Creating an educational partnership between school and home.

Meaningful understanding of young children's learning requires setting the best early learning standards possible, asking the right questions about children's growth and development, deciding which assessment strategies will best answer those questions, and using the results in ways that promote effective teaching and improved learning. Yet none of this can be developed and sustained without strong leadership that sets the goals, provides the resources to meet the goals, and promotes and fosters assessment literacy to ensure that teachers and administrators understand the assessment process and know how to use it thoughtfully so that, ultimately, all children experience success in school and throughout their lives.

Critical Thinking

1. One of the assessment tools described by the author on the last page of the article is "Measures of Environmental Quality and Adult-Child Interaction." What specifically would you look for when evaluating the environment of a kindergarten classroom? What materials would you want to see in those classrooms?
2. What makes assessing young children so challenging compared to children in the older grades? What can teachers do to ensure an accurate assessment picture of each child is compiled?

Create Central

www.mhhe.com/createcentral

Internet References

Association for Childhood Education International (ACEI)
    www.acei.org
Common Core State Standards Initiative
    www.corestandards.org
HighScope Educational Research Foundation
    www.highscope.org
Idea Box
    http://theideabox.com
Mid-Continent Research for Education and Learning
    www2.mcrel.org/compendium
National Association for the Education of Young Children
    www.naeyc.org
The Perpetual Preschool
    www.perpetualpreschool.com

JACQUELINE JONES is the senior adviser to the secretary for early learning at the U.S. Department of Education.

Jones, Jacqueline. From *Principal*, vol. 90, no. 5, May/June 2011, pp. 13–15. Copyright © 2011 by National Association of Elementary School Principals. Reprinted by permission.

Article Prepared by: Karen Menke Paciorek, *Eastern Michigan University*

Rough Play

One of the Most Challenging Behaviors

FRANCES M. CARLSON

Learning Outcomes

After reading this article, you will be able to:

- Plan for large motor physical play experiences for young children on a daily basis.

- Explain to families why young children need opportunities to engage in big body play.

Young children enjoy very physical play; all animal young do. This play is often vigorous, intense, and rough. You may know this "big body play" as *rough-and-tumble play, roughhousing, horseplay,* or *play fighting.* In its organized play forms with older children, we call it many names: King of the Mountain, Red Rover, Freeze Tag, Steal the Bacon, Duck-Duck-Goose, and so on.

From infancy, children use their bodies to learn. They roll back and forth, kick their legs, and wave their arms, sometimes alone and sometimes alongside another infant. They crawl on top of each other. They use adults' bodies to stand up, push off, and launch themselves forward and backward.

As toddlers, they pull each other, hug each other tightly, and push each other down. As children approach the preschool years, these very physical ways of interacting and learning begin to follow a predictable pattern of unique characteristics: running, chasing, fleeing, wrestling, open-palm tagging, swinging around, and falling to the ground—often on top of each other.

Sometimes young children's big body play is solitary. Preschoolers run around, dancing and swirling, rolling on the floor or on the ground, or hopping and skipping along. Children's rough play can include the use of objects. For example, early primary children might climb up structures and then leap off, roll their bodies on large yoga balls, and sometimes tag objects as "base" for an organized game. More often, this play includes children playing with other children, especially with school-age children who often make rules to accompany their rough play.

Children's big body play may resemble, but does not usually involve, real fighting (Schafer & Smith 1996). Because it may at times closely resemble actual fighting, some adults find it to be one of the most challenging of children's behaviors. In spite of its bad reputation, rough play is a valuable and viable play style from infancy through the early primary years—one teachers and families need to understand and support.

Misconceptions about Rough Play

Teachers and parents often mistake this play style for real fighting that can lead to injury, so they prohibit it (Gartrell & Sonsteng 2008). This play style has also been neglected and sometimes criticized at both state and national levels.

The Child Development Associate (CDA) *Assessment Observation Instrument,* which is used to observe and evaluate a CDA candidate's classroom practices, states, "Rough play is minimized. Example: defuses rough play before it becomes a problem; makes superhero play more manageable by limiting time and place" (Council for Professional Recognition 2007, 31). In Georgia, a 2010 statewide licensing standards revision includes a rule change that states, "Staff shall not engage in, or allow children or other adults to engage in, activities that could be detrimental to a child's health or well-being, such as, but not limited to, horse play, rough play, wrestling" (Bright from the Start 2010, 25). Standards or expectations like these are based on the assumption that play fighting typically escalates or that children are often injured while playing this way. Neither assumption is true (Smith, Smees, & Pellegrini 2004).

Play fighting escalates to real fighting less than one percent of the time (Schafer & Smith 1996). And when it does, escalation typically occurs when participants include children who have been rejected (Schafer & Smith 1996; Smith, Smees, & Pellegrini 2004). (Children who are rejected are those "actively avoided by peers, who are named often as undesirable playmates" [Trawick-Smith 2010, 301].)

Attempts to ban or control children's big body play are intended to protect children, but such attempts are ill placed because children's rough play has different components and consequences from real fighting (Smith, Smees, & Pellegrini 2004). Rather than forbidding rough-and-tumble play, which can aid in increasing a child's social skills, teachers' and parents' efforts are better directed toward supporting and supervising this type of play, so that young children's social skills and friendship-making skills can develop (Schafer & Smith 1996).

What It Is and What It Is Not

Big body play is distinctly different from fighting (Humphreys & Smith 1987). Fighting includes physical acts used to coerce or control another person, either through inflicting pain or through the threat of pain. Real fighting involves tears instead of laughter and closed fists instead of open palms (Fry 2005). When open palms are used in real fighting, it is for a slap instead of a tag. When two children are fighting, one usually runs away as soon as possible and does not voluntarily return for more. With some practice, teachers and parents can learn to discern children's appropriate big body play from inappropriate real fighting.

In appropriate rough play, children's faces are free and easy, their muscle tone is relaxed, and they are usually smiling and laughing. In real fighting, the facial movements are rigid, controlled, stressed, and the jaw is usually clenched (Fry 2005). In rough play, children initiate the play and sustain it by taking turns. In real fighting, one child usually dominates another child (or children) and the other child may be in the situation against his or her will. In rough play, the children return for more even if it seems too rough to adult onlookers. In real fighting, children run away, sometimes in tears, and often ask the teacher or another adult for help.

Why It Matters

Rough-and-tumble play is just that: play. According to Garvey, all types of play

- are enjoyable to the players;
- have no extrinsic goals, the goal being intrinsic (i.e., pursuit of enjoyment);
- are spontaneous and voluntary; and
- involve active engagement by the players (1977, 10).

Rough play shares these characteristics; as in all appropriate play, when children involve their bodies in this vigorous, interactive, very physical kind of play, they build a range of skills representing every developmental domain. Children learn physical skills—how their bodies move and how to control their movements. They also develop language skills through signals and nonverbal communication, including the ability to perceive, infer, and decode. Children develop social skills through turn taking, playing dominant and subordinate roles, negotiating, and developing and maintaining friendships (Smith, Smees, & Pelligrini 2004; Tannock 2008). With boys especially, rough play provides a venue for showing care and concern for each other as they often hug and pat each other on the back during and after the play (Reed 2005). Rough play also allows young children to have their physical touch needs met in age- and individually appropriate ways (Reed 2005: Carlson 2006), and provides an opportunity for children to take healthy risks.

From an evolutionary developmental perspective, play-fighting allows children to practice adult roles (Bjorklund & Pellegrini 2001). That is, big body play helps prepare children for the complex social aspects of adult life (Bjorklund & Pellegrini 2001). Other researchers speculate that it is practice for future self-defense, providing vital practice and the development of critical pathways in the brain for adaptive responses to aggression and dominance (Pellis & Pellis 2007). There is a known connection between the development of movement and the development of cognition (Diamond 2000), and researchers believe there is a connection between this very physical, rowdy play style and critical periods of brain development (Byers 1998). Rough play between peers appears to be critical for learning how to calibrate movements and orient oneself physically in appropriate and adaptive ways (Pellis, Field, & Whishaw 1999). There is evidence that rough-and-tumble play leads to the release of chemicals affecting the mid-brain, lower forebrain, and the cortex, including areas responsible for decision making and social discrimination; growth chemicals positively affect development of these brain areas (Pellis & Pellis 2007). In other words, rough-and-tumble play, this universal children's activity, is adaptive, evolutionarily useful, and linked to normal brain development.

Supporting Rough Play

One of the best ways teachers can support rough play is by modeling it for children. When adults model high levels of vigorous activity, the children in their care are more likely to play this way. Children also play more vigorously and more productively when their teachers have formal education or training in the importance of this type of play (Bower et al. 2008; Cardon et al. 2008).

Besides modeling, teachers can do three specific things to provide for and support rough play while minimizing the potential for injury: prepare both the indoor and outdoor environment, develop and implement policies and rules for rough play, and supervise rough play so they can intervene when appropriate.

Environments That Support Big Body Play

The learning environment should provide rich opportunities for children to use their bodies both indoors and outdoors (Curtis & Carter 2005). When planning for big, rough, vigorous body play, give keen, thoughtful attention to potential safety hazards. Children need to play vigorously with their bodies, but they should do so in a safe setting.

To support rough play with infants during floor time, provide safe, mouthable objects in a variety of shapes, colors, and textures. Place the items near to and away from the baby to encourage reaching and stretching. Also provide a variety of large items—inclined hollow blocks, large rubber balls, sturdy tubes, exercise mats—so infants can roll on, around, over, and on top of these items. Get on the floor, too so infants can crawl around and lie on you. Allow babies to be near each other so that they can play with each other's bodies. Supervise their play to allow for safe exploration.

Indoor environments encourage big body play when there is ample space for children to move around freely. Cramped or restricted areas hamper children's vigorous play. When usable space is less than 25 square feet per child, children tend to be more aggressive (Pellegrini 1987). Boys, especially play more actively when more space is available (Fry 2005; Cardon et al. 2008).

Some teachers find it helpful to draw or mark off a particular section of the room and dedicate it to big body play. One teacher shares the way she established a "wrestling zone" in her preschool classroom:

> First, I cleared the area of any furniture or equipment. Next, I defined the area with a thick, heavy comforter and pillows. After setting up the area, I posted guidelines for the children's rough play on the wall near the wrestling zone.

Designate an area for rough play where there is no nearby furniture or equipment with sharp points and corners. Firmly anchor furniture so that it doesn't upturn if a child pushes against it. All flooring should be skid-free, with safety surfaces like thick mats to absorb the shock of any potential impact.

Policies and Rules for Rough Play

Programs need policies about rough play. Policies should define this type of play, explain rules that accompany it, specify the level of supervision it requires, and include specific types of staff development or training early childhood teachers need to support it. In addition, policies can address how to include it in the schedule and how to make sure all children—especially children with developmental disabilities and children who are socially rejected—have access to it. Clear policies about supervision are vital, as this play style requires constant adult supervision—meaning the children are both seen and heard at all times by supervising adults (Peterson, Ewigman, & Kivlahan 1993).

Even with its friendly nature and ability to build and increase children's social skills, this play style is more productive and manageable when guidelines and rules are in place (Flanders et al. 2009). Children can help create the rules. By preschool age, children are learning about and are able to begin participating in games with rules. Involving the children in creating rules for their play supports this emerging ability.

The rules should apply to children's roughhousing as well as to big body play with equipment and play materials. Wrestling, for example, may have rules such as wrestling only while kneeling, and arms around shoulders to waists but not around necks or heads. For big body play with equipment, the rules may state that the slide can be used for climbing on alternate days with sliding, or that a child can climb up only after checking to make sure no one is sliding down, and that jumping can be from stationary structures only and never from swings. Other rules may say that tumbling indoors always requires a mat and cannot be done on a bare floor,

and that children may only roll down hills that are fenced or away from streets and traffic.

Some general rules for big body play might be

- No hitting
- No pinching
- Hands below the neck and above the waist
- Stop as soon as the other person says or signals stop
- No rough play while standing—kneeling only
- Rough play is optional—stop and leave when you want (A Place of Our Own, n.d.)

Write the rules on white poster board, and mount them near the designated rough play area.

Supervise and Intervene

Teachers should enforce the rules and step in to ensure all children are safe, physically and emotionally. It's important to pay attention to children's language during rough play and help them use words to express some of the nonverbal communication. For example, if two boys are playing and one is on top of the other, say, "He is pushing against your chest! He wants you to get up!" Help the larger boy get up if he needs assistance. Instead of scolding, simply point out, "Because you are larger than he is, I think he felt uncomfortable with you on top of him." Allow the smaller boy to say these words, too. Help children problem solve about ways to accommodate their size differences if they are unable to do so unassisted. Say, "How else can you wrestle so that one of you isn't pinned under the other one?"

Children Who are Rejected

When supervising children with less developed social skills, remember that for these children, big body play can more easily turn into real fighting. Many children who are socially rejected lack the language skills needed to correctly interpret body signals and body language, which makes rough play difficult for them. The children often lack the social skill of turn taking or reciprocity. A child may feel challenged or threatened by another child's movement or action instead of understanding that rough play involves give-and-take and that he or she will also get a turn.

Although more difficult for them, engaging in big body play can help such children build social skills. When supervising these children, remain closer to them than you would to other children. If you see or sense that a child may be misunderstanding cues or turn taking, intervene. Help clarify the child's understanding of the play so it can continue. Strategies like coaching, helping the child reflect on cues and responses, and explaining and modeling sharing and reciprocity help a child remain in the play and ultimately support his or her language and social competence.

Communicating with Families

Some children already feel that their rough body play is watched too closely by their early childhood teachers (Tannock 2008). Not all parents, though, find children's rough play unacceptable. Several mothers, when interviewed, stated that rough

Sample Handbook Policies for Big Body Play

Big Body Play for Preschool and School-Age Children

Here at [name of school or program], we believe in the value of exuberant, boisterous, rough-and-tumble play to a child's overall development. This vigorous body play allows children opportunities to use language—both verbal and nonverbal—and learn how to negotiate, take turns, wait, compromise, sometimes dominate and sometimes hold back, and make and follow rules. They are learning about cause and effect and developing empathy. Big body play also supports optimum physical development because it is so vigorous and because children—since they enjoy it so much—tend to engage in it for an extended amount of time.

To support the use of big body play, we do the following:

- Provide training to all staff on the importance of big body play and how to supervise it
- Prepare both indoor and outdoor environments for this play style
- Establish classroom and playground rules with the children to keep them safe and help them know what to expect

- Encourage staff to use big body games with the children
- Supervise the play constantly, which means ensuring an adult is watching and listening at all times
- Model appropriate play; coach children as they play so that they are able to interact comfortably with each other in this way

The following indoor and outdoor environmental features of our program support big body play:

- At least 50 square feet of usable indoor play space per child, free from furniture and equipment so that children can tumble and wrestle (for example, a wrestling area for two children would consist of at least 100 square feet with no furnishings in the area)
- At least 100 square feet of usable outdoor play space per child, free from fixed equipment so that children can run, jump, tag, roll, wrestle, twirl, fall down, and chase each other (for example, a group of six children playing tag would have at least 600 square feet in which to play)
- Safety surfaces indoors under and around climbers, and furniture that children might use as climbers (a loveseat, for example)
- Safety surfaces outdoors under and around climbers, slides, balance beams, and other elevated surfaces from which children might jump

From F.M. Carlson, *Big Body Play: Why Boisterous, Vigorous, and Very Physical Play Is Essential to Children's Development and Learning* (Washington, DC: NAEYC 2011). 87–88. © 2011 by NAEYC.

---

play is empowering for their daughters and that they appreciate how this play style makes their girls feel strong ("Rough and Tumble Play" 2008). In industrialized countries, rough play is probably the most commonly used play style between parents and their children after the children are at least 2 years old (Paquette et al. 2003).

If children learn that rough play is acceptable at home but not at school, it may be difficult for them to understand and comply with school rules. Children are better positioned to reap the benefits of rough play when both home and school have consistent rules and messages. Children thrive in early childhood programs where administrators, teachers, and family members work together in partnerships (Keyser 2006). Partnership is crucial for children to feel supported in their big body play.

Teachers who decide to offer big body play must make sure that families are aware of and understand why rough play is included. Communicate program components to families when they first express interest in the program or at events such as an open house before the first day of school. Explain the use of and support for big body play in a variety of ways:

- Include in your family handbook a policy on big body play—and how it is supported and supervised in the program or school (see "Sample Handbook Policies for Big Body Play").
- Send a letter to families that explains big body play and its many benefits.

- Show photographs of children engaged in big body play
  - — in newsletters
  - — in documentation panels
  - — in promotional literature, like brochures and flyers
  - — on bulletin boards at entryways

Going Forward

Most children engage in rough play, and research demonstrates its physical, social, emotional, and cognitive value. Early childhood education settings have the responsibility to provide children with what best serves their developmental needs. When children successfully participate in big body play, it is "a measure of the children's social well-being and is marked by the ability of children to . . . cooperate, to lead, and to follow" (Burdette & Whitaker 2005, 48). These abilities don't just support big body play; these skills are necessary for lifelong success in relationships.

References

A Place of Our Own, n.d. "Rough Play Area." http://aplaceofourown.org/activity.php?id=492.

Bjorklund, D., & A. Pellegrini. 2001. *The Origins of Human Nature.* Washington, DC: American Psychological Association.

Bower, J.K., D.P. Hales, D.F. Tate, D.A. Rubin, S.E. Benjamin, & D.S. Ward, 2008. "The Childcare Environment and Children's Physical Activity." *American Journal of Preventive Medicine* 34 (1): 23–29.

Bright from the Start. Georgia Department of Early Care and Learning. 2010. "Order Adopting Amendments to Rule Chapter 591-1-1. Rule Chapter 290-2-1 and Rule Chapter 290-2-3." 25. http://decal.ga.gov/documents/attachments/OrderAdoptingAmendments080510.pdf.

Burdette, H.L., & R.C. Whitaker. 2005. "Resurrecting Free Play in Young Children: Looking Beyond Fitness and Fatness to Attention, Affiliation, and Affect." *Archives of Pediatrics & Adolescent Medicine* 159 (1): 46–50.

Byers, J.A. 1998. "The Biology of Human Play." *Child Development* 69 (3): 599–600.

Cardon, G., E. Van Cauwenberghe, V. Labarque, L. Haerens, & I. De Bourdeaudhuij. 2008. "The Contributions of Preschool Playground Factors in Explaining Children's Physical Activity During Recess." *International Journal of Behavioral Nutrition and Physical Activity* 5 (11): 1186–192.

Carlson, F.M. 2006. *Essential Touch: Meeting the Needs of Young Children.* Washington, DC: NAEYC.

Council for Professional Recognition. 2007. "Methods for Avoiding Problems Are Implemented." *CDA Assessment Observation Instrument.* Washington. DC: Author.

Curtis, D., & M. Carter. 2005. "Rethinking Early Childhood Environments to Enhance Learning." *Young Children* 60 (3): 34–38.

Diamond, A. 2000. "Close Interrelation of Motor Development and Cognitive Development and of the Cerebellum and Prefrontal Cortex." *Child Development* 71 (1): 44–56.

Flanders, J.L., V. Leo, D. Paquette, R.O. Pihl, & J.R. Seguin. 2009. "Rough-and-Tumble Play and Regulation of Aggression: An Observational Study of Father-Child Play Dyads." *Aggressive Behavior* 35: 285–95.

Fry, D. 2005. "Rough-and-Tumble Social Play in Humans." In *The Nature of Play: Great Apes and Humans,* eds A.D. Pellegrini & P.K. Smith, 54–85. New York: Guilford Press.

Gartrell, D., & K. Sonsteng. 2008. "Promote Physical Activity—It's Proactive Guidance." Guidance Matters. *Young Children* 63 (2): 51–53.

Garvey, C. 1977. *Play.* Cambridge, MA: Harvard University Press.

Humphreys, A.P., & P.K. Smith. 1987. "Rough and Tumble, Friendships, and Dominance in School Children: Evidence for Continuity and Change with Age." *Child Development* 58: 201–12.

Keyser, J. 2006. *From Parents to Partners: Building a Family-Centered Early Childhood Program.* Washington, DC: NAEYC: St. Paul, MN: Redleaf.

Paquette, D., R. Carbonneau, D. Dubeau, M. Bigras, & R.E. Tremblay, 2003. "Prevalence of Father-Child Rough-and-Tumble Play and Physical Aggression in Preschool Children." *European Journal of Psychology of Education* 18(2): 171–89.

Pellegrini, A.D. 1987. "Rough-and-Tumble Play: Developmental and Educational Significance." *Educational Psychology* 22 (11): 23–43.

Pellis, S.M., & V.C. Pellis. 2007. "Rough-and-Tumble Play and the Development of the Social Brain." *Association of Psychological Science* 16 (2): 95–8.

Pellis, S.M., E.F. Field, & I.Q. Whishaw, 1999. "The Development of a Sex-Differentiated Defensive Motor Pattern in Rats: A Possible Role for Juvenile Experience." *Developmental Psychobiology* 35 (2): 156–64.

Peterson, L., B. Ewigman, & C. Kivlahan. 1993. "Judgments Regarding Appropriate Child Supervision to Prevent Injury: The Role of Environmental Risk and Child Age." *Child Development* 64: 934–50.

Reed, T.L. 2005. "A Qualitative Approach to Boys' Rough and Tumble Play: There Is More Than Meets the Eye." In *Play; An Interdisciplinary Synthesis,* eds F.F. McMahon, D.E. Lytle, & B. Sutton-Smith, 53–71. Lanham, MD: University Press of America.

"Rough-and-Tumble Play." Ontario: TVO, 2008. Video, 10 min. www.tvo.org/TVO/WebObjects/TVO.woa?videoid?24569407001.

Schafer, M., & P.K. Smith. 1996. "Teachers' Perceptions of Play Fighting and Real Fighting in Primary School." *Educational Research* 38 (2): 173–81.

Smith, P.K., R. Smees, & A.D. Pellegrini. 2004. "Play Fighting and Real Fighting: Using Video Playback Methodology with Young Children." *Aggressive Behavior* 30: 164–73.

Tannock, M. 2008. "Rough and Tumble Play: An Investigation of the Perceptions of Educators and Young Children." *Early Childhood Education Journal* 35 (4): 357–61.

Trawick-Smith, J. 2010. *Early Childhood Development: A Multicultural Perspective.* Upper Saddle River, NJ: Pearson Merrill Prentice Hall.

Critical Thinking

1. Observe young children in an organized program playing outside on a playground. What opportunities are available for large muscle play and how is it encouraged?

2. Write a paragraph that could be included in a newsletter to families about the importance of rough play and how you will supervise that play with the children in your care.

Create Central

www.mhhe.com/createcentral

Internet References

Action for Healthy Kids
www.actionforhealthykids.org

American Academy of Pediatrics
www.aap.org

American Alliance of Health Physical Education Recreation and Dance
www.aahperd.org

Global SchoolNet Foundation
www.gsn.org

Kid Fit
http://kid-fit.com

National Association for the Education of Young Children
www.naeyc.org

Frances M. Carlson, MEd, is the lead instructor for the Early Childhood Care & Education department at Chattahoochee Technical College in Marietta, Georgia. She is the author of a book from NAEYC, *Big Body Play: Why Boisterous, Vigorous, and Very Physical Play Is Essential to Children's Development and Learning* (2011). francescarlson@bellsouth.net.

Unit 5

UNIT

Prepared by: Karen Menke Paciorek, *Eastern Michigan University*

Educational Practices That Help Children Thrive in School

We all can remember outstanding teachers from our past and list certain practices by that teacher or administrator that make us remember with great fondness the experiences we had in that school or classroom. There are evidence-based practices in education that are more successful in helping learners maximize their potential. It is our job to search out the best practices and make sure they are a part of what happens in the places where we work.

When planning your classroom activities, make sure that action is a part of the class pace. The children should be actively questioning and investigating while the teachers are supporting the exploration and discussions. Children who approach learning with wonder and awe are those who will spend their life seeking answers and looking for solutions to problems. These traits can be introduced and fostered during the early childhood years. Teachers can plan effectively by purposefully providing materials, activities, and opportunity for students to come to know and truly understand their learning. If teachers understand how young children learn, they can be successful in engaging their students in developmentally appropriate activities and in avoiding the risks of early academic instruction.

A practice that is increasing across the country as kindergarten teachers focus more on academic content is academic redshirting, named after the practice of a college athlete sitting out a year to develop and grow stronger. This practice involves the parents not enrolling children in kindergarten when they are age eligible to attend. Parents are interested in having their children be the most academically ready for school and the oldest in the class. However, this practice has some potential long-term costs. Educators and economists are weary of parents holding their children back and not considering all of the ramifications of this practice that involves 11 percent of children. Early childhood organizations have all recommended that children start kindergarten when they are age eligible. The responsibility to be ready to start school does not belong to the student, for it is the school and teachers' responsibility to meet the child's educational needs. Early childhood educators knowledgeable about differentiation

and their role in accommodating the learning setting to meet the needs of all children need to speak up and encourage all children to enter school when they are eligible. It is not the job of a four- or five-year-old to get ready for school. It is the job of the teacher and educational setting to meet the needs of each child who attends.

When discussing educational practices, the idea of rushing or pushing is an uninvited pressure that has crept into the policies and decisions made for young children. Children born today have an excellent chance of living long lives into their 90s. There is no need to rush and acquire skills that can easily be learned when the child is older, especially at the expense of valuable lifetime lessons that are learned best when children are young. Preschoolers and kindergartners need to learn lifelong social skills such as getting along with others, making wise choices, negotiating, developing compassion and empathy, and communicating needs, to name a few. The basics are a solid foundation to understanding how things work, the exploration and manipulation of materials, and the many opportunities for creative expressions. A walk down any toy store aisle by someone not familiar with toys on the market today will be the foundation for a rich discussion on the new materials available and their effects on young children. Creativity is one word often associated with teachers and many envy the opportunities for engaging in creative endeavors effective teachers provide for their students. Early childhood educators must continue to provide a variety of opportunities for children to explore, create, and problem solve using a variety of materials. Many of the key issues facing our society will be solved by creative solutions only developed after much exploration.

This unit has a variety of different articles that highlight the many practices that help our students thrive in school. Children and families should see the educational setting as a safe and supportive environment. There are many issues that are critical to teachers being effective with their students in the classroom and beyond. Be a thoughtful, intentional educator as you work to understand practices, implement them, and provide optimal opportunities for young children to thrive under your care.

Article   Prepared by: Karen Menke Paciorek, *Eastern Michigan University*

10 Ways Kindergarten Can Stop Failing Our Kids

LAURIE LEVY

Learning Outcomes

After reading this article, you will be able to:

- Advocate for a child-centered environment in kindergarten.

- Explain to others the importance of kindergarten teachers being knowledgeable about child development.

- Discuss why social/emotional needs of five-year-olds are so important.

My grandson, like millions of other five- and six-year-olds across the country, is about to start his formal education in kindergarten. Like most kids, he's a bit worried. He has three important questions about what his new school will be like:

- Will my teacher be nice?
- Can I get cookies?
- Do they have a tiger robot in their toys?

Those are great, age-appropriate questions for a five-year old to be asking, and I hope starting school brings him and his cohorts enough happy moments to fill those cute, overlarge backpacks they proudly carry around. But I'd be lying if I said I'm not a little worried for him, and for his peers—worried about our current educational climate and the demands it makes on these littlest learners.

Kindergarten has changed so much over the past decade; it is so much more work and so much less play. No Child Left Behind and Race to the Top have brought learning standards with higher (and not necessarily developmentally appropriate) expectations of these young children, and the partner of these standards, assessment, plays a huge role in today's kindergarten

classrooms. The validity of using this testing, often administered to five-year-olds before or at the very beginning of kindergarten, to track learning is questionable at best. Children this age aren't necessarily "test-ready": they may hesitate to answer a strange adult's questions, or prefer to stare out the window, and many don't understand that giving a complete answer actually matters. Sadly, it does.

In short, kindergarten has become the new first (or even second) grade, with kids anxiously filling in bubbles and receiving reading instruction when many can't even decode words yet. A dozen years ago, the play kitchens and imaginative free play areas disappeared, followed by the loss of blocks and easel paints and most other toys. Time for socialization and play has vanished. We seem to have forgotten that *how* children learn at this age matters—facts drilled into their heads that have no connection to their life experience, or regard for their development, are both meaningless and quickly forgotten. But it doesn't have to be that way.

Once upon a time we had a different vision for what the kindergarten year should be: a time for play and experimentation and the sorting out of self that leads to further learning. How can we create those kinds of learning environments again? Here are 10 ways schools can stop failing our kids in their earliest years, and begin building passionate learners from the start.

1. **Ensure time to learn through play and time to play for fun.** This should be obvious to educators who know anything about child development, but standards for what kids should know generally don't come with directions about the best way to teach them. Kids learn by doing, manipulating and playing. And in order to learn, they need time to play to recharge their batteries and discover important social skills.

2. **Grant permission to color outside of the lines.** Five-year-olds are amazingly creative if we allow them to express themselves. Worksheets and expectations of conformity undermine this. One of my granddaughters was berated in kindergarten for not finishing her "work" because she spent too much time coloring the pictures in the early squares. As my daughter explained it, she had no idea going fast was important—it never had been before.

3. **Employ educators who have patience with developing skills.** Zipping, shoe-tying, nose-wiping, opening lunch-foods, and even toileting independently can challenge a five-year-old. Many teachers have told me that dealing with these issues is the worst part about teaching kindergarten. So I wish the kindergarten class of 2015 teachers who both expect and don't mind these challenges.

4. **Understand that not all kindergarteners are going to be developmentally ready to read, write or take tests.** Even though we wish all kids could be readers and writers when they leave kindergarten, some will not be able to do this yet. And that's okay. When a child's mind is ready for reading, the light bulb goes on. Before then, the child is more of a parrot than a reader. Unless there is an underlying problem, kids learn to read when they are ready. There's no shame in not getting it until age 6, or even 7.

5. **Expect occasional squirrelly behavior.** It's really hard for these little kids to sit still all day doing work—and not all of them have ADHD and need to be medicated. Early childhood educators understand that kids need hours of free playtime from their earliest days to develop healthy sensory systems that enable their brains to learn. Valerie Strauss recently posted a piece on this issue by Angela Hanscom titled, *Why So Many Kids Can't Sit Still in School Today.* It's worth reading Hanscom's answer, as she is a pediatric occupational therapist as well as an advocate for more creative play in children's lives.

6. **Insist that teachers are trained in child development.** I always think of kindergarten as the year of sorting everything out. Children generally span over a year age-wise, from the child who just turned five to the child who is already six and was held back. Add to that the huge range of skills and social/emotional ability among children this age; the fact that there will be kids with special needs and learning challenges yet to be indentified; and the reality that, for some children, this is their first exposure to any kind of formal group learning, and you've got a challenging mix for any teacher to handle. The best tool a kindergarten teacher can possess is the ability to look at this wide range of behavior, development, experience, skill, and maturity through the eyes of someone well-trained in child development.

7. **Realize that the hardest parts of kindergarten have little to do with academic learning (parents too!).** Arrival, lunch, recess, transitions, bathroom routines, and rules in general are really challenging for children this age. Untrained personnel who often have little patience for the needs of five- and six-year-olds often supervise arrival and lunch times. Recess (if allowed) can resemble *Lord of the Flies,* as kids with developing social skills are left pretty much on their own to negotiate peer interactions. The rules in general often don't make sense to kindergarteners. In particular, many have trouble figuring out when it is okay to use the bathroom, leading to accidents. If there are specialists (gym, music, art, drama, etc.), these teachers will have different rules and not really know the kids as well as their kindergarten teacher. All in all, it's a lot to manage for such young children.

8. **Develop a kindergarten curriculum that meets the developmental and social/emotional needs of 5-year-old learners.** Kindergarten is definitely the year to differentiate expectations and instruction, as there will be huge differences in what children know and how they behave. The curriculum should still be based in early childhood best practices, not merely a push down of what was formerly first or second grade work. Teaching kids in large groups and expecting them to sit for long periods of time is unrealistic. Learning activity stations and play-based activities are definitely the way to go.

9. **Welcome parents as part of a team working in the best interests of the child.** Parents must advocate for their young children because they cannot do it themselves. School principals need to be available to parents and require teachers to listen when parents share anything unique about their child's needs, learning style, behavior, or life situation. Asking for and allowing help from parents will benefit everyone.

10. **Be sensitive to the child who is chronologically young or has special needs.** Among my eight grandkids, I have both issues. Two of the boys have June birthdays, which can be a disadvantage these days because of kids who are red-shirted (held back) and current educational expectations that may not be developmentally appropriate, especially for the youngest students. And kids with special needs who are included in general education classes still have different learning and social challenges that must be understood and addressed.

School districts need to avoid pressuring teachers to expect all children to meet standards at the same pace and time, thus ensuring better test scores. And teachers need to walk the talk of differentiated instruction, and be especially empathic to those who may struggle due to age or ability.

Getting back to my grandson's three questions about kindergarten: with regret, I've informed him that cookies will not be served for snack (unhealthy), and there will not be tiger robots in the classroom (in fact, there probably won't be any toys). But I hope I will eventually be able to respond with a resounding yes to his first question: Will the teacher be nice? In fact, I expect the teacher to honor my grandson's energy, curiosity, zest for life, and unique interests. I'm not really worried about how much "stuff" he learns. I simply want him to learn to love learning, and be happy, as he begins his formal education. That's what kindergarten should be all about.

Critical Thinking

1. What would you add to the list Levy developed?
2. How would you help parents of a soon-to-be kindergartener prepare their child for kindergarten? What do children need to be able to do to be successful in kindergarten?

Internet References

Association for Childhood Education International
http://acei.org/

National Association for the Education of Young Children
http://naeyc.org/

PBS Parents
http://www.pbs.org/parents/education/going-to-school/grade-by-grade/kindergarten/

Article   Prepared by: Karen Menke Paciorek, *Eastern Michigan University*

It's Play Time!

The value of play in early education, and how to get teachers on board.

JOAN ALMON

Learning Outcomes

After reading this article, you will be able to:

- Describe why play is so important in the early childhood classroom and why it is vanishing.

- Provide strategies for those wanting to advocate for more play opportunities for our youngest learners.

Play is one of the primary approaches to learning available to young students. Sensory impressions and ideas bubble up from within them, much as they do in an artist or a composer. Children use the arts as a form of expression, but most often they use play itself to express their ideas. Through play, they try on every role and situation they've encountered in life. They explore the world around them and make it their own. Their play is often serious, but it is also enjoyable and deeply satisfying.

Yet despite its importance for cognitive, social-emotional, and physical growth, play has largely been pushed out of kindergarten classrooms and is currently vanishing from preschool classrooms as well. It has been replaced with teacher-led instruction. Research and commentary about this situation can be found in the Alliance for Childhood's report "Crisis in the Kindergarten: Why Children Need to Play in School," and in an article, "The Crisis in Early Education," both by me and Edward Miller.

Play vs. Reading Instruction

One contributing factor that has moved early education in the United States away from play and toward cognitive instruction is the prevalent belief that children should learn to read at age 5. The assumption is that they will be better readers than if they wait until age 6 or 7. But there is essentially no evidence that this is true.

Fortunately, the Common Core Standards are a bit vague on this point. They call for kindergarten children to read "emergent-reader texts with purpose and understanding." But there does not seem to be widespread recognition of what emergent-reader texts are, which leaves room for interpretation. The primary goal should be that young children begin building the bridge toward print literacy, not that they cross the bridge and stand firmly on the other side.

Many other countries do not begin formal reading until age 6 or 7. They use guidelines similar to those proposed by Bank Street College in New York. Bank Street, a highly respected college for early childhood educators, identifies three stages of reading: emergent readers in preschool, kindergarten, and first grade; early readers in first and second grade; and early fluent/fluent readers in second and third grade. Using this approach allows time for preschool and kindergarten children to slowly, but effectively, build a bridge from oral language to written language. And it allows time for play-based learning.

What the Research Reveals

Play-based learning is a term that embraces two approaches simultaneously. One is that children are given ample time to carry their own ideas into play—with assistance from teachers as needed. The other is that their knowledge of the world has been enriched through appropriate content offered in interesting and experiential ways by their teachers. This can include reading books, storytelling, puppetry, music, and the arts, as well as encouraging hands-on activities and exploration of nature. The children's own play and the content offered by teachers enhance one another. One child succinctly expressed it this way: "At recess, I remember everything I learned."

Many studies documenting the value of play in early learning have been summarized in *A Mandate for Playful Learning in Preschool: Presenting the Evidence* (2008), by Kathy Hirsh-Pasek and others. Among the studies they report is one by Herb Ginsburg of Columbia University. He and Kyoung-Hye Seo filmed 90 preschool children during free play. Each film lasts 15 minutes. The researchers found that regardless of children's social class, about half of the play scenarios contained mathematical activity, including patterns and shapes, magnitude of different objects, and number or quantity. No one assigned them these themes; they arose spontaneously.

A Mandate for Playful Learning in Preschool also reports on several studies that indicate that heightened language skills are exhibited in connection with children's play. For example, a longitudinal study by David Dickinson and Patton Tabors, the Home-School Study of Language and Literacy Development, followed 74 children from low-income homes from age 3 through middle school. The research shows a clear relationship between the children's use of language during early childhood play and their later literacy outcomes.

There are other studies that show long-term gains for children in play-based programs. A striking example is the High-Scope Preschool Curriculum Comparison Study (PCCS). It was a companion study to the well-known Perry Preschool study that shows the importance of preschool education for children from low-income homes. The PCCS goes further and shows that play-based programs can lead to much better long-term outcomes for children than instructional programs.

PCCS researchers assigned 68 at-risk children to one of three preschool programs. The HighScope program and the traditional nursery were both play-based and yielded similar outcomes. The third classroom was heavily cognitive in orientation and used a scripted program. At the end of the first year, it seemed that all students advanced equally, but the youngsters were followed until age 23. Over time, the children who attended the cognitive class needed special education far more often than those from the play-based programs (47 percent compared with 6 percent). The students from the cognitive class were also more likely to later commit felonies (34 percent versus 9 percent) and more likely to be suspended from work (27 percent compared with 0 percent).

"At recess, I remember everything I learned."

Long-term gains for children from play-based classrooms were also found in Germany in a study done in the 1970s. In that case, children from 50 kindergarten classes that were play-based were compared with the same number from cognitively oriented kindergartens. The children were followed until age 10. The study, reported by Linda Darling-Hammond and Jon Snyder in the *Handbook of Research on Curriculum*, found that children from the play-based kindergarten classes excelled over those in the cognitive classrooms in all 17 measures used, including creativity, oral expression, and "industry." The study was so convincing that Germany, which was moving rapidly toward academic kindergarten classes, switched back to play-based programs.

Play and Early Learning

Why is play so important in early learning? Play has been likened to the inquiry-based approach of a scientist because both engage in "what if" thinking. The child is continually trying out new possibilities and learns as much from failure and mistakes as from positive outcomes. It is this process that is of great importance to the child rather than the outcome. However, it is difficult to assess this process, which is one reason that play has fallen out of favor in schools.

Creativity, curiosity, play, and problem-solving are all intertwined in early childhood. Social negotiation is also frequently part of the mix. It starts with "Let's play this way" and "No, let's do it my way," and then the conversation begins. At age 3 it might end in a tussle. But by age 5 children have become adept in their use of language in play and in their ability to negotiate socially. This holds true for children from all socioeconomic backgrounds.

It is increasingly the case, however, that children from all backgrounds enter preschool with poor play skills. One reason is that they have too many hours of screen time during which they view other people's creativity rather than developing their own. In addition, modern toys are often related to films or television shows and come with a clear story line, making it difficult for children to create their own stories. Instead, it is helpful for children to engage with open-ended play materials. Almost anything becomes a good toy in the hands of a playful child—blocks and other building materials, ropes, cloths, household items, and simple dress-ups are used in new ways every day.

Incorporating Play

Many children play well in school as soon as they realize it is allowed. Others need help from teachers, who themselves need to understand play and ways to cultivate it in children. Young teachers often did not grow up with much playtime and benefit from experiences with creative play. Even older teachers who did play as children may need some prompting to recall open-ended play strategies. Sharing play memories with one another is helpful, as is engaging in actual play.

Many teachers are fearful of play in the classroom. In their minds, play is synonymous with chaos. But when children are deeply engaged in play, they tend to be focused and fairly quiet. There is a "hum" of play that fills the room, with occasional loud voices that then quiet down again. This is true of young children, but also of school-age children.

For the PBS documentary *Where Do the Children Play?* (2008), we organized a play session for fifth graders at a public school in Flint, Michigan. At the end of the hour-long film shoot, the teacher, who had been quite apprehensive about play, remarked that it had not been chaotic at all. The children had played with enormous concentration using cardboard boxes, old sheets, ropes, and tape, and they played with children with whom they did not usually socialize.

Given all the benefits of play, as well as hesitance on the part of some teachers, what can principals do to support play in early education? Here are five suggestions:

- **Create opportunities for teachers** to learn about play in early education from mentors, visits to programs with effective play-based approaches, and workshops.
- **Provide time for teachers** to observe each other during playtime and to share play experiences with one another.
- **Create beautiful play environments,** indoors and outdoors. Equip them with simple, open-ended play materials, but avoid clutter and overstimulation.
- **Schedule time for play every day.** Ideal playtimes last 45 minutes or longer to give children a chance to enter deeply into play.
- **Help teachers address the concerns of parents** who think young children should master more cognitive skills than is developmentally appropriate.

Make No Excuses

The Common Core State Standards do not preclude play for kindergarten students. And they should not serve as an excuse for removing it from preschool classrooms even though anecdotal reports indicate that that is happening. Research by Sara Smilansky, described in her book with Edgar Klugman, *Children's Play and Learning,* showed that children who engaged well in socio-dramatic play experienced more gains in language usage and in understanding what others meant than children who were not strong players. Such abilities are needed to meet standards calling for written expression and for comprehension of what is meant in a text.

The Common Core Standards were created to help graduates enter the workplace and college. A recent IBM Institute study asked 1,500 CEOs around the world what they most sought in employees. The answer was simple: Creativity. There is no better way to foster creativity than to keep it alive in early childhood when it is naturally strong and expresses itself through play. Yet, teachers tell us that if they give their children time to play, some have no ideas of their own, or do not know how to engage in make-believe play.

Further, Kyung Hee Kim at William and Mary College, using scores on the Torrance Test of Creative Thinking, found that creativity levels had risen from the 1950s to 1990, but then began to decline, especially among children. She is now frequently asked by business schools to help them develop courses that will stimulate creative thinking. The irony is not lost on her that we are driving creativity out of young children and then trying to restore it in college students.

Play-based education in preschool and kindergarten gives children a chance to develop their creativity in balanced ways. It supports the overall healthy development of children and prepares them for the 21st century workplace where creativity is highly valued.

Critical Thinking

1. How would you respond to a kindergarten teacher who told you they didn't have time in the day to allow the children to play.

2. Why do you think this article published in the journal *Principal*?

Internet References

Alliance for Childhood
   http://www.allianceforchildhood.org/

National Association for the Education of Young Children
   http://naeyc.org/

National Association of Elementary School Principals
   http://www.naesp.org/

Joan Almon is co-founder of the Alliance for Childhood.

Article   Prepared by: Karen Menke Paciorek, *Eastern Michigan University*

Let's Get Messy!

Exploring Sensory and Art Activities with Infants and Toddlers

It's raining lightly in the infant yard, and the babies are outside examining the wet grass and splashing in puddles. Aziz (17 months) picks up a ball and tosses it into a muddy puddle. He squeals in delight, bends down, and lifts the ball back up. He touches the mud, watching as it oozes onto his finger. He then drops the ball back into the puddle. Next, he walks over to a nearby shelf and grasps another ball, walks back, then drops that one into the puddle as well.

Fascinated by his messy discovery, Aziz continues to drop balls and other toys into the muddy water until it is time to go inside. Meanwhile, several other infants wobble over and imitate the game. Having observed the infants' interest, the next day the staff place a tub of water and balls in the indoor art/sensory area to extend the children's investigation.

TRUDI SCHWARZ AND JULIA LUCKENBILL

Learning Outcomes

After reading this article, you will be able to:

- Explain the importance of very young children participating in sensory activities.

- Develop a list of possible creative activities for infants and toddlers.

Visitors to our classrooms who observe scenarios like the one described above often make surprised comments, such as, "You let them get that messy?" But these projects are commonplace in our infant and toddler classrooms. As infant/toddler teachers we take a child-centered, emergent approach, meaning that we observe the children at play, ask ourselves what they are interested in learning, and design developmentally appropriate curricula to meet and extend those interests. This curriculum development technique leads to "possibilities for the child to develop deeper understandings" of how the world works (Curtis & Carter 1996, 52). The activities in our classroom interest areas and our play yards change weekly, though the content in the areas remain in the same locations. When children arrive in the morning, they tend to beeline to their favorite areas to see what has changed. One of the preferred areas inside and outside is the art/sensory area.

We believe that art and sensory projects are integral to the curriculum, and that children develop key skills through these types of activities. This belief is supported by the Arts Education Partnership (Goldhawk 1998) and by the Infant/Toddler

Environment Rating Scale—Revised (Harms, Cryer, & Clifford 2007). We provide art and sensory activities every day and give children ample time to explore them. Why? "Children must explore to know. A direct connection exists between sensory experiences and the development of creativity" (Miller 1999, 157). Smith and Goldhaber (2004) note, "Young children actively test out their theories [ideas] many times before accommodating their own theories to knowledge gained from new experiences" (18–19). Through hands-on play, even infants are developing rudimentary theories (schemas) to explain their world. In other words, infants construct an idea of how things work in their heads, and then refine it over time through experience. For example, giving infants time to paint leads to them discovering that they have made marks on the paper. Over time, this understanding becomes more systematic and the children become capable of integrating new tools and media into their art.

Learning and Growing through Art and Sensory Activities

Children benefit by engaging in hands-on exploration of materials. They add many vital "tools" to their school readiness toolbox through art/sensory play.

Motor Skill Development

- Poking, smashing, pinching, squeezing, cutting, and rolling playdough and real clay improves hand strength and fine motor skills.

- Grasping a crayon or marker and scribbling supports future writing and drawing skills. Toddlers initially use their whole arms to make scribble marks on paper. With practice they refine these skills and begin to make vague shapes. These early experiences support the ability to plan their artwork and draw things they know from their environment, usually during their preschool years (Cryer, Harms, & Riley 2004).

Social-Emotional Skills

- Painting together on a see-through easel or a shared piece of paper encourages children's ability to use materials together and supports prosocial interactions.
- Splashing side by side at the water table teaches toddlers about sharing spaces and leads to conversations about other children's feelings (for example, if a child did not want to get wet).

Engaging in art and sensory play supports the emergence of children's new skills, while observing children's play provides vital information about children's developmental progress.

In this article, we share the experiences of the infant and toddler art/sensory program at our school. We begin with issues to consider when planning the curriculum, and provide ideas about where to find inexpensive, high-quality materials. Finally, we share some examples from our classrooms and offer suggestions for yours.

Planning a Curriculum

Visitors to our youngest classrooms are often surprised to discover that we have daily art and sensory activities, just as preschool classrooms do. However, there are essential differences between planning art/sensory activities for preschoolers and activities for infants and toddlers. Following are some things to consider when planning art/sensory activities.

Encourage Experimentation

Infants enjoy using their senses to learn and are very oral. It's best to design activities with this in mind. Infants love to gradually explore the texture, scent, taste, sight, and sound of the art materials. They often are messy in their use of the materials (for example, crawling through paint). Projects must use materials that are washable, nontoxic, and do not contain small parts. Activities should be open-ended so that children have the time and space to construct their own understanding of the materials and their properties. Allow ample time for play and for cleanup.

Some adults are concerned that infants and young toddlers might eat the art materials. While we don't encourage this behavior, we understand that tasting the materials is part of the children's exploratory process. We have found that after a small sample, children realize that the materials are not tasty, and teachers can then redirect them to a more appropriate use. For example, after an infant puts a (non-toxic) paint-covered finger in his mouth, a caregiver might say, "That doesn't taste so good. You can rub the paint on the paper instead." If you find that infants are eating large amounts of homemade play-dough,

switch to commercially made playdough or salt-free recipes, because an excess of salt is harmful to young children.

Supervise Exploration

As infants become toddlers, they use materials with more intentionality. They are less likely to eat the art materials, though they may still experiment by tasting them. Toddlers do not understand conservation of volume. They will squeeze a glue bottle until it is empty or shake all the colored sand out of the salt shaker and then demand more. They explore the nature of paint by decorating not only the paper, but also the table and themselves. Toddlers' explorations require close supervision from caregivers and enough space to be messy.

Affirm the Process

Infants and toddlers are *process* rather than *product* oriented. Placing cotton balls on the back of a die-cut sheep is less satisfying to them than finger painting. Coloring in a coloring book is less exciting than playing with playdough. Infants and toddlers want to feel the paint as it covers their fingers, smell the mint in the scented playdough, and taste the basil leaves in the tub on the table.

Use Culturally Diverse Materials

Use an antibias approach to all projects. Materials that reflect the cultures and backgrounds of the children you serve send a message that everyone is valued in the classroom (Derman-Sparks & Olsen Edwards 2010). For example, offer brown and tan playdough as well as pink shades, and training chopsticks to explore the play-dough instead of plastic knives. Ask the children's parents to donate materials that reflect their backgrounds, such as origami or wrapping paper for use in collage. The more you keep the families in mind, the more inclusive and welcoming your program will be.

Make Accommodations for Special Needs

Art/sensory projects must be accessible to all children in your care and address a range of skills and abilities. This may mean making accommodations for children with special needs. For instance, you can place materials directly on the floor for children with mobility challenges or for those who cannot stand at a table. You can provide paintbrushes with extra-large handles for children with fine motor difficulty. To create them, wind self-adhering first aid wrap on the handle of the brush to make it easier to grasp.

Modify Activities for Sensory Avoiders

Differences in temperament impact each child's response to art and sensory materials. For example, some children love the feel of gooey wet paint on their hands, while other children shy away from such slimy activities. If you have children in your care who avoid sensory experiences, you can include them by modifying sticky and gooey projects. For example, add brushes in the finger paint or cups with oobleck (a corn-starch

A Note on Cultural Sensitivity

It is offensive in some cultures to use food as an art material—in particular, rice. Avoid this kind of activity, as you cannot be sure who may be offended by the waste of food. It is not always obvious if a child or their extended family have experienced food scarcity (Derman-Sparks & Olsen Edwards 2010). We have found that birdseed is a good nontoxic alternative to rice in a sensory table, and that fish tank gravel and cornstarch-based packing peanuts (they melt in your mouth) work just as well as beans and pasta for gluing on collages.

and water mixture) so these children can explore the materials at their own pace and in a way that feels right to them. When sensory-avoidant children are exposed to art materials in a way that respects their unique temperaments, they may become more comfortable touching the materials as they become familiar with textures. Playing with finger paint, bubble water, and other sensory materials is part of a healthy "sensory diet" for all children. Engaging in these activities can help a child with sensory processing disorder (and children without the disorder as well) more easily interpret the environment (Arnwine 2007, 4).

Display Children's Artwork

Display the children's artwork at their eye level. This allows them to admire their creations and feel ownership of the classroom. Families also appreciate seeing their children's creations valued. Display 3-D art, such as playdough sculptures, in addition to paper collages and paintings. Children's art displays are an indicator of a high-quality classroom in the NAEYC accreditation standards and in both the Infant/Toddler and the Early Childhood Environment Rating Scale—Revised (ITERS-R/ECERS-R), which are tools used to assess the quality of early childhood learning environments (Harms, Clifford, & Cryer 2005; Harms, Cryer, & Clifford 2007).

Art and Sensory Activities In the Infant Room

It is wise to plan activities for young children in order to avoid chaotic transitions. When teachers plan curriculum based on their observations of children's interests, children's learning experiences are extended. Below is an example from our infant room.

Choosing the Activity

At snack time, we noticed 11-month-old Alice smearing her sweet potato on the table and gazing intently at the color. Other infants were also smearing their food while eating. Since the infants were clearly interested in spreading color, we decided that finger paint was a good extension.

Designing the Activity

We decided to introduce nontoxic foam paint in the art/sensory area. We placed the paint in a low bin on the floor and put wipes on a table near the paint.

Implementing the Activity

On the first day, several infants crawled or wobbled over to the paint bin. Some reached in, grasping and smearing the paint. Others poked it lightly with a finger or avoided it. We continued for several days with adults modeling that it was safe to touch the paint. Over the course of the week we saw more infants join in.

Changing the Activity

In response to the children's initial reaction to the project, we planned the following extensions:

1. We added round-ended paint-brushes (like shaving brushes), inviting infants to engage with the paint without smearing their fingers. Teachers allowed the children to explore the materials, and modeled using the brushes without requiring infants to try.
2. The following week, we observed the infants still showing interest in the paint. We changed the project very little, substituting finger paint for foam paint. The finger paint was more slippery than the foam paint. The infants continued to engage with the paint.
3. We noticed that when we washed the paint off the infants' hands, they enjoyed the bubbles and water. We changed the paint to soapy water. More infants joined in this exploration—splashing, dumping items in the water, and even crawling in. The children engaged in this activity outside as well as inside.
4. We decided to explore oobleck. Oobleck looks a lot like paint and contains water, but it behaves differently than both substances. The infants were initially hesitant around this substance. They gradually joined in, especially after plastic cups were introduced so they could examine the substance without touching it, if they preferred to explore in this way.

Making a Record

To share the children's explorations with families and the wider community, we documented each infant art/sensory activity in our classroom photo essay, "Adventures in the Infant Room." The photo essays help parents and caregivers look back on infant and toddler learning. It also helps capture the range of process-based activities and models how they might be tried at home. Here is an excerpt from the infant room's oobleck documentation:

Julia is observing Leo (15 months) and the oobleck. She has noticed that he avoids touching many sensory materials, using towels, cups, or brushes to engage with them instead. She locates cups as Leo joins the activity. Next she observes Leo touching the cups. She knows that he likes to enter play slowly.

Julia notes Leo's gaze shifting from the cup to the oobleck. He lightly touches the oobleck. His finger comes back clean but wet. She responds by using parallel talk, a teaching technique where teachers describe aloud what children are doing in order to connect with them and expand their ideas. Julia says, "You touched it and now your finger got wet. Oobleck is wet." She imitates his action. Leo pushes his cup back into the oobleck, bottom first. Julia says, "If you want to pick up the oobleck, you can use the cup." She models this by filling her own cup with oobleck. She pours the oobleck out. "It comes out slowly," she comments. "Do you want to try?" Leo reaches out and grasps her cup and pours out the oobleck.

The oobleck falls in puddles. Leo now appears comfortable with the substance. He grasps handfuls of it, pinches and squeezes it, and puts it back into his cup. Julia, still observing him, continues to facilitate his play, moving the oobleck back into the cups for further pouring. She narrates the action of the oobleck—how slowly it moves—and she talks about how Leo can pinch it to pick it up. She also steps back again, allowing him to feel autonomous in his exploration.

Art and Sensory Activities in the Toddler Room

We use the same techniques to design and expand curriculum in both the infant and toddler programs. Following is an example of a curriculum designed for older children.

Choosing the Activity

Playdough was a passion in the toddler room. Each day children would ask for it by name, and they would crowd around the trays as we placed them on the tables, reaching for playdough and tools. We provided cookie cutters, butter knives, pizza cutters, and rolling pins to use with the dough. We noticed several toddlers putting globs of playdough on the butter knives and declaring them to be "Popsicles."

Designing and Implementing the Activity

We put out a range of materials, from Popsicle sticks and pipe cleaners to feathers and leaves, and then watched what the toddlers did and made. They excitedly created many "birthday cakes" by poking items into the playdough. They enjoyed singing "Happy Birthday" to themselves, their peers, and their caregivers.

Changing the Activity

In response to the children's initial reaction to the project, we planned the following extensions:

1. Noting the toddlers' interest in cakes, we set up a bakery shop. We added brown playdough, birthday candles, whisks, measuring cups, cupcake tins and wrappers, salt-filled shakers, and other baking tools to the trays.

When We Talk about "Art"

When we use the term *art* in this context, we are discussing activities that result in finished products, such as a painting on paper. The term *sensory* in this context refers to activities with no end product, such as running hands through a bin of birdseed. Art projects are sensory based, and sensory projects could be considered art. For this article, we use the terms interchangeably.

The toddlers jumped right in, making more cakes and cupcakes. They were particularly interested in the salt shakers and sometimes got into conflicts over taking turns using them.

2. We decided to make salt shaker art. We filled small glue bottles with about a tablespoon of glue apiece. We placed construction paper on trays, anticipating glue puddles. We placed colored sand in several recycled spice shakers and taped over some of the holes to make the sand come out slowly. The toddlers made small glue lakes and shook all the sand out into colorful piles. We scooped the excess sand up, refilled the spice containers, and repeated the process. The toddlers did not understand that the glue made the sand stick, or that if they used too much glue the sand would fall off, but they loved the process. As expected, this was a developmentally appropriate outcome. Although children at this age do not carefully use glue, they do enjoy the experience of emptying, squeezing, and making a mess.

3. We added food coloring to the glue in the bottles after observing that the toddlers enjoyed using the glue puddles as paint.

4. The toddlers did not want to stop using shakers—it was so much fun! We took the activity outside to the dramatic play table beside the sandbox. Here the toddlers could make a mess using filled shakers without getting the classroom salty or sandy. They could also refill the shakers with sand. We knew the toddlers would "ruin" the playdough with the sand, but we accepted this as part of the process. This project included the initial playdough and accessories, salt shakers filled with various substances, and glue with and without food color.

Making a Record

To share the children's explorations with parents and visitors to our school, we documented each toddler art/sensory activity in the classroom in a photo essay. "Adventures in the Toddler Room." Here is an excerpt from the toddler room's glue-and-sand activity:

We introduced glue-and-sand painting. This was a direct extension of last week's bakery shop project. We noticed that the toddlers loved using shakers and enjoyed decorating with sand.

Sensory and Art Activities for Infants and Toddlers

Nontoxic material	Nontoxic items to place on or in the material	Surface	Tools	Ages and notes
Tempera paint, foam paint, finger paint	Colored sand and liquid soap	Paper, Plexiglass, wood, cardboard items, natural items, body parts, bubble wrap	Paintbrushes, stamps, sponges, plastic cars, plastic balls	Infants and toddlers
Watercolor block paint or liquid paint	None	Paper, coffee filters	Water, brushes, bottles for liquid watercolor	Toddlers
Contact paper	Colored sand, regular sand, natural materials, paper scraps, pictures from magazines, photos, recycled wrapping paper, pipe cleaners, tissue paper	Table or floor	Scotch tape or similar to affix contact paper to the table	Infants and toddlers
Stickers, tape	None	Paper or skin	None	Infants and toddlers
Construction paper, cardboard, tissue paper, newspaper, butcher paper, etc.	None	Paper can be used as a surface.	Tape to affix to the paper or materials to decorate it	Infants and toddlers Crumpling, tearing, climbing into containers of crumpled paper, and making balls of paper.
Glue	None	Table with trays and paper or cardboard to hold collage	Glue bottles	Toddlers
Playdough, purchased or homemade. (*Note:* Limit how much playdough children eat due to the high salt content or make salt-free playdough, or purchase commercial playdough.)	Colored sand; liquid watercolor, food color, or extract (e.g., vanilla or peppermint); pipe cleaners; Popsicle sticks; leaves, sticks, shells, etc.	Table with trays to define each child's space, or a bin if a group of infants shares the playdough	Cookie cutters, cutting tools, baking tools, ceramic tools, tortilla presses, garlic presses, plastic toys as props	Infants and toddlers
Natural clay	Pipe cleaners, Popsicle sticks, nontoxic branches, water if clay is dry	Table or bin, trays optional	See above	Infants and toddlers Clean up well after using clay to prevent dust buildup.
Water	Liquid watercolor or food color, soap, large ice blocks (but remove when they become smaller), cornstarch (oobleck), wool	Bins on or off a table. Towels taped to floor around this project.	Cups, funnels, bath toys, measuring cups, whisks, items that sink and float, eye droppers for toddlers	Infants and toddlers
Birdseed, sand, soil	Hidden toys or shells under the material. Water in the sand or soil.	Bins inside or outside to decrease mess. Water table.	Containers, sand mills, plastic vehicles or animals. Various sizes of tubes. Plastic beakers.	Infants and toddlers
Nontoxic leaves, pinecones, seedpods, flowers	Water, soil, clay	Table, bin, piles outside	Scissors (for toddlers only)	Infants and toddlers
Stamping ink/dot markers	None	Table with individual papers or butcher paper if this is a communal artwork. Wall with butcher paper.	Stamps for stamp pad. Both age groups are more likely to use hands.	Infants and toddlers
Crayons, colored pencils, markers, nontoxic oil pastels, chalk	None	Table with individual papers or butcher paper if this is a communal artwork. Wall with butcher paper.	None	Older infants and toddlers. Use chalk outside or with ventilation to prevent dust buildup.
Fabric	None	Can be connected into a "sensory blanket" with other materials such as bubble wrap for young infants to crawl over. Older children can use it on a table for collage.	Scissors (for toddlers only)	Infants and toddlers Invites open-ended dramatic play and dance for toddlers.

Peter is using both hands to squeeze out colored glue from the bottle. He has placed his sand down before the glue. This shows us that he does not understand that the glue will make the sand stick to the paper, but that he is testing out the properties of both materials on the paper.

Andy and Joo are engaging in a similar process, testing the materials without being told how to use them by an adult. They are developing strong fine motor skills as they handle the tools.

Conclusion

We have found that the art and sensory investigations in the infant and toddler classrooms are some of the most exciting that we provide. Well-planned projects that include time for exploration and a way to control—or at least contain—the mess allow everyone to relax and enjoy the process. We encourage you to try art and sensory activities with the infants and toddlers in your care. There is nothing like seeing a child realize that she has caused a mark on a paper, or watching a toddler discover for himself that mixing blue and red makes purple. While art explorations with infants and toddlers are certainly more work for caregivers, they have a strong positive impact on young children's development and learning.

Sources for Art/Sensory Materials

Materials available commercially: Tempera paint, foam paint, watercolor paint, glue, Popsicle sticks, colored sand, paper, contact paper, tape, stamp pads and stamps, bird-seed, feathers, soap, sponges.

Materials found at thrift stores: Cups and funnels, magazines for clipping images for collage, and kitchen utensils.

Nontoxic natural materials (bleach them before children put them in their mouths, using the ratio of bleach to water recommended by your state's licensing protocol): Straw, non-toxic leaves and seeds, flowers and sticks, wool, shells, rocks, gourds, pinecones, sand, mud.

Using these materials is beneficial to young children—handling nontoxic pinecones and leaves in a bin encourages a love of nature and engages all of a child's senses (White & Stoecklin 2008).

Materials found in the home or classroom: Paper towel/toilet paper rolls, yogurt containers, plastic water bottles, recycled paper, newspaper, cardboard boxes of all sizes, egg cartons, canning jar lids, water, old towels to make rags.

Materials created from scratch: Playdough, finger paint, oobleck, "clean mud," colored salt/sand. There are many recipes for these online and in the library.

References

Arnwine, B. 2007. *Starting Sensory Integration Therapy: Fun Activities That Won't Destroy Your Home or Classroom.* Arlington, TX: Future Horizons.

Cryer, D., T. Harms, & C. Riley. 2004. *All about the ITERS-R.* Lewisville, NC: Pact House.

Curtis, D. & M. Carter. 1996. *Reflecting Children's Lives: A Handbook for Planning Child-Centered Curriculum.* Saint Paul, MN: Redleaf.

Derman-Sparks, L., & J. Olsen Edwards. 2010. *Anti-Bias Education for Young Children and Ourselves.* Washington, DC: NAEYC.

Goldhawk, S. 1998. *Young Children and the Arts: Making Creative Connections. A Report of the Task Force on Children's Learning and the Arts, Birth to Age Eight.* Washington, DC: The Arts Education Partnership. www.eric.ed.gov./PDFS/ED453968.pdf.

Harms, T., R.M. Clifford, & D. Cryer. 2005. *Early Childhood Environment Rating Scale Revised.* New York: Teachers College Press.

Harms, T., D. Cryer, & R.M. Clifford. 2007. *Infant/Toddler Environment Rating Scale Revised Edition.* New York: Teachers College Press.

Miller, K. 1999. *Simple Steps: Developmental Activities for Infants, Toddlers, and Two-Year-Olds.* Beltsville, MD: Gryphon House.

Smith, D., & J. Goldhaber. 2004. *Poking, Pinching and Pretending: Documenting Toddlers' Explorations with Clay.* Saint Paul, MN: Redleaf.

White, R., & V.L. Stoecklin. 2008. "Nurturing Children's Biophilia: Developmentally Appropriate Environmental Education for Young Children." *Collage: Resources for Early Childhood Educators,* Nov. www.whitehutchinson.com/children/articles/nurturing.shtml.

Critical Thinking

1. Write a culturally sensitive policy on the use of food products in your classroom.

2. Choose two of the materials listed on the chart of sensory and art activities in the article and extend and develop an activity that you could use with infants and toddlers.

Create Central

www.mhhe.com/createcentral

Internet References

Idea Box
   http://theideabox.com

Make Your Own Webpage
   www.teacherweb.com

Meet Me at the Corner
   www.meetmeatthecorner.org

Teacher Planet
   http://teacherplanet.com

Teacher Quick Source
   www.teacherquicksource.com

Teachers Helping Teachers
   www.pacificnet.net/~mandel

Zero to Three
   zerotothree.org

Let's Get Messy! Exploring Sensory and Art Activities with Infants and Toddlers by Trudi Schwarz and Julia Luckenbill

143

TRUDI SCHWARZ, MS, is the infant room head teacher at the University of California–Davis Center for Child and Family Studies' NAEYC-Accredited Early Childhood Lab School. She has presented at California AEYC and local early childhood education conferences. Her professional interests include infant language development and creating innovative infant curricula. tkschwarz@ucdavis.edu.

JULIA LUCKENBILL, MA, is the infant and toddler program coordinator for the Early Childhood Lab School at UC–Davis. She has directed several preschool programs in California. In addition to her classroom and lecture responsibilities at the school, she presents on a range of child development topics for parents, teachers, and students. Her interests include sensory activities and integrating Reggio Emilia philosophy into US schools. jaluckenbill@ucdavis.edu.

Schwarz, Trudi; Luckenbill, Julia. From *Young Children*, September 2012, pp. 26–34. Copyright © 2012 by National Association for the Education of Young Children. Reprinted by permission. www.naeyc.org.

Article   Prepared by: Karen Menke Paciorek, *Eastern Michigan University*

Time for Play

A new movement of parents and childhood experts want to save an endangered human behavior: joyful, spontaneous play unaided by electronic screens and hovering parents.

STEPHANIE HANES

Learning Outcomes

After reading this article, you will be able to:

- Chronicle how play has evolved over the past half century.

- Explain to administrators and families why play should be an integral part of the curriculum.

H avely Taylor knows that her two children do not play the way she did when she was growing up.

When Ms. Taylor was a girl, in a leafy suburb of Birmingham, Ala., she climbed trees, played imaginary games with her friends, and transformed a hammock into a storm-tossed sea vessel. She even whittled bows and arrows from downed branches around the yard and had "wars" with friends—something she admits she'd probably freak out about if her children did it today.

"I mean, you could put an eye out like that," she says with a laugh.

Her children—Ava, age 12, and Henry, 8—have had a different experience. They live in Baltimore, where Taylor works as an art teacher. Between school, homework, violin lessons, ice-skating, theater, and play dates, there is little time for the sort of freestyle play Taylor remembers. Besides, Taylor says, they live in the city, with a postage stamp of a backyard and the ever-present threat of urban danger.

"I was kind of afraid to let them go out unsupervised in Baltimore . . . ," she says, of how she started down this path with the kids. "I'm really a protective mom. There wasn't much playing outside."

This difference has always bothered her, she says, because she believes that play is critical for children's developing emotions, creativity, and intelligence. But when she learned that her daughter's middle school had done away with recess, and even free time after lunch, she decided to start fighting for play.

"It seemed almost cruel," she says. "Play is important for children—it's something so obvious it's almost hard to articulate. How can you talk about childhood without talking about play? It's almost as if they are trying to get rid of childhood."

Taylor joined a group of parents pressuring the principal to let their children have a recess, citing experts such as the US Centers for Disease Control and Prevention, which recommends that all students have at least 60 minutes of physical activity every day. They issued petitions and held meetings. And although the school has not yet agreed to change its curriculum, Taylor says she feels their message is getting more recognition.

She is not alone in her concerns. In recent years, child development experts, parents, and scientists have been sounding an increasingly urgent alarm about the decreasing amount of time that children—and adults, for that matter—spend playing. A combination of social forces, from a No Child Left Behind focus on test scores to the push for children to get ahead with programmed extracurricular activities, leaves less time for the roughhousing, fantasizing, and pretend worlds advocates say are crucial for development.

Meanwhile, technology and a wide-scale change in toys have shifted what happens when children do engage in leisure activity, in a way many experts say undermines long-term emotional and intellectual abilities. An 8-year-old today, for instance, is more likely to be playing with a toy that has a computer chip, or attending a tightly supervised soccer practice, than making up an imaginary game with friends in the backyard or street.

But play is making a comeback. Bolstered by a growing body of scientific research detailing the cognitive benefits of different types of play, parents such as Taylor are pressuring school administrations to bring back recess and are fighting against a trend to move standardized testing and increased academic instruction to kindergarten.

Public officials are getting in on the effort. First lady Michelle Obama and US Secretary of Education Arne Duncan, for instance, have made a push for playgrounds nationwide. Local politicians from Baltimore to New York have participated in events such as the Ultimate Block Party—a metropolitan-wide play gathering. Meanwhile, business and corporate groups, worried about a future workforce hampered by a lack of creativity and innovation, support the effort.

"It's at a tipping point," says Susan Magsamen, the director of Interdisciplinary Partnerships at the Johns Hopkins University School of Medicine Brain Science Institute, who has headed numerous child play efforts. "Parents are really anxious and really overextended. Teachers are feeling that way, too."

So when researchers say and can show that "it's OK to not be so scheduled [and] programmed—that time for a child to daydream is a good thing," Ms. Magsamen says, it confirms what families and educators "already knew, deep down, but didn't have the permission to act upon."

But play, it seems, isn't that simple.

Scientists disagree about what sort of play is most important, government is loath to regulate the type of toys and technology that increasingly shape the play experience, and parents still feel pressure to supervise children's play rather than let them go off on their own. (Nearly two-thirds of Americans in a December *Monitor* TIPP poll, for instance, said it is irresponsible to let children play without supervision; almost as many said studying is more important than play.) And there is still pressure on schools to sacrifice playtime—often categorized as frivolous—in favor of lessons that boost standardized test scores.

"Play is still terribly threatened," says Susan Linn, an instructor of psychiatry at Harvard Medical School and director of the nonprofit Campaign for a Commercial-Free Childhood. But, she adds, "what is changing is that there's a growing recognition that the erosion of play may be a problem . . . we need to do something about."

One could say that the state of play, then, is at a crossroads. What happens to it—how it ends up fitting into American culture, who defines it, what it looks like—will have long-term implications for childhood, say those who study it.

Some go even further: The future of play will define society overall and even determine the future of our species.

"Play is the fundamental equation that makes us human," says Stuart Brown, the founder of the California-based National Institute for Play. "Its absence, in my opinion, is pathology."

Can You Define "Play"?

But before advocates can launch a defense of play, they need to grapple with a surprisingly difficult question. What, exactly, is play?

It might seem obvious. Parents know when their children are playing, whether it's a toddler scribbling on a piece of paper, an infant shaking a rattle, or a pair of 10-year-olds dressing up and pretending to be superheroes.

But even Merriam-Webster's Collegiate Dictionary definition, "recreational activity; especially the spontaneous action of children," is often inaccurate, according to scientists and child development researchers. Play for children is neither simply recreational nor necessarily spontaneous, they say.

"Play is when children are using something they've learned, to try it out and see how it works, to use it in new ways—it's problem solving and enjoying the satisfaction of problems

solv[ed]," says Diane Levin, a professor of education at Wheelock College in Boston. But Ms. Levin says that, in her class on the meaning and development of play, she never introduces one set definition.

"This is something that people argue about," she says.

Scientists and child advocates agree that there are many forms of play. There is "attunement play," the sort of interaction where a mother and infant might gaze at each other and babble back and forth. There is "object play," where a person might manipulate a toy such as a set of marbles; "rough and tumble play"; and "imaginative play." "Free play" is often described as kids playing on their own, without any adult supervision; "guided play" is when a child or other player takes the lead, but a mentor is around to, say, help facilitate the LEGO castle construction.

But often, says Dr. Brown at the National Institute for Play, a lot is happening all at once. He cites the time he tried to do a brain scan of his then-4-year-old grandson at play with his stuffed tiger.

"He was clearly playing," Brown recalls.

"And then he says to me, 'Grandpa, what does the tiger say?' I say, 'Roar!' And then he says, 'No, it says, "Moo!"'" and

Evolution of Play

1950s:

- **Outdoor play** without adult supervision was common in both urban and rural US settings.
- **Different ages** played together.
- **Bicycles and balls** were the main outdoor toys, and board games were the most common inside.
- **Much of play** revolved around traditional games such as baseball, modified to fit space and materials.

1980s:

- **Use of toys increased,** and many were 'branded'—connected to TV characters—Barbies, Power Rangers, My Little Ponies, etc.
- **Outdoor play** was likely to be adult-supervised or part of an 'organized activity.'
- **TV viewing** was increasingly a part of free time.
- **Athletics become more formal** and age-based—such as soccer camp for 7-year-olds rather than neighborhood pickup soccer in a vacant lot.

2010s:

- **Toys are the center** of play; most are connected to media characters and are somehow electronic.
- **Most free time** is screen time spent in front of the TV, computer, etc.
- **Unsupervised outdoor time** is almost nonexistent. Physical activity of any kind has decreased.
- **Multi-age,** cross-gender play is disappearing, even among siblings.

—Stephanie Hanes

then laughs like crazy. How are you going to track *that*? He's pretending, he's making a joke, he's interacting."

This is one reason Brown says play has been discounted—both culturally and, until relatively recently, within the academic community, where detractors argue that play is so complex it cannot be considered one specific behavior, that it is an amalgamation of many different acts. These scientists—known as "play skeptics"—don't believe play can be responsible for all sorts of positive effects, in part because play itself is suspect.

"It is so difficult to define and objectify," Brown notes.

But most researchers agree that play clearly exists, even if it can't always be coded in the standard scientific way of other human behaviors. And the importance of play, Brown and others say, is huge.

Brown became interested in play as a young clinical psychiatrist when he was researching, somewhat incongruously, mass murderers. Although he concluded that many factors contributed to the psychosis of his subjects, Brown noticed that a common denominator was that none had participated in standard play behavior as children, such as interacting positively with parents or engaging in games with other children. As he continued his career, he took "play histories" of patients, eventually recording 6,000. He saw a direct correlation between play behavior and happiness, from childhood into adulthood.

It has a lot to do with joy, he says: "In the play studies I'd find many adults who had a pretty playful childhood but then confined themselves to grinding, to always being responsible, always seeing just the next task. [They] are less flexible and have a chronic, smoldering depression. That lack of joyfulness gets to you."

Brown later worked with ethologists—scientists who study animal behavior—to observe how other species, from honeybees to Labrador retrievers, play. This behavior in a variety of species is sophisticated—from "self-handicapping," so a big dog plays fairly with a small dog, to cross-species play, such as a polar bear romping with a sled dog. He also studied research on play depravation, noting how rat brains change negatively when they are deprived of some sorts of play.

Brown became convinced that human play—for adults as well as children—is not only joyful but necessary, a behavior

---

A 2-Year-Old's Dilemma: Angry Birds or Plain Old Blocks?

The Games Kids No Longer Play

Once upon a time, a typical gift for a child was a set of blocks. Plain old blocks with no batteries or screens, no electronic voice asking to be friends, no game of Angry Birds somehow embedded in their cubic walls.

No longer.

As anyone who braved toy stores this past holiday season knows, the bulk of gear for children these days is far more technologically decked out, with everything from flashing lights to 3-D computer screens to disembodied voices. And this, say child development experts, is turning into a massive problem.

High-stimuli toys, even many of those advertised as "educational" or "interactive," actually serve to diminish children's creativity, many experts say. Instead of using their minds to imagine how to use a toy—how to build a castle with blocks, say—they simply push a button or watch a flashing light. The toy is doing the work, which is the reverse of what researchers say is ideal.

"The best toy is 90 percent child and 10 percent toy," says Susan Linn, a Harvard University psychiatry instructor and cofounder of the Campaign for a Commercial-Free Childhood. "The [perfect] toy's meaning and its use changes at the child's behest."

At the same time, a large percentage of children's toys are based on media characters—Transformers, for instance, were top sellers this past holiday season. The problem with this, says Diane Levin, an education professor at Wheelock College in Boston, is that when a child plays with a toy that already has a character description, the play tends to be limited; the child doesn't invent the figure's personality or actions because those characteristics are already determined.

"Play material is very important," Ms. Levin says. "When they have something that is just something they saw on TV, they will use it the same way. They will imitate."

And of course, there is the issue of screen time. According to the Kaiser Family Foundation, 8-to-18-year-olds now spend 7.5 hours a day in front of one or more screens. This, according to the American Academy of Pediatrics, is too much. It recommends no screen time for children 2 years old and younger, and no more than two hours a day for older ones.

But some top-selling toys this past season—including infant toys—were screen-based. (Teachers Resisting Unhealthy Children's Entertainment named a tablet computer for babies the worst toy of the year; a similar device was in the Toys "R" Us Top 15 Christmas gifts for 2011.)

Many of these screen toys advertise themselves as educational, tapping into parents' desire to help children get ahead in a technologically focused world. In a December *Monitor* TIPP poll, for instance, two-thirds of Americans agreed with the statement "the earlier a child can use technology, the better off he or she will be." Yet numerous studies have found no educational benefit—and possibly some harm—in early screen time.

It comes down, child advocates say, to money.

"One of the reasons that creative play has been diminishing in the United States is that it's not lucrative," Dr. Linn says. "Companies make less money when children play creatively. Children who play creatively need less stuff, and they can use the same thing over and over again—mud, water, blocks, dolls that don't do anything."

—Stephanie Hanes

that has survived despite connections in some studies to injury and danger (for example, animals continue to play even though they're likely to be hunted while doing so) and is connected to the most ancient part of human biology.

'Executive' Play

Other scientists are focusing on the specific impacts of play. In a small, brick testing room next to the "construction zone" at the Boston Children's Museum, for instance, Daniel Friel sits with a collection of brightly colored tubing glued to a board. The manager of the Early Childhood Cognition Lab in the Department of Brain and Cognitive Sciences at the Massachusetts Institute of Technology (MIT), he observes children at play with puppets and squeaky toys, rubber balls and fabulously created pipe sculptures. Depending on the experiment, Mr. Friel and other researchers record such data as the time a child plays with a particular object or what color ball is picked out of a container. These observations lead to insights on how children form their understanding of the world.

"We are interested in exploratory play, how kids develop cause and effect, how they use evidence," he says.

The collection of tubing, for instance, is part of a study designed by researcher Elizabeth Bonawitz and tests whether the way an object is presented can limit a child's exploration. If a teacher introduces the toy, which has a number of hidden points of interest—a mirror, a button that lights up, etc.—but tells a child about only one feature, the child is less likely to discover everything the toy can do than a child who receives the toy from a teacher who feigns ignorance. Without limiting instruction from an adult, it seems, a child is far more creative. In other words, adult hovering and instruction, from how to play soccer to how to build the best LEGO city, can be limiting.

Taken together, the MIT experiments show children calculating probabilities during play, developing assumptions about their physical environment, and adjusting perceptions according to the direction of authority figures. Other researchers are also discovering a breathtaking depth to play: how it develops chronological awareness and its link to language development and self-control.

The latter point has been a hot topic recently. Self-regulation—the buzzword here is "executive function," referring to abilities such as planning, multitasking, and reasoning—may be more indicative of future academic success than IQ, standardized tests, or other assessments, according to a host of recent studies from institutions such as Pennsylvania State University and the University of British Columbia.

Curriculums that boost executive function have become increasingly popular. Two years ago, Elizabeth Billings-Fouhy, director of the public Children's Place preschool in Lexington, Mass., decided to adopt one such program, called Tools of the Mind. It was created by a pair of child development experts—Deborah Leong and Elena Bodrova—in the early 1990s after a study evaluating federal early literacy efforts found no positive outcomes.

"People started saying there must be something else," Dr. Leong says. "And we believed what was missing was self-regulation and executive function."

She became interested in a body of research from Russia that showed children who played more had better self-regulation. This made sense to her, she says. For example, studies have shown that children can stand still far longer if they are playing soldier; games such as Simon says depend on concentration and rule-following.

"Play is when kids regulate their behavior voluntarily," Leong says. Eventually, she and Dr. Bodrova developed the curriculum used in the Children's Place today, where students spend the day in different sorts of play. They act out long-form make-believe scenes, they build their own props, and they participate in buddy reading, where one child has a picture of a pair of lips and the other has a picture of ears. The child with the lips reads; the other listens. Together, these various play exercises increase self-control, educators say.

This was on clear display recently at the Children's Place. Nearly half the children there have been labeled as special needs students with everything from autism to physical limitations. The others are mainstream preschoolers—an "easier" group, perhaps, but still not one typically renowned for its self-control.

But in a brightly colored classroom, a group of 3-, 4-, and 5-year-olds are notably calm; polite and quiet, sitting in pairs, taking turns "reading" a picture book.

"Here are scissors, a brush. . .," a boy named Aiden points out to his partner, Kyle, who is leaning in attentively.

"Oh, don't forget the paint," Kyle says, although he's mostly quiet, as it's his turn to listen.

Aiden nods and smiles: "Yes, the paint."

When Aiden is finished, the boys switch roles. Around them, another dozen toddlers do the same—all without teacher direction. The Tools classrooms have the reputation of being far better-behaved than mainstream classes.

"We have been blown away," says Ms. Billings-Fouhy, the director, comparing how students are doing now versus before the Tools curriculum. "We can't believe the difference."

Educators and scientists have published overwhelmingly positive analyses since the early 2000s of the sort of curriculum Tools of the Mind employs. But recently the popularity of the play-based curriculum has skyrocketed, with more preschools adopting the Tools method and parenting chat rooms buzzing about the curriculum. Two years ago, for instance, Billings-Fouhy had to convince people about changing the Children's Place program. Now out-of-district parents call to get their children in.

> **"Play is the fundamental equation that makes us human. Its absence, in my opinion, is pathology."**
>
> —Stuart Brown, founder of the National Institute for Play

"I think we're at this place where everyone is coming to the conclusion that play is important," Leong says. "Not just because of self-regulation, but because people are worried about the development of the whole child—their social and emotional development as well."

Today's Kids Don't Know How to Play

But not all play is created equal, experts warn.

The Tools of the Mind curriculum, for instance, uses what Leong calls "intentional mature play"—play that is facilitated and guided by trained educators. If children in the class were told to simply go and play, she says, the result probably would be a combination of confusion, mayhem, and paralysis.

"People say, 'Let's bring back play,'" Leong says. "But they don't realize play won't just appear spontaneously, especially not in preschool. . . . The culture of childhood itself has changed."

For a host of reasons, today's children do not engage in all sorts of developmentally important play that prior generations automatically did. In her class at Wheelock College, Levin has students interview people over the age of 50 about how they played. In the 1950s and '60s, students regularly find, children played outdoors no matter where they lived, and without parental supervision. They played sports but adjusted the rules to fit the space and material—a goal in soccer, for instance, might be kicking a tennis ball to the right of the trash can. They had few toys, and older children tended to act as "play mentors" to younger children, instructing them in the ways of make-believe games.

That has changed dramatically, she says. In the early 1980s, the federal government deregulated children's advertising, allowing TV shows to essentially become half-hour-long advertisements for toys such as Power Rangers, My Little Ponies, and Teenage Mutant Ninja Turtles. Levin says that's when children's play changed. They wanted specific toys, to use them in the specific way that the toys appeared on TV.

Today, she says, children are "second generation deregulation," and not only have more toys—mostly media-based—but also lots of screens. A Kaiser Family Foundation study recently found that 8-to-18-year-olds spend an average of 7.5 hours in front of a screen every day, with many of those hours involving multiscreen multitasking. Toys for younger children tend to have reaction-based operations, such as push-buttons and flashing lights.

Take away the gadgets and the media-based scripts, Levin and others say, and many children today simply don't know what to do.

"If they don't have the toys, they don't know how to play," she says.

The American educational system, increasingly teaching to standardized tests, has also diminished children's creativity, says Kathy Hirsh-Pasek, a professor of psychology and director of the Infant Language Laboratory at Temple University in Philadelphia. "Children learn from being actively engaged in meaningful activities," she says. "What we're doing seems to

be the antithesis of this. We're building robots. And you know, computers are better robots than children."

Other countries, particularly in Asia, she notes, have already shifted their educational focus away from test scores, and Finland—which is at the top of international ranking—has a policy of recess after every class for Grades 1 through 9.

But as Dr. Hirsh-Pasek points out, children spend most of their time out of school. A playful life is possible if parents and communities know what to do.

The Ultimate Block Party, which Hirsh-Pasek developed with other researchers, is one way to involve local governments, educators, and institutions in restoring play and creativity, she says. The Ultimate Block Party is a series of play stations—from blocks to sandboxes to dress-up games to make-believe environments—where kids can play with their parents. Meanwhile, the event's staff helps explain to caregivers what sorts of developmental benefits the children achieve through different types of play.

The first Ultimate Block Party in New York's Central Park in October 2010 attracted 50,000 people; Toronto and Baltimore held parties last year. Organizers now say they get multiple requests from cities every month to hold their own block parties; Hirsh-Pasek says she hopes the movement will go grass roots, with towns and neighborhoods holding their own play festivities.

"It's an exciting time," she says. "We're starting to make some headway. It's time for all of us to find the way to become a more creative, thinking culture."

Critical Thinking

1. Interview three of your peers not taking early childhood or child development classes and ask them to name some of their favorite childhood play memories. Were there similarities among their responses? If so, how did their memories compare to your memories of play experiences when you were young?

2. With all of the evidence that supports children having ample opportunities to engage in freely chosen play, why do you think there is such backlash to children playing, both in school and during their out of school time? How did play become a negative way to use one's time?

Create Central

www.mhhe.com/createcentral

Internet References

HighScope Educational Research Foundation
www.highscope.org

National Association for the Education of Young Children
www.naeyc.org

National Institute for Play
www.nifplay.org

Unit 6

UNIT

Prepared by: Karen Menke Paciorek, *Eastern Michigan University*

Teaching Practices That Help Children Thrive in School

This unit focuses on teachers, administrators, and the practices they perform to ensure student success. We know that teachers possess and exert significant power and control over what occurs in their classrooms. That is a huge responsibility, and teachers should receive all of the support necessary to enable them to carry through with the many requirements of the job. The influence teachers have over the students in their classroom continues to have a strong impact even with the influx of technology and media sources. There has been much debate over the choice of materials and curriculum content, but teachers can trump all these by what they say or do in the classroom. We need to give teachers the strategies and skills to lead with the understanding of what is best for children and what will encourage the students' development and learning. I get frustrated when I visit schools and am in classrooms in which I would not want to spend one hour, let alone the three to eleven hours some young children spend in formal education settings each and every day. I see classrooms with all life and joy sucked right out of them and instead occupied by children void of energy or excitement for learning. If zest and passion for teaching is not part of what you bring to your job each and every day, then consider another profession. Children's success depends on highly motivated and skilled teachers who understand the importance of what they do. As Abraham Lincoln said, "Whatever you are, be a good one."

In a recent conversation I had with a parent the woman said her husband picked up their daughter during lunch time and noticed their daughter's face getting red as she ran to greet her father. He then saw she was eating humus she got from a classmate. He quickly got her EpiPen and administered the required medication. After things calmed down he had a conversation with the lead teacher and new-to-the-job assistant teacher who said she checked the list and saw Riley was allergic to chick peas and she thought it was ok since she was eating humus. The assistant teacher didn't realize that humus is made from chick peas. A few years ago teachers only focused on academic content but now teachers of young children have a whole host of issues about which they must be well informed and then use that information to best support the children in their classrooms.

The struggle between doing what is right for students and what state standards mandate has become an issue teachers face more often in these days of high stakes testing and accountability. Teachers face a great challenge as they balance the needs of the child with the demands of the curriculum. The state standards can challenge teachers who are trying to make meaningful and engaging learning opportunities a common occurrence in the classroom. Policies, standards, and understanding of child development demand a teacher's attention on a daily basis.

Taking the time to play, tinker around, or freely explore is so crucial to figuring things out and learning. The opportunities of play afforded time to the great inventors like Orville and Wilbur Wright, Thomas Edison, Henry Ford, Steve Jobs, Bill Gates, and Mark Zuckerberg, to discover and let their minds create. Can you imagine the stifling of creativity that passive learning would have done to these contributors to our modern conveniences? Their play allowed them to imagine planes, lights, automobiles, computers, and social media! We appreciate their inventions, and children today need the same opportunities to manipulate and interact with a variety of materials. Who knows what they will imagine and create? In my five trips to China in the past eight years I have observed in over 500 classrooms and have heard of the interest of the Chinese government to move to more creativity in teaching, yet educators in China struggle to allow students the freedom to explore and investigate. Creativity doesn't just happen without the fertile ground that is laid starting when a child is very young.

It is my hope this unit will encourage teachers to hone their skills and strategies. Teachers, you have the power. You have the power to inspire, encourage, and teach. Use your power wisely. Read these articles with the commitment that you will use your power for the good. Read these articles with the goal of reflecting on your practice and improving on your skills. The students want to thrive in their learning, but will you help them?

Good Thinking! Fostering Children's Reasoning and Problem Solving by Jessica Vick Whittaker

151

Article   Prepared by: Karen Menke Paciorek, *Eastern Michigan University*

Good Thinking!

Fostering Children's Reasoning and Problem Solving

JESSICA VICK WHITTAKER

Learning Outcomes

After reading this article, you will be able to:

- Explain to others why developing critical thinking skills in young children is important for future learning.

- Articulate how problem solving ability is helpful to learning in other domains.

- Describe significant findings from the research on children's thinking.

Sandy teaches 3- and 4-year-old children in a Head Start classroom. She often asks children to be investigators and to solve problems or questions that arise. For example, during outside time one day, Sandy notices Keira and Amir playing on the slide. Sandy hears Keira say, "Hey, Amir, you're going really fast down that slide! How come I'm not going so fast?" Sandy comments, "Keira, you made a really interesting observation. You noticed that Amir is going down the slide faster than you. Why do you think that might be?" "Well," Keira says thoughtfully, "maybe because his pants are more slippery than mine." Sandra responds, "That is really good thinking! You've made a guess, a hypothesis. Can you think of some way we could test out whether Amir's clothing is making him go faster?"

Keira decides that she can test whether clothing makes a difference by using clothes from the dramatic play area. She finds two pairs of pants: one pair from a wizard outfit that is very shiny and made of what Keira calls "slippery" material, and the other a pair of jeans from the construction worker outfit. They look rough and less slippery. Sandy times Keira as she goes down the slide to see whether the slippery pants make her go faster. They find that Keira can indeed slide faster with the slippery pants on.

From this experience Keira learns several things. She learns, for example, that the texture of a material—whether it is smooth or rough—affects how quickly or slowly an object (in this case, a person) moves down a ramp. She learns that if she doesn't know the answer to a question she can make a guess and then test that guess to determine if it is correct (she also discovers that another word for *guess* is *hypothesis*). If something puzzles Keira, she now knows that she can ask her teacher for help and information.

If asked, sandy could identify particular content areas she supported during this interaction. She could respond that she fostered Keira's knowledge about the physical world and how things work (science), encouraged her thinking about inclined planes (mathematics), and expanded her communication skills by teaching her new words and how to explain her thinking (language). As important as these skills are, however, there was more to this learning experience than just science, mathematics, and language. In this interaction, Sandy encouraged Keira to construct a possible explanation, a hypothesis, and then test that explanation to better understand cause-and-effect relationships. Sandy promoted "good thinking," the ability to logically think and reason about the world.

Critical thinking skills span multiple domains. They include focusing to pursue knowledge, using self-control to define a problem and determine goals, making connections to brainstorm solutions, and communicating to justify actions and share evaluations (Galinsky 2010).

Forty-four percent of the preschool day is spent on learning activities, primarily literacy and writing activities (Early et al. 2005). Too often, such activities focus on skill attainment and not on the critical thinking, reasoning, and problem solving that are foundational to learning and development. Such skills warrant attention, and it is important that teachers foster them *intentionally*. This article summarizes research on the development of preschool children's critical thinking skills and suggests practical, research-based strategies for supporting them.

Reasoning and Problem-Solving Skills

Definitions of critical thinking skills vary, although nearly all include reasoning, making judgments and conclusions, and solving problems (Willingham 2008; Lai 2011). Although it was previously believed that these were higher-order thinking skills that developed only in older children and adults (Piaget 1930), research demonstrates that children reason and problem solve as early as infancy (e.g., Woodward 2009). Between ages 3 and 5 children form complex thoughts and insights, and during the preschool years their cognitive abilities—including logical thinking and reasoning—develop substantially (Amsterlaw & Wellman 2006). These skills enable children to recognize, understand, and analyze a problem and draw on knowledge or experience to seek solutions to the problem (USDHHS 2010). Some researchers conclude that reasoning and problem-solving skills are domain specific (e.g., reasoning skills in science do not necessarily transfer to mathematics); others, however, argue that teachers can foster young children's general critical thinking skills (see Lai 2011 for a review).

Reasoning and problem-solving skills are foundational for lifelong learning. Analyzing arguments, making inferences, reasoning, and implementing decisions to solve problems are important skills across all content areas and thus critical for school success. The ability to efficiently gather, understand, analyze, and interpret information is increasingly necessary to function in school and in the workplace (Schneider 2002). Educators and policy makers, now more than ever, recognize the need to foster critical thinking skills in young children. This is evidenced in the Common Core State Standards, which emphasize the importance of reasoning and problem-solving skills in preparing children for "college, workforce training, and life in a technological society" (NGA Center & CCSSO 2010, 4).

Key Ideas about Children's Thinking

Three key ideas emerge from the research on young children's thinking:

1. Young children are capable of developing reasoning and problem-solving skills.
2. Children's early reasoning and problem-solving skills support their later development and learning.
3. Early childhood educators can foster children's reasoning and problem solving.

Research suggests how these ideas relate to everyday practice.

Young Children Can Develop Reasoning and Problem-Solving Skills

Scholars long believed that true logical reasoning does not develop until adolescence (Piaget 1930). However, recent research suggests that logical thinking and reasoning begin in infancy and develop gradually throughout childhood (Gopnik et al. 2004; Hollister Sandberg & McCullough 2010). From infancy on, children pay attention to people's intentions and goals, and infants as young as 6 months old demonstrate rudimentary reasoning skills (Woodward 2009).

Early reasoning skills. Woodward and her colleagues explored how infants make sense of their physical and social worlds and develop reasoning skills (e.g., Hamlin, Hallinan, & Woodward 2008; Cannon & Woodward 2012). The researchers tested whether 7-month-olds would copy an experimenter's actions if they understood the experimenter's intention (Hamlin, Hallinan, & Woodward 2008). Infants were shown two toys, and then they watched as the experimenter reached for one of the toys and grasped it. The experimenter pushed the toys within reach of the infants and said, "Now it's your turn!" Infants reliably touched the same object the experimenter had grasped. This was not the case when the experimenter simply brushed the toy with the back of her hand rather than grasped it (suggesting that the touch was unintentional, not goal directed). In both cases the experimenter's actions drew attention to the object, but infants responded only when they interpreted the experimenter's actions as goal directed. These results, along with others from a series of studies Woodward and colleagues conducted, demonstrate that infants as young as 7 months old can analyze others' intentions and use this information to reason about things in their world (Woodward 2009).

Understanding of causality. Between 9 and 12 months, infants begin to understand that one event or behavior causes another (Woodward 2009), and 2-year-olds are adept at using causality in their thinking (McMullen 2013). Gopnik and colleagues (2000; 2001) designed a series of experiments to explore how young children construct and test explanations for events. They showed children a "magical" light box that glowed when it was activated. Although the experimenter controlled the box, the box appeared to be activated by placing a block on top of it. The experimenter showed 2- to 4-year-old children different blocks, some that turned the box on (the experimenter called these *blickets*) and some that did not (not blickets). The children were asked which block was the blicket. Children as young as 2 were able to draw causal conclusions about which object was the blicket, correctly choosing the block that had "activated" the light. In another experiment with 3- and 4-year-old children, the task was modified so two blocks were placed on the machine and children were asked which block to remove to make the machine stop lighting up. Children correctly predicted which object they should remove from the box to make it stop.

The blicket studies are important because they demonstrate that very young children understand how one thing affects another and that as children get older, their reasoning skills are more sophisticated. Children are increasingly able to generate theories about the causal effects of objects and to test those theories by asking questions and making predictions.

Inductive and deductive reasoning. Understanding cause and effect is an important component of both inductive and deductive reasoning, which develop between the ages of 3 and 6 (Schraw et al. 2011). Young children use *inductive reasoning* when they generalize the conclusions they draw from the consequences of their own behaviors or experiences. *Deductive reasoning* is the process by which individuals use facts or general rules to draw a conclusion, being able to understand the premise "If *P* happens, then *Q* will too" (Schraw et al. 2011).

Three-year-old Maya has a fireplace at home and has learned through experience that fires are hot and should not be touched. When she sees the flame on a gas stove in the kitchen at her early childhood program, she reasons that the stove is also hot and should not be touched. "Hot," she says to her friend. "Don't touch!" Maya uses inductive reasoning in this situation, generalizing and extending her knowledge about fire and heat to a new situation.

Although young children's deductive reasoning becomes more sophisticated with age, their development of this reasoning is complex.

Three-year-old Brandon knows that if it is nighttime, it is time for him to take a bath (if *P*, then *Q*). Through repeated experiences—nighttime (P), then bath (Q)—Brandon connects these two events using deductive reasoning, the basis for making predictions. Inductive and deductive reasoning skills grow substantially during the preschool years as a result of children's increasing knowledge and varied experiences and interactions with the world around them.

Analogical reasoning. Goswami and Pauen (2005) have spent many years researching how *analogical reasoning,* a form of inductive reasoning that involves making and understanding comparisons, develops in young children (Goswami 1995; Goswami & Pauen 2005). In a series of three experiments, they tested the ability of 3- and 4-year-olds to make comparisons, or relational mappings, based on size (Goswami 1995). An experimenter read *Goldilocks and the Three Bears* to a child, and then said they were going to play a game about choosing cups. The experimenter said, "We are each going to have a set of cups, a daddy-bear-size cup, a mummy-bear-size

cup, and a baby-bear-size cup, and you have to choose the same cup from your set that I choose from mine." The experimenter named the cups in her set (e.g., "I'm choosing the Mummy cup") but not in the child's set. To choose the correct cup, the child had to work out the size relationship between the two sets of cups using one-to-one correspondence. Not only did 3- and 4-year-old children choose the correct cup, they could do so even when the positions and colors of their cups were different from those of the experimenter's cups.

However, when experimenters asked 3- and 4-year-olds to make analogies (comparisons) involving concepts rather than physical characteristics (e.g., *A* is hotter than *B* is hotter than *C,* or *A* is louder than *B* is louder than *C*), only the 4-year-olds were successful (Goswami 1995; Goswami & Pauen 2005). Goswami concluded that children as young as 3 can use analogies as a basis for reasoning only if the analogy is based on a familiar structure, such as the characters in *Goldilocks*. This skill develops and becomes more sophisticated over time, doing so rather rapidly during the brief time between ages 3 and 4.

Reasoning with abstract ideas. Research demonstrates that although young children's deductive reasoning becomes more sophisticated with age and that 4-year-olds can reason using abstract ideas, their development of this reasoning is complex. For example, a teacher is working with a small group of children. She says, "We're going to think about some silly stories together. Some of the stories may sound funny, but I want you to think carefully about them. For each story, I'm going to ask you to use your imagination and make a picture in your head. In this story, all cats bark. So the cats that are in your head, are they barking? Are they meowing? Now, Jeremy is a cat. Is Jeremy barking? Is Jeremy meowing? How do you know?" Problems like this actually get more difficult for children as they get older and acquire more real-world experience, because they are more likely to know of counterexamples ("I know a cat that can't 'meow'!"). However, children eventually overcome this and draw the correct conclusions from complex, even absurd, premises (Hollister Sandburg & McCullough 2010).

Children's Early Reasoning and Problem-Solving Skills Support Their Later Development and Learning

Cognitive learning. Children's reasoning and problem-solving skills are associated with a range of important literacy learning (e.g., Tzuriel & Flor-Maduel 2010) and mathematics outcomes (Grissmer et al. 2010). In an analysis of six longitudinal data sets, researchers found that general knowledge at kindergarten entry was the strongest predictor of children's science and reading skills and a strong predictor of math skills (Grissmer et al. 2010). General knowledge includes children's thinking and reasoning skills, in particular their ability to form questions about the natural world, gather evidence, and communicate conclusions (USDOE 2002).

Social-emotional learning. Children's reasoning and problem-solving skills are also important components of social and emotional competence. Social problem-solving skills include generating a number of alternative solutions to a conflict and understanding and considering the consequences of one's behaviors (Denham & Almeida 1987; Denham et al. 2012). These skills are linked to children's long-term behavioral outcomes (Youngstrom et al. 2000), school adjustment (Bierman et al. 2008), and academic success (Greenberg, Kusché, & Riggs 2001).

To see how reasoning and problem solving apply to the social-emotional domain, let's return to Sandy's classroom a couple of months after Keira's first experience with creating an experiment to test a hypothesis:

> Keira notices Andy and Eric creating a zoo with animals and blocks in the block area and asks, "Can I play with you?" Andy responds, "No, there's not enough animals for three people!" Upset, Keira says to her teacher, Sandy, "Andy won't play with me because I'm a girl." Sandy bends down to Keira's eye level and says, "Are you sure? I saw you and Andy playing together just this morning on the playground. Can you think of any other reasons Andy might not want to play with you right now?" Keira says, "Well, maybe because there aren't enough animals for me too." Sandy asks Keira where she might find some other animals to add to the zoo. Keira finds several animal puppets in the book area and takes them to the block area.

As this situation demonstrates, children's daily experiences offer opportunities to construct explanations about cause and effect. When teachers provide enriching experiences and materials and support children's interactions with each other, they enable children to develop their reasoning.

In addition to these general teaching practices, there are specific strategies that promote preschool children's reasoning and problem-solving skills. These strategies, described in detail in the following three sections, promote "thoughtful decision

---

Checklist of Teaching Practices and Strategies to Support Preschool Children's Problem Solving and Reasoning

- **Facilitate children's play.** Support children's exploratory play experiences by providing challenging, varied materials that appeal to all of the senses—sight, sound, smell, touch, and taste. Encourage communication during play by extending children's language with their peers and with you. Ask them to talk about their play both during and after their play experiences.

- **Help children understand the difference between guessing and knowing.** A guess, or hypothesis, needs to be tested. Assist children with simple experiments in which they make predictions based on their hypotheses, gather evidence by making observations that they document (e.g., through pictures, dictated stories, graphs), and seek information to help them support or reject their original hypotheses and make conclusions. Do they prove their hypotheses, or do they need to do additional experimenting?

- **Foster categorization skills.** Provide materials that allow children to explore, compare, and sort by a variety of attributes (size, shape, sound, taste, etc.). With younger children, use objects that differ in just one attribute (e.g., balls of different colors). Ask children to describe the similarities and differences and to put the objects into categories. Use and reinforce vocabulary that helps children describe their comparisons (e.g.,

short, round, loud, quiet, blue, red, smooth, bumpy) and use problem-solving language (e.g., hypothesis, compare, observe, interpret). During play, notice how children use materials. Do they sort them? Do they comment on similarities and differences?

- **Encourage children to think before responding.** Help children learn to freeze—to take a moment before answering a question to think about their best or most reasonable response to a problem and how they would test it. With a group of children, discuss different ways they solved a problem to demonstrate that there is often more than one way to do so. Point out that children sometimes think about and approach things differently, but that everyone's ideas should be respected.

- **Model and promote scientific reasoning, using the language of problem solving.** Teachers demonstrate good habits of problem solvers when they encourage children to use their senses to observe the world around them, help children form questions about what they observe and make predictions, share their own thinking and problem-solving processes aloud with children, model and conduct experiments to test predictions, and facilitate discussion about the results of children's experiments.

making" by developing children's planning and reflecting skills (Epstein 2014). (See "Checklist of Teaching Practices and Strategies to Support Preschool Children's Problem Solving and Reasoning," for further explanation of strategies.)

Foster categorization skills. Understanding how to compare and contrast, categorize, and sort enables children to generalize information from one category or situation to another—to reason inductively (Hollister Sandberg & McCullough 2010). Generalizing helps children determine how to approach new objects or events with confidence. For example, 4-year-old Justin was once bitten by a dog and now is afraid of all dogs. During neighborhood walks, his parents have helped him categorize dogs by watching for behavioral signs: a dog with a wagging tail and relaxed demeanor is most likely friendly, but a dog that is barking and has its ears pinned back and teeth bared should be given some space. When they visit the park, Justin generalizes the information he learned about which dogs he can feel safe with based on how he categorizes their behavior.

To promote categorizing, provide children with objects or sets of objects that have contrasting qualities and encourage them to explain how the objects are alike and not alike (Loewenstein & Gentner 2001; Mix 2008; Christie & Gentner 2010). Challenge children to categorize by attributes beyond size and shape; for example, ask them to group objects according to color, width, or function (e.g., "find tools that can cut") (Kemler Nelson, Holt, & Egan 2004). Also, notice how children spontaneously categorize during play; what attributes are they using to categorize in sets they create?

Teachers also foster categorization skills by modeling strategies for children. Children as young as 3 can understand and imitate categorization strategies they see a teacher use without the teacher explicitly stating the strategies (Williamson & Markman 2006; Williamson, Meltzoff, & Markman 2008; Williamson, Jaswal, & Meltzoff 2010). For example, with a group of children watching, Sandy arranges several toys in front of her. Some of the toys make noise and some do not. Without telling children what characteristic she is using to sort, she carefully picks up each toy, shakes it and listens to it, and then puts the toy in the appropriate group. For the last few unsorted toys, she picks them up one at a time and says to a child, "Sort the toys the way I did." To do so, the child must have attended to what Sandy did, understood her goal, and learned her sorting rule as she modeled the strategy (shaking the toys and listening). This requires deeper-level mental processes and more complex problem solving than if Sandy had simply told the children her sorting rule.

Encourage children to brainstorm multiple solutions to problems. Young children tend to act on their first impulse in a situation or on the first thing that comes to mind. But to be good thinkers, they need to develop *inhibitory control,* "the ability to ignore distractions and stay focused, and to resist making one response and instead make another" (Diamond 2006). Inhibitory control helps children regulate their emotions and behavior and problem solve more effectively. Teachers can help children learn this important skill by encouraging them to pause before acting; consider multiple solutions to questions, tasks, or problems; and then choose a solution to try out.

Model and promote scientific reasoning. Scientific reasoning involves constructing hypotheses, gathering evidence, conducting experiments to test hypotheses, and drawing conclusions (Hollister Sandberg & McCullough 2010). It requires children to distinguish between various explanations for events and determine whether there is evidence to support the explanations. Although this is a complex type of reasoning for young children, teachers can support it through modeling and scaffolding. For example, after encouraging children to construct multiple reasonable explanations for events (hypotheses), teachers can help children talk through the steps they will take to test their hypotheses, as Sandy did in the first scenario with Keira and the slide. As children test their hypotheses, teachers should encourage them to use their senses (i.e., smell, touch, sight, sound, taste) to observe, gather, and record data (e.g., through pictures or charts). Finally, teachers can help children summarize the results of their investigation and construct explanations (i.e., verbalize cause and effect) for their findings. When teachers ask children questions such as "Why do you think that?" or "How do you know?," they help children become aware of their own thinking processes, reflect on the results of their experiments, and evaluate outcomes.

Conclusion

Children's ability to problem solve and reason is integral to their academic as well as social success. Each day, early childhood teachers support these skills in numerous ways—for example, by facilitating children's play, scaffolding learning, and offering interesting and challenging experiences. With a better understanding of how young children's reasoning and problem-solving skills develop, and a plan for implementing strategies to support them, teachers will become more intentional in helping children become good thinkers.

References

Amsterlaw, J., & H.M. Wellman. 2006. "Theories of Mind in Transition: A Microgenetic Study of the Development of False Belief Understanding." *Journal of Cognition and Development* 7 (2): 139–72.

Bierman, K.L., C.E. Domitrovich, R.L. Nix, S.D. Gest, J.A. Welsh, M.T. Greenberg, C. Blair, K.E. Nelson, & S. Gill. 2008. "Promoting Academic and Social-Emotional School Readiness: The Head Start REDI Program." *Child Development* 79 (6): 1802–17. www.ncbi.nlm.nih.gov/pubmed/19037591

Cannon, E.N., & A.L. Woodward. 2012. "Infants Generate Goal-Based Action Predictions." *Developmental Science* 15 (2): 292–98. www.ncbi.nlm.nih.gov/pubmed/22356184

Christie, S., & D. Gentner. 2010. "Where Hypotheses Come From: Learning New Relations by Structural Alignment." *Journal of Cognition and Development* 11(3): 356–73.

Denham, S.A., & C.M. Almeida. 1987. "Children's Social Problem-Solving Skills, Behavioral Adjustment, and Interventions: A Meta-Analysis Evaluating Theory and Practice." *Journal of Applied Developmental Psychology* 8 (4):391–409. http://nichcy.org/research/summaries/abstract29

Denham, S.A., H.H. Bassett, M. Mincic, S. Kalb, E. Way, T. Wyatt, & Y. Segal. 2012. "Social-Emotional Learning Profiles of Preschoolers' Early School Success: A Person-Centered Approach." *Learning and Individual Differences* 22 (2): 178–89. www.ncbi.nlm.nih.gov/pmc/ articles/PMC3294380

Diamond, A. 2006. "The Early Development of Executive Functions." Chap. 6 in *Lifespan Cognition: Mechanisms of Change,* eds. E. Bialystok & F.I.M. Craik, 70–95. New York: Oxford University Press.

Early, D., O. Barbarin, D. Bryant, M. Burchinal, F. Chang, R. Clifford, G.M. Crawford, C. Howes, S. Ritchie, M.E. Kraft-Sayre, R.C. Pianta, W.S. Barnett, & W. Weaver. 2005. "Pre-Kindergarten in Eleven States: NCEDL's Multi-State Study of Pre-Kindergarten & Study of State-Wide Early Education Programs (SWEEP): Preliminary Descriptive Report." NCEDL working paper. National Center for Early Development & Learning. http://fpg.unc.edu/sites/fpg.unc.edu/files/resources/reports-and-policy-briefs/NCEDL_PreK-in-Eleven-States_Working-Paper_2005.pdf

Epstein, A.S. 2014. *The Intentional Teacher: Choosing the Best Strategies for Young Children's Learning.* Rev. ed. Washington, DC: NAEYC.

Galinsky, E. 2010. *Mind in the Making: The Seven Essential Life Skills Every Child Needs.* New York: HarperCollins. Available from NAEYC.

Gopnik, A., C. Glymour, D.M. Sobel, L.E. Schulz, T. Kushnir, & D. Danks. 2004. "A Theory of Causal Learning in Children: Causal Maps and Bayes Nets." *Psychological Review* 111 (1):3–32. www.ncbi.nlm.nih.gov/pubmed/14756583

Critical Thinking

1. Prepare a list of strategies teachers can use in the classroom to foster problem solving skills.

2. Think how you would respond to a job interview question about what you might do in the classroom to encourage critical thinking and what are sometimes called executive functioning skills.

Internet References

Critical Thinking Foundation
http://www.criticalthinking.org/

Duke University: Talent Identification Program
http://tip.duke.edu/node/822

Early Childhood and Parenting Collaborative
http://ecap.crc.illinois.edu/eecearchive/digests/1993/britz93.html

JESSICA VICK WHITTAKER, PhD, is a research assistant professor at the Center for Advanced Teaching and Learning, University of Virginia, in Charlottesville. Her work focuses on developing and evaluating professional development aimed at improving teacher-child interaction quality to support children's math and science skills. She also studies children's self-regulation.

Whittaker, Jessica Vick. From *Young Children,* vol. 69, no. 3, July 2014, 80–87. Copyright © 2014 by National Association for the Education of Young Children. Used with permission.

Article   Prepared by: Karen Menke Paciorek, *Eastern Michigan University*

Happy 100th Birthday, Unit Blocks!

KARYN W. TUNKS

Learning Outcomes

After reading this article, you will be able to:

- Provide three reasons why blocks and block play belong in an early childhood setting.

- Advocate for teachers to intentionally plan for appropriate block play that fosters development in many domains.

- Describe three of the more popular types of blocks on the market today.

A small group of 5-year-olds gathers in the block play area. Dorothy and Tomás work together to build a house. They use quadruple unit blocks as the foundation, and then they carefully add standard unit blocks for walls. After experimenting with making windows, they decide to make doors instead, and leave spaces between the blocks. After placing a board on top for the roof, they see that they need more blocks to cover the top of the house completely. They barter and trade with children playing nearby so they have enough double units to cover the top. After finishing, they step back and admire their work. Their teacher joins them and asks them about their block house.

Nearby, Frank and Latoya are re-creating a race-track and garage they made last week. Having already worked through the design, they quickly begin placing unit blocks end to end, adding elliptical curves to make an oval for the racetrack. They use double units to make the garage floor, and place ramps side by side on one end for vehicles to enter. They embellish the structure by adding pillars on either side of the track and topping them with a unit arch. After a suggestion from their teacher, they create a tunnel for cars to pass through by repeating the pillar-and-arch structure.

Scenes such as these take place every day in preschool and kindergarten classroom block centers. What some teachers may not realize is that similar scenarios have been occurring for 100 years! Caroline Pratt (1867–1954), founder of New York's City and Country School, devised the system of blocks widely recognized as *unit blocks* in 1913, making this year the centennial celebration of her significant contribution to early childhood play and learning.

While other play and learning materials have come and gone, blocks continue to be a mainstay in early childhood settings. Their smooth wooden surfaces and standard proportions make them inviting to young builders. The resiliency of the material enables a set of blocks to last for generations. Although unit blocks are among the most recognizable blocks, they were not the first building materials used in early childhood settings (Wellhousen & Kieff 2001). Since we are celebrating a century of unit block play, it is the perfect time to revisit the evolution of these popular play materials and take a look at construction play in the 21st century.

Building Materials in the First Kindergarten

The first use of blocks for learning and play in early childhood education is attributed to Friedrich Froebel (1782–1852). The German educator is recognized as the "father of the kindergarten" for his many contributions to educating children from 2 to 7 years. For nearly a century, the Froebel kindergarten was the only kindergarten curriculum in existence. One of his most significant creations was a set of toy-like materials known as "gifts" (Hinitz 2013). Among these were six sets of wood blocks, each carefully housed in its own wooden container with a sliding lid. The blocks were based on a modular system, with each set fitting together to create a six-inch cube (Brosterman 1997).

In Froebel's kindergarten curriculum, children used the blocks in specific ways to create representations of familiar objects, as well as to study mathematical concepts and copy creative designs that the teacher demonstrated (Wiggin & Smith [1895] 2010). Froebel's disciples, many of whom immigrated to the United States, continued using the materials and methods (Snyder 1972).

Changes in Blocks during the Child Study Movement

The child study movement, which spanned the 1930s through the 1950s, had a dramatic impact on early education and forever changed Froebel's original kindergarten curriculum. This scientific approach to studying child development resulted in a change in methods and materials used to educate young children. Patty Smith Hill (1868–1946), a proponent of the child study movement (Snyder 1972), devised a set of blocks 16 times larger than the Froebel blocks. According to Hill, the larger blocks were better suited for young children and helped develop large muscles and physical strength. Because of the large and awkward size of the blocks, cooperation between children was needed to build (Fowlkes 1984). The blocks used a peg-hole-groove system to keep them in place, unlike the Froebel blocks, which required balancing. Over time, the Hill blocks became obsolete and were replaced by blocks of more manageable size.

We now return to Caroline Pratt, inventor of the blocks still in use today. Pratt, a student of Hill, saw the need for a block system with a more organized approach than the cumbersome blocks designed by her mentor. After carefully observing children at play, Pratt designed blocks that were larger than Froebel's but smaller than Hill's, making them easier for young children to handle. She based them on a standard proportion to promote children's understanding of mathematical relationships (Hirsch 1996). The unit block is the standard that all other block shapes are based on. The unit block is 5½" (L) × 3¾" (W) × 1⅜" (D). A half-unit is half the length of the unit block, a double unit is twice the length of the unit block, and so on. The entire system includes more than 20 block shapes. Each shape is carefully cut to specific dimensions and sanded to a smooth finish so they stack uniformly.

Montessori's Influence on Blocks

While Pratt was developing unit blocks, in Italy Maria Montessori (1870–1952) was inventing a very different system of blocks for teaching. The materials were based on her philosophy that children benefit from an orderly, carefully prepared environment that encourages independence in thinking and behavior (Hinitz 2013). Montessori's block sets are systematic and self-correcting—that is, when a piece is left over or does not fit, a child can see the error and solve the problem independently (Epstein, Schweinhart, & McAdoo 1996; Helfrich 2011).

Pratt saw the need for a block system with a more organized approach.

One of Montessori's most recognizable materials is the pink tower, which includes 10 pink wooden cubes ranging in size from 1 to 10 centimeters. Children begin with the largest cube as a base block and stack the remaining cubes in ascending order by size. Another example is the brown stair, a set of 10 blocks that are identical in length but vary in height and width. When arranged in a certain way, the blocks form a representation of a stairway (Montessori [1912] 1964). The red rods are another example of how Montessori designed blocks to teach specific concepts. Red rods are blocks that are equal in diameter (and of the same color) and vary only in length to teach the concept of long and short.

The initial response to Montessori's method was very positive, because children using the materials demonstrated cognitive improvement (Morgan 2011). Her approach to teaching young children spread quickly as teacher training was made available. The Montessori method was accepted with much enthusiasm in the United States. It was short-lived, however, after the 1914 publication of Kilpatrick's *The Montessori System Examined*. This pamphlet criticized the materials and methods in the Montessori system as too restrictive of children's imaginations because there is a definite and expected outcome. Montessori was further criticized because her emphasis was on the development and learning of the individual child. Kilpatrick, along with other advocates of the progressive education movement of the early 20th century, emphasized the need for children to experience freedom and spontaneity in their play, as well as learn skills for democratic living and learning. Pratt subscribed to the philosophy of the progressive movement, and since her unit blocks facilitated experimentation and group play, they were viewed as consistent with the progressive approach and their popularity continued to grow. A renewed interest in Montessori schools in the United States began in the 1960s, following the establishment of the American Montessori Society.

Blocks and Construction Play in the 21st Century

Today, the early care and education field is less rigid and more accepting of the benefits and learning possibilities of various methods and materials. Teachers are willing to try new approaches to learn what works best for children. Now a wide variety of construction materials is available, offering valuable play and learning experiences. Alongside unit blocks, children choose from an array of building materials (see "Additional Contemporary Construction Materials") and accessories—such as craft sticks and toy cars, people, and animals—as they imagine, plan, and build.

Planning for Block Play

Teachers today have a better understanding of child development and the value of block play for learning. The first step in planning for block play involves setting up and organizing classroom space. When creating an area for children to experiment and build, it is important that teachers consider construction materials and building accessories to include, storage of materials, and guidelines for using and caring for construction materials.

Selecting Materials

It is important for teachers to choose the materials that best accommodate the age and ability of the children using them (Giles & Tunks 2013). In preschool and kindergarten, teachers often supplement unit blocks with other construction materials such as LEGOs or DUPLOs (or similar brands), which are among the most popular contemporary construction sets. The bright, colorful plastic pieces are designed so that they interlock to stay in place. Original LEGOs are best suited for children with developed fine motor skills, while DUPLO blocks (the larger version of LEGOs) are more easily manipulated by younger children.

Storage

A well-organized storage system helps children find specific items as they build, and makes clean-up time easier. Ample shelving for blocks and accessories is important. Larger blocks and accessories can be displayed on shelves, while smaller pieces can be organized in clear, labeled containers. Providing outlines of the various unit block shapes, adhered to shelves, helps to keep the area organized and reinforces the sizes and shapes of blocks.

Guidelines for Use and Care

Guidelines minimize disruptions and enable children to concentrate on their block building. Teachers can encourage children to build in areas where structures won't be accidentally knocked over. Allowing enough time for cleanup helps children learn how to handle blocks with care. A set of simple guidelines posted in the block center reminds children of proper block play etiquette. For example:

- Blocks are for building
- Keep blocks in construction zone
- Unbuild your construction only.

Teachers' Role in Block Play

The degree of teacher involvement in block play will depend on program goals, the age and developmental abilities of the children (Chalufour & Worth 2004), and the specific situation. The least intrusive approach is to set up the area, observe and record children's play, and make comments such as, "I see you made two bridges using six unit blocks." More active involvement includes asking questions about children's play or offering suggestions, such as, "Have you tried using the colored cubes to make a walkway?" An example of the most direct involvement is physically assisting or even taking part in the block play. Teachers also may be directly involved to help resolve a conflict or to model how to clean up the area. Common dilemmas during block play that may require teacher intervention include children fighting over blocks, structures being accidentally knocked down, and children resisting cleaning up after block play (Tunks 2009).

By taking a developmentally appropriate perspective and devising a plan of action, dilemmas can be resolved and peace restored to any block center (Tunks 2009). For example, when the children's block structures are knocked over, the teacher can change the environment and introduce a new rule. Using tape to create a one-foot border on the floor between the block shelf and the building area minimizes the risk of structures falling down when children reach for blocks from the shelf. Children can easily understand the benefit of the rule of building only in the designated zone.

Meaningful Learning through Block Play

When Caroline Pratt devised the unit block system a century ago, it was readily accepted that blocks were important for helping children develop mathematical and spatial concepts, as well as for creativity and pleasure (Leeb-Lundberg 1996). Today the value of play, even in some early childhood classrooms, is questioned in response to pressure for children to meet standardized benchmarks. Teachers of young children may find themselves defending the need for children's play. Justifying specific types of learning that are derived through play is an effective way to promote and protect play in early childhood settings. Block play offers essential opportunities for promoting children's social and emotional development. Through building together, children learn to share, take turns, and collaborate in meaningful ways. In addition, construction play provides opportunities for children to learn problem solving, math, science, and language skills.

Math Concepts

Pratt designed unit blocks with a standard proportion in mind to promote children's understanding of mathematical relationships. As children manipulate the blocks, they develop a deeper cognitive understanding of the relationships between objects. This type of learning is known as *logico-mathematical knowledge* (Kamii 1990), and it enables children to master skills such as counting, sorting, classifying, and identifying shapes. These skills form the foundation on which mathematical processes are learned. Chalufour and Worth (2004) suggest these specific strategies for promoting math skills in the block center:

- Count and record the number of blocks used to build a tower.
- Measure the height of a structure using measuring tools such as measuring tape, string, or Unifix cubes (small interlocking cubes used to teach measurement).
- Encourage descriptions of structures using mathematical attributes such as shape, number, size, and order.

Science Constructs

Children can learn scientific constructs such as height, gravity, balance, action/reaction, and cause and effect through block play. Children can make further discoveries as they experiment with cardboard tubes, lengths of PVC pipe, straws, string, small boxes, table tennis balls, and toy cars. Provide a variety of surfaces for children to build on, such as tile, cardboard, sponges, bubble wrap, and carpet squares (Giles & Tunks 2013). Guiding children by asking open-ended questions as they experiment opens the door for further discoveries. For example, "What can you use to connect these two blocks?" or "What would happen if you tried to balance a block on top?"

Language Skills

Opportunities for using language and increasing vocabulary are an authentic outcome of block play. Children engage in conversations with each other during block play (Chalufour & Worth 2004). They negotiate ideas as they build cooperatively and, once a structure is complete, might role-play with the block structure as the center for their play (Wellhousen & Keiff 2001). For example, following a field trip to a firehouse, three children construct a fire station from unit blocks. They

Additional Contemporary Construction Materials

Block Type	Features
Mega Bloks First Builders (ages 1–5 years)	• Large size of blocks make it easy for small hands to grasp • Bright, primary colors • Easy to stack
DUPLOs (ages 18 months to 5 years)	• Slightly larger than LEGOs • Easier for young children to put together and pull apart
Waffle blocks (ages 2–4 years)	• Waffle-shaped plastic pieces that snap together • Bright colors in various sizes
Cardboard blocks (ages 2–6)	• Lightweight, easy to stack • Crush resistant • Sets include varied sizes and colors
Bristle blocks (ages 2 and up)	• Soft, flexible interlocking plastic bristles are used to connect blocks • Can be attached to 6" × 7" building plate • Bright colors
Foam building blocks (ages 2 and up)	• Multicolored blocks in various shapes and sizes • Chunky foam pieces are easy to grip
Large interlocking blocks (ages 2 and up)	• Flexible plastic pieces in four shapes • Rectangular shape measures 4.5" × 9" • Durable and washable
Soft unit blocks (ages 2 and up)	• Built to the same scale as unit blocks • Made of dense foam • Lightweight, colorful, and safe if thrown
Building bricks (ages 3 and up)	• 2" plastic cubes that snap together • Made of bright, colorful plastic
Large hollow blocks (ages 3 and up)	• Wooden blocks • Used to make child-size structures such as forts • Five different sizes and shapes, plus boards
Tabletop building blocks (ages 3 and up)	• Variety of shapes • Smaller version of unit blocks • May be natural wood or wood painted bright colors
LEGOs (ages 4 and up)	• Bright colors • Small, interlocking pieces • Require fine motor skills

share ideas about adding accessories, including a toy fire truck, a plastic dalmatian, and a piece of surgical tubing that serves as a fire hose. They adjust the size of the fire station to accommodate the fire truck. Once complete, they put on plastic firefighter hats and become firefighters. Imagination and language energizes their play. Next, they build a house from spare blocks so they can rush into action to save lives and put out fires.

Conclusion

Thanks to Caroline Pratt and the many early childhood educators who followed, unit blocks have enjoyed a long and rich history in early childhood education. They have stood the test of time and the ever-evolving philosophy and approaches in early childhood education. Generations of young children have explored and learned through playing with unit blocks over the past century, and there is little doubt that playing with unit blocks will continue to be a favorite activity among young children for the next 100 years!

References

Brosterman, N. 1997. *Inventing Kindergarten.* New York: Abrams.

Chalufour, I., & K. Worth. 2004. *Building Structures With Young Children.* St. Paul, MN: Redleaf.

Epstein, A.S., L.J. Schweinhart, & L. McAdoo. 1996. *Models of Early Childhood Education.* Ypsilanti, MI: HighScope.

Fowlkes, M.A. 1984. "Gifts From Childhood's Godmother: Patty Smith Hill." *Childhood Education* 61 (1): 44–49.

Giles, R., & K. Tunks. 2013. "Building Young Scientists: Developing Scientific Literacy Through Construction Play." *Early Years: Journal of the Texas Association for the Education of Young Children* 34 (2): 22–27.

Helfrich, M.S. 2011. *Montessori Learning in the 21st Century: A Guide for Parents and Teachers.* Troutdale, OR: NewSage.

Hinitz, B.F. 2013. "History of Early Childhood Education in Multicultural Perspective." Chap. 1 in *Approaches to Early Childhood Education,* 6th ed., eds. J. Roopnarine & J.E. Johnson, 3–33. Boston: Pearson.

Hirsch, E.S., ed. 1996. *The Block Book.* 3rd ed. Washington, DC: NAEYC.

Kamii, C. 1990. "Constructivism and Beginning Arithmetic (K–2)." In *Teaching and Learning Mathematics in the 1990s: 1990 Yearbook,* eds. T.J. Cooney & C.R. Hirsch, 22–30. Reston, VA: National Council of Teachers of Mathematics.

Kilpatrick, W.H. 1914. *The Montessori System Examined.* New York: Houghton Mifflin. http://archive.org/details/montessorisystem00kilprich

Leeb-Lundberg, K. 1996. "The Block Builder Mathematician." In E.S. Hirsch, 30–51.

Montessori, M. [1912] 1964. *The Montessori Method.* Trans. A.E. George. New York: Stokes. http://digital.library.upenn.edu/women/montessori/method/method.html

Morgan, H. 2011. *Early Childhood Education: History, Theory, and Practice.* 2nd ed. New York, NY: Rowman & Littlefield.

Snyder, A. 1972. *Dauntless Women in Childhood Education, 1856–1931.* Washington, DC: Association for Childhood Education International

Tunks, K.W. 2009. "Block Play: Practical Suggestions for Common Dilemmas." *Dimensions of Early Childhood* 37 (1): 3–8.

Wellhousen, K., & J. Kieff. 2001. *A Constructivist Approach to Block Play in Early Childhood.* Stamford, CT: Cengage.

Wiggin, K.D., & N.A. Smith. [1895] 2010. *The Republic of Childhood: Froebel's Gifts.* New York: Houghton Mifflin. http://archive.org/details/froebelsgifts00wiggrich

Critical Thinking

1. If your administrator gave you $1,000 to purchase blocks for your preschool classroom, what would you buy and why? You may use the internet references below to assist you in developing the list of materials.

2. How have blocks and block play changed over the 100+ years they have been available for young children?

3. Write a one paragraph note to the families of children in your kindergarten class describing why you have blocks in the kindergarten room and what their children will learn from block play.

Internet References

City and Country School Blocks
http://www.cityandcountry.org/page/Programs/Blocks-Program

Community Play Things
http://www.communityplaythings.com/products/blocks

Early Childhood News
http://www.earlychildhoodnews.com/earlychildhood/article_view.aspx?ArticleID=397

Play and Playground Encyclopedia
http://www.playgroundprofessionals.com/b/block-play

KARYN W. TUNKS, PhD, is an associate professor of education at the University of South Alabama, in Mobile. She has published widely on the topic of block play and is the coauthor of the book *A Constructivist Approach to Block Play in Early, Childhood.*

Article

Prepared by: Karen Menke Paciorek, *Eastern Michigan University*

Want to Get Your Kids into College? Let Them Play

ERIKA CHRISTAKIS AND NICHOLAS CHRISTAKIS

Learning Outcomes

After reading this article, you will be able to:

- Explain the value of play for children, young and old.
- Name some of the skills children acquire through play.

Every day where we work, we see our young students struggling with the transition from home to school. They're all wonderful kids, but some can't share easily or listen in a group.

Some have impulse control problems and have trouble keeping their hands to themselves; others don't always see that actions have consequences; a few suffer terribly from separation anxiety.

We're not talking about preschool children. These are Harvard undergraduate students whom we teach and advise. They all know how to work, but some of them haven't learned how to play.

Parents, educators, psychologists, neuroscientists, and politicians generally fall into one of two camps when it comes to preparing very young children for school: play-based or skills-based.

These two kinds of curricula are often pitted against one another as a zero-sum game: If you want to protect your daughter's childhood, so the argument goes, choose a play-based program; but if you want her to get into Harvard, you'd better make sure you're brushing up on the ABC flashcards every night before bed.

We think it is quite the reverse. Or, in any case, if you want your child to succeed in college, the play-based curriculum is the way to go.

In fact, we wonder why play is not encouraged in educational periods later in the developmental life of young people—giving kids more practice as they get closer to the ages of our students.

Why do this? One of the best predictors of school success is the ability to control impulses. Children who can control their impulse to be the center of the universe, and—relatedly—who can assume the perspective of another person, are better equipped to learn.

Psychologists call this the "theory of mind": the ability to recognize that our own ideas, beliefs, and desires are distinct from those of the people around us. When a four-year-old destroys someone's carefully constructed block castle or a 20-year-old belligerently monopolizes the class discussion on a routine basis, we might conclude that they are unaware of the feelings of the people around them.

The beauty of a play-based curriculum is that very young children can routinely observe and learn from others' emotions and experiences. Skills-based curricula, on the other hand, are sometimes derisively known as "drill and kill" programs because most teachers understand that young children can't learn meaningfully in the social isolation required for such an approach.

How do these approaches look different in a classroom? Preschoolers in both kinds of programs might learn about hibernating squirrels, for example, but in the skills-based program, the child could be asked to fill out a worksheet, counting (or guessing) the number of nuts in a basket and coloring the squirrel's fur.

In a play-based curriculum, by contrast, a child might hear stories about squirrels and be asked why a squirrel accumulates nuts or has fur. The child might then collaborate with peers in the construction of a squirrel habitat, learning not only about number sense, measurement, and other principles needed for engineering, but also about how to listen to, and express, ideas.

The child filling out the worksheet is engaged in a more one-dimensional task, but the child in the play-based program interacts meaningfully with peers, materials, and ideas.

Programs centered around constructive, teacher-moderated play are very effective. For instance, one randomized, controlled trial had 4- and 5-year-olds engage in make-believe play with adults and found substantial and durable gains in the ability of children to show self-control and to delay gratification. Countless other studies support the association between dramatic play and self-regulation.

Through play, children learn to take turns, delay gratification, negotiate conflicts, solve problems, share goals, acquire flexibility, and live with disappointment. By allowing children to imagine walking in another person's shoes, imaginative play also seeds the development of empathy, a key ingredient for intellectual and social-emotional success.

The real "readiness" skills that make for an academically successful kindergartener or college student have as much to do with emotional intelligence as they do with academic preparation. Kindergartners need to know not just sight words and lower case letters, but how to search for meaning. The same is true of 18-year-olds.

As admissions officers at selective colleges like to say, an entire freshman class could be filled with students with perfect grades and test scores. But academic achievement in college requires readiness skills that transcend mere book learning. It requires the ability to engage actively with people and ideas. In short, it requires a deep connection with the world.

For a five year-old, this connection begins and ends with the creating, questioning, imitating, dreaming, and sharing that characterize play. When we deny young children play, we are denying them the right to understand the world. By the time they get to college, we will have denied them the opportunity to fix the world too.

Critical Thinking

1. How has playing around at something allowed you to learn a new skill? Observe a child playing with something and watch for the ah-ha moment of discovery when they figure something out through play.

2. What advice would you give to parents who are pushing their child into academics and limiting the amount of time for free-play?

Create Central

www.mhhe.com/createcentral

Internet References

Mid-Continent Research for Education and Learning
www2.mcrel.org/compendium

National Association for the Education of Young Children
www.naeyc.org

National Education Association
www.nea.org

National Institute for Play
www.nifplay.org

Article   Prepared by: Karen Menke Paciorek, *Eastern Michigan University*

Animal Attraction: Including Animals in Early Childhood Classrooms

CLARISSA M. UTTLEY

Learning Outcomes

After reading this article, you will be able to:

- Advocate to acquire an animal for your classroom or your child's classroom.

- Describe the benefits for children when they have an animal in their classroom.

- List the pros and cons of having a classroom animal.

Animals and children have been intricately connected throughout history. Some parents bring home a pet to help their children gain a sense of responsibility and to encourage social-emotional development. Children learn to care for others, increase their ability to empathize, and gain self-esteem as they care for pets. Early childhood educators recognize the benefits of including animals in the classroom to address the developmental and educational goals of the children they teach.

Educators use a variety of strategies to include animals in support of the curriculum. They maintain classroom pets as permanent residents, welcome family pets for short visits, host guest visitors from local zoos or farms, and schedule field trips to environmental education facilities. Teachers have included animals in programs to encourage children to read (Shaw 2013), increase environmental stewardship (Bailie 2010; Torquati et al. 2010), support cultural education (Dubosarsky et al. 2011), enhance curriculum goals (Gee et al. 2012; Hachey & Butler 2012), and address challenging behaviors (Nielson & Delude 1989; Wedl & Kotrschal 2009).

A Survey of Animals in the Classroom

There is limited research on the numbers and types of animals found in early childhood classrooms, so I conducted a study to examine early childhood educators' use of animals in their classrooms. This article presents survey results describing the types of animals included in respondents' programs. It offers practical strategies to help educators decide whether to include animals in the classroom, select the right animals, engage children with animals to support learning goals, and assess whether the children and animals are benefitting from these experiences. The article provides examples from my own experiences and from the experiences of study participants.

More than 1,400 NAEYC-accredited programs for young children, with classrooms for birth through third grade, participated in the study. (Some birth-through-kindergarten NAEYC-accredited programs have after-school or older classrooms as extra components.) Nearly two-thirds (879) of the participants reported having animals in their classrooms.

There are many types of animals in these classrooms. Fish are by far the most common—approximately 50 percent. Watching fish can reduce blood pressure and ease anxiety, especially when used in a medical office (Jackson 2012). Fish can be extremely beneficial in educational settings too. Several participants mentioned how easy it is to care for fish and how well children react to seeing these colorful creatures.

A lead teacher in a preschool classroom in Washington, DC, says,

We have a variety of fish swimming happily in the tank. We have black lace angel fish, moonlight gouramis, gold tetras, sucker fish, and salt and pepper catfish. The children *love* them! There is only one sucker fish, so whenever they spot it they get very excited. There is a bench around the tank so the children can hang out there whenever they're feeling out of sorts.

Amphibians and reptiles are also well represented in the study. Teachers use frogs, toads, and lizards to support educational activities and to ease classroom transitions. Animals can change the classroom environment and engage children in ways many children have not previously experienced. Classroom pets can be the support that some children need and a vehicle for educators to use in reaching children with challenging behaviors.

Serious Considerations for Teachers

There are some important points to consider before bringing animals into an early childhood classroom. First, think about your own comfort level with animals and your knowledge of how to care for specific animals. According to the study, educators who have had positive experiences with their own pets are more likely to include animals in the classroom. More than 67 percent of respondents who have classroom pets also have pets at home. One center director in Georgia emphasized the importance for educators of being familiar with the needs of any animal in the classroom to prevent its inadvertent mistreatment. Having seen such cases, she feels strongly that "in centers where we have animals, it is of primary importance that the teacher has actually cared for a pet before."

Second, carefully articulate and examine the intended educational and developmental outcomes. Remember that multiple lives (animals' and people's) are affected when keeping classroom pets, so it is essential to give careful thought to how to safely and appropriately include animals in the curriculum.

For example, a first grade teacher at a university-based early care and education program in California wanted to extend the university's focus on environmental sustainability to his classroom curriculum. To help the children learn how they and their families could set up compost piles at home, he writes that he "created a worm farm that was used daily to recycle snack food wastes (peels, leftovers, and such). Caring for this farm (and learning about recycling) has become an important part of the class routine." Working with invertebrates was an appropriate choice to meet the curriculum's educational goals.

Discuss the financial resources available to care for an animal well before deciding whether to acquire classroom pets or which type to include.

And third, be mindful of the resources necessary for keeping any kind of animal in the classroom. As many study participants noted, financial and space resources are limited in most early childhood classrooms, and adding animals to the environment may further strain the budget. Costs can include veterinarian expenses, housing and food supplies, and materials to support the healthy development of the animals. One respondent, a kindergarten teacher in Colorado, shares that "because of our economy and a reduced budget, we have limited our classroom pets to hermit crabs. Typically, we also have fancy mice; however, the cost of appropriate materials, such as bedding, has prevented us from acquiring new mice." Discuss the financial resources available to care for an animal well before deciding whether to acquire classroom pets or which type to include.

More Considerations and Challenges

In addition to the considerations regarding personal experiences with pets, the animal—curriculum connections, and the potential strain on the budget, there are a few other points that respondents expressed as concerns.

Animal Well-Being

Animals have certain needs in terms of natural light, heat, privacy, and so on. To meet those needs and ensure that an animal feels as comfortable as possible, establish an area of the room specifically for the pet. Consider the placement of the animal's enclosure and how the children will engage with it. An adult must be able to easily view the children's interactions with both the animal and the enclosure. A case in point from a teacher in Nevada:

> When we first introduced an aquarium to a toddler classroom, a new child, on his first day, broke the front of the aquarium with a wooden truck. We had water and fish everywhere! Fortunately, there was an aquarium in the next class, so all the fish survived.
>
> The teachable moment was explaining to children how fish need water to live and breathe; it also gave us a chance to go over classroom rules and how trucks work better on the floor instead of in the air. We replaced the aquarium, and children still enjoy watching the fish.

Lifespan

Remember that animals are living beings, and as such they have a lifespan. Thoughtfulness in preparing for a pet's end-of-life care is important. This includes a plan to deal with any common illnesses that a particular animal species tends to contract (for example, rats typically grow tumors, fish commonly get ich [*Ichthyophthirius multifiliis*]). It also involves thinking about ways to discuss the death of a pet with the children and their families.

Several educators reported that although discussing the death of a classroom pet was not a welcome experience, they felt that being honest with the children and their families about life cycles helped some children deal with their relatives' deaths. A touching story provided by a center director from New Hampshire describes the class's experience with the death of their classroom pet:

> Last year we had a rabbit in our 4-year-olds class. Unfortunately, the rabbit died halfway through the school year. We were all sad, but realized that his death helped some children open up to us and to their parents about their fear of dying or losing a loved one. One child spoke for the first time about her mom being sick with cancer.
>
> The rabbit's death was an experience that allowed us all to show our true emotions. Some parents said their children cried at home; some children prayed for the rabbit and some children saw him happily hopping in their dreams! We shared books about dying with the children—one being *All Dogs Go To Heaven*—and the teacher changed the wording to fit the rabbit.

Ethics

Even center directors and educators who see the value of including animals in early childhood classrooms raise major concerns regarding the ethics of keeping animals in classrooms. Study participants expressed worries about issues such as finding the time to properly care for the animal, acquiring enough knowledge to be responsible for the animal, and maintaining a high level of engagement between the children and the animal so the animal does not get abandoned or become just another piece of furniture.

Be aware of times when animals are stressed, and the possible reasons for the stress. A stressed animal is likely to behave differently and to become ill (Fine 2010). To maintain a safe and engaging classroom for both children and animals, learn what is necessary to maintain animals' emotional well-being.

Think also about the experiences of families' and staff's pets that visit the classroom. Pets that enjoy visiting the early childhood classroom get excited about their "work" and have been known to display behaviors that indicate they anticipate these visits. For example, my dog, Nina, gets excited when I take her working vest out of the closet; she seems to understand we are going to visit children. She runs to the door with her tail wagging and eagerly jumps into the backseat of the car. If or when the visits cease, it is common for the pets to experience depression (Kwong & Bartholomew 2011). Animal caregivers need to be aware of the psychological impacts, both positive and negative, that classroom visits may have on the pets.

Health and Hygiene

It is very important for children and educators to use proper hygiene when interacting with animals of any type. All who touch an animal or its food, bedding, or enclosure should wash their hands immediately after the encounter. The animal enclosure should be well maintained and cleaned regularly by an adult. Proper disposal of animal waste ensures a healthy classroom environment for the children and the animal.

Check national accreditation standards and state licensing guidelines, and consult with veterinarians and other animal specialists, when selecting classroom pets. Large-beaked birds can inflict serious injury to tiny fingers, even when playing or taking food from a child's hand. Reptiles, hedgehogs, and certain types of birds (parrots, for example) may not be permitted due to the potential for biting or the increased risk of transmitting salmonella.

Overcoming the Challenges

Even with the many challenges associated with including animals in the early childhood classroom, 70 percent of study participants believe that classroom pets create a positive learning environment for the children. Some are indifferent to having animals in the classroom, and others think maintaining them is too challenging.

Check national accreditation standards and state licensing guidelines, and consult with veterinarians and other animal specialists, when selecting classroom pets.

The Threat of Salmonella

Salmonella is a bacterium that can be transmitted several ways. When animals are involved, salmonella can be transferred to humans through contaminated water or animal feces. Reptiles, amphibians, snakes, and other animals can be carriers and may transmit salmonella bacteria to humans. Several organizations, including the American Academy of Pediatrics, the Centers for Disease Control and Prevention, and NAEYC, advise not having these animals around children.

One center director from Vermont makes a strong case for the benefits:

Animals play an important role for many, many reasons. Children are small in the world and have little power of their own. Caring for an animal provides the experience of taking care of a living being even smaller and more vulnerable than they are.

I spent five and a half years working in a day treatment center for dysfunctional families. My part of the program was providing therapeutic care for young children in an early childhood classroom setting. I worked with young children whose stories still make me weep 30 years later. Many of these children had shut down and were unable to let in an adult human being. Yet I saw them lovingly care for the class pets—a guinea pig, rabbit, and hamster. I saw them sit for hours holding, stroking, cuddling, and talking to these animals, telling them the stories that they were unable to share with adults. I would never have a classroom without a pet, even if it was only a fish.

What Are Some Options?

Early childhood educators are creative and resourceful. If, after thoroughly reviewing the considerations, teachers decide not to include a pet as a permanent resident of the classroom, there are still many ways to bring animals into the setting and curriculum.

Projects Based on Animals

Consider the children's interests and the intended learning outcomes when exploring ways to relate animals to the curriculum. In no other story was the children's interest more evident than in this example provided by an early childhood center director in New Mexico:

I was a kindergarten teacher during 9/11. The children in my classroom expressed an interest in the rescue dogs, so we began a yearlong project on dogs and rescue dogs. The children collected pennies to send to the rescue foundation to support a rescue dog. We took a field trip to the bank to cash in the pennies, then to the post office to mail off the check, and then to the park, where we had a picnic and were visited by a rescue dog team.

Annual Animal Events

Special occasions are great opportunities to safely, and with little investment of resources, include animals in a program. Consider this activity at a private early childhood center in Kentucky:

We have a pet blessing every October to celebrate St. Francis Day. The children and their families are invited to bring their pets for a blessing from our priest. Various animals attend this blessing, and it is one of the most fun family activities we offer. It is always very well attended.

And from Texas:

One year during NAEYC's Week of the Young Child (in April), we asked families to bring in pets and other animals. We sent out a blanket notice to all families about animal visits (addressing allergies and fear of animals, and assuring heavy supervision) and collected current pet vaccination information. All sorts of animals visited. We had one or two days of horses, turtles, dogs, ferrets, lambs, goats, birds, gerbils, pigs, cats, snakes, and so on. It was a lot of fun and excitement for the young children.

Close-ups with Nature

Encouraging natural wildlife such as birds, squirrels, insects, and deer to spend time in the view of the children can lead to numerous teachable moments. Hanging a bird feeder outside a window is an easy way to invite birds. Other ways to incorporate animals in the curriculum include taking field trips to farms or zoos, inviting representatives from zoos or animal shelters to visit the classroom, going on nature hikes, or creating a natural area outside.

In Closing

As the number of animals in early childhood classrooms increases, it is critical that educators of young children provide meaningful interactions between children and animals to enhance classroom experiences. Study participants have shared several considerations for maintaining positive environments for both children and animals. While concerns and benefits vary based on curriculum and behavioral needs, it is clear that including animals in the early childhood classroom has the potential to engage and inspire both educators and young children.

References

Bailie, P.E. 2010. "From the One-Hour Field Trip to a Nature Preschool: Partnering With Environmental Organizations." *Young Children* 65 (4): 76–82.

Dubosarsky, M., B. Murphy, G. Roehrig, L.C. Frost, J. Jones, & S.P. Carlson, with N. Londo, C.J.B. Melchert, C. Gettel, & J. Bement. 2011. "Animosh Tracks on the Playground, Minnows in the Sensory Table: Incorporating Cultural Themes to Promote Preschoolers' Critical Thinking in American Indian Head Start Classrooms." *Young Children* 66 (5): 20–29.

Fine, A.H., ed. 2010. *Handbook on Animal-Assisted Therapy: Theoretical Foundations and Guidelines for Practice.* New York: Academic Press.

Gee, N.R, J.M. Belcher, J.L. Grabski, M. Dejesus, & W. Riley. 2012. "The Presence of a Therapy Dog Results in Improved Object Recognition Performance in Preschool Children." *Anthrozoös* 25 (3): 289–300.

Hachey, A.C., & D. Butler. 2012. "Creatures in the Classroom: Including Insects and Small Animals in Your Preschool Gardening Curriculum." *Young Children* 67 (2): 38–42. www.naeyc.org/tyc/files/tyc/file/V5N5/HacheyButler.%20 Creatures%20in%20the%20Class room.pdf

Jackson, J. 2012. "Animal-Assisted Therapy: The Human-Animal Bond in Relation to Human Health and Wellness." Capstone paper, Winona State University. www.winona.edu/ counseloreducation/images/justine_jackson_capstone.pdf

Kwong, M.J., & K. Bartholomew. 2011. "Not Just a Dog: An Attachment Perspective on Relationships With Assistance Dogs." *Attachment & Human Development* 13 (5): 421–36.

Nielson, J.A., & L.A. Delude. 1989. "Behavior of Young Children in the Presence of Different Kinds of Animals." *Anthrozoös* 3 (2): 119–29.

Shaw, D.M. 2013. "Man's Best Friend as a Reading Facilitator." *The Reading Teacher* 66 (5): 365–71. www.therapyanimals. org/Research_&_Results_files/Shaw%20Mans%20Best%20 Friend%20Doogan%20 1.13.pdf

Torquati, J., with M.M. Gabriel, J. Jones-Branch, & J. Leeper-Miller. 2010. "Environmental Education: A Natural Way to Nurture Children's Development and Learning." *Young Children* 65 (6): 98–104.

Wedl, M., & K. Kotrschal. 2009. "Social and Individual Components of Animal Contact in Preschool Children." *Anthrozoös* 22 (4): 383–96.

Critical Thinking

1. Develop a plan of action you would implement if you decided to have an animal in your classroom serving young children.
2. What life skills would you expect children to gain by interacting with a classroom animal?
3. Share your feelings about having an animal in your classroom. Are those based on experiences you had as a child?

Internet References

Classroom Animals and Pets
http://www.teacherwebshelf.com/classroompets/HomeTOC.htm
Humane Society
http://www.humanesociety.org/parents_educators/classroom_pet.html
Massachusetts Society for the Prevention of Cruelty to Animals
http://www.mspca.org/programs/humane-education/resources-for-educators/animals-in-education/school-policy-on-classroom.html
Pets in the Classroom
http://www.petsintheclassroom.org/

CLARISSA M. UTTLEY, PhD, is a professor of early childhood studies at Plymouth State University in Plymouth, New Hampshire. Clarissa's research focuses on ethically including animals in early childhood classrooms to support the learning and development of young children.

Article

Prepared by: Karen Menke Paciorek, *Eastern Michigan University*

Food Allergy Concerns in Primary Classrooms

Keeping Children Safe

PEGGY THELEN AND ELIZABETH ANN CAMERON

Learning Outcomes

After reading this article, you will be able to:

- Describe at least three safe food policies.

- Plan ways to include all children in safe and healthy eating environments in a school setting.

Food-allergy awareness and management have only lately come to the forefront in early childhood settings, although advocacy organizations have been working on the issue for more than a decade (FAAN, n.d.). A national poll (C.S. Mott Children's Hospital 2009) asked parents with children in early education settings if they were aware of what their program does to protect children with food allergies. The poll results indicate that more than three-quarters of these parents knew of one or more preventive actions offered in those settings. Of these actions, the ban on treats or food brought from home was the measure cited most frequently. About half of all parents responded that their children's program or school offered staff training specifically for food allergies, with more food allergy plans seen in early childhood programs (56 percent) than in elementary schools (37 percent).

Schools have a legal and ethical responsibility to be prepared for children with food allergies, so organization and implementation of allergy policies and procedures should receive the importance and time they deserve. This article reviews administrative policies and procedures, child development concerns, and classroom realities related to food allergies.

School Policies and Classroom Procedures

Policies that focus on preventing children from consuming or being exposed to food that may trigger allergic reactions often include banning certain foods from the school, a "no sharing" component, or an "exclusion" component (Behrmann 2010). While banning food may seem to be an easy solution, most experts do not recommend this type of action. Such a policy can be difficult for families whose children do not have food allergies, and can create a false sense of security. Sharing or trading food or utensils must be forbidden due to the obvious possible presence of offending allergens. Creating an allergen-free zone, such as a peanut-free table in the cafeteria, is an alternative strategy (Hay, Harper, & Moore 2006).

Emergency preparedness policies for a child with allergies should include the following (Muñoz-Furlong 2003; Behrmann 2010):

- Each child who has an allergy has a medical information file (such as the model provided by the Food Allergy and Anaphylaxis Network, www.foodallergy.org/files/FAAP.pdf) filled out in cooperation with the child's physician. The file outlines the causes of the child's allergic reactions, states what medication should be administered, and includes a photo of the child, a list of emergency contacts, preferred hospital, copies of medical cards, and a list of trained staff members.

- The child's medical information file includes injectable, prefilled intramuscular epinephrine (common brand names include EpiPen) readily available in case of an allergic reaction, and a diagram and written directions about when and how to administer epinephrine (for example, EpiPens are often administered in the thigh).

- Teaching and support staff (such as food service staff) receive routine training in reading labels, recognizing anaphylactic symptoms, and correctly administering epinephrine.

Administrators should familiarize staff with the program's or school's current allergy policies. Administrators and school nurses should ensure that the appropriate teaching and support staff receive the training needed to respond to specific children with food allergies each school year (Behrmann 2010).

Additionally, as new staff, volunteers, and substitute teachers become part of the educational setting, they too must receive allergy-preparedness training. The medical information files of children with allergies should be readily available. Copies of the medical files should be placed in the children's classrooms and in the school nurse's office. If there is no nurse's office, the main office is an appropriate place for a second file and EpiPen.

The medical information files of children with allergies should be readily available.

Guidelines and recommendations, such as those from the American Academy of Allergy, Asthma, and Immunology (AAAAI), www.aaaai.org, and the National School Boards Association, www.nsba.org, provide information on both the prevention of consumption and exposure to allergens, and preparation for emergencies in case a severe food reaction occurs.

Working with Families

Create an allergy procedure for each child. Beyond school policy, individual procedures for children with allergies may be jointly established by their parents and teachers. Families whose children were recently diagnosed with a food allergy may be on a learning path right along with the teachers. Therefore, it is beneficial for families of children in the primary grades to work with teachers, the school administrator, and the school health professional to create an allergy procedure for each child with allergies. Parents who have more experience dealing with food allergies can share suggestions with the school and other families.

Have emergency medical kits. Require parents of children with food allergies to prepare at least one emergency medical kit, clearly marked on the outside with the child's name, grade, medical alert insignia, and photo. Ideally, families leave two emergency kits—one for the classroom and one for the school nurse. While schools are not responsible for the items in the kit, the school administration is responsible for making sure that staff are trained to use them.

Store emergency medical kits in a safe, easily accessible location out of the reach of children. All staff should be aware of the location of these kits. The kits should contain the child's medical information file and injectable epinephrine (EpiPens). Parents should check expiration dates on the epinephrine shots regularly.

Notify all families. Before the school year starts, the administrator can send a letter, or ask the classroom teacher to send a letter, to all parents explaining that in their child's classroom there will be a child with allergies who cannot be exposed to or eat nuts (or whatever the allergen is). The letter states that the classroom will be allergen free and requires all parents to agree in advance to be supportive and work with the teacher to ensure a safe classroom. The letter should include a list of acceptable snacks and unacceptable snacks. This is a good opportunity to inform families about safety procedures that must be followed in the setting, such as washing hands frequently to avoid *cross-contamination*, sanitizing surfaces routinely, and not sharing food or school tools (pencils, erasers, and so on) with the child with allergies. (Cross-contamination occurs when food that does not contain any allergens is exposed to an allergen during food preparation, such as through unwashed cutting boards or knives.)

The National Association of School Nurses website, www.nasn.org, offers a tool kit that includes suggestions for preparing, training, and organizing for allergen prevention and emergencies. This site also contains many helpful checklists and training guides for families, school staff, and school health professionals.

For families that may have difficulty following the outlined policies and procedures, the letter should explain that the school can switch their children to a classroom without children with allergies. (See the FAAN website for a sample letter—www.foodallergy.org/page/sample-letter.)

Minimizing Allergen Exposure Schoolwide

Administrators, teachers, the school nurse, and parents should plan strategies to minimize allergen exposure throughout the school. It is important that children be equally safe when participating in activities in the library, gym, and computer, music, art, and other rooms children visit (such as speech/language therapy or English as a second language). As in the child's home classroom, these spaces must be made allergen free by sanitizing the surfaces, requiring frequent hand washing by other children and staff who use the spaces, and checking to ensure objects in the spaces do not contain allergens.

Preparing Staff for Possible Emergencies

All staff who work with children, including teaching assistants, ancillary staff, lunchroom staff, specialty-subject teachers, recess staff, and bus drivers, need training to know which children have allergies and how to recognize reactions. They should understand how to respond quickly and appropriately in emergencies. When a child with acute food allergies says "I don't feel good," adults must respond immediately. Adults should not wait for symptoms to appear before taking action. (See "Recognizing and Responding to an Emergency.")

Children seeking assistance in the lunchroom, during class, or outdoors at recess should be taken immediately to the nurse's station, the office, or the adult in charge of medical care. We may think that a child is not sick when in fact the child has recognized an allergic reaction at the earliest stage. Anaphylactic shock may occur if medical responses are not timely, especially for children with severe nut or seafood allergies (AAAAI 2010).

Reviewing Preparedness Plans

It's important to regularly assess and adjust prevention and response strategies as new information on dealing with allergic reactions becomes public. Up-to-date information can be found on the websites for the American Academy of Allergy, Asthma, and Immunology (AAAAI) (www.aaaai.org) and FAAN (www .foodallergy.org). Frequent conversations with families help in the information-sharing process. This allows all involved in the child's care to learn tips about new foods and to be aware of products found to have allergens or cross-contamination.

Recognizing and Responding to an Emergency

Symptoms of an anaphylactic reaction may occur within seconds of exposure or be delayed 15 to 30 minutes, or even an hour or more after exposure. The child may not understand what is happening and might simply say, "I don't feel good." Or he may present symptoms such as flushing, itching, hives, or anxiety. More serious symptoms, such as swelling of the throat and tongue, resulting in hoarseness, difficulty swallowing, and difficulty breathing, frequently occur. If some or any of these symptoms are present, take action immediately.

If allergy symptoms are life threatening, do not take a child in an anaphylactic reaction to the hospital. First, get the child's emergency kit, checking for the appropriate dose of epinephrine. Inject the child with the EpiPen, call emergency services (911), and then call the parents and physician.

Developmental Concerns

Research-based information about the psychological effects of certain food allergies is limited (Mandell et al. 2005). What there is suggests that severe food allergies may have significant implications for children's appropriate and healthy development (DunnGalvin, Gaffney, & Hourihane 2009; Gupta et al. 2011). The following are examples of social-emotional challenges that children with a food allergy may experience, and ways teachers can support these children.

Peer Relations and Social Isolation

Peer relationships may be problematic for children with food allergies (Muñoz-Furlong 2003; Mandell et al. 2005). Classmates and parents may view the children as having "something wrong with them." Children may be afraid to play with or eat lunch with a child who has allergies. Many children with severe food allergies must eat at a separate table in the cafeteria or in a different room to keep them safe. This separates a child from classmates and friends. Children may find out that they can't bring in certain foods because of another child's allergies and be resentful, leading to bullying or teasing. Some children may be jealous of the child who sits at her own table, viewing her as receiving special treatment.

Adults need to explain to children what food allergies are, how a severe allergy can affect a classmate, and why their classmate must eat lunch at a separate table. Hold a class brainstorming session to generate ideas on how to fairly choose tablemates for the child with allergies, ensuring that the child has at least one person to eat with every day. This process allows interested children to feel successful in helping a classmate or friend.

Teachers must talk to parents about any changes in a child's behavior that may be attributable to her allergies.

Depression and Anxiety

Recent research looking at children between the ages of 6 and 15 who have allergies asserts that a food allergy "impacts directly on children's normal trajectory of psychological development in both an age- and disease-specific manner" (DunnGalvin, Gaffney, & Hourihane 2009, 560). So it is not surprising that children with food allergies may develop disordered eating (eating in a way that harms a child physically or psychologically) (Muñoz-Furlong 2003) or depression and anxiety (Masia, Mullen, & Scotti 1998).

Common symptoms of depression and anxiety include poor sleep or nervousness. Teachers must talk to parents about any changes in a child's behavior that may be attributable to her allergies. Ongoing family–school communication is essential for maintaining a team approach to supporting the social-emotional development of a child with allergies. Talk with the child about her fears and anxieties and brainstorm together ideas about how to feel safer in school.

Obsessive-Compulsive Disorder

Children with allergies may mistrust other people, even an otherwise-trusted adult who accidentally exposes them to an allergen (Masia, Mullen, & Scotti 1998). As a result, some children might develop symptoms of obsessive-compulsive disorder (OCD), such as frequent hand washing, refusal to eat for fear of unsafe food preparation, not eating lunch away from home, or avoidance of lunch staff, school personnel, and other children.

Some children who develop OCD or OCD-like behavior may be less likely to touch, hold hands, or shake hands with someone else, because they are aware that they can have a reaction by cross-contamination. Teachers can help alleviate mistrust by being patient with children who exhibit these behaviors. Again, talking to a child about his fears is an important part of supporting his development of coping skills. For example, ask the child directly what makes him feel anxious. If the child is nervous about touching another child's hand, remind him that everyone has washed their hands and that it is safe to hold hands. Or suggest that partners hold on to a piece of rope or elastic band.

Classroom Realities

It takes time and planning to minimize the potentially dangerous situations that children with a food allergy encounter during

Strategies for Promoting Inclusion

Adults should address isolation and exclusion issues early in the year to facilitate acceptance of children with special needs. Community building and education about allergies can help classmates understand why it is important for a child with allergies to feel accepted.

Sharing a book about allergies with all children can increase their understanding of the situation. A wonderful, age-appropriate book to help primary-age children (and their families) become aware of the significance of a food allergy is *The Peanut-Free Café,* written by Gloria Koster and illustrated by Maryann Cocca-Leffler. Reading this book to the class and allowing children to take it home to share with family members can open up conversations about what it means to have a food allergy. It may even generate inventive inclusion ideas.

Asking a child with allergies to explain how it feels to have a food allergy can help other children learn to empathize. Classmates could make posters that remind everyone to share in the responsibility to keep their classmates safe. Sharing websites and book lists are good ways to help families understand the impact of food allergies at school. Schools could hold a family night where children and families share books and information on understanding allergens. Offer a healthy snack or have the children make one using an allergen-free recipe.

A Note About Classroom Pets

While many classrooms have pets, allergy-prone children may be allergic to pets with hair and dander. If a pet visits, sanitize the classroom after the visit. If children with allergies must leave the classroom during the pet visit, advise them in advance and provide another engaging activity, so they are less likely to feel isolated or disappointed. A better idea is to allow a pet to visit the playground, where children with allergies can keep a safe distance from the animal and contamination is less likely. Remind children who have handled pets at home to wash their hands and eliminate pet hair on their clothing with a lint roller before entering the classroom.

the school day. The following list includes cross-contamination issues that teachers and classroom assistants must think about and plan for daily:

Personal school supplies. Children with a food allergy should have their own containers of school supplies (paper, pencils, crayons, scissors, rulers, and so on) that they do not share with other children.

Reviewing children's work. Always be conscientious about washing your hands *before* reviewing children's papers, both at home and at school. Many airborne allergens, such as nut dust, can remain on papers long after someone touches them. Even this seemingly innocuous cross-contamination could result in an allergic reaction (Young, Muñoz-Furlong, & Sicherer 2009).

Hand-washing procedures. Food allergens can be transmitted through the air and via skin contact. The Centers for Disease Control and Prevention (2012) encourages both children and adults to wash their hands for at least 20 seconds after cooking or handling food. This minimizes the spread of allergens. Alcohol-based hand sanitizers, while found to be effective for killing germs, do not clean hands as well as warm soapy water, unless the alcohol content of the sanitizer is at least 60 percent (Duda 2011; Centers for Disease Control and Prevention 2012).

Classroom surfaces. Tables, toys, computer keyboards, and other surfaces must be systematically cleaned. Use a mixture of water and bleach—1 part bleach to 10 parts water or 1 cup of bleach to 5 gallons of water. For quick cleanups, use pop-up sanitizing wipes.

Food in the classroom. Snacks, birthday treats, and holiday celebration foods must be free of allergens (for example, nuts, milk, and gluten).

Even though families receive a letter explaining the allergen situation in the classroom, send a reminder to parents that even healthy snacks from home can be dangerous due to cross-contamination from cutting boards. And while many parents will remember to send in snacks that all students can safely eat, staff must still inspect snacks or treats meant for all children. Be aware that many foods labeled "gluten free" or "free of nut oils" may still contain the allergen. If you are unsure of the contents of a food item, always err on the side of safety and offer an alternative, safe item to the child with a food allergy.

A more comprehensive list of possible allergens, along with allergen-free recipes to share with parents and staff, can be found on the FAAN website: www.foodallergy.org.

Classroom items. Everyday items in the classroom may have nut oils or allergens in them, including facial tissue (several are made with lotion containing nut oils), hand soaps, and some sunscreens. As families send in such classroom supplies, read the labels to make sure each is allergen free.

The FAAN website is a good resource for understanding how to read food and other labels: www.foodallergy.org/section/understanding-food-labels1.

It takes time and planning to minimize the potentially dangerous situations that children with a food allergy encounter during the school day.

Cubbies or lockers. Thoughtful planning should go into the location of cubbies or other areas where children keep their food. The best locker location for a child with food allergies limits exposure to cross-contamination from sources such as other children's hands or bag lunches. Locate the child's cubby at the end of a row to decrease exposure.

Field Trips

Planning is especially important when considering field trips. Remember the following to be as safe as possible:

- The location of the field trip should be as free as possible of allergens, so all children can enjoy the experience. For example, if a trip to a museum includes eating lunch in a cafeteria or restaurant, where food allergens cannot be controlled, the child with allergies would have to eat elsewhere. For that child to enjoy lunch with his classmates and discuss new experiences, schedule lunch for all of the children in an allergen-free space.
- Staff should bring the child's emergency medical kit on all field trips.
- Snack foods, either brought along or purchased on site, should be allergen free.
- The transportation vehicle should be free of allergens.
- Group children ahead of time, when you have time to think about whether, for example, the child with allergies needs a smaller group, rather than during the hectic time of leaving for a field trip.
- All chaperones should have adequate knowledge to handle allergic situations.

Conclusion

While having children with food allergies in early childhood settings can be challenging, it can also be very rewarding. These children are frequently very healthy eaters and have a high level of independence. And while children with allergies

are often very cautious and accepting of their personal challenges, they also learn at an early age to accept differences in others. Well-prepared and well-trained adults create safe and inclusive environments for all children.

References

AAAAI (American Academy of Allergy, Asthma, and Immunology). 2010. "Guidelines for the Diagnosis and Management of Food Allergy in the United States: Report of the NIAID-Sponsored Expert Panel." *Journal of Allergy and Clinical Immunology* 126 (6): 51–58. www.jacionline.org/article/S0091-6749(10)01566-6/fulltext.

AAFA (Asthma and Allergy Foundation of America). 2011. "State Honor Roll: Asthma and Allergy Policies for Schools." www.aafa.org/pdfs/2011%20State%20Honor%2Roll%20Full%20Report%20Final.pdf.

Behrmann, J. 2010. "Ethical Principles as a Guide in Implementing Policies for the Management of Food Allergies in Schools." *Journal of School Nursing* 26 (3): 183–93.

Centers for Disease Control and Prevention. 2012. "Handwashing: Clean Hands Save Lives." www.cdc.gov/handwashing.

C.S. Mott Children's Hospital. 2009. "Are Schools Doing Enough for Food-Allergic Kids?" National Poll on Children's Health. www.mottnpch.org/reports-surveys/are-schools-doing-enough-food-allergic-kids.

Duda, K. 2011. "Is Hand Sanitizer Better Than Hand Washing?" About.com Guide. http://coldflu.about.com/old/prevention/qt/handsanitizer.htm.

DunnGalvin, A., A. Gaffney, & J.O. Hourihane. 2009. "Developmental Pathways in Food Allergy: A New Theoretical Framework." *Allergy* 64 (4): 560–68.

FAAN (Food Allergy and Anaphylaxis Network). n.d. "About Us." www.foodallergy.org/about.html.

Gupta, R.S., E.E. Springston, M.R. Warrier, B. Smith, R. Kumar, J. Pongracic, & J.L. Holl. 2011. "The Prevalence, Severity, and Distribution of Childhood Food Allergy in the United States." *Pediatrics* 128 (1): e9–e17.

Hay, G.H., T.B. Harper III, & T.G. Moore. 2006. "Assuring the Safety of Severely Food Allergic Children in School." *Journal of School Health* 76 (9): 479–81.

Mandell, D., R. Curtis, M. Gold, & S. Hardie. 2005. "Anaphylaxis: How Do You Live with It?" *Health & Social Work* 30 (4): 325–35.

Masia, C.L., K.B. Mullen, & J.R. Scotti. 1998. "Peanut Allergy in Children: Psychological Issues and Clinical Considerations." *Education and Treatment of Children* 21 (4): 514–31.

Muñoz-Furlong, A. 2003. "Daily Coping Strategies for Patients and Their Families." *Pediatrics* 111 (Supplement 3): 1654–61.

Young, M.C., A. Muñoz-Furlong, & S.H. Sicherer. 2009. "Management of Food Allergies in Schools: A Perspective for Allergists." *Journal of Allergy and Clinical Immunology* 124 (2): 175–82. http://integrativehealthconnection.com/wp-content/uploads/2011/11/Management-of-food-allergies-in-schools-A-perspective-for-allergists.pdf.

The following topics are included in the expanded version of this article, which is online at www.naeyc.org in the NAEYC Members Only area:
- Food Allergy Checklist
- Legal Issues
- Lunch Considerations
- Resources for Children and Families

Critical Thinking

1. Read through the Food Allergy Checklist in the article and reflect how these could be carried out in a classroom that

has a number of staff working in the room on a rotating basis.

2. What role do families play in keeping the environment safe for all children?

Create Central

www.mhhe.com/createcentral

Internet References

Allergy Kids Foundation
http://allergykids.com

American Academy of Pediatrics
www.aap.org

American College of Allergy, Asthma and Immunology
www.acaai.org/allergist/allergies/Types/food-allergies/Pages/default.aspx

Food Allergy Research and Education
www.foodallergy.org

U.S. Food and Drug Administration
www.fda.gov/Food/ResourcesForYou/Consumers/ucm079311.htm

Peggy Thelen, PhD, is an associate professor of education and director of the early childhood program at Alma College in Alma, Michigan. She teaches courses on human growth and development, diverse learners, and all aspects of early childhood education. thelen@alma.edu. **Elizabeth Ann Cameron, JP** MBA, is a professor of business administration at Alma College. She teaches business and health care courses and is the 2011 Midwest Academy of Legal Studies in Business Master Teacher. She is also an attorney who advocates for young children and the mother of a child with food allergies. cameron@alma.edu. An expanded version of this article (including a food allergy checklist) is available online at www.naeyc.org/yc in the Members Only area.

Thelen, Peggy; Cameron, Elizabeth Ann. From *Young Children,* September 2012, pp. 106–112. Copyright © 2012 by National Association for the Education of Young Children. Reprinted by permission. www.naeyc.org.

Article　　　　Prepared by: Karen Menke Paciorek, *Eastern Michigan University*

Supporting Children's Learning While Meeting State Standards

Strategies and Suggestions for Pre-K–Grade 3 Teachers in Public School Contexts.

In Jenny Aster's kindergarten classroom, the 30-minute "literacy stations" block is coming to a close. Stragglers finish their daily journal entries, put their completed handwriting worksheets in the All Done basket, and staple the *at* word family booklets they've created. Jenny claps rhythmically to get the children's attention: "It's time to clean up so we can have centers. The quicker we clean up, the sooner we can start." The children scurry around the room picking up scraps of paper and returning supplies to their proper locations.

When center time begins, it is easy to see why the children were so motivated to get started. The centers transform the space from a teacher-directed environment to a buffet of child-directed learning opportunities. A pair of bland, unmarked cupboard doors swings open to reveal a large assortment of unit blocks, all of which are eagerly—and noisily—pulled onto the speckled linoleum floor and immediately used to construct a racing tower. Several robber–pirates dart out of the housekeeping area, scarves tied around their heads and clutching treasure-filled sacks. Children pull puzzles and games onto the carpet, reminding each other of the rules and procedures.

A businesslike group of clipboard-holding girls moves purposefully through the room, engaging briefly with each small group of busy children. The girls apologize for interrupting, ask a few questions, make notes, and move on. A quick peek at their clipboards reveals each girl using invented spelling and cues from environmental print, such as entries on the classroom word wall, to record classmates' names and responses.

LISA S. GOLDSTEIN AND MICHELLE BAUML

Learning Outcomes

After reading this article, you will be able to:

- Identify three traits common to teachers who successfully balance an understanding of the students' needs with curricular demands.

- Describe three strategies presented in the article that would enhance teaching and learning.

The current emphasis on standards-based education and accountability in public schools in the United States has had a significant impact on early childhood teachers' practices. States, school districts, and administrators may require teachers to cover certain academic content standards and/or use particular instructional materials. But many teachers at the prekindergarten, kindergarten, and primary grade levels are concerned about the ways in which these new expectations limit their ability to meet the needs of individual children and to promote the learning of all the children they teach (Goldstein 2007a, 2007b; Valli & Buese 2007).

Asking teachers to stop making decisions about what to teach and how best to teach it is as unrealistic as asking artists to stop choosing which colors to use on their canvas: making intentional decisions about curriculum and instruction is the signature responsibility that defines teaching as a profession (Hawthorne 1992). Even when school districts enact policies with explicit expectations for curriculum content and instructional practices, teachers rarely follow those lesson plans or pacing guides exactly as they are written (Ehly 2009); early childhood educators seek every available opportunity to provide meaningful, engaging learning experiences that support all children (DeVault 2003; Geist & Baum 2005; Bauml 2008).

Early childhood educators seek every available opportunity to provide meaningful, engaging learning experiences that support all children.

Most public school teachers have a repertoire of strategies for modifying the requirements in ways that allow them to do what they know will be most effective in advancing children's learning. Perhaps they replace the storybook suggested in the Teachers' Edition with one they believe to be more suitable. Or they incorporate sheltered instructional strategies, such as the use of visual aids or concrete materials to support dual language learners' comprehension of the academic content in a science lesson. They might supplement a required mathematics lesson on addition with a range of math games that help children practice and integrate the concepts introduced in the lesson. Maybe their administrators have given them permission to make these departures from their districts' policies and expectations. Possibly they have colleagues with whom they discuss and share strategies for tweaking the required plans.

Our goal in this article is to bring these strategies into the open. We encourage all pre-K–grade 3 teachers to consider their need to develop effective strategies for teaching state standards in appropriate, responsive ways as a challenge to be embraced explicitly and overtly. In discussions about the findings of our individual research projects—Lisa's with experienced kindergarten teachers (Goldstein 2007a, 2007b, 2008) and Michelle's with preservice teachers in grades pre-K–grade 4 (Bauml 2008, 2009)—we identified three traits common to those teachers who successfully balance "the child and the curriculum" (Dewey 1902) in today's complex public school environments. These teachers acquire detailed and thorough knowledge of the policies, procedures, and requirements shaping their work; they consider the district-adopted materials to be a starting point for curriculum and instruction; and they actively showcase children's learning and academic progress. In this article we discuss each of these traits, providing examples and suggestions to help all early childhood teachers find new ways to work within existing constraints and to continue to make the decisions about curriculum and instruction that will be most beneficial to young learners.

Trait 1: Acquire Detailed and Thorough Knowledge of Policies and Expectations

A strong knowledge base is essential for making effective decisions. Today it may seem that new obligations, demands, and expectations are coming at teachers from all directions. Having the information you need, being clear about requirements, and understanding the implications of the policies shaping your practice allow you to make curricular and instructional decisions that meet the needs of the children you teach, as well as the expectations of your school or district. Here are a few ways to develop your knowledge base:

Know the Law

Build a strong understanding of the relevant aspects of the federal and state legislation governing your practices. Your curricular and instructional decisions should be principled and intentional (Epstein 2007), grounded in the real details of the laws that govern your responsibilities. You can find information about state

policy on your state education agency website, and information about federal requirements at the US Department of Education's website (www.ed.gov) or in books written to inform parents, teachers, and others about the details and demands of recent education policies and reform efforts (David & Cuban 2010).

> The long list of content standards in each area of the curriculum can seem daunting, but there are ways to manage the scope of this endeavor.

Know Your State's Content Standards

In classrooms from pre-K to grade 12, public school teachers are expected to move their students to mastery of their state's content standards. A detailed, thorough knowledge of exactly which skills and what knowledge comprise the content standards makes this goal much more attainable. The long list of content standards in each area of the curriculum can seem daunting, but there are ways to manage the scope of this endeavor. For example, grade level study groups can explore the state standards for each content area in greater depth (Ehly 2009). During this exploration, study group members might make note of cross-disciplinary connections that can create and enhance standards-based thematic curriculum units (Helm 2008). Likewise, teachers might agree to identify the specific content standards in each subject that they consider most significant for children's future success and commit to placing the greatest emphasis on those prioritized standards throughout the year (Ainsworth & Viegut 2006).

Know the Policies in Your District

Closely examine the school district policies relevant to your grade level to find out exactly what the district expects of its teachers. It is critical to have accurate information about which practices are required, which are strongly recommended, and which are optional. Consult your district's website, as well as key administrators in the district office—such as the head of curriculum and instruction—to clarify exactly what the district requires.

Know Your Principal's Stance on District Policies and State/National Laws

Talk to your principal. How does she understand and interpret the district's requirements? Find out whether he holds personal expectations that depart from those of the district, and determine the degree of curricular and instructional flexibility your principal supports. Aligning your decisions not only with state and district policy, but also with the principal's goals and priorities, will help you to continue to do what you know will be most effective in supporting children's learning.

Develop Your Assessment Literacy

Avoid becoming intimidated by the mountains of data available about the children's skills and knowledge. Test scores from locally developed and statewide assessments provide important information about learning and development that has significant implications for your teaching and your curriculum. Consider these assessment data to be a source of critical feedback on the effectiveness of your practices, and use this feedback to inform your future instructional decisions. In addition, supplement the "scientific" evidence of children's skills provided by test scores with authentic documentation of the children's capabilities, such as anecdotal observations, annotated work samples or photographs of children involved in learning activities, such as science explorations or building with pattern blocks, and other types of teacher-developed assessment tools. Considering and discussing formal and informal assessment data side by side can broaden your knowledge of children as learners and help you make curricular and instructional decisions tailored precisely to their strengths and needs.

Aligning your decisions not only with state and district policy, but also with the principal's goals and priorities, will help you to continue to do what you know will be most effective in supporting children's learning.

A strong knowledge base will help you determine which expectations and practices are suggested and which are mandatory. Solicit information from many different authoritative sources, and talk with colleagues and administrators. Synthesize what you learn, and you will strengthen your ability to support the children's learning and progress.

Trait 2: Consider the Required Materials to Be a Starting Point

For many teachers, choosing what content and skills to teach and planning meaningful learning activities are deeply rewarding professional experiences. Rather than allowing new expectations to eliminate this aspect of your work, think of the required materials and content as the small seeds from which you can grow engaging, meaningful lessons expressly for the children in your class. In our work as researchers and teacher educators, we have seen public school prekindergarten, kindergarten, and primary grade teachers customize district-adopted curricula using a wide range of strategies that can be applied at any grade level. Teachers can:

Substitute

Teach the concepts presented in the recommended lesson, but use different materials or instructional approaches to reach the objectives. For example, transform a letter-sorting worksheet into a game or hands-on activity to increase children's interest and engagement. Use technology resources such as DVDs, streaming, podcasts, and computer games to create captivating substitutes for mundane activities.

Supplement

Augment the required lessons with additional materials and activities. Bring in extra books at various reading levels (and, when possible, in the home languages of dual language learners); offer a broader range of learning experiences; add new materials; integrate meaningful opportunities for children to engage with technology; and incorporate the visual and performing arts. These strategies can help you meet all children's developmental needs while addressing content standards.

Enrich

Add depth, complexity, and opportunities for creative thinking and expression to mandated lessons. Treat all children like gifted children, encouraging them to explore activities typically reserved for high-achieving learners. Design open-ended activities that allow students to investigate and practice content area concepts through the arts and movement. Give children opportunities to experiment, to problem-solve and theorize, and to manage ambiguity and possibility by working at engaging, challenging intellectual tasks.

Adjust the Pace

Allow children time to explore materials, activities, and ideas more deeply. Strategic placement of materials in learning centers can encourage prolonged engagement and enhanced learning opportunities throughout the year. Accelerating the pace of lessons and activities can also be an effective curriculum management strategy. This can be achieved by determining how much work is needed to provide sufficient evidence of student mastery, and stopping when children reach that point—even if it means some children complete only half of a worksheet. Applied carefully, acceleration can buy precious classroom time for other activities that are sometimes squeezed out of the daily schedule—such as outdoor play—without shortchanging children's learning.

Cherry-Pick

Extract the best activities and ideas from mandated texts and programs and use them as cornerstones for new units. District-required materials, already aligned with the standards, may contain excellent activities for you to build on as you develop the most appropriate learning experiences for the children you teach. Also, you can replace lackluster activities in one unit with high-interest activities cherry-picked and modified from another.

Shoehorn

Pack as many standards as possible into those powerful thematic units that have proven successful with children in past years. Although every lesson you teach must incorporate knowledge and skills specified by the state, it might not be necessary to eliminate effective, engaging units because they do not immediately appear to be aligned directly to the current standards. Creative, resourceful shoehorning can allow you to adapt your best time-tested activities and use them to teach today's standards in meaningful ways.

Strategic placement of materials in learning centers can encourage prolonged engagement and enhanced learning opportunities throughout the year.

Our experiences suggest that even when teachers are expected to teach the mandated curriculum using district-adopted textbooks and lessons, they are rarely told they must use *only* those materials. Strategies like these enable you to both satisfy official policies and bring the standards to life for young children.

Trait 3: Showcase Children's Engagement in Substantive Learning

Learning and growth for all children have always been the early childhood teacher's primary goal, and this still holds true today. However, today it also is vitally important that pre-K–grade 3 teachers are able to present concrete evidence of children's learning. Parents, principals, district administrators, and other teachers—all of whom are important stakeholders in children's educational futures and have a strong interest in their achievement and progress—may wonder whether the children in your classroom are really learning or "just playing." Wise early childhood teachers should be proactive in showcasing the significant learning taking place in their classrooms and explicit in drawing connections between the children's work and the state's standards and expectations for academic achievement. Here are a few ideas teachers can use to increase the visibility of children's learning and success:

Develop Language for Talking About Your Decisions, Your Practices, and Children's Learning

When you modify mandated materials to benefit the children you teach, you might find that colleagues, administrators, or parents will ask questions about your decisions. Having effective language to describe the reasoning behind your decisions will allow others to understand your strategic application of professional knowledge. This is especially effective when you discuss your decisions using terms that make sense to your listeners. A phrase like *developmentally appropriate* might not help parents, administrators, or others without an early childhood background see the value in the children's work. Making simple changes in the words you choose—saying *progress* rather than *growth,* for example—can go a long way toward making your decisions accessible and meaningful to others. Listen closely to conversations at your school or at district events to identify commonly used buzzwords, such as *learning outcomes, accountable talk, mastery,* and so on. Your judicious use of those terms to describe your own practices (when relevant and appropriate) may help your colleagues identify

and acknowledge the real learning that is taking place in early childhood classrooms.

Communicate with the Principal

Principals want to know that all the children in the school are learning. Because many principals have little or no experience teaching in early childhood settings, it makes sense for teachers to take deliberate steps to demonstrate the learning that is taking place in their classrooms. Invite your principal to visit during learning center time when, for example, you can offer commentary about children's engagement in problem solving and language development. Provide copies of parent newsletters featuring topics of study and their connections to the standards. Most principals are eager to learn more about developmentally appropriate practices and are committed to playing an active role in supporting the academic success of their schools' youngest students.

Communicate with Colleagues

Upper grade teachers who may lack the knowledge base to understand the unique learning needs of young children may not realize that early childhood teachers are engaged in complex, demanding work. Put an end to this misconception by finding opportunities to teach your colleagues about the relationship between your practices, children's learning, and the state standards. For example, supplement hallway displays of children's work with explanatory labels that describe the purpose of the activity on display and explain the activity's explicit connection to the standards. You might even place arrows and text strategically around the work to highlight specific evidence of children's skills and abilities. Another way to communicate with colleagues about your curricular and instructional choices is to invite a class of older children into your room as reading buddies. While children read in pairs, you and your colleague can discuss classroom activities and the progress children are making.

Supplement hallway displays of children's work with explanatory labels that describe the purpose of the activity on display and explain the activity's explicit connection to the standards.

Communicate with Families

The popular media's focus on standardized test scores, school performance, and accountability has heightened the general public's awareness of—and concern about—young children's academic achievement. In today's educational climate you might encounter parents who express concern that their young children are not experiencing enough academic rigor, as well as parents who mourn the loss of the play-centered, child-directed learning they expected their children to experience in the early grades. Can a teacher hope to satisfy everyone? Opening lines of communication with children's families—reaching out, helping to connect them to your classroom curriculum, and inviting questions, comments, and suggestions—is an important place to start. Trust and partnership between teachers and families is particularly important when the public conversations about what's best for young learners can be so contentious and confusing.

Communicate with the Children

The children you teach become your greatest publicists when they are able to take classroom learning conversations home to their families. Teach them to reflect on their experiences and to think about their thinking. Help them develop language for describing their learning by asking them to discuss what they did and what they learned after activities such as story time or explorations in learning centers. Make process-oriented learning goals explicit to children by using strategic compliments to reinforce learning episodes, such as effective collaboration or oral expression.

Having effective language to describe the reasoning behind your decisions will allow others to understand your strategic application of professional knowledge.

Although pre-K–grade 3 are early childhood settings, states' standards-based education policies position these grade levels as the foundation of "a progressing, expanding, non-repeating curriculum of increasing complexity, depth, and breadth" (Ardovino, Hollingsworth, & Ybarra 2000, 91) that extends up through the final year of high school. Now that teachers in grades pre-K–grade 3 are expected to be full participants in much larger conversations about public school students' learning and achievement, it is critically important that you demonstrate and talk about young children's experiences and growth in terms that can be understood outside of early childhood education. It is in your best interest to help colleagues at all grade levels understand not only the unique curricular and instructional terrain of the school's youngest learners, but also the significant commonalities that unite your professional practices, challenges, and goals with theirs.

Regardless of the grade they teach, teachers are professional decision makers committed to supporting children's learning. Making decisions about what to teach and how to teach it best is simply a nonnegotiable feature of your job: only teachers have the specialized knowledge and professional training required to design meaningful learning experiences that build sturdy, flexible bridges between the academic content mandated by the state or district and a particular, specific group of children with a unique constellation of intellectual capabilities, cultures, home languages, life experiences, and aspirations. Even in schools where curricular and instructional freedoms are limited, there are always opportunities for resourceful teachers to use their professional judgment to devise learning

experiences that meet children's needs. Develop the traits and use the strategies presented in this article to make confident, informed decisions; to strengthen your ability to teach the standards to children in engaging and appropriate ways; and to support public school early learning environments that are focused on the learning and growth of all children.

References

Ainsworth, L., & D. Viegut. 2006. *Common Formative Assessments: How to Connect Standards-Based Instruction and Assessment.* Thousand Oaks, CA: Corwin Press.

Ardovino, J., J. Hollingsworth, & S. Ybarra. 2000. *Multiple Measures: Accurate Ways to Assess Student Achievement.* Thousand Oaks, CA: Corwin Press.

Bauml, M. 2008. "The 'X-Factor': Early Childhood Preservice Teachers' Perceptions of the Professional Characteristics of Effective Teachers." Paper presented at the Annual Meeting of the American Educational Research Association, New York, 24–28 March.

Bauml, M. 2009, "Examining the Unexpected Sophistication of Preservice Teachers' Beliefs about the Relational Dimensions of Teaching." *Teaching and Teacher Education* 25 (6): 902–8.

David, J.L. & L. Cuban. 2010. *Cutting through the Hype: The Essential Guide to School Reform.* Cambridge, MA: Harvard Education Press.

DeVault, L. 2003. "The Tide Is High but We Can Hold On: One Kindergarten Teacher's Thoughts on the Rising Tide of Academic Expectations." *Young Children* 58 (6): 90–93.

Dewey, J. 1902. *The Child and the Curriculum.* Chicago: University of Chicago Press.

Ehly, S.Y. 2009. *The Learning-Centered Kindergarten: 10 Keys to Success for Standards-Based Classrooms.* Thousand Oaks, CA: Corwin Press.

Epstein, A.S. 2007. *The Intentional Teacher: Choosing the Best Strategies for Young Children's Learning.* Washington, DC: NAEYC.

Geist, E., & A.C. Baum. 2005. "Yeah, But's That Keep Teachers from Embracing an Active Curriculum: Overcoming the Resistance." *Young Children* 60 (4): 28–36. Washington, DC: NAEYC. www.naeyc.org/files/yc/file/200507/03Geist.pdf.

Goldstein, L.S. 2007a. "Embracing Pedagogical Multiplicity: Examining Two Teachers' Instructional Responses to the Changing Expectations for Kindergarten in U.S. Public Schools." *Journal of Research in Childhood Education* 21 (4): 378–99.

Goldstein, L.S. 2007b. "Beyond the DAP Versus Standards Dilemma: Examining the Unforgiving Complexity of Kindergarten Teaching in the United States." *Early Childhood Research Quarterly* 22 (1): 39–54.

Goldstein, L.S. 2008. "Kindergarten Teachers Making 'Street-Level' Education Policy in the Wake of No Child Left Behind." *Early Education and Development* 19 (3): 448–78.

Hawthorne, R.K. 1992. *Curriculum in the Making: Teacher Choice and the Classroom Experience.* New York: Teachers College Press.

Helm, J.H. 2008. "Got Standards? Don't Give Up on Engaged Learning." *Young Children* 63 (4): 14–20. www.naeyc.org/files/yc/file/200807/BTJJudyHarrisHelm.pdf.

Valli, L., & D. Buese. 2007. "The Changing Roles of Teachers in an Era of High-Stakes Accountability." *American Educational Research Journal* 44 (3): 519–58.

Critical Thinking

1. Get a copy of your state's content standards for the age level or grade(s) you teach or want to teach. Choose one area and develop an activity that you could plan for the children in your class that would meet that standard.

2. Develop a letter to the parents of the children in your class explaining your philosophy on how you think children best learn and the kinds of activities you plan on providing for the children this year.

Create Central

www.mhhe.com/createcentral

Internet References

Association for Childhood Education International (ACEI)
www.acei.org

Common Core State Standards Initiative
www.corestandards.org

National Association for the Education of Young Children
www.naeyc.org

LISA S. GOLDSTEIN, PhD, is professor and director of teacher education at Santa Clara University in Santa Clara, California. Lisa's current research focuses on primary grade teachers' curricular and instructional decision making in today's highly regulated school environments. MICHELLE BAUML, PhD, is an assistant professor of early childhood/social studies education at Texas Christian University in Fort Worth, Texas. Her research interests include new teacher development, teacher thinking and decision making, and early childhood elementary curriculum and instruction.

Goldstein, Lisa S.; Bauml, Michelle. From *Young Children*, May 2012, pp. 96–103. Copyright © 2012 by National Association for the Education of Young Children. Reprinted by permission. www.naeyc.org.

Article Prepared by: Karen Menke Paciorek, *Eastern Michigan University*

The Potential of the Project Approach to Support Diverse Young Learners

Mr. Robinson's inclusive preschool classroom is full of activity and chatter as the 4- and 5-year-olds gather around the rug for their morning meeting. Two children with identified special needs are enrolled in the class: Ginelle and Rylee. Ginelle, who has global developmental delays, engages in some parallel play with other children, particularly if painting is involved, but rarely initiates interactions with peers or adults. Her mother works in a nearby grocery store. Rylee, who was recently diagnosed with autism, loves books and prefers interacting with adults rather than peers. Additionally, Darnell, who is a dual language learner, recently joined the class. Darnell enjoys swinging, running, and playing with blocks.

Sallee J. Beneke and Michaelene M. Ostrosky

Learning Outcomes

After reading this article, you will be able to:

- Explain how teachers plan using the project approach.
- Describe how children are engaged in the learning when in a classroom using the project approach.

Just as universal design encourages architects to design environments that benefit all users, UDL helps early childhood educators select and implement teaching approaches that benefit all learners.

What curriculum approach does Mr. Robinson use to teach this diverse group of children effectively? What are some culturally and linguistically relevant and developmentally appropriate practices and strategies that meet the needs of dual language learners, like Darnell, and the needs of children with developmental delays, like Rylee and Ginelle, as well as children without special needs? Is there one approach that works best with young learners with a variety of strengths and needs in the same setting?

Inclusion of children with special needs in early childhood classrooms is identified as best practice in early childhood education, enabling children who have special needs and children who do not have special needs to learn and develop together in the same class (Odom 2000; Sandall et al. 2007). Yet many early childhood educators struggle to plan optimal educational experiences for all of the children in their classrooms without separating them into ability groups or having them taken out of class for instruction. Early childhood educators understand the importance of building a classroom community of diverse learners and their families, and they know that it is important to find approaches that provide access to learning experiences in which all children can fully participate while receiving individualized support (DEC & NAEYC 2009).

The Division for Early Childhood (DEC) of the Council for Exceptional Children and NAEYC developed a joint position statement, "Early Childhood Inclusion," to serve as "a blueprint for identifying the key components of high quality inclusive programs" (2009, 1). The position statement discusses Universal Design for Learning (UDL) and designates *access* as a defining feature of inclusion. It explains how UDL "reflects practices that provide multiple and varied formats for instruction and learning" that can be used to ensure that every child has access to the curriculum (1).

This article considers ways early childhood educators can increase the quality of instruction for all children in inclusive classrooms by linking principles of UDL with the project approach. As we discuss providing access to learning through key UDL principles, we highlight examples of practice from the grocery store project that Mr. Robinson implements in an inclusive preschool classroom.

Universal Design for Learning

Originally conceptualized as a principle of architectural design, universal design guides the development of architectural features that benefit everyone, including individuals with physical disabilities. For example, everyone enjoys the advantages of curb cuts, which make it easier to move from street to sidewalk for a person pushing a stroller, walking with a cane, rolling a wheelchair, or pulling a suitcase. Educators have adopted this principle, with UDL providing a framework for creating instructional goals, methods, materials, and assessments that work for everyone.

Rather than waiting to make adaptations until a child is struggling, the idea behind UDL is that teachers begin by considering what instructional features make a situation—that is, a learning activity—accessible to all children. For example, when planning a field trip to a nearby grocery store where children will record observations and collect artifacts for their classroom project, Mr. Robinson worked with children beforehand. He helped Ginelle learn to use the classroom tablet so she could take photographs to document the visit. He also selected vocabulary words related to grocery stores and reviewed them with Darnell.

UDL is "not a single, one-size-fits-all solution but rather flexible approaches that can be customized and adjusted for individual needs" (CAST 2012). Just as universal design encourages architects to design environments that benefit all users, UDL helps early childhood educators select and implement teaching approaches that benefit all learners (Conn-Powers et al. 2006). UDL promotes access to learning through multiple means of engagement, representation, and expression—UDL principles (CAST 2012).

To learn more about Universal Design for Learning, visit the CAST website, www.cast.org/udl/.

The Project Approach

Projects are investigations of one overarching topic that typically last eight weeks or longer. They create an environment of coherence as children engage in activities that satisfy their curiosity and help them make sense of the world around them.

The project approach is a child-initiated, firsthand, in-depth investigation on a topic of interest undertaken by a group of children. There are many opportunities for children to take part in the investigation, learn about the topic, and express what they understand in different ways. Children can participate in project work on a variety of levels, building on their interests, using their strengths, and improving their abilities and skills.

A project typically proceeds through three phases (Katz & Chard 2000). In Phase 1 the teacher introduces the topic—in this case, grocery stores—and children explore their past experiences with and current knowledge of the topic. They generate questions or indicate their curiosity about the topic through their drawings, constructions, stories, and dramatic play. In Phase 2, the longest segment of a project, the children actively investigate the topic. They may interview experts, investigate firsthand by taking a field trip to a topic-related site, or use their senses to explore topic-related objects and artifacts teachers have added to the classroom environment. Children learn more about the topic by examining nonfiction books and creating observational drawings. They generate additional information as they discuss their experiences with one another and with the teacher. In Phase 3 the children summarize what they have learned by taking part as a class in a group production, such as

a construction, mural, play, video, report, book, song, or story. They plan a culminating event to celebrate their accomplishments, such as holding an open house for families or inviting another class to attend a presentation about their project.

Project work is not the whole curriculum, nor is it meant to take the place of systematic instruction for children with special needs. It is intended to complement and enhance what children learn from spontaneous play and systematic instruction (Katz & Chard 2000). It is an approach to curriculum that exemplifies the UDL principles, offering all children multiple means of engagement, representation, and expression (CAST 2012).

Teachers interested in learning more about the project approach can visit the Illinois Projects in Practice website (http://illinoispip.org), a free resource designed to support teachers in implementing the approach.

Multiple Means of Engagement

The UDL principle *multiple means of engagement* is defined as learning opportunities that "stimulate interest and motivation for learning" (CAST 2012). The observant educator learns about the interests of the children in her classroom. If their interests are not obvious, then she has conversations with family members or others who know them and can provide insight into activities the children are particularly drawn to at home or in the community.

Opportunities for Engagement

The project approach provides many opportunities to promote children's engagement by increasing their interest motivation, and attention span. These opportunities create entry points for teachers to use strategies to involve diverse learners. Features of the project approach that foster engagement include topic selection, the ongoing nature of projects, opportunities for firsthand investigation, the various ways children can show what they have learned, and the teacher's ability to document children's learning and interests (Beneke & Ostrosky 2009).

Teachers typically select topics for project work that are of high interest to many of the children in the class. Mr. Robinson had recently observed several children playing grocery store in the dramatic play area, and he knew that all of the children in the class had likely been to a grocery store with their families. Based on the children's common experience, the opportunity for firsthand investigation, and the variety of aspects of a grocery store they might investigate, he decided that it was a topic rich enough to support a long-term investigation. Mr. Robinson knew that Darnell likes being physically active, Rylee loves reading, and Ginelle enjoys painting and playing with blocks. The grocery store project could address all three children's interests.

Children's interest in the topic and the project's extended nature give children time to become experts on the topic of study, which benefits diverse learners.

Children's interest in the topic and the project's extended nature give children time to become experts on the topic of study, which benefits diverse learners. For example, children who do not typically engage in dramatic play activities have more time to consider the roles associated with the topic (What does the bagger do at the grocery store? What does the cashier say and do?). Children develop a better understanding about how to enter topic-related play after spending sustained time engaged in a project. The children might then enact the roles in pretend play with other children. For example, Rylee had repeated opportunities to observe the roles of grocery store workers and the shoppers and to listen to Mr. Robinson and other children describe these jobs. Two weeks after the class grocery store opened in the dramatic play center, Rylee began standing by the checkout counter and bagging the groceries for the customers.

The length of the project also enables the teacher to observe children's participation and interest in various aspects of the project, and to gather ongoing assessment data as children develop and learn. And it gives the teacher time to develop rich, topic-related experiences he can provide in classroom centers. For example, Mr. Robinson initially set up an area with shelves for groceries and a checkout counter. Following a class field trip to the local grocery store, the children expressed interest in the bakery, so he added a bakery section to the dramatic play center, complete with white aprons, food preparation gloves, and baking trays.

Over time Mr. Robinson made many more connections and extensions in other classroom learning centers. For example, he hole-punched laminated cards with grocery store words and images, put them on a book ring, and placed them in the writing area. He added books such as *The Baker's Dozen,* by Dan Andreasen, and *Growing Vegetable Soup,* by Lois Ehlert, to the library center.

Strategies for Engagement

Sometimes teachers choose topics that are likely to appeal to particular children in order to draw them into more active roles (Beneke 2011). For example, Ginelle's mother told Mr. Robinson that Ginelle often asked to visit the grocery store where she worked. Mr. Robinson believed that selecting the grocery store as a topic of study might encourage Ginelle's participation in dramatic play.

The richness of the grocery store play environment increased the possibilities for all the children to engage in project work. For example, knowing that Darnell likes to be physically active, Mr. Robinson provided a broom and plastic crates Darnell could use to carry groceries as he stocked the shelves. (See "Facilitating Engagement," for more strategies.)

Multiple Means of Representation

Learning experiences like projects incorporate multiple means of representation—that is, they "present information and content in different ways" (CAST 2012). Project work presents information to children in a variety of ways as a project unfolds, since some modes of learning are more effective than others for individual children. A teacher can plan multiple ways to investigate a topic, considering each child's preferred mode of learning.

Opportunities for Representation

Throughout a project, children have opportunities to learn through hands-on experiences. To get the project under way and open up discussion, a teacher might tell a simple story or present an artifact related to the topic. For example, to start a conversation about grocery stores, Mr. Robinson brought in different types of produce (eggplant, artichoke, pineapple, corn on the cob) for the children to feel, smell, draw, and talk about.

Through project work, teachers plan and provide sources of information and experiences over time to help children satisfy their curiosity and learn more about the topic. These may include props and costumes for dramatic play, nonfiction literature, software, Internet sites, visits from guest experts, and field trips. During the children's field trip to the grocery store, the manager invited them to walk inside a tractor trailer truck that was backed up to the loading bay. Days later, as the children discussed what they would like to construct, several expressed interest in building a truck. Mr. Robinson invited a local truck driver to visit the school with his semitrailer.

Powerful firsthand experiences like these provided many more ways for children—and particularly children with special needs—to learn than if they had seen just a picture, or even a video, of a semi. Mr. Robinson asked Ginelle to pick a partner to tour the cab of the semi with her. Ginelle and Shaniece shared the experience of sitting in the cab, holding the steering wheel, and discovering that the semi cab had a bed for sleeping. Later that day Mr. Robinson provided a steering wheel and prompted Ginelle and Shaniece to play semi driver.

As the children explored the semi, Mr. Robinson took photographs and later made a book about the truck driver's visit. He asked Rylee to assist him in writing the narrative. He prompted children to ask Rylee to read the book to them, thereby increasing her interaction with peers.

Darnell stood next to one of the semi's wheels and reached up to feel the relative difference in height. Mr. Robinson spoke to Darnell in Spanish to reinforce the mathematical concept of taller and shorter. Darnell heard Mr. Robinson emphasize the English words for these terms as other children compared their height to that of the wheel.

Strategies for Representation

Teachers can take advantage of varied project experiences to support the ways children learn most effectively. Because project work is flexible, some or all of the materials and experiences can be simplified or made more complex. The teacher can use these strategies with children who have a range of abilities, adjusting materials to enable all children to participate with success. For example, Mr. Robinson hoped to increase Ginelle's social interactions with other children. Knowing that Ginelle loved to paint, he proposed that the children paint the grocery store shelves in teams. Mr. Robinson arranged for Ginelle and a socially skilled peer to share a container of paint, and they spent 30 minutes painting their shelf orange and talking about their work. (See "Supporting Representation," for more strategies.)

Multiple Means of Action and Expression

In project work there are many opportunities and ways for all children to express their growing understanding about the topic under investigation. Children may draw, paint, sculpt, tell stories, add to class-created web diagrams, make signs, engage in pretend play, make up songs, and work on individual and group constructions. Mr. Robinson made available a variety of drawing and writing utensils, including thick and thin crayons, markers, and colored pencils with grippers, so that all of the preschoolers could draw their ideas and observations related to the project. Following the trip to the grocery store, each child dictated a memory of something observed at the store. Mr. Robinson wrote the memories on separate pieces of paper, and the children drew illustrations of their memories. Later, Mr. Robinson put these pages together as a class book that children could check out from the classroom lending library and explore with their family. When it was his turn, Darnell said he had really liked the walk-in refrigerator with the green curtain in front of it. Mr. Robinson gave Darnell a set of markers and named the colors in English and Spanish, highlighting the name of the green marker Darnell chose to color the curtain.

All three phases of the project approach offer children opportunities to engage in different types of expression about their knowledge and learning.

Opportunities for Action and Expression

To some extent, all three phases of the project approach offer children opportunities to engage in different types of expression about their knowledge and learning. In Phase 1 the teacher prompts children to show what they currently know about the project topic by telling, pretending, drawing, and painting about it. The teacher helps the children express their curiosity about different aspects of the project by inviting them to develop a list of research questions. To support Rylee's participation in the first phase of the grocery store project, Mr. Robinson paired her with a peer and asked them to come up with five questions they might ask a grocer.

The investigation of the project topic gets under way in Phase 2, when the teacher provides many opportunities for children to communicate their observations in a variety of ways. Mr. Robinson supported Darnell's emerging ability to communicate in dual languages by providing labeled picture cards on a book ring, placed where Darnell could easily access them. When Darnell is unsure of a word, he can find the picture and ask a teacher or peer to say the word for him. Mr. Robinson further supported Darnell's emerging abilities using the grocery artifacts in the dramatic play center to act out situations that include the word (for example, *money*).

Facilitating Engagement

- Communicate with families to determine children's interests and experiences
- Add topic-related artifacts to the environment, to increase participation
- Ask questions about topic-related objects or artifacts that have been added to the environment—tailor them to individual children
- Prompt children to participate in unfamiliar aspects of the project exploration and acknowledge their participation
- Feature each child's work or contributions in the project's documentation

Supporting Representation

- Place artifacts related to the topic in the classroom for children to explore
- Add photos of topic-related images to centers (e.g., block, dramatic play areas)
- Place tools related to the project topic in the discovery area
- Plan a field trip that is accessible to all children so they can learn from firsthand observation

Promoting Action and Expression

- Place topic-related props in dramatic play and block areas to spark dramatic play, with adaptations that ensure all children can use them (e.g., aprons with Velcro closures)
- Pair a child with a more competent peer to express their learning together
- Provide open-ended media that children can use to express their findings (e.g., glue, tape, paint, cardboard, clay) in 2- and 3-dimensional products
- Prompt children during fieldwork to notice aspects of the environment that might be desirable to record; point out attributes that will help them understand how to record it (e.g., drawing, tallying, photographing, tracing, making a rubbing)
- Help children with limited verbal ability participate in webbing and creating lists by describing their interests in particular objects

In Phase 3 children have learned a great deal, and their curiosity about and interest in the project wane noticeably. This final phase is a time for the children to summarize what they have learned by creating or participating in a group production. For the culmination of the grocery store project, Mr. Robinson's class invited the children across the hall to tour the giant trailer truck they had constructed using cardboard boxes. Group constructions provide opportunities that fit a range of abilities. Ginelle used a wide paintbrush to help paint the truck green, and Rylee painted *Grocery Store* on the side.

Strategies for Action and Expression

Teachers can use the many opportunities inherent in project work to support the action and expression of diverse learners (see "Promoting Action and Expression" for ideas). These opportunities help children develop in areas that need improvement and excel in areas of strength. For example, Mr. Robinson had observed Ginelle's interest in using the date stamper. He supported Ginelle's participation in creating the class web about grocery stores during Phase 1 by describing her interest ("Ginelle is interested in the date stamper. I'm going to add, 'What does the grocer do with the date stamper?' to our list of questions."). In view of Darnell's interest in block play, Mr. Robinson helped him make small laminated signs with the logos of local English and Spanish stores to place in the block area. Mr. Robinson rehearsed the names of the stores with Darnell. Soon Darnell was interacting with peers during block play as they constructed and labeled a variety of stores.

Conclusion

The project approach is a useful addition to teaching that exemplifies the key principles of Universal Design for Learning. It provides a framework that can help teachers like Mr. Robinson create learning experiences that give *all* children access to full participation in optimal learning experiences while also providing opportunities for individualized support.

References

Beneke, S. 2011. "Rearview Mirror: Reflections on a Preschool Car Project." In *Projects to Go!* (disc 2), eds. L.G. Katz & J.A. Mendoza. Urbana-Champaign, IL: Clearinghouse on Early Education and Parenting.

Beneke, S., & M.M. Ostrosky. 2009. "Teachers' Views of the Efficacy of Incorporating the Project Approach Into Classroom Practice With Diverse Learners." *Early Childhood Research & Practice* 11 (2). http://ecrp.uiuc.edu/v11n1/ostrosky.html.

CAST (Center for Applied Special Technology). 2012. Universal Design for Learning. "About UDL." www.cast.org/udl.

Conn-Powers, M., A.F. Cross, E.K. Traub, & L. Hutter-Pishgahi. 2006. "The Universal Design of Early Education." *Young Children* archives. www.naeyc.org/files/yc/file/200609/ConnPowersBTJ.pdf.

DEC (Division for Early Childhood) & NAEYC. 2009. "Early Childhood Inclusion: A Joint Position Statement of the Division for Early Childhood (DEC) and the National Association for the Education of Young Children (NAEYC)." Chapel Hill: The University of North Carolina, FPG Child Development Institute. www.naeyc.org/files/naeyc/file/positions/DEC_NAEYC _updatedKS.pdf.

Katz, L.G., & S.C. Chard. 2000. *Engaging Children's Minds: The Project Approach.* 2nd ed. Stamford, CT: Ablex.

Odom, S.L. 2000. "Preschool Inclusion: What We Know and Where We Go From Here." *Topics in Early Childhood Special Education* 20 (1): 20–27.

Sandall, S., M.L. Hemmeter, B.J. Smith, & M.E. McLean. 2007. *DEC Recommended Practices: A Comprehensive Guide for Practical Application.* Longmont, CO: Sopris West.

Critical Thinking

1. Observe a classroom of young children, or talk to their teacher, and find out their current interests that could be developed into a project-based investigation.

2. Describe to a teacher not familiar with the project approach the role of the teacher in initiating and supporting an area of investigation.

Create Central

www.mhhe.com/createcentral

Internet References

Child Care Lounge
www.childcarelounge.com/curriculum/project-approach.php

National Association for the Education of Young Children
www.naeyc.org

Project Approach
www.projectapproach.org

Reggio Emilia
http://reggioalliance.org

Future of Children
www.futureofchildren.org

SALLEE J. BENEKE, PhD, is associate professor of early childhood education at St. Ambrose University in Davenport, Iowa. Sallee conducts research in, writes about, and provides training in the project approach, inclusion, professional development, and early childhood math and science. BenekeSalleeJ@sau.edu. **MICHAELENE M. OSTROSKY,** PhD, is a Goldstick Family Scholar and the department head of special education at the University of Illinois at Urbana-Champaign. She conducts applied research and participates in curriculum development on social interaction interventions, social-emotional competence, challenging behavior, and communication interventions. ostrosky@illinois.edu.

Beneke, Sallee J.; Ostrosky, Michaelene M. From *Young Children*, May 2013, pp. 22–28. Copyright © 2013 by National Association for the Education of Young Children. Reprinted by permission. www.naeyc.org.

Unit 7

UNIT

Prepared by: Karen Menke Paciorek, *Eastern Michigan University*

Curricular Issues

Teachers possess the power to inspire, encourage, and influence the young lives in their classrooms. They lay the foundation for all future learning in formal and informal settings. Therefore, preschool teachers have become increasingly more aware of the tremendous responsibility to plan learning experiences that are not only aligned with state and national standards, but also provide opportunities for children to develop a lifelong love for learning along with the necessary skills to be successful in life. The curriculum and the choices made within are pressing in on these decisions and opportunities that teachers facilitate in their classrooms. Through everyday moments, teachers are able to build and expand the natural interests of their students. The use of questions and the act of wondering are a part of this approach and a way to help the students and the teachers look at the world in a new way. Again, teachers have this power to inspire. Inspiring our young students to think critically and to look at things from different points of view not only gives them a firm foundation in learning but also encourages them to consider the act of learning as a fun and natural activity.

For example, young children approach a sand box with curiosity and readiness to manipulate the sand with their hands, shovels, buckets, or any tool that is available. Inherently, a child will use scientific thinking as they scoop, measure, and move the sand from container to container. A teacher can support this play and learning by the materials provided, the questions posed during the exploratory play, and the additional explorations facilitated at later times. Knowing how children make meaning in their play will guide teachers in planning and implementing science activities that are rich in context and fun for the children.

Providing appropriate early literacy, scientific, social, and numeracy experiences is a major focus for teachers of young children. Teachers who use the standards to plan learning experiences that will enable the children to master the standards are setting their students up for learning success in the future. The standards, experiences, and assessments go hand in hand and lead to successful teaching and learning.

Opportunities for the student to participate in authentic learning experiences that allow children to investigate, explore, and create while studying a particular curricular area such as math, science, or writing should be a part of the daily education offerings. Make children work for their learning or, as noted early childhood author Lilian Katz says, "Engage their minds." As a teacher of young children, acquaint yourself with the importance of firsthand experiences. Teachers often confuse firsthand and hands-on experiences but they are very different. Firsthand experiences are those where the children have a personal encounter with an event, place, or activity. Firsthand experiences include having the local fire department stop by with their hook and ladder truck for a visit to your school, looking for the life at the end of a small pond, or touring a local pet store. After children have these firsthand experiences, they are then able to incorporate them into their play, investigating, and exploring in the classroom. Hands-on experiences allow the children to actually use their hands and body to manipulate materials as they learn about the activity such as making a batch of play-dough, building a tall tower with blocks, or investigating bubbles in the water table. The theme of this unit is clear: Hands on = Minds on!

Professional organizations, researchers and educators are reaching out to teachers of young children with the message that what they do in classrooms with young children is extremely important for children's future development and learning capabilities. Of course, the early childhood community will continue to support a hands-on experiential learning environment, but teachers must be clear in their objectives and have standards firmly in mind that will lead to future success. Only when we are able to effectively communicate to others the importance of early childhood and receive recognition and support for our work, will the education of young children be held in high regard. We are working toward that goal, but we need adults who care for and educate young children, as well as view their job as building a strong foundation for children's future learning. Think of early childhood education as the extremely strong and stable foundation for a building that is expected to provide many decades of active service to thousands of people. If we view our profession in that light, we can see the importance of our jobs. Bring passion and energy to what you do with young children and their families. Your reward will be great. Enjoy your work; use your power to promote the love of learning in our young children's lives.

Article   Prepared by: Karen Menke Paciorek, *Eastern Michigan University*

Social Studies in Preschool? Yes!

Ann S. Epstein

Learning Outcomes

After reading this article, you will be able to:

- Discuss with others the importance of social studies being included in the curriculum for preschool children.

- Explain the components of social systems and social concepts.

- Share teaching strategies for the social studies with other teachers.

The preschoolers in Ms. Sharif's class take a walk around the block at outside time. They pass the bodega, a fish store, the pharmacy, a produce stand, and a used clothing store. In front of the produce stand, Adam waves to Mr. and Mrs. Torricelli, the owners, who are piling fruit on the carts. "They live upstairs from me!" Adam announces. Concetta points to the fruit and says, *"Manzanas* and *plátanos,"* and Ms. Sharif replies, "Yes, apples and bananas." The children talk about the neighborhood places they visit with their families and the people who work there (for example, the man at the shoe store, the money lady [cashier] at the corner store, and the popcorn guy at the movies).

Later that day, at choice time, Adam sets up a fruit store, and the other children make purchases. Ms. Sharif asks for some less common fruits (such as plantains, mangoes, rambutan), and the children talk about the vegetables and fruits they eat at home with their families.

Often young children's first sense of community outside the home comes from attending an early childhood setting. As children learn to get along, make friends, and participate in decision making, they are engaging in social studies learning. Typically, the social studies curriculum also expands children's horizons beyond the school into the neighborhood and the wider world.

According to the National Council for the Social Studies (NCSS), "the aim of social studies is the promotion of *civic competence*—the knowledge, intellectual processes, and democratic dispositions required of students to be active and engaged participants in public life" (2010, 1). Although state standards for social studies in early childhood vary, they address the following common themes: (1) membership in a democratic classroom community, (2) location and place relationships, (3) similarities and differences in personal and family characteristics, (4) basic economic principles as they relate to children's lives, and (5) appreciation of one's own and other cultures in a diverse society (Gronlund 2006). Early childhood teachers help children begin to understand these concepts so they can later generalize the ideas to school and eventually the larger society.

Social studies draws on several disciplines, including history, geography, economics, and ecology. Although these subjects sound abstract when applied to young children, preschoolers deal with them in concrete ways (Seefeldt, Castle, & Falconer 2010). For example, children between 4 and 7 years old become aware of personal time—that is, how past, present, and future are sequentially ordered in the history of their own lives. By age 6 or 7, they have rudimentary clock and calendar skills. The components of geography include spatial relations and the places people occupy. An awareness of nature and the importance of taking care of animals and plants in one's immediate environment give real meaning to an appreciation of ecological diversity and interdependence.

Young Children's Development in Social Studies

Beginning with their interactions with the individuals in their families, neighborhoods, and schools, young children establish a foundation that will later enable them to branch out to encounter new people and settings when they become older and eventually take their place in the adult world. Aside from their families, early childhood settings are where young children typically first learn to become responsible citizens.

For example, preschoolers learn about human diversity—language and culture, beliefs and practices, living environments and relationships, abilities and needs—by interacting with a wide range of adults and peers. They take on different roles during pretend play, read stories and informational books about interesting people and situations, explore the arts of different cultures, and go on field trips in their communities. When young children solve problems collaboratively in the classroom, it is a microcosm of the democratic process (Gartrell 2012).

Components of Social Studies

Social studies learning in early childhood has two components. *Social systems* are the norms, values, and procedures that affect human relationships in our day-to-day lives. For preschoolers, they include experiencing the diversity of people and cultures, becoming aware of the roles people perform at home and in the community, understanding the need to have rules for group behavior, and beginning to participate in the democratic process.

The second component is *social concepts,* or the standard topics taught later in school. They include economics, which for preschoolers involves gaining a rudimentary understanding of how money works. History at this age focuses on the sequence of events, as young children are increasingly able to recall the past and anticipate the future. Preschool geography is about locations and their relationship to one another, especially direction and distance. Preschoolers are also interested in the lives of people from other parts of the world, provided these are made concrete and connected to their own lives (e.g., customs related to food, housing, games children enjoy, family relationships). In recent years, ecology—how human behavior affects nature and the health of the planet—has been added to the mix. While mastering these subjects might seem like a tall order for preschoolers, meaningful early experiences can have a positive impact on the rest of their lives.

> **Aside from their families, early childhood settings are where young children typically first learn to become responsible citizens.**

Social Systems

Because of their observant natures and their curiosity about people, children become aware of human diversity on their own, although they depend on adults to help them develop sensitivity in responding to the differences they encounter among people. Likewise, young children are very attuned to the roles performed in their own families and, as they venture out into the world, to roles in the community. When it comes to creating and following rules, however, adults need to play a more active role in helping preschoolers see how and why rules might apply to them. Involving children in making reasonable decisions about how the classroom should be run (adults still decide matters related to health and physical and emotional safety) helps them appreciate and follow rules voluntarily. Related to this practice is encouraging children to help establish and participate in the democracy of the classroom. With adult guidance, they can learn to listen to others, contribute their own ideas, and accept majority decisions that affect the group as a whole.

Valuing diversity

Diversity can take many forms, including gender, ethnicity, age, religion, family structure, ability levels, body shape, hair/eye color, culture, language, ideas, esthetic preferences, and so on. Valuing diversity means accepting and appreciating the differences of ourselves and of others as normal and positive. It means treating people as individuals and not as stereotypes and recognizing that preferences are not always value judgments (for example, if Daiwik brings curried lentils for lunch and Ramon brings macaroni and cheese, it does not mean each child can refer to the food the other one likes as "yucky" or "bad").

Teaching strategies. Teachers can help children accept and even embrace diversity in the classroom and community (as well as other cultures they may encounter through the media) in ways such as these:

- Model respect for others by the way you listen to and accept children's ideas and feelings. Let them see you treat everyone equally and fairly, including children, families, and your coworkers.
- Avoid judgmental comparisons. Instead, comment on specific attributes and accomplishments without labeling one as better than the other. For example, instead of saying to Yolanda, "I like red hair," offer an observation such as, "Yolanda has short, red hair, and Nicole has her brown hair in braids."
- Hang reproductions of artwork in diverse media and representing different cultures at eye level throughout the room. At large group time, explore different styles of music and dance, again being sure to include the many styles that children's families enjoy. Grow different (and unfamiliar) vegetables and flowers in the school garden.

Learning about community roles

The first roles preschoolers become aware of are those played by the people in their families. At first, they are concerned about the roles that affect them directly, such as who cooks their meals, provides comfort when they are hurt or upset, or reads to them at bedtime. Provided they feel secure about having their basic needs met, young children next begin to pay attention to the roles family members perform outside the home, such as their jobs or the volunteer work they do. As their world expands, preschoolers also take an interest in the services performed by people outside the family, such as doctors, firefighters, police officers, teachers, bus drivers, zookeepers, performing artists, and barbers and hair stylists. These roles often appear in their pretend play. Over time, the number of roles and the details included in acting them out become more elaborate.

Teaching strategies. Materials and experiences inside and outside the classroom can support children's interest in learning about community roles. Here are some ideas:

- Create opportunities for children to learn about and act out different community roles. Provide materials for pretend play (dress-up clothes, housewares, shop and garden tools, office equipment). Talk about what family members do at home (for example, "Sean's daddy made dinner last night" or "Mattie did the laundry with her mom. She helped sort the *calcetines,* the socks") and the roles they play outside the home (for example, "Jerome's uncle is a teacher like me" or "Charlotte's grandmother sings in the choir at church"). Make a class book with photos of children's families performing different roles (planting a garden, taking the bus to the library).
- Take field trips and invite visitors to the classroom so children can expand their awareness of people and roles in their community. On neighborhood walks point out people at work—for example, people who are driving trash and recycling trucks, selling produce at the farmers' market, or fixing cars at the corner garage. Visit various places of work, especially those that often show up in children's pretend play, such as the fire station or supermarket. Bring back materials (grocery bags, receipt pads) they can incorporate in their play scenarios.

Creating and following rules

A rule is an authoritative direction for how to act or what to do. Just as licensed programs must follow health and safety rules, programs and teachers have rules that children must concern themselves with, such as who will pass out snacks, feed the hamster, sit next to the teacher, choose the song for circle time, use the computer, and so on. Children may create rules for games they invent, such as the start and finish line in a race or what constitutes inbounds in a beanbag toss. Sometimes the group feels the need to establish policies for preserving quiet areas, respecting block structures built by others, or protecting work in progress overnight. Setting rules also can be a way to deal with interpersonal conflicts, especially if they affect groups of children or the whole class.

Teaching strategies. Like a personal code of morality, competence in respecting and making rules begins in childhood and continues to develop into adolescence and early adulthood. Teachers can be instrumental in laying the foundation for this development by carrying out practices such as the following:

- Make children aware of basic health and safety rules that have everyday meaning to them. Be concrete and positive. Children relate mostly to the *what* of behavior (for example, "Always wash your hands after using the bathroom"), although they can also benefit from a simple explanation of *why* (for example, "Soap and water get rid of the germs so they don't make us sick"). After discussing a few simple rules with children, write them out in short words and pictures, and post them at children's eye level. Be sure to demonstrate the important rules rather than assuming that all of the preschoolers understand them based simply on your discussion. For dual language learners, write them in their home language (for example, *lávese las manos* [*wash your hands*]), which will help them learn key words as well as the rules themselves.

> We do not always get our way, but the democratic process does provide the satisfaction of being heard and knowing that decisions and policies can be reviewed and revised if needed.

- During small group time or a class meeting, describe a problem that affects everyone and invite children to suggest one or more rules to solve it. (Children may also use small group time or class meetings to allow the whole group to resolve problems that involve just a few children, provided those directly affected agree to using this strategy.) Encourage children to discuss the pros and cons of each suggestion. Write down and post the rules they decide to try. Revisit the rules as a group in a few days to see whether or not they are working.

Creating and participating in democracy

Democracy in the early childhood classroom means conditions of equality and respect for the individual. "Education that teaches children the skills they need to be contributing members of a civil society begins with classroom communities that embrace inclusive—mutually respectful—communication" (Gartrell 2012, 5). Developing a sense of democracy grows out of experiences with rule making and social problem solving. For young children, it means learning that everyone has a voice, even those with minority opinions. Democracy entails compromise and negotiation. We do not always get our way, but the democratic process does provide the satisfaction of being heard and knowing that decisions and policies can be reviewed and revised if needed.

Teaching strategies. Participating in a democratic society and in a democratic classroom require similar skills, such as solving problems, making decisions, managing emotions, taking the perspectives of others, and pursuing and achieving goals. To bring about these understandings in ways that make sense to young children, teachers can use strategies such as these:

- Ask children to consider alternative ways to reach a goal; for example, "What do you think would happen if . . . ?" or "Can you think of another way to do that?" Encourage them to plan more than one way to accomplish a task. Pose questions to help them anticipate consequences and reflect on outcomes; for example, "What will you do if the children who are making the refrigerator box into an airplane don't follow the rules tomorrow that you came up with today?"

- Build children's skills of perspective taking and turn taking. Remind children to listen before they add their ideas to the discussion. Ask them to repeat back what they hear and check it out with the speaker.

- Introduce other ideas and vocabulary words that are at the core of democratic principles and actions. Carry out mathematics activities to help children develop the concepts of *more/greater* versus *less/fewer,* which are foundational to the principle of majority rule. For example, ask children to indicate their preferences (for instance, for a color or food) by a show of hands. Count and record the results on chart paper, using the appropriate vocabulary words.

Social Concepts

Some social concepts, such as economics and history, tend to emerge from children's own observations and experiences. For example, as they accompany family members on errands, they encounter people exchanging money for goods and services. Looking at photos of a family vacation or a trip to their home country, preschoolers begin to recall what happened at a time in the past, when they took their trip. They also begin to anticipate events, such as an upcoming birthday, although their sense of time is still shaky. Understanding other standard social studies topics, such as geography, requires more active

adult intervention. Children are so used to being taken places, for example, that they may only become aware of where they are coming from or going to if adults call their attention to it. Likewise, preschoolers often take nature for granted. They may not consider how their actions, let alone those of others, affect the plants and animals around them.

> **Research shows that young children are capable of engaging with three areas of geography: reading simple maps, identifying familiar locations and landmarks, and recognizing prominent features in the landscape.**

Understanding simple economics

While the field of economics can seem abstract, even for adults, preschoolers know many things about this aspect of social studies. Observing the roles of family members and others in the community, they develop basic ideas about reciprocity, including the exchange of money (Seefeldt, Castle, & Falconer 2010). For example, young children can grasp that people work to earn money to buy food, medicine, and movie tickets. They know that money, or its equivalent, comes in various forms (paper and coins, checks, plastic cards). Overhearing comments from adults or in the media, they gather that certain goods and services are more valuable than others.

Teaching strategies. Money often assumes a prominent role in children's pretend play. For example, children pay for food at the restaurant; the more they order, the more it costs. Adult guidance can help preschoolers begin to think about the connections that underlie a society's economic system. Try the following strategies:

- Provide materials and props so children can incorporate money and the exchange of goods and services into their pretend play. Build on typical family experiences, such as going to the grocery store, paying the doctor or babysitter, or purchasing new shoes. Provide strips of paper, rocks, beads, and other small items for preschoolers to use as pretend money.

- Make comments and pose occasional questions to help children consider simple economic principles, such as the relationship between work and money. For example, you might ask, "*How much more* will it cost if I order the large salad instead of the small one?" When you read books that include stories with people buying and selling things, briefly engage children in discussing the transactions.

Understanding history

Children's understanding of history is closely tied to their ideas about time. At first it is a highly personal understanding, associated with events in their daily lives. By late preschool, however, children begin to apply logic to understanding time. They know time moves forward, are able to look backward, and understand that the past and present can affect the future (for example, they can wear the jacket they bought yesterday to school today). A growing vocabulary (words such as *before* and *after, first* and *last, then* and *next*) enables preschoolers to understand and talk about time. They begin to grasp that a minute is shorter than an hour, and a day is shorter than a year.

Teaching strategies. With a consistent schedule, children become aware of the daily sequence of events in the classroom on their own. However, it helps if adults occasionally point out "what we just did" or "what comes next," especially to children who are new to the group. Materials and books also provide many opportunities to help children develop a sense of time. Try these strategies:

- Play sequencing games at group times. For example, at circle time, have the children do two movements in order (for example, "First tap your ears; next tap your shoulders"). Do the same with sounds.
- Use concrete representations, such as books, artwork, and music, to make children aware of the distant past and far future. (To see how one preschool classroom set up an old-fashioned general store inspired by the *Little House* books, see Miles 2009.) Media images might similarly encourage them to think about futuristic settings where people have superpowers, travel in unusual vehicles, and use fantastic equipment to accomplish their goals. Talk about the characters in stories that feature spaceships, robots, or odd-looking houses and vehicles, and compare their lives with life today.
- Use and encourage children to use an expanding vocabulary of time and sequence words. Begin with terms such as *before* and *after, first* and *last, yesterday* and *tomorrow;* include their home-language equivalents for dual language learners.

Understanding geography.

Geography is "a field of study that enables us to find answers to questions about the world around us—about where things are and how and why they got there" (GESP 1994, 11). The challenge for early educators is to introduce young children to geography concepts that are meaningful to them. Research shows that young children are capable of engaging with three areas of geography: reading simple maps (Liben & Downs 1993), identifying familiar locations and landmarks (Mayer 1995), and recognizing prominent features in the landscape (Seefeldt, Castle, & Falconer 2010).

Teaching strategies. The perspective taking that allows young children to solve problems with materials and peers can also help them acquire simple concepts in geography. Help preschoolers engage with geography by beginning with their daily experiences—where they go, what they do there—and then branching out to a wider range of places and features. The following strategies will make learning about geography interesting and appropriate for young children:

- Draw simple maps or diagrams of the classroom, school, and neighborhood. Include obvious features such as doors and windows, the playground and parking lot, benches, bus stops, and stores. Talk about the maps with the children, emphasizing how the various places are related (for example, the direction and distance one must travel when getting from one place to another). Provide the children with flags, stickers, or other symbols they can use to mark places on the map.
- Display a map of the neighborhood near the block area and encourage children to use it to work together to re-create the neighborhood using blocks and other props (such as cars, people, animals, signs; [Colker 2013]).

Children must develop a love for nature before they can think about the environment abstractly and become its guardians.

Appreciating ecology.

Learning about ecology involves understanding our roles as caretakers of the planet. For young children, this begins with regular and enjoyable encounters with the natural world. As members of the classroom community, preschoolers can take responsibility for its physical care, such as picking up litter, feeding pets, or planting a garden. Their growing capacity for empathy makes them capable of showing concern for wildlife. Children must develop a love for nature before they can think about the environment abstractly and become its guardians (Sobel 2008). Therefore, "during early childhood, the main objective of environmental education should be the development of empathy between the child and the natural world" (White & Stoecklin 2008, n.p.). This includes opportunities to play in nature, take care of plants, and cultivate relationships with animals.

Teaching strategies. Connecting children to the environment can be as simple as getting out into nature. Because children may take these experiences for granted, however, it is important to help them become aware of the diversity of plants and animals around them. Being indoors also presents many opportunities for helping children learn the importance of taking care of things if we want those things to remain available to ourselves and others. Use the following strategies to inspire young children to care about the environment and to make ecology a meaningful subject for them:

- Help children become aware of and appreciate nature. The more young children enjoy the sensations of the natural world, the more meaningful their concerns about ecology will become as they get older. Except during days of extreme weather conditions, include time to go outside each day. Call attention to the feel of the sun and wind on children's faces, and examine the plants and animals native to your area. Plant a garden together or make and hang a simple bird feeder.

- Encourage children to take care of the indoor classroom and outdoor learning environment, such as putting tops on markers so they do not dry out, treating dress-up clothes carefully so they do not tear, and planting, watering, and weeding the class garden. When children play a meaningful role in taking care of the settings where they play and interact every day, it supports the development of empathy and the sense of community that undergirds ecological awareness.

Social studies is the "new kid on the block" when it comes to content areas in the early childhood curriculum, yet it is also the oldest area of study in general. The preschool classroom is a microcosm of the larger society. As concerns mount about the unraveling of civil behavior in the fabric of our social world, early childhood educators, in partnership with families, can help to lay the foundation for a future that guarantees that all of us have an opportunity to fulfill our human potential while respecting the rights of others and the sustainability of our planet.

References

Colker, L.J. 2013. "A Place for Building Your Community." *Teaching Young Children 7* (1): 18–19.

Gartrell, D. 2012. *Education for a Civil Society: How Guidance Teaches Young Children Democratic Life Skills.* Washington, DC: NAEYC.

GESP (Geography Education Standards Project). 1994. *Geography for Life: National Education Standards—1994.* Washington, DC: GESP.

Gronlund, G. 2006. *Make Early Learning Standards Come Alive: Connecting Your Practice and Curriculum to State Guidelines.* St. Paul, MN: Redleaf; Washington, DC: NAEYC.

Liben, L.S., & R.M. Downs. 1993. "Understanding Person-Space-Map Relations: Cartographic and Developmental Perspectives." *Developmental Psychology 29* (4): 739–52.

Mayer, R.H. 1995. "Inquiry Into Place as an Introduction to World Geography—Starting With Ourselves." *Social Studies 86* (2): 74–77.

Miles, L.R. 2009. "The General Store: Reflections on Children at Play." *Young Children 64* (4): 36–41.

NCSS (National Council for the Social Studies). 2010. *National Curriculum Standards for the Social Studies: A Framework for Teaching, Learning, and Assessment.* Silver Spring, MD: NCSS.

Seefeldt, C., Castle, S., & Falconer, R. 2010. *Social Studies for the Preschool/Primary Child.* 8th ed. Englewood Cliffs, NJ: Prentice Hall.

Sobel, D. 2008. *Children and Nature: Design Principles for Educators.* Portland, ME: Stenhouse.

White, R., & V.L. Stoecklin. 2008. "Nurturing Children's Biophilia: Developmentally Appropriate Environmental Education for Young Children." *Collage: Resources for Early Childhood Educators.* November. www.communityplaythings.com/resources/articles/2008/nurturing-childrens-biophilia-environmental-education-for-young-children

Critical Thinking

1. Develop a list of the critical skills you believe young children should learn related to social studies. Why are these skills so critical for future development?

2. How do young children first develop an understanding of their self and their role in society?

Internet References

Head Start Social Studies: Knowledge and Skills
http://eclkc.ohs.acf.hhs.gov/hslc/hs/sr/approach/cdelf/ssk_skills.html

National Council for the Social Studies
http://www.socialstudies.org/

Social Studies for Kids
http://www.socialstudiesforkids.com/

ANN S. EPSTEIN is the senior director of Curriculum Development at HighScope Educational Research Foundation in Ypsilanti, Michigan. This article is adapted from the forthcoming NAEYC Comprehensive Member benefit *The Intentional Teacher,* revised edition, by Ann S. Epstein, being copublished by NAEYC and HighScope.

Epstein, Ann S. From *Young Children,* vol. 69, no. 1, March 2014, 78–83. Copyright © 2014 by National Association for the Education of Young Children. Used with permission.

Article   Prepared by: Karen Menke Paciorek, *Eastern Michigan University*

Starting Out Practices to Use in K–3

Look for these seven features in primary classrooms that teach beginning reading and writing with an emphasis on informational text.

Nell K. Duke

Learning Outcomes

After reading this article, you will be able to:

- Share the importance of informational text for children learning to read.

- Explain how the Common Core State Standards are changing the way teachers teach reading.

For decades, U.S. educators have believed that children first *learn to read,* and then, around 4th grade, they begin to *read to learn.* This belief has long been reflected in K–3 classrooms, where beginning reading materials have largely consisted of stories and where informational books have rarely been read aloud to young children.

The Common Core State Standards call for a major shift in this thinking. The standards expect children to be reading to learn as well as learning to read from the very beginning of schooling. Dozens of research studies suggest that young children can handle this shift (for example, Pappas, 1993; Reutzel, Smith, & Fawson, 2005). In fact, many children appear to be highly engaged by opportunities to read about the world around them and to demonstrate their expertise on topics through their writing (Guthrie, McRae, & Klauda, 2007).

Here are seven things we should expect to see in primary classrooms that are effectively using informational text to help students learn to read and write.

1 Informational Text Used from the Beginning

No longer should Dick, Jane, and Spot—or modern-day characters such as Mrs. Wishy-Washy or Fly Guy—provide the only grist for beginning reading instruction. About half of the time, materials should be informational texts. Although it's harder to find them, informational texts appropriate for beginning reading instruction are available.

Patterned-predictable texts, which are often used when children are still developing an understanding of basic print concepts and print-to-speech match, can be informational.

For example, the book *What Grows Here?* by Santina Bruni (National Geographic Society, 2003) follows this pattern: "What grows here? Cactuses grow here. What grows here? Water lilies grow here," and so on.

Decodable texts, which can help address Common Core State Standards related to decoding, can also be informational. For example, the book *Who Has a Bill?* by Judy Nayer (Scholastic, 1997) notes the uses of different types of bird bills, as in "The bird will sip with it" . . . "The bird will tap with it" (pp. 2–3). The website TextProject.org has many sets of free, downloadable, four-page informational and other books written especially for beginning readers. (It also offers sets of free downloadable informational texts for older children to read over the summer months.)

In these examples, as in many informational texts for beginning readers, much of the information is conveyed through the photographs or illustrations. Through these graphics as well as the written text, children learn *through* reading while they are learning *to* read.

2 Informational Text Read-Alouds

Even with information-rich graphics, there are limits to the content knowledge that young children can comprehend through texts that are easy enough for them to read themselves. For this reason, approximately half of read-alouds should involve informational text.

Such read-alouds should be combined with engaging instructional activities—asking students questions about the text, having them discuss the text with partners and then share with the group, having them fill out graphic organizers as the teacher reads text aloud, and so on. Figure 1 gives some examples of how teachers can design such instruction to support students in working toward Common Core English language arts and literacy standards.

3 Sets of Related Texts

Gone are the days of reading a text on one topic, then another text on another unrelated topic, and so on. The Common Core standards explicitly call for reading sets of related texts: "Within a grade level, there should be an adequate number of titles on a single topic that would allow children to study that topic for a sustained period" (National Governors Association Center for Best Practices [NGA] & Council of Chief State School Officers [CCSSO], 2010, p. 33).

Text sets not only build students' knowledge, but also allow us to focus on specific Common Core State Standards, most notably Standard 9, which deals with multiple-text reading. For instance, Standard 9 asks that 1st grade children "identify basic similarities in and differences between two texts on the same topic (e.g., in illustrations, descriptions, or procedures)" (NGA & CCSSO, 2010, p. 13). Educators can compile sets of texts in advance on topics to use in read-alouds and small-group reading.

A K–3 classroom should immerse children in informational as well as literary texts.

Figure 1 Using Informational Text Read-Alouds to Meet Common Core Standards

Grade Level	Sample Common Core Reading Standard for Informational Text	Possible Instructional Technique during Read-Aloud
Kindergarten	#2: With prompting and support, identify the main topic and retell key details of a text.	Ask open-ended, higher order questions: • What is this text mostly about? • What are the three most important things the author has told us? Have students use turn-and-talk to share their initial thinking, then discuss as a whole class.
1st Grade	#3: Describe the connection between two individuals, events, ideas, or pieces of information in a text.	Provide clipboards with graphic organizers, such as a Venn diagram or chronological order chart, for students to complete and discuss as they listen to the text read aloud.
2nd Grade	#7: Explain how specific images (e.g., a diagram showing how a machine works) contribute to and clarify a text.	Use sticky notes to cover an image in the text being read aloud. Read the written text and ask children what they can learn from it alone. Then uncover the image and ask students what more they can learn.
3rd Grade	#1: Ask and answer questions to demonstrate understanding of a text, referring explicitly to the text as the basis for the answers.	Establish a consistent follow-up question, such as, "How do you know?" to ask students after they initially respond to a question. Encourage students to ask that same question of you and of one another. Eventually, they are likely to automatically include how they know in their initial responses.

Editor's note: Standards referenced above are from National Governors Association Center for Best Practices & Council of Chief State School Officers. (2010). Common Core State Standards. Washington, DC: Authors. Retrieved from www.corestandards.org/ELA-Literacy

4 An Informational-Text-Rich Environment

Researchers and educators have long emphasized the importance of the classroom literacy environment for young children (for example, Wolfersberger, Reutzel, Sudweeks, & Fawson, 2004). Following this thinking, a K–3 classroom should immerse children in informational as well as literary texts. The classroom library should include large numbers of informational texts. Classroom walls should include lots of informational text: posters (museums and public agencies are a good source); informational articles in high-traffic spots (for example, where children line up); and children's own informational writing. Teachers can post directions—which the Common Core State Standards identify as among the genres that K–5 children should read—throughout the room.

For younger grades, dramatic play settings can include informational texts related to the theme, such as maps for a camping play theme. Older children can populate a "Did You Know?" bulletin board with interesting facts from texts they have read.

Technology in the classroom should also direct students' attention to informational text. Websites with informational text for young children, such as National Geographic's *Young Explorer!* magazine for grades K–1 (http://ngexplorer.cengage.com/ngyoungexplorer), should be book-marked on the computers students use. A listening center should include recordings of informational books as well as literary texts.

5 A Lexically Curious Environment

Informational text for children typically includes a number of unfamiliar words. In kindergarten and 1st grade, the Common Core State Standards expect students to ask and answer questions about unknown words in informational text. Teachers should model and praise questions about words. So often in U.S. schools, children are praised for displaying what they *do* know; in this case, we want to praise children for revealing what they *don't* know—what they need to learn.

In grades 2–3, children are asked to "determine the meaning of words and phrases in a text relevant to a grade 2 [or 3] topic or subject area" (NGA & CCSSO. 2010, pp. 13–14). Even much older students have difficulty with this task, so explicit instruction is key. The teacher can use anchor charts to remind children of key questions to ask themselves as they make informed guesses about word meaning:

- Does the author explain what the word means?
- Does the rest of the page help?
- Do the graphics provide clues?
- Is there a glossary?

Coaching or guided practice is also important. In a lesson for 2nd graders, a teacher gave students excerpts from beloved author Jim Arnosky's book *All About Manatees* (Scholastic. 2008). The students' task was to use the context to try to figure out the meaning of specific words. For example, the teacher asked students to make informed guesses about the meaning of the underlined word in the following passage: "A manatee uses its highly flexible snout and upper lip to grasp vegetation to eat. Its diet consists of green aquatic plants." Notably, this vocabulary work had a larger purpose: Students were studying manatees and other endangered species to inform a writing project.

6 Teaching about Text

Even in kindergarten, you should see children talking about text itself—being metatextual. For example, the Common Core standards ask that kindergartners "with prompting and support, identify the reasons an author gives to support points in a text" (NGA & CCSSO, 2010, p. 13). Specific text features named in the standards for K–3 include:

Kindergarten: front cover, back cover, title page, author, illustrator
Grade 1: headings, tables of contents, glossaries, electronic menus, icons
Grade 2: subheadings, captions, bold print, glossaries, indexes, electronic menus, icons, diagrams
Grade 3: key words, sidebars, hyperlinks (pp. 13–14).

Across grade levels, the standards also refer to other components of text, including illustrations, topics, details, paragraphs, descriptions, procedures, individuals, events, ideas, and other pieces of information within a text.

Unfortunately, little research has been conducted on how to teach these text features to young children. In my experience, young children most thoroughly learn many of these features by producing the features themselves, either for their own texts or to add to published texts. For 2nd and 3rd graders, acquisition of text features may also be facilitated by engaging children with real-world texts for authentic purposes (Purcell-Gates, Duke, & Martineau, 2007).

7 Opportunities to Share Information through Writing

One of the most important characteristics of Common Core–aligned K–3 classrooms is abundant opportunities for writing. This includes not only the narrative writing so common in primary classrooms, but also opinion or argument writing (30 percent of writing) and informative/explanatory writing

(35 percent of writing). From kindergarten on, students are expected to participate in shared research and writing projects (independently in grade 3), recalling experiences and gathering information from sources. They are expected to use digital tools to produce, publish, and revise writing.

Clearly, the Common Core State Standards set ambitious goals for writing. Theory and research suggest that establishing compelling purposes and audiences for children's writing helps a great deal (Duke, Caughlan, Juzwik, & Martin. 2012). Although a story can arguably be of interest to any audience, informative/explanatory texts are written, outside schools at least, with a purpose in mind—to convey information to someone who doesn't already know that information and wants or needs to know it. In the classroom, we need to establish this kind of purpose for children's informational writing. And we need to pay careful attention to audience. A recent study of 2nd graders (Block, 2013) found that children wrote more effectively when they had an audience other than their teacher.

Some informational writing projects can involve children in writing about what they already know well. For example, 1st grade teachers Sonali Deshpande, Mallory Kairys, and Wendy Rothman had their students write guides to 1st grade for kindergartners. The teachers used read-alouds and discussions to remind students of their own feelings and questions when they entered 1st grade. They shared examples of published guides to serve as mentor texts. They routinely reminded students of their purpose and audience for writing. On the day when the 1st graders delivered their guides to the kindergartners, the excitement was palpable. (To view samples of students' guides, go to www.ascd.org/ell113duke.)

Other writing projects can involve students in writing about topics for which they need to conduct research. For example, students might read texts about sea creatures and then write pamphlets about those creatures for the city aquarium. Or students might conduct interviews to learn about notable people, places, and events in the community, and then use this information to write articles for a class magazine to be distributed at city hall.

Even in kindergarten, you should see children talking about text itself.

Regardless of topic, informational writing lessons and coaching should focus on specific attributes of writing called for in the Common Core State Standards—for example, the 2nd grade standards that require students to "introduce a topic, use facts and definitions to develop points, and provide

a concluding statement or section" (NGA & CCSSO, 2010, p. 19). In addition. I recommend teaching students about other valued qualities of informational writing, such as grabbing and sustaining the reader's attention.

From the Past to the Future

The notion that children must learn to read before they can read to learn is a relic of the past. The Common Core State Standards hold high expectations for students around informational text, and research suggests that even young children can meet these expectations.

K–3 classrooms that implement the seven components described here, among others, not only give young children a jump-start on learning content knowledge but also engage them in reading and writing that establishes a firm foundation for their future literacy development.

References

Block, M. K. (2013). *The impact of identifying a specific purpose and external audience for writing on second graders' writing quality.* Unpublished doctoral dissertation, Michigan State University, East Lansing.

Duke, N. K., Caughlan, S., Juzwik, M. M., & Martin, N. M. (2012). *Reading and writing genre with purpose in K–8 classrooms.* Portsmouth, NII: Heinemann.

Guthrie, J. T., McRae, A., & Klauda, S. L. (2007). Contributions of Concept-Oriented Reading instruction to knowledge about interventions for motivations in reading. *Educational Psychologist, 42,* 237–250.

National Governors Association Center for Best Practices & Council of Chief State School Officers. (2010). *Common core state standards for English language arts and literacy in history/ social studies, science, and technical subjects.* Washington, DC: Authors. Retrieved from www.corestandards.org/assets/CCSSI_ELA%20Standards.pdf

Pappas, C. C. (1993). Is narrative "primary?" Some insights from kindergarteners' pretend readings of stories and information books. *Journal of Reading Behavior, 25,* 97–129.

Purcell-Gates, V., Duke, N. K., & Martineau, J. A. (2007). Learning to read and write genre-specific text: Roles of authentic experience and explicit teaching. *Reading Research Quarterly, 42,* 8–45.

Reutzel, D. R., Smith, J. A., & Fawson, P. C. (2005). An examination of two approaches for teaching reading comprehension strategies in the primary years using science information texts. *Early Childhood Research Quarterly, 20,* 276–305.

Wolfersberger, M. E., Reutzel, D. R., Sudweeks, R., & Fawson, P. C. (2004). Developing and validating the Classroom Literacy Environmental Profile (CLEP): A tool for examining the "print richness" of early childhood and elementary classrooms. *Journal of Literacy Research, 36,* 211–272.

Critical Thinking

1. Interview a K–3 teacher and ask him or her for the differences noticed in the reading materials provided for the children in a class today as opposed to those provided five years ago. What differences were noticed in the reading ability of the children?

2. Explain to new parents why reading every day to their new baby will better prepare the child for the early literacy experiences they will encounter in elementary school.

3. Why is the old adage that children must learn to read before they can read to learn no longer applicable in schools?

Internet References

International Reading Association
http://www.reading.org/
National Council for Teachers of English
http://www.ncte.org/
Text Project
http://textproject.org/

NELL K. DUKE is a professor of language, literacy, and culture and faculty associate in the combined program in education and psychology at the University of Michigan, Ann Arbor.

Article Prepared by: Karen Menke Paciorek, *Eastern Michigan University*

Every Child, Every Day

The six elements of effective reading instruction don't require much time or money—just educators' decision to put them in place.

RICHARD L. ALLINGTON AND RACHAEL E. GABRIEL

Learning Outcomes

After reading this article, you will be able to:

- Describe six research-based elements that support reading instruction.

- Explain why child choice is important to the development of early literacy skills.

"Every child a reader" has been the goal of instruction, education research, and reform for at least three decades. We now know more than ever about how to accomplish this goal. Yet few students in the United States regularly receive the best reading instruction we know how to give.

Instead, despite good intentions, educators often make decisions about instruction that compromise or supplant the kind of experiences all children need to become engaged, successful readers. This is especially true for struggling readers, who are much less likely than their peers to participate in the kinds of high-quality instructional activities that would ensure that they learn to read.

Six Elements for Every Child

Here, we outline six elements of instruction that every child should experience every day. Each of these elements can be implemented in any district and any school, with any curriculum or set of materials, and without additional funds. All that's necessary is for adults to make the decision to do it.

1. Every Child Reads Something He or She Chooses

The research base on student-selected reading is robust and conclusive: Students read more, understand more, and are more likely to continue reading when they have the opportunity to choose what they read. In a 2004 meta-analysis, Guthrie and Humenick found that the two most powerful instructional design factors for improving reading motivation and comprehension were (1) student access to many books and (2) personal choice of what to read.

We're not saying that students should never read teacher- or district-selected texts. But at some time every day, they should be able to choose what they read.

The experience of choosing in itself boosts motivation. In addition, offering choice makes it more likely that every reader will be matched to a text that he or she can read well. If students initially have trouble choosing texts that match their ability level and interest, teachers can provide limited choices to guide them toward successful reading experiences. By giving students these opportunities, we help them develop the ability to choose appropriate texts for themselves—a skill that dramatically increases the likelihood they will read outside school (Ivey & Broaddus, 2001, Reis et al., 2007).

Some teachers say they find it difficult to provide a wide selection of texts because of budget constraints. Strangely, there is always money available for workbooks, photocopying, and computers; yet many schools claim that they have no budget for large, multileveled classroom libraries. This is interesting because research has demonstrated that access to self-selected texts improves students' reading performance (Krashen, 2011), whereas no evidence indicates that workbooks, photocopies, or computer tutorial programs have ever done so (Cunningham & Stanovich, 1998; Dynarski, 2007).

There is, in fact, no way they ever could. When we consider that the typical 4th grade classroom has students reading anywhere from the 2nd to the 9th grade reading levels (and that later grades have an even wider range), the idea that one workbook or textbook could meet the needs of every reader is absurd (Hargis, 2006). So, too, is the idea that skills developed through isolated, worksheet-based skills practice and fill-in-the-blank vocabulary quizzes will transfer to real reading in the absence of any evidence that they ever have. If school principals eliminated the budget for workbooks and worksheets and instead spent the money on real books for classroom libraries, this decision could dramatically improve students' opportunities to become better readers.

2. Every Child Reads Accurately

Good readers read with accuracy almost all the time. The last 60 years of research on optimal text difficulty—a body of research that began with Betts (1949)—consistently demonstrates the importance of having students read texts they can read accurately and understand. In fact, research shows that reading at 98 percent or higher accuracy is essential for reading acceleration. Anything less slows the rate of improvement, and anything below 90 percent accuracy doesn't improve reading ability at all (Allington, 2012; Ehri, Dreyer, Flugman, & Gross, 2007).

Although the idea that students read better when they read more has been supported by studies for the last 70 years, policies that simply increase the amount of time allocated for students to read often find mixed results (National Reading Panel, 2000). The reason is simple: It's not just the time spent with a book in hand, but rather the intensity and volume of *high-success* reading, that determines a student's progress in learning to read (Allington, 2009; Kuhn et al., 2006).

When students read accurately, they solidify their word-recognition, decoding, and word-analysis skills. Perhaps more important, they are likely to understand what they read—and, as a result, to enjoy reading.

In contrast, struggling students who spend the same amount of time reading texts that they can't read accurately are at a disadvantage in several important ways. First, they read less text; it's slow going when you encounter many words you don't recognize instantly. Second, struggling readers are less likely to understand (and therefore enjoy) what they read. They are likely to become frustrated when reading these difficult texts and therefore to lose confidence in their word-attack, decoding, or word-recognition skills. Thus, a struggling reader and a successful reader who engage in the same 15-minute independent reading session do not necessarily receive equivalent practice, and they are likely to experience different outcomes.

Sadly, struggling readers typically encounter a steady diet of too-challenging texts throughout the school day as they make their way through classes that present grade-level material hour after hour. In essence, traditional instructional practices widen the gap between readers.

3. Every Child Reads Something He or She Understands

Understanding what you've read is the goal of reading. But too often, struggling readers get interventions that focus on basic skills in isolation, rather than on reading connected text for meaning. This common misuse of intervention time often arises from a grave misinterpretation of what we know about reading difficulties.

The findings of neurological research are sometimes used to reinforce the notion that some students who struggle to learn to read are simply "wired differently" (Zambo, 2003) and thus require large amounts of isolated basic skills practice. In fact, this same research shows that remediation that emphasizes comprehension can change the structure of struggling students' brains. Keller and Just (2009) used imaging to examine the brains of struggling readers before and after they received 100

hours of remediation—including lots of reading and rereading of real texts. The white matter of the struggling readers was of lower structural quality than that of good readers before the intervention, but it improved following the intervention. And these changes in the structure of the brain's white matter consistently predicted increases in reading ability.

Numerous other studies (Aylward et al., 2003; Krafnick, Flowers, Napoliello, & Eden, 2011; Shaywitz et al., 2004) have supported Keller and Just's findings that comprehensive reading instruction is associated with changed activation patterns that mirror those of typical readers. These studies show that it doesn't take neurosurgery or banging away at basic skills to enable the brain to develop the ability to read: It takes lots of reading and rereading of text that students find engaging and comprehensible.

The findings from brain research align well with what we've learned from studies of reading interventions. Regardless of their focus, target population, or publisher, interventions that accelerate reading development routinely devote at least two-thirds of their time to reading and rereading rather than isolated or contrived skill practice (Allington, 2011). These findings have been consistent for the last 50 years—yet the typical reading intervention used in schools today has struggling readers spending the bulk of their time on tasks other than reading and rereading actual texts.

Students read more, understand more, and are more likely to continue reading when they have the opportunity to choose what they read.

Studies of exemplary elementary teachers further support the finding that more authentic reading develops better readers (Allington, 2002; Taylor, Pearson, Peterson, & Rodriguez, 2003). In these large-scale national studies, researchers found that students in more-effective teachers' classrooms spent a larger percentage of reading instructional time actually reading; students in less-effective teachers' classrooms spent more time using worksheets, answering low-level, literal questions, or completing before-and-after reading activities. In addition, exemplary teachers were more likely to differentiate instruction so that all readers had books they could actually read accurately, fluently, and with understanding.

4. Every Child Writes about Something Personally Meaningful

In our observations in schools across several states, we rarely see students writing anything more than fill-in-the-blank or short-answer responses during their reading block. Those who do have the opportunity to compose something longer than a few sentences are either responding to a teacher-selected prompt or writing within a strict structural formula that turns even paragraphs and essays into fill-in-the-blank exercises.

As adults, we rarely if ever write to a prompt, and we almost never write about something we don't know about. Writing is called *composition* for a good reason: We actually *compose* (construct something unique) when we write. The opportunity to compose continuous text about something meaningful is not just something nice to have when there's free time after a test or at the end of the school year. Writing provides a different modality within which to practice the skills and strategies of reading for an authentic purpose.

When students write about something they care about, they use conventions of spelling and grammar because it matters to them that their ideas are communicated, not because they will lose points or see red ink if they don't (Cunningham & Cunningham, 2010). They have to think about what words will best convey their ideas to their readers. They have to encode these words using letter patterns others will recognize. They have to make sure they use punctuation in a way that will help their readers understand which words go together, where a thought starts and ends, and what emotion goes with it. They have to think about what they know about the structure of similar texts to set up their page and organize their ideas. This process is especially important for struggling readers because it produces a comprehensible text that the student can read, reread, and analyze.

5. Every Child Talks with Peers about Reading and Writing

Research has demonstrated that conversation with peers improves comprehension and engagement with texts in a variety of settings (Cazden, 1988). Such literary conversation does not focus on recalling or retelling what students read. Rather, it asks students to analyze, comment, and compare—in short, to think about what they've read. Fall, Webb, and Chudowsky (2000) found better outcomes when kids simply talked with a peer about what they read than when they spent the same amount of class time highlighting important information after reading.

Similarly, Nystrand (2006) reviewed the research on engaging students in literate conversations and noted that even small amounts of such conversation (10 minutes a day) improved standardized test scores, regardless of students' family background or reading level. Yet struggling readers were the least likely to discuss daily what they read with peers. This was often because they were doing extra basic-skills practice instead. In class discussions, struggling readers were more likely to be asked literal questions about what they had read, to prove they "got it," rather than to be engaged in a conversation about the text.

Time for students to talk about their reading and writing is perhaps one of the most underused, yet easy-to-implement, elements of instruction. It doesn't require any special materials, special training, or even large amounts of time. Yet it provides measurable benefits in comprehension, motivation, and even language competence. The task of switching between writing, speaking, reading, and listening helps students make connections between, and thus solidify, the skills they use in each. This makes peer conversation especially important for English language learners, another population that we rarely ask to talk about what they read.

6. Every Child Listens to a Fluent Adult Read Aloud

Listening to an adult model fluent reading increases students' own fluency and comprehension skills (Trelease, 2001), as well as expanding their vocabulary, background knowledge, sense of story, awareness of genre and text structure, and comprehension of the texts read (Wu & Samuels, 2004).

Yet few teachers above 1st grade read aloud to their students every day (Jacobs, Morrison, & Swinyard, 2000). This high-impact, low-input strategy is another underused component of the kind of instruction that supports readers. We categorize it as low-input because, once again, it does not require special materials or training; it simply requires a decision to use class time more effectively. Rather than conducting whole-class reading of a single text that fits few readers, teachers should choose to spend a few minutes a day reading to their students.

Things That Really Matter

Most of the classroom instruction we have observed lacks these six research-based elements. Yet it's not difficult to find the time and resources to implement them. Here are a few suggestions.

First, eliminate almost all worksheets and workbooks. Use the money saved to purchase books for classroom libraries; use the time saved for self-selected reading, self-selected writing, literary conversations, and read-alouds.

Second, ban test-preparation activities and materials from the school day. Although sales of test preparation materials provide almost two-thirds of the profit that testing companies earn (Glovin & Evans, 2006), there are no studies demonstrating that engaging students in test prep ever improved their reading proficiency—or even their test performance (Guthrie, 2002). As with eliminating workbook completion, eliminating test preparation provides time and money to spend on the things that really matter in developing readers.

It's time for the elements of effective instruction described here to be offered more consistently to every child, in every school, every day. Remember, adults have the power to make these decisions; kids don't. Let's decide to give them the kind of instruction they need.

First, eliminate almost all worksheets and workbooks.

References

Allington, R. L. (2002). What I've learned about effective reading instruction from a decade of studying exemplary elementary classroom teachers. *Phi Delta Kappan, 83*(10), 740–747.

Allington, R. L. (2009). If they don't read much . . . 30 years later. In E. H. Hiebert (Ed.), *Reading more, reading better* (pp. 30–54). New York: Guilford.

Allington, R. L. (2011). Research on reading/learning disability interventions. In S. J. Samuels & A. E. Farstrup (Eds.), *What research has to say about reading instruction* (4th ed., pp. 236–265). Newark, DE: International Reading Association.

Allington, R. L. (2012). *What really matters for struggling readers: Designing research-based programs* (3rd ed.). Boston: Allyn and Bacon.

Aylward, E. H., Richards, T. L., Berninger, V. W., Nagy, W. E, Field, K. M., Grimme, A. C., Richards, A. L., Thomson, J. B., & Cramer, S. C. (2003). Instructional treatment associated with changes in brain activation in children with dyslexia. *Neurology, 61*(2), E5–6.

Betts, E. A. (1949). Adjusting instruction to individual needs. In N. B. Henry (Ed.), *The forty-eighth yearbook of the National Society for the Study of Education: Part II, Reading in the elementary school* (pp. 266–283). Chicago: University of Chicago Press.

Cazden, C. B. (1988). *Classroom discourse: The language of teaching and learning.* Portsmouth, NH: Heinemann.

Cunningham, A. E., & Stanovich, K. E. (1998). The impact of print exposure on word recognition. In J. Metsala & L. Ehri (Eds.), *Word recognition in beginning literacy* (pp. 235–262). Mahwah, NJ: Erlbaum.

Cunningham, P. M., & Cunningham, J. W. (2010). *What really matters in writing: Research-based practices across the elementary curriculum.* Boston: Allyn and Bacon.

Dynarski, M. (2007). *Effectiveness of reading and mathematics software products: Findings from the first student cohort.* Washington, DC: Institute for Education Sciences, U.S. Department of Education. Retrieved from http://ies.ed.gov/ncee/pubs/20074005.

Ehri, L. C., Dreyer, L. G., Flugman, B., & Gross, A. (2007). Reading Rescue: An effective tutoring intervention model for language minority students who are struggling readers in first grade. *American Educational Research Journal, 44*(2), 414–448.

Fall, R., Webb, N. M., & Chudowsky, N. (2000). Group discussion and large-scale language arts assessment: Effects on students' comprehension. *American Educational Research Journal, 37*(4), 911–941.

Glovin, D., & Evans, D. (2006, December). How test companies fail your kids. *Bloomberg Markets,* 127–138. Retrieved from http://timeoutfromtesting.org/bloomberg_education.pdf.

Guthrie, J. T. (2002). Preparing students for high-stakes test taking in reading. In A. Farstrup & S. J. Samuels (Eds.), *What research has to say about reading instruction* (pp. 370–391). Newark, DE: International Reading Association.

Guthrie, J. T., & Humenick, N. M. (2004). Motivating students to read: Evidence for classroom practices that increase motivation and achievement. In P. McCardle & V. Chhabra (Eds.), *The voice of evidence in reading research* (pp. 329–354). Baltimore: Paul Brookes.

Hargis, C. (2006). Setting standards: An exercise in futility? *Phi Delta Kappan, 87*(5), 393–395.

Ivey, G., & Broaddus, K. (2001). Just plain reading: A survey of what makes students want to read in middle schools. *Reading Research Quarterly, 36,* 350–377.

Jacobs, J. S., Morrison, T. G., & Swinyard, W. R. (2000). Reading aloud to students: A national probability study of classroom reading practices of elementary school teachers. *Reading Psychology, 21*(3), 171–193.

Keller, T. A., & Just, M. A. (2009). Altering cortical activity: Remediation-induced changes in the white matter of poor readers. *Neuron, 64*(5), 624–631.

Krafnick, A. J., Flowers, D. L., Napoliello, E. M., & Eden, G. F. (2011). Gray matter volume changes following reading intervention in dyslexic children. *Neuroimage, 57*(3), 733–741.

Krashen, S. (2011). *Free voluntary reading.* Santa Barbara, CA: Libraries Unlimited.

Kuhn, M. R., Schwanenflugel, P., Morris, R. D., Morrow, L. M., Woo, D., Meisinger, B., et al. (2006). Teaching children to become fluent and automatic readers. *Journal of Literacy Research, 38*(4), 357–388.

National Reading Panel. (2000). *Teaching children to read: An evidence-based assessment of the scientific research literature on reading and its implications for reading instruction.* Rockville, MD: National Institutes of Child Health and Human Development. Retrieved from www.nationalreadingpanel.org/publications/summary.htm.

Nystrand, M. (2006). Research on the role of classroom discourse as it affects reading comprehension. *Research in the Teaching of English, 40,* 392–412.

Reis, S. M., McCoach, D. B., Coyne, M., Schreiber, F. J., Eckert, R. D., & Gubbins, E. J. (2007). Using planned enrichment strategies with direct instruction to improve reading fluency, comprehension, and attitude toward reading: An evidence-based study. *Elementary School Journal, 108*(1), 3–24.

Shaywitz, B., Shaywitz, S., Blachman, B., Pugh, K., Fulbright, R. K., Skudlarski, P., et al. (2004). Development of left occipitotemporal systems for skilled reading in children after phonologically based intervention. *Biological Psychiatry, 55*(9), 926–933.

Taylor, B. M., Pearson, P. D., Peterson, D. S., & Rodriguez, M. C. (2003). Reading growth in high-poverty classrooms: The influence of teacher practices that encourage cognitive engagement in literacy learning. *Elementary School Journal, 104,* 3–28.

Trelease, J. (2001). *Read-aloud handbook* (5th ed.). New York: Viking-Penguin.

Wu, Y., & Samuels, S. J. (2004, May). *How the amount of time spent on independent reading affects reading achievement.* Paper presented at the annual convention of the International Reading Association, Reno, Nevada.

Zambo, D. (2003). The importance of providing scientific information to children with dyslexia. *Dyslexia* [online magazine]. Retrieved from Dyslexia Parents Resource at www.dyslexia-parent.com/mag47.html.

Critical Thinking

1. Teach a writing mini-lesson that focuses on a self-selected text that the child can write about. Observe the connections that suggest comprehension between what was written and what was read.

2. Visit a classroom with a large classroom library. Observe the order of the texts, the accessibility by the students, and the kinds of books that the teacher has in her library.

Create Central

www.mhhe.com/createcentral

Internet References

Common Core State Standards Initiative
www.corestandards.org

Grade Level Reading Lists
www.gradelevelreadinglists.org

International Children's Digital Library
http://en.childrenslibrary.org/index.shtml

International Reading Association
www.reading.org

RICHARD L. ALLINGTON is a professor at the University of Tennessee in Knoxville; richardallington@aol.com. RACHAEL E. GABRIEL is assistant professor at the University of Connecticut in Storrs; rachael.gabriel@uconn.edu.

Allington, Richard L.; Gabriel, Rachael E. From *Educational Leadership*, March 2012, pp. 10–15. Copyright © 2012 by ASCD. Reprinted by permission. The Association for Supervision and Curriculum Development is a worldwide community of educators advocating sound policies and sharing best practices to achieve the success of each learner. To learn more, visit ASCD at www.ascd.org.

Article   Prepared by: Karen Menke Paciorek, *Eastern Michigan University*

Developing Fine Motor Skills

On a crisp September morning during my first year teaching kindergarten, Mrs. Lucio and I [Michelle] met to discuss her son's progress. I eagerly shared that Mario was inquisitive, creative, and quite intelligent. His literacy skills were emerging rapidly. He could identify all upper- and lowercase letters, was phonemically aware, and recognized many sight words. However, Mario had great difficulty writing his name.

Mrs. Lucio's frustration and confusion were evident. The family had provided Mario with pencils, paper, and hand-over-hand writing demonstrations. They had done all they knew to do to help him master this skill. How could it be that this child was not able to write his name?

J. MICHELLE HUFFMAN AND CALLIE FORTENBERRY

Learning Outcomes

After reading this article, you will be able to:

- List activities that specifically target fine muscle development.

- Name the four stages of fine motor development.

Early childhood is the most intensive period for the development of physical skills (NASPE 2007). Writing progress depends largely on the development of fine motor skills involving small muscle movements of the hand. Muscle development for writing is a comprehensive process that begins with movements of the whole arm and progresses toward very detailed fine motor control at the fingertips (Adolph 2008). Much like an amateur runner who cannot run a marathon without proper training, a child cannot master the art of conventional writing without the proper foundation of muscle development.

Muscle development for writing is a comprehensive process that begins with movements of the whole arm and progresses toward very detailed fine motor control at the fingertips.

Young children need to participate in a variety of developmentally appropriate activities intentionally designed to promote fine motor control. Fine motor skills are difficult for preschoolers to master, because the skills depend on muscular control, patience, judgment, and brain coordination (Carvell 2006). Children develop motor skills at different rates. Teachers must encourage motor development with developmentally appropriate tasks that are achievable at any age or with any skill set (Bruni 2006).

Stages of Fine Motor Development

Just as there is a progression in gaining cognitive abilities, so too there is a sequence in developing muscles. Four stages of fine motor development set the stage for early writing success—whole arm, whole hand, pincher, and pincer coordination (Carvell 2006). Fine motor development begins with strengthening and refining the muscles of the whole arm. As young children participate in large arm movements, such as painting a refrigerator box with paint rollers and water or tossing a beach ball into a laundry basket, they use their entire arm. This full arm movement is a precursor to muscle development of the hand.

Pouring water from one container to another and squeezing water from a turkey baster develop the muscles of the whole hand. Strengthening the hand muscles leads to the ability to coordinate the finer movements of the fingers. Children develop the pincher movements by pressing the thumb and index finger together. Clipping clothespins on a plastic cup, stringing beads, and tearing paper are activities that support this development.

Pincer control is the final stage of fine motor development. With other skills in place, children are now prepared to properly grasp markers, pencils, and other writing utensils as they engage in authentic writing activities. This coordination allows the thumb, index, and middle fingers to act as a tripod, supporting the writing utensil and enabling small, highly coordinated finger movements.

Activities That Promote Fine Motor Development

These simple activities engage children in different levels of motor development in preparation for writing.

Muscle development	Activity and materials	Description
Whole arm	**Under-the-Table Art** Large sheet of drawing paper, tape, and crayons	Tape the paper to the underside of a table. Children lie on their backs under the table, extend the arm with crayon or chalk in hand, and draw on the paper.
	Ribbons and Rings Set of plastic bracelets and 12 inches of colored ribbon for each bracelet	Attach a ribbon to each bracelet using a simple slipknot. Play music. Children wear or hold their bracelet, using their bracelet arm to make big circles, wave the ribbons high and low, and perform other creative movements.
	Stir It Up! Large pot, long wooden spoon, and dry beans, pebbles, or pasta	Put the dry ingredients and the spoon in the bowl, and place them in the dramatic play area. Children "stir the soup" using a large circular arm motion.
Whole hand	**Sponge Squeeze** Small sponge, divided food dish, and water	Fill one side of the dish with water. Children transfer the water from side to side by dipping and squeezing the sponge.
	Lid Match Two baskets and a collection of plastic containers with matching lids (spice jars, margarine tubs, yogurt cups, shampoo containers, hand cream jars, and such)	Sort the containers and lids into separate baskets. Children match and attach the lids to the right containers.
	Cornmeal Sifting Crank-style sifter, 1-cup plastic measuring cup, large bowl, and cornmeal	Place the empty sifter in the bowl. Children use two hands to pour the cornmeal into the sifter, then turn the crank handle to sift the cornmeal into the bowl.
Pincher	**Button Drop** Four plastic containers with lids, and buttons	Cut a slit in each lid and label each container with a color. Children sort the buttons by color and drop them into the appropriate containers.
	Color Transfer Eyedroppers, muffin tin, food coloring, water, and a section of rubber bath mat backed with suction cups	Fill the muffin tin compartments with water of different colors. Children use the eyedroppers to transfer drops of colored water into each suction cup.
	Using Tongs Spring-handle metal tongs, sorting trays (ice cube trays, egg cartons, divided dishes, small containers), and items to sort (counting bears, acorns, buttons, pom-poms)	Show children how to use their thumb and middle and index fingers to manipulate the tongs. Children use the tongs to pick up the items and sort them into separate compartments or containers.
Pincer	**Capture the Cork!** Corks in a variety of sizes, a bowl of water, and tweezers	Put the corks in the bowl of water. Children use the tweezers to try to capture the floating corks.
	Locks & Keys A variety of small locks with keys	Close the locks. Children try to determine which keys work with which locks and unlock them.
	Clip It A variety of small barrettes, hair clips, and elastic bands; dolls with hair, brushes, combs, and a tray for materials	Children use the hair fasteners or elastic bands to divide the dolls' hair into small sections. Clips that fasten in different ways and small elastic bands support a range of motor skill levels.

Adapted with permission from Nell R. Carvell, *Language Enrichment Activities Program* (LEAP), vol. 1 (Dallas, TX: Southern Methodist University, 2006).

In the Classroom

As noted in the NAEYC Early Childhood Program Standards, teachers can give children multiple and varied opportunities to support their physical development. The daily routine, frequency of activities that foster fine motor development, and types of materials teachers provide all influence children's muscle development (NAEYC 2007). In "Activities That Promote Fine Motor Development," we suggest a number of easily implemented activities teachers can use that enhance young children's fine motor development.

Conclusion

Many kindergartners feel frustrated when they face the daunting task of conventional writing. In Mario's case, we identified the root of his writing difficulty—lack of motor development in his hands. We planned ways to support his developmental needs. Rather than asking Mario to write, we replaced paper and pencil tasks with developmentally appropriate experiences that helped him develop his fine motor skills.

Classroom environments can build children's whole-arm, whole-hand, pincher, and pincer coordination in preparation for learning to write.

When preschool teachers observe children, they have endless opportunities to gather information about each child (Owocki & Goodman 2002). Throughout the day, perceptive teachers use their keen sense of observation to note how children use their arms, hands, and fingers. Responsive teachers can alleviate frustration and nurture emerging fine motor skills by providing materials and activities that support differentiated instruction for each stage of physical development. With intentional planning and preparation, classroom environments can build children's whole-arm, whole-hand, pincher, and pincer coordination in preparation for learning to write.

References

Adolph, K.E. 2008. "Motor/Physical Development: Locomotion." In *Encyclopedia of Infant and Early Childhood Development*, 359–73. San Diego, CA: Academic Press.

Bruni, M. 2006. *Fine Motor Skills for Children with Down Syndrome: A Guide for Parents and Professionals*. Bethesda, MD: Woodbine House.

Carvell, N.R. 2006. *Language Enrichment Activities Program (LEAP)*, vol. 1. Dallas, TX: Southern Methodist University.

NAEYC. 2007. *NAEYC Early Childhood Program Standards and Accreditation Criteria: The Mark of Quality in Early Childhood Education*. Rev. ed. Washington DC: NAEYC.

NASPE (National Association for Sport and Physical Education) & AHA (American Heart Association) 2007. *2006 Shape of the Nation Report: Status of Physical Education in the USA*. Reston, VA: NASPE.

Owocki, G., & Y. Goodman. 2002. *Kidwatching: Documenting Children's Literacy Development*. Portsmouth, NH: Heinemann.

Critical Thinking

1. Write a pamphlet with information on fine motor skills to give to parents who have preschoolers moving onto kindergarten. List activities that the parents can do during the summer and reasons why their children need to develop their fine motor muscles.

2. Investigate which activities from the chart would be important for students to carry out activities such as coloring, cutting, and shoe tying.

Create Central

www.mhhe.com/createcentral

Internet References

American Alliance of Health Physical Education Recreation and Dance
www.aahperd.org

Busy Teacher's Café
www.busyteacherscafe.com

Idea Box
http://theideabox.com

J. Michelle Huffman, MS, is the Early Reading First grant facilitator for the Child Development Center in Mount Pleasant, Texas. Michelle has worked in the early childhood field for over 20 years and is a doctoral candidate at Texas A&M University, Commerce. jhuffman@mpisd.net. **Callie Fortenberry**, EdD, is associate professor of education and reading at Texas A&M University–Texarkana. Callie teaches education and emergent literacy courses and works closely with preservice early childhood teachers.

Huffman, J. Michelle; Fortenberry, Callie. From *Young Children*, September 2011, pp. 100–103. Copyright © 2011 by National Association for the Education of Young Children. Reprinted by permission. www.naeyc.org.